D1567908

Flight of the

VIN FIZ

Flight of the

VIN FIZ

by E. P. STEIN

ARBOR HOUSE
New York

Manufactured in the United States of America

10 9 8 7 6 5 4 3 2 1

This book is printed on acid-free paper. The paper in this book meets the
guidelines for permanence and durability of the Committee on Production
Guidelines for Book Longevity of the Council on Library Resources.

Library of Congress Cataloging in Publication Data

Stein, E. P.
  Flight of the Vin Fiz.

  1. Aeronautics—United States—Flights. 2. Rodgers,
Calbraith Perry. I Title.
TL721.R54S778 1985 629.13'0973 84-24521
ISBN 0-87795-672-3

CONTENTS

U.S.A ROUTE OF THE VIN FIZ

ATLANTIC OCEAN

GULF OF MEXICO

PACIFIC OCEAN

CANADA

MEXICO

NEW YORK
Sheepshead Bay
Middletown
Hancock
Elmira
Salamanca
Meadville
Kent PENNSYLVANIA
Marion
OHIO
Huntington
INDIANA
Chicago
Springfield
ILLINOIS
Marshall
MISSOURI
Kansas City
McAlester
Moran
Russell Creek
KANSAS
OKLAHOMA
Dallas
Fort Worth
Austin
TEXAS
San Antonio
Del Rio
Rio Grande
Fort Hancock
El Paso
Lordsburg
NEW MEXICO
Tucson
Phoenix
ARIZONA
Imperial Junction
Banning
Pasadena
CALIFORNIA
Los Angeles
Long Beach

Mississippi River
Missouri River

PREFACE

At the end of 1911, the most celebrated person in America was Calbraith Perry Rodgers. His name symbolized the spirit of valiant adventure. His activities were chronicled on the front pages of major newspapers. He presided over Pasadena's New Year's Day Rose Parade and proved its star attraction. President William Howard Taft certified his fame with a handshake and a gold-plated medal. Such honors were accepted as simply the consequence of his birthright.

Shortly after his birth—in January 1879—Cal Rodgers was accorded the ritual of prophecy traditional for male heirs to the Rodgers and Perry bloodlines. His mother, Maria Chambers Rodgers, substituting for the father who had died five months earlier, held up the swaddled infant before a gathering of the clan and proclaimed that one day her Calbraith would surpass the achievements of his illustrious forebears—including such champions of American history as Commodores Matthew Calbraith Perry and Oliver Hazard Perry. Mrs. Rodgers regarded history not merely as a record of events but as an imperative for the future. "This child has the mark of greatness on him," she declared grandiloquently, "and all the world shall know it."

The world, at first, showed itself inattentive and otherwise preoccupied. Cal Rodgers grew up unable—or unwilling—to navigate the channel carved out so deeply for him. Through his twenties and into his thirties he remained dependent on his mother's largesse, haunted by ancestral ghosts, a gladiator without an arena, a mountain climber without a mountain to climb.

Then, drawn by an iron chain of events, as if the Fates had belatedly recognized their obligation, came his introduction to the airplane. Here, Rodgers understood immediately, was the machine that held his destiny, the engine that would lift him to the heights ordained by his inheritance. As the airplane was to transform the world, so it usurped the being of Calbraith Rodgers, directed his life, and prescribed his death.

Since the first human eyes turned upward, the air—dynamic, invisible, beckoning—had been a natural metaphor for the soaring spirit of man. Until the Wright brothers forged dream into reality, the impossibility of flight was one of the immutable certainties, one of nature's inviolable laws. The fact of powered flight released shock waves into the culture—for if such an immutability were mutable, what other dogma or authority might be challenged? What, people wondered, will they think of next?

Yet for some years after the Wrights' preeminent achievement—December 17, 1903—the airplane only gradually gained acceptance. Newspapers featured the exploits of those few daring "drivers" or "birdmen" who risked their lives in "flying machines" or "aeroplanes" (a "plane" was a set of wings; two sets constituted a "biplane") and carried accounts of altitude records, speed records, air meets, and, more frequently, deaths in airplane crashes. But less than 2 percent of America's populace had seen a flying machine by the end of the century's first decade. People clung to an entrenched skepticism until their own eyes, quickened with wonderment, actually beheld the rumored invention. Not until then—and sometimes not even then—did they credit its existence.

Still, the airplane, its miraculousness notwithstanding, was generally regarded as an impracticality—fit for exhibition at county fairs or for the gratification of thrill-seekers, with little or no sensible application. Aviation's most ardent enthusiasts were adolescents. Youngsters, unburdened by past failures and lacking comprehension of the intricacies of flight, sensed in the ungainly, spidery craft a shadow of the future. Adults knew better.

America's first air meet, in January 1910, drew the presence of one of the nation's most influential personages: publisher and politician William Randolph Hearst. When Hearst, seeking a means to promote the cause of aviation—and the circulation of his newspapers—broached the notion of a transcontinental air journey, experts warned that such a preposterous proposition would inspire only a torrent of scorn and ridicule. Each take-off, Hearst was told, was still an adventure; each landing a triumph; more than a score of individual flights might be required to cross the country. Nonetheless, in October 1910, he tendered a $50,000 prize for the first aviator to fly coast to coast in thirty days or less. The proposal was instantly hailed as one of imaginative genius; Hearst was awarded the Aeronautical Society's medal for his "contribution and inspiration toward the advancement of aeronautics."

Several aviators filed intentions to compete for the Hearst prize. But faced with the realities of low-powered unreliable engines, inadequate controls, fragile structures, and lack of navigational facilities, none attempted to solidify intentions into actual flight. Hearst's offer languished, largely forgotten, until September 1911 (it was valid for one year). Then, three men prepared to coax their flying machines across the nation. First into the air was Robert Fowler, a racing-car driver who had purchased a Type B biplane from the Wright brothers; Fowler sallied forth from San Francisco on September 11, aiming toward New York City (precise routes were not laid out in advance). Two days later Jimmy Ward, an erstwhile jockey, lifted off from Governors Island, New York, in a Curtiss biplane and fixed himself on a westward course. Four days after Ward's takeoff, the third contestant set out—this time from Sheepshead Bay, Long Island —with the goal of traversing the continent to Los Angeles, California. That aviator was Calbraith Perry Rodgers.

Financial backing for Cal Rodgers's enterprise was secured from the Armour Meat-Packing Company of Chicago and its newly formed subsidiary, the Vin Fiz soft-drink company. Rodgers's airplane, a Model EX biplane negotiated with Orville Wright, was accordingly christened the *Vin Fiz.* Armour and Vin Fiz Company officials agreed to lease a private train that Cal would follow across the continent (Fowler had previously arranged for a supply train). The three-car Vin Fiz special would carry Cal's wife, Mabel; his now twice-widowed mother (uninvited but inescapable); managers; mechanics ("mechanicians"); workmen; representatives of the Armour and Vin Fiz companies; a revolving contingent of reporters; plus spare parts, a machine shop to effect repairs, an automobile, and a second airplane.

For eighty-four days Cal Rodgers pursued his odyssey across the continental United States. Supported by his wife and nagged by his mother to abandon the flights that were risking his life daily, he was impervious to outside forces, pro or con. Compulsively, through crashes, injuries, adverse weather, he answered only to the interior demons that beset him. As he pressed onward, his name appeared more and more in the headlines of the country's newspapers. As he neared the West Coast, Americans to a man rose to cheer him on. Thousands gathered at each stop for a glimpse of his figure and to inscribe their names on the fabric of the *Vin Fiz*. Rodgers was acknowledged as the quintessential American hero, destined for enshrinement in the history books. That he was instead slighted by history diminishes not at all the testament to his courage, his perseverance, his quality of transcendence that stirred the emotions of his countrymen. He had ventured into the unknown and emerged with a map for others to follow.

The year—1911—in which Cal Rodgers launched his journey was an age of faith, an age of blinkers, a time of fading innocence when life moved to a deliberate metronome. The world of 1911 was larger—manifoldly—than it is today. In that world, New York and Los Angeles were separated not by 3,000 miles but, as it were, by 3 million miles. Only in that world can the wonder of a transcontinental flight be understood. . . .

1

Sheepshead Bay— Up and Away

CALBRAITH PERRY RODGERS fell in love with flying in June 1911. He was thirty-two years of age. The object of his passion, born at Kitty Hawk, North Carolina, seven and a half years earlier, was too immature, too maladroit to respect or reciprocate that passion. He would nonetheless— as with all true love affairs—honor his commitment. Wheresoever it led, he would follow.

It led, on September 17, 1911, to Sheepshead Bay, Long Island, where Cal Rodgers prepared for the initial leg of a flight that would culminate, so he fervently professed, in the first air crossing of the United States.

Most of the crowd assembled at the Sheepshead Bay racetrack for the Sunday afternoon takeoff was drawn more by the newfangled flying machine than by its driver. Airplanes and New Yorkers were not unacquainted. Both the Nassau Boulevard Field, where a nine-day international aviation meet would begin the following weekend, and that at Brighton Beach, currently hosting a three-day meet, had been operating for over a year. Such renowned birdmen as Thomas Sopwith and George W. Beatty had successfully negotiated the seventeen-mile air course between Brighton and Nassau Boulevard. Attitudes of big-city dwellers to such stunts approached the blasé—even among the nonhuman populace; as New York horses were the first of their species to accommodate the automobile, so New York birds were first to accept the noisy intruder into their previously exclusive domain. Still, a craft heralded as a potential cross-country flier could attract adolescents, curious onlookers, and—if only to scoff—a scattering of sophisticates. Almost 2,000 persons paid the $1.50 admission price to the racing grounds where the flying machine reposed under guard. Several hundred others patrolled or picnicked on nearby beaches.

Cal Rodgers, driver of the airship, was known to comparatively few. A month before—in August—he had entered his first aviation meet, in Chicago, and to the surprise of spectators and fellow contestants alike emerged as the third-place money winner, capturing the prize for endurance aloft. That feat certified his solitary credential as a bona-fide birdman. His accumulated air time was yet less than sixty hours.

Throughout the middle hours of the seventeenth, Cal Rodgers lay asleep in his room at the Hotel Martinique in downtown Manhattan. He had labored continuously through the previous night until 4:00 A.M., readying his machine for flight. A prostrating blunder had led Cal and his crew to assemble the airplane in a farmyard almost a mile from Sheepshead Bay. With the darkness and the scant guideposts of south Brooklyn, the wagon transporting the airplane parts—from a railway car at Jersey City—was driven astray by a wagoner who had presumed upon his all too casual acquaintance with the area. The Rodgers party—including Cal, mechanicians Frank Shaffer and Charlie Wiggin, and Jimmy Dunn, chauffeur of the expedition's official automobile, a Palmer-Singer racer— trailed the wagon, blithely relying on its guidance.

It was well past three o'clock in the morning when the farm's resident, roused from sleep by the sounds of hammering and cursing, ventured out to investigate the curious activity on his property.

"Isn't that there a flying machine?" asked the farmer, swinging his lantern in the direction of the array of planes, propellers, wire, and engine components.

Someone in the crew languidly assured him that he would, indeed, shortly behold a full-fledged airplane.

"That so?" said the farmer. "Well, if that there is the Mr. Rodgers who's fixin' to fly for the Hearst money, he sure picked a strange place to start from."

In such manner did Cal and his crew learn that they had been deposited not at the Sheepshead Bay racetrack but near the park at Brighton Beach.

A volley of lively oaths ensued. "Never mind, boys," Cal said finally, surmounting a surge of anger and frustration, "it takes a few bumps to make the game worth the sweat." It was resolved that Cal should return to his hotel for a vital few hours' rest while workmen and mechanicians carried the biplane to its prescribed takeoff site.

Jimmy Dunn settled Cal with a lap rug in the rear seat of the Palmer-Singer and struck out across Brooklyn to the East River and the Brooklyn Bridge. Behind them, as they motored into Manhattan, the darkness peeled back from the fresh light of a new day. Taciturn by nature and tempered by a slight speech impediment, Cal sat huddled with his thoughts; an unsociable wind and exhaustion from long hours' work further discouraged conversation. Wordlessly, Jimmy Dunn delivered the aviator to the Herald Square entrance of the Hotel Martinique, then directed the sports car back across the East River to resume its duties as a transporter of airplane parts.

The Martinique, at Thirty-second Street and Broadway, a seventeen-story brick-facade structure of architectural stolidity, was host to Cal, his wife Mabel, and several other members of the Rodgers entourage. Located only a few doors from the Perry family residence at 38 West Thirty-second Street (built for Commodore Matthew Calbraith Perry in the 1850s), it had stood as a convenient hostelry for Cal during previous sojourns in New York City. Exigent schedules on this occasion permitted no visits with the Perry relatives, most of whom were on holiday abroad.

In the two-story, marble-paneled lobby, Cal found the night clerk dozing, shook him into semiconsciousness, and ordered a wake-up call for ten o'clock.

The Rodgerses' suite on the twelfth floor boasted porcelain W.C. and washing facilities and a recently installed cast-iron, roll-rim, claw-foot bathtub, a feature proudly proclaimed by the management. Cal banged his knee on the steamer trunk blocking the vestibule, collided with a tasseled, Tiffany-glass lampshade in the parlor, and stumbled into the bedroom. On one of the twin beds lay Mabel Rodgers, her head and darksome blonde tresses protruding from layers of quilts.

"An hourglassful of bubbly Champagne," so Cal described his wife, she was drained nearly flat by a final round of activity and by the 5:00 A.M. hour. She stirred and squinted into the darkness to ask, "What time is it?" In five years of married life, Cal had not once answered a rhetorical question from his wife; this occasion proved no exception. He and Mabel, each preoccupied with separate preparations, had rarely crossed paths during the past several days. He dropped his cigar stub, missing a convenient cuspidor, removed his boots, and curled up his six-foot-four-inch frame within the bed's dimensions.

For a brief moment he lay, eyes open, staring vacantly at the past, unable to envision the future despite the comfort of the dark. Then, quickly, the future canceled out the past.

By 7:30 A.M. Mabel was fully awake. She hastened through her morning ablutions, dressed herself, and worked a plumed hat over the tightly bound rats in her coiffure. By 8:30 she had packed her remaining clothes and personal articles into the steamer trunk. Several obligations awaited her attention before she was to board the special train in the Jersey City yards: an eleventh-hour list of accessories to be purchased; a sister, Mrs. Irene Stegmeyer, visiting New York from Vermont; a hasty look-in at the tea party for John Butler Yeats at the Petitpes sisters' boardinghouse on West Twenty-ninth Street (a social affair too select to be missed).

Cal awoke shortly before two in the afternoon; his pocket watch confirmed the hour and the night clerk's incompetence. He jiggled the telephone hook for the hotel's "hello girl" and, while lighting a fresh cigar, was connected to the clubhouse office at the Sheepshead Bay racetrack. Fred Felix Wettengel, business manager and, with Stewart deKrafft, general coordinator for the transcontinental enterprise, grabbed the receiver at the first ring. Cal was overdue, he noted superfluously, and proceeded to enumerate concerns of ceremony, finance, and scheduling, all slighted in his absence.

"Never mind the gingerbread," Cal interrupted. "Is the machine ready?"

"All in one piece and fit as a fiddle," said Wettengel, adding that engine tests had revealed a defectively soldered seam in the gasoline tank. Chief Mechanician Frank Shaffer and Charlie Wiggin were repairing and remounting the tank.

Cal arranged with Wettengel to dispatch Jimmy Dunn to the hotel and hung up. He pulled on his vest and coat, pitched his boots and leather jacket atop the steamer trunk (which held his spare suit and—mostly—the overflow from Mabel's two Saratoga trunks and numerous hatboxes), and left the suite to pace back and forth at the hotel entrance, impatiently awaiting the Palmer-Singer racer.

He handed a newsboy 5¢ for a copy of the *New York American*—principally to ascertain standings in the National League pennant race. Saturday's win for the Giants over Pittsburgh coupled with Chicago's loss to the Brooklyn Superbas boosted the Giants' lead over the Cubs to five games. In the American League, Connie Mack's Philadelphia Athletics enjoyed an eight-game advantage and were considered a "shoo-in." Cal scanned the front pages in the remaining moments before Jimmy Dunn arrived. News from abroad—food riots in Vienna, the assassination of the Russian premier in Kiev, friction between France and Germany over their Moroccan interests, threats of war between Italy and Turkey—could only reinforce the reader's appreciation for American culture and the two oceans that immunized it from foreign contagion. Events in America were more comforting if less stirring: President Taft, on the occasion of his fifty-fourth birthday (September 15), closed a three-week vacation and boarded the Taft Special train in Boston for his second tour across the forty-six states; designed to muster support for the following year's elections, his itinerary encompassed 13,000 miles in forty-six days, concluding in Washington on November 1.

Driving down Broadway, Dunn reassured Cal that his crew had toiled through the morning to tune the flying machine to tip-top fitness. Cal merely nodded in response. They passed along the edge of Union Square, by the spacious Georgian mansions to the north of Washington Square, past the grand bay-windowed buildings of lower Broadway guarded by balustrades of black wrought iron. City streets, this last Sunday of summer, enticed motorists by the thousands from their homes. To an increasing extent, the "man in the street" had abandoned his bicycle and was becoming the "man in the car." Proud members of the automotive age, costumed in dusters and goggles, motoring tools and repair kits at the ready, set their sparks and throttles, and cranked up their machines to sally forth like streams of soldier ants along avenues newly topped with macadam. "Traffic in New York is becoming insufferable," muttered Dunn as he turned the sports car onto Chambers Street, past City Hall Park, and onto the approach to the Brooklyn Bridge.

At Sheepshead Bay, a sizable crowd had already gained admission to the infield. Wettengel, beset by the clamor of the restless throng that milled about the grounds, ordered the airplane removed from the betting-ring enclosure into public view. Frank Shaffer endorsed the decision, and the machine was hitched to an automobile and towed across the dirt track onto the grassy infield of the racecourse.

It was immediately engulfed by excited spectators. Six policemen hired for the event proved inadequate to restrain them. Reinforced by mechanicians, crew members, and officials, they were yet unable to deter the zealots who fingered the controls, tugged at the chains and propellers, and inscribed their names on the fabric. Pleas for the safety of the machine and threats to cancel the takeoff went unheard or discredited by the enthusiastic mob.

Most of those present had been waiting, unheeded, for three or more hours and were not to be denied their moment of quittance. They were, largely, determined rather than destructive. They had come from Manhattan, from Brooklyn, from Queens, with a small percentage from outlying areas or visiting from other states. A few patrons of Mulrenan's Saloon strolled over to the track, discovered nothing of interest, and withdrew to their male retreat.

Anthony Cassara, age fourteen, had bicycled in from his home at the far end of Rockaway Avenue, promising to return before sunset; a smart caning awaited him when, in the fervor of his first close view of a flying machine, that promise went unfulfilled.

Harold Watkins, owner of a small export-import company and amateur photographer, had returned from a European business trip only the previous night aboard the Cunard liner *Lusitania.* An admirer of all aviators, whom he glorified as the times' true heroes, Watkins had photographed, two years earlier, Harry Houdini's flights from the Hufaron parade grounds in Hamburg, Germany. He bore with him—to memorialize Rodgers's takeoff—a Houghton-Butcher brass-backed folding camera and a swivel-top tripod.

Of all the spectators at the racetrack, Eddie Lynch had traveled the shortest distance to reach the site. His home, a farmhouse on the estate of the wealthy stockbroker and horse breeder Ben Ali Haggin, was located directly across the road from the racetrack. After attending early mass at St. Mark's in the village of Sheepshead Bay, he and his parents were repairing to their home when a friend animatedly apprised him of the news: Another aviator—this one named Cal P. Rodgers—was about to undertake a transcontinental voyage for the William Randolph Hearst prize. At the age of fourteen, Eddie Lynch was familiar with fliers and their machines. He had frequented exhibitions by Glenn Curtiss, Eugene Ely, and J. C. ("Bud") Mars from the Sheepshead Bay field and had watched Lawrence Sperry experiment with his home-built glider. Through reports at school and from acquaintances, he was following the progress of Jimmy Ward and Robert Fowler in the cross-country air race. For Eddie Lynch and other youths of his milieu, it was an honor to run errands for such renowned birdmen. To touch the machines, to be granted a glance of recognition, forged memories hoarded and recounted as treasures. Without a thought of breakfast, Eddie

Lynch scampered to the racing grounds for the promised spectacle.

At three o'clock Wettengel signaled to begin the preliminary ceremonies, a decision hotly welcomed by the crowd. Pleading for attention, he recited the data familiar to everyone in his audience: that the airship before him, the *Vin Fiz*, had been especially constructed for Calbraith Perry Rodgers by the Wright brothers of Dayton, Ohio; that Rodgers was about to embark in this machine on a transcontinental passage; and that the $50,000 prize for completion of the passage in thirty days or less had been posted by William Randolph Hearst. Regrettably, said Wettengel, Mr. Hearst's current travels abroad precluded a personal send-off for any of the contestants in the cross-country air race.

Cal Rodgers, although third to attempt the crossing, would be first to achieve it, Wettengel predicted. He announced that the birdman would depart with 263 pieces of mail, the most notable a card from J. Ogden Armour, president of Armour & Company, the prosperous meat-packing concern; Mr. Armour had pinned a $100 check to his card. The distinguished actor Fred Niblo had entrusted the enterprise with a letter and a $5 donation. A broach of perfume was addressed to the celebrated songwriter Carrie Jacobs Bond. Official communiqués had been received from the honorable William J. Gaynor, mayor of the boroughs of Greater New York, to Mayor George Alexander of Los Angeles* and from the army and navy commanders in the East to their counterparts in the West. These items were stowed in a mail pouch lashed to the lower plane; each letter or postcard had been guaranteed aerial transport over at least part of the transcontinental route. His announcements having failed to spark a flicker of interest, Wettengel introduced Miss Amelia Swift of Memphis, Tennessee, a buxom if otherwise ungifted lass who had been selected to christen the flying machine.

Miss Swift stepped forward gingerly. In one hand she held a bottle of Armour & Company's new carbonated grape drink, Vin Fiz. She regarded the airplane with some apprehension. The words *Vin Fiz* were drawn in scrolled characters on the fabric of the rudder and elevator surfaces; painted clusters of purple grapes separated the two words. Another bottle of the Vin Fiz drink was strapped to an upright brace on the forward plane edge, affixed there by Charles Davidson, president of the Armour &

---

*Uninspired by its potential status in history, the letter dated Sept. 16, 1911, read: "Honorable George Alexander, Mayor, Los Angeles, California. Dear Sir: This letter will be carried by Mr. Calbraith P. Rodgers, who starts from this city tomorrow in an attempt to fly across the country to Los Angeles. I trust that he will successfully make the trip and be able to hand you this letter in person. Very truly yours, Wm. Gaynor, Mayor."

Company subsidiary. A corset lace (for attitude reckoning) donated by Mabel Rodgers hung from the front cross brace. Miss Swift glanced at it and snickered.

"I christen thee *Vin Fiz!*" Miss Swift pronounced the line she had rehearsed and committed to memory.

She splashed a stream of grape juice over one skid, having been forewarned that standing too close to one of the twin propellers could prove injurious to her body and that breaking the bottle against a spar could prove injurious to the airplane.

This ritual apparently stimulated the throng, which launched a concerted rush forward. For a moment it appeared as if the machine might be trampled, but policemen and officials rallied to hold back the charge.

Harry Sanger, the Vin Fiz barker, stepped forward and raised his megaphone to holler forth the virtues of the sponsoring product. Clad in black-and-white-checkered suit, purple vest, and orange tie bearing a hand-painted portrait of Lillian Russell, Sanger was adroit at the art of compelling attention. This time, however, jostled by the crush around the airplane, he was unable to vent more than a few words of his advertising patter. Wettengel attempted to recapture the crowd's heed by introducing officers from the Brooklyn Navy Yard. He then presented Cal's mother, the imperious and imposing Mrs. Harry Sweitzer; Cal's sister, Mrs. Albert Pease; and Cal's cousin, Miss Jane Hone Lewis. He was casting about for another official or relative when, at nearly 3:30, he caught sight of the Palmer-Singer automobile entering the track alongside the 500-foot, two-tier grandstand.

A few derisive hoots of "Get a horse!" were heard, but they were drowned in a roar of salutations. Cal was besieged instantly by a score of boys in knickers and cloth caps and girls in pinafores and Mary Janes who had slipped the reins of parental restraint to race alongside his car. The youngsters soon gave way to the determination of Cal's associates— Wettengel; Stewart deKrafft; Charles Davidson; Andre Roosevelt, representing the Wright brothers; and half a dozen others.

Of those surrounding Cal, Stewart deKrafft easily appeared the most commanding. At six feet two inches—with metallic features and a sometimes unnerving fixity of gaze—he was nearest to Cal in height and nearest in temper and creed. He exercised his authority with an air of purpose, meting out his words in efficacious dosages. In organizing the projected cross-country odyssey, he controlled without effort a cat's cradle of connections between the business and operational ends of the enterprise. On his detachable cuffs, he frequently scribbled notes to remind himself of intended actions.

"Isn't John here yet? We're already late by an hour." Cal addressed deKrafft, lighting another cigar and ignoring questions and directions from the other men.

Lieutenant John Rodgers, Cal's cousin, closest friend, and fellow birdman, slated to assist in preparing the *Vin Fiz* for takeoff, had been denied permission to aviate the navy's Wright machine from Annapolis to New York, so deKrafft informed Cal. From the Naval Aviation Field at Greenberry Point, he had sent a telegram pledging to reach New York by train; if he failed to arrive before takeoff, he would catch up with them that evening when Cal and the full party would be resting in Middletown.

Plans for an air escort to the Hudson River by Lieutenant Rodgers and by Thomas Sopwith in their respective flying machines had consequently been canceled. Sopwith was committed to the Brighton Beach Meet and had notified manager deKrafft that he could not adjust his schedule to the delayed departure.

"Let's get on with it," Cal declared. He strode through the people crowding around him to the infield where the *Vin Fiz* stood, beset like a beached whale by a swarm of curious landsmen. Wettengel announced his presence—an unnecessary observance. Cal's lanky figure—six feet four inches and 200 pounds—towered over the general populace (despite his tendency to stoop when exposed to the public spotlight). With his new brown business suit, blue tie tucked into his vest, and white handkerchief jauntily protruding from his breast pocket, he embodied the popular notion of the daring birdman. Dark brown hair smoothed back flatly beneath his cap, graphic deep-set blue eyes, and cleanly chiseled contours lent the impression of sincerity. A lengthy nose matched the proportions of his face. His ruddy complexion suggested to some a fondness for alcoholic spirits—understandable in the face of his hazardous pastime. He was, so he steadfastly maintained, a teetotaler.

To many of those present, to the youngsters in particular, he was the authentic American hero. In his bearing they could perceive the framework of native metal. They respectfully opened a space for him whenever he moved.

His mother greeted him with a clutching, proprietary hug and kiss. Her husband, Harry Sweitzer—Cal's stepfather—had died Thursday and had been buried only the day before in Pittsburgh's Allegheny Cemetery; a veil, in token thereof, covered Mrs. Sweitzer's uncompromising features and muted the force of her kiss. "You look so handsome in that suit," she said, adjusting his tie while faintly acknowledging his condolences for her loss. Cal's sister, Martha ("Patty") Pease, frail, reserved in her mother's presence, awaited her turn to bestow a second hug. Next came her two children, Perry Pease, age seven, and Patty Pease, age six. Cal swooped his nephew and niece into his arms for an affectionate embrace. He clasped hands with several other acquaintances and accepted a red rose from his cousin Jane. A navy lieutenant, J. T. Abbott, strapped a compass onto Cal's wrist, a gift from officers at the Brooklyn Yard.

Under Cal's supervision, final adjustments were administered to the engine and chain controls. Frank Shaffer pronounced the airship ready for fueling.

A photographer pleaded for a few more poses. Cal lifted his nephew and niece together and plunked them onto the driver's seat of the airplane. "Take their picture," he ordered, "just for luck."

"What news of Ward or Fowler?" he asked deKrafft while the photographer set up his equipment. DeKrafft had received only sparse reports: Ward was downed in Owego, New York, unable to proceed, his motor wholly disabled; Fowler's Wright biplane had been fully repaired, but the aviator was still halted in Colfax, California, awaiting clearance for Reno. DeKrafft promised to collect the afternoon's newspapers and read through the pertinent accounts while the special train was traveling to Middletown. At the moment Ward was ahead of Cal by 208 miles. Fowler had traversed 140 miles along his course eastward from the Pacific Coast.

Cal dictated a telegram for Jimmy Ward in Owego: "Am taking to air in my Vin Fiz Flyer. Look out or I will catch you Tuesday."

Vin Fiz president Charles Davidson, having ascertained for the third time that the bottle of Vin Fiz was securely bound to its brace, confronted the aviator with bundles of Vin Fiz leaflets. "Drop these out over the field," he ordered. Cal stared at him without expression and turned back to deKrafft. Davidson thrust the leaflets into Cal's coat pockets: "When we pay the piper, we expect a tune. . . ."

DeKrafft intervened with a summary of the weather report: a light, easterly breeze with rougher winds forecast. Conditions would be slightly "puffy" aloft, he cautioned. "Just head into the wind and let her fly."

A stepladder was brought up and deployed in front of the airplane. Several boys scuffled for the opportunity to hold it in place; the junior mechanician, seventeen-year-old Charlie Wiggin, turned an officious manner and his piping voice on them to dismiss their efforts. His orders disregarded—as expected—he hauled a five-gallon container of gasoline up the ladder, draining the fuel into a tank suspended above the engine. With a second container handed up by his young "helpers," he filled the tank's ten-gallon volume.

Mechanician Frank Shaffer, deKrafft, Wettengel, and three crew members crammed themselves into the Palmer-Singer racer with Jimmy Dunn at the wheel. Davidson and other representatives of the Armour and Vin Fiz companies sprang into a Buick touring car. The two automobiles drove off, dashing for the Jersey City railroad yards and the Vin Fiz special train. Of the entourage accompanying Cal, only young Charlie Wiggin remained on the field. He would board a later passenger train to Middletown. Wiggie, "The Kid," five feet nine inches of unflagging devotion, stayed close to the aviator who overshadowed him. "That's my pal, Cal," he proclaimed to anyone within earshot.

A correspondent from the Hearst newspapers approached Rodgers and asked for a quote. "I am confident I will reach the coast and win the $50,000 prize offered by Mr. Hearst," said Cal. "I hope to overtake Jimmy Ward before I reach Chicago. I hope to alight first at Middletown." The words were spoken with only his mouth animated, as if his face did not agree with—and indeed despised—such simplistic prognostication.

"There are two others ahead of you in this race," the reporter pointed out as Cal turned away. "Why is it so important for you to fly to the coast?"

Cal found resource for one more artless comment: "It's important . . . because everything else I've done was not important."

A young woman in garibaldi and velveteen jacket, Mrs. J. B. Harris of Terrell, Texas, was emboldened by her tourist status in New York to weave through the crowd and press on the aviator a four-leaf clover and a wish of good luck. "What you are doing is the bravest thing in the world," she stammered before retreating awkwardly.

Cal directed Lieutenant Abbott and Charlie Wiggin to position the airplane for takeoff. With the aid of five or six youngsters, they pushed and pulled the machine up and down the field, maneuvering unsuccessfully with the crowd for a clear pathway. Repeatedly they yelled at the spirited assembly that, for the most part, did not comprehend the airplane's need for a running start. Without the restraint of policemen and other officials, a swarm of rowdies and souvenir hunters attacked the machine, bent on stripping away pieces of fabric or wire. The unruly spoilers were pulled from the airship and held at bay by volunteers who understood that even slight damage to the airplane could risk the death of its driver.

For twenty minutes Cal suffered these proceedings, all the while puffing smoke from an expiring cigar stub, seemingly to screen the offending scene from his view. Then, chafing at the delay and disgusted with those continuing to hem in the machine, he turned his cap around, adjusted his goggles, marched to the front of the plane, climbed onto the seat, and signaled to Lieutenant Abbott and Charlie Wiggin for their assistance. "Stand back," he bellowed, "or you'll all get killed." He discarded his burnt-out stub and from his vest pocket extracted the fifth cigar of the past two and a half hours. He borrowed a match from a bystander, lit the stogie, and clamped his teeth into its wrappings. He threw open the switch shorting the magneto spark and yanked at the compression-release cable. Abbott and Wiggin counted out in unison, "One, two, three," and pulled down on the propellers. The engine coughed, spluttered, then quickened into pulsating existence. The cloud of black smoke and the whirring of the huge blades produced their intended effect, and the crowd fell back.

The staccato roar from the drive chains fired the insides of everyone present. A prickly tension clutched at every throat. Away from the airplane, people doffed their caps and pulled out their handkerchiefs, prepared to wave them, and drew in deep breaths, primed to cheer their hero.

Cal reached back and swiveled the lug that restored compression; the black smoke dispersed, and the engine's hiss and irregular beat flattened to a steady roar. Abbott and Wiggin moved to restrain the fidgety, impatient flying machine. After a few moments Cal placed his hand on the radiator; its warmth confirmed the engine's readiness.

Directly ahead, several people stood watching, witlessly blocking the takeoff run. The aviator gestured at them—to no avail.

He called out for the airplane to be released, threw a last salute to his mother and sister, twisted the hinged rudder-control, and maneuvered the machine 800 feet toward the west end of the racetrack infield, "blinking" the magneto-shorting switch off and on to control his speed.

Only a few youngsters stayed with him; the remaining throng strung out in his wake. He moistened a finger and held it up, sensitive to the air currents, then angled the airship toward the east—facing the wind. Fifty yards along his path, he noted the bent figure of Harold Watkins peering through the Houghton-Butcher camera on its tripod. He glanced to either side. At one end of the lower plane stood Eddie Lynch,[1] at the other end Tony Cassara, two lads obviously knowledgeable about flying principles.

For an instant he stared without focus. The journey he was about to launch was a journey traveled in his mind for years—before the invention that would carry him, before a destination existed or a place to start from. It was, until now, a blind man's vision: fuzzy, shapeless, nondimensional, unlit by colors of reality. Now the past collided with the present and jarred it into focus. "All right, Betsy," Cal told the machine, "let's get crackin'."

"Let her go, boys," he yelled out. He gripped the lever controls, stepped on the spark-advance treadle, and the craft lurched forward under full power, the two youths sprinting alongside, each steadying it with a hand on a wing tip. As it gained speed, one boy dropped away, then the other.

As ever at these moments of suspended time, Cal again felt the seminal current of transmutation—an almost spiritual charge—of evolution from sluggish worm to soaring eagle. He felt the machine shudder, the fabric stiffen against the wind, the spars and struts vibrate in sympathy. Wood, metal, wire, and fabric became flesh, bone, and sinew. Where there was coldness, there was now fire. Where there was plainness, there was now beauty. Where there was but inert matter, there was now life. The *Vin Fiz* breathed. It sang. It rejoiced in its being. It pledged its covenant with man. Where there was nothing, there was now flight.

The *Vin Fiz* was airborne.

2

Love at First Flight

"A CURIOUS HAPPENING," John Rodgers said of his cousin's first-ever view of an airplane. "He seemed to experience some sort of transformation, as if he were about to sprout a pair of wings himself."

That happening—one link in the chain of circumstances that set Cal Rodgers to the launch of his transcontinental flight—took place the afternoon of April 14, 1911, at the Wright Flying School at Simms Station, eight miles northeast of Dayton, Ohio.

The first link in the chain had been cast three months earlier while Lieutenant John Rodgers, USN, was stationed aboard the USS *Pennsylvania*[1] in San Francisco Bay. As assistant to the senior engineer, Lieutenant Rodgers was privileged to witness at close hand Eugene Ely's landing of a Curtiss biplane on the *Pennsylvania*'s deck.* Enthralled by the event, he had volunteered to man an experimental box-kite array[2] moored to the

*Ely's flight (Jan. 17) was the first to terminate aboard ship. (Earlier, Nov. 14, 1910, he had achieved the first flight from ship to shore—from the USS *Birmingham* to Willoughby Spit, Va., two and a half miles distant.) On the *Pennsylvania*, a platform 85 feet long and 25 feet wide was constructed. To arrest the flying machine, a cable was stretched across the platform and tied at both ends to weighted sandbags.

stern and on January 30 was lifted 400 feet in the kite's "boatswain's chair" as the ship steamed across the bay. He remained aloft for fifteen minutes, swaying and bobbing on the wind to the protests of his stomach, yet fixing his sight on vessels as far as forty miles distant and signaling to officers below.

On February 15, Lieutenant Rodgers was detached from sea duty to his home in Washington, D.C., arriving on February 23 to await further orders.

To renew their friendship, Cal and Mabel motored down from New York for a week's lodging at the Rodgerses' twenty-room red-brick colonial mansion (named Sion Hill) in Havre de Grace, Maryland. John Rodgers's fiancée, Ethel Greiner, a resident of Annapolis, also accepted an invitation to Sion Hill despite the qualms of her mother. The two couples occupied themselves strolling the country lanes of Maryland's eastern shore, racing their twenty-four-foot sloops in the chill winds of Chesapeake Bay off the mouth of the Susquehanna, picnicking at the fairgrounds, attending the Sunday ice-cream social, and discussing John's career in the navy and Cal's prospects as a race-car driver.

John Rodgers, pencil-straight, slightly smaller, slightly heavier than Cal, was a stiffer, more thin-lipped version of his cousin. His inclinations aimed toward further concentration on engineering; he was persuaded that the modern navy would increasingly rely on skilled technical officers. Cal was yet adrift—"a professional without a profession," John called him. Success at motorcycle and automobile racing remained fugitive, although he could claim a distinct flair for engines, structures, and their design. If only he knew where to search for his destiny, Cal asserted, he would hasten there at once to begin the search.

John's parents (Cal's uncle and aunt), Admiral John Rodgers and Elizabeth Chambers Rodgers, were hosts to this family reunion. On occasional evenings, Vice Admiral Frederick Rodgers and other navy associates from Washington or Annapolis joined the group for supper or postprandial conversation. With the ladies excused and cigars distributed from a mahogany humidor, serious matters could be raised and debated: the need to fortify the soon-to-be-completed Panama Canal; the treaty with Japan just ratified by the Senate.

On Sunday, March 5, Lieutenant John Rodgers returned to his Washington, D.C., residence. On March 16 he received his new orders, transferring him "to Dayton, Ohio, to confer with Wright Bros. for instruction in Art of Aviation, report progress, and when qualified report."

This assignment was not unexpected. His skill and courage in manning

the box kite had been reported to Captain W. I. Chambers,* and rumors
floated that special orders were in the offing. Further, he was aware of the
envy aroused by the army's acquisition of three heavier-than-air machines.
Lieutenant Theodore Ellyson had become the navy's first aviator by dint
of his enrollment at the Glenn Curtiss School. John Rodgers, now appointed the second naval birdman, promptly boarded a train in Washington for the overnight journey to Dayton.

Letters from his cousin in Dayton reached Cal at his sister's home in
Hempstead, Long Island. They spoke of the Wright brothers, of Al
Welsh and Cliff Turpin (the two flying instructors), of the civilian student
Howard W. Gill, and of John's struggles with the capricious flying machine. The tone of the letters was euphoric—not in keeping with John's
usual judicious character. Cal was invited to the school to observe the
activity for himself.

"What is so special about flying?" asked Cal. "Birds do it; bats and bugs
do it; even a few fish." Nevertheless, what with dismal weather in New
York and no other matters pressing, it was decided that Cal would quit
New York for Dayton while Mabel would pass the week with her father
in Bennington, Vermont. Cal stepped from a Pennsylvania Railroad train
at Dayton, Ohio, on April 14; John Rodgers was waiting at the station
to greet him.

Public conveyance in Dayton—a quiet, residential town of less than
150,000 people—was served by trolley cars, open at the rear, one of which
ran by the Wright factory, a small (four-room) brick building at city's
edge. Even before depositing Cal's luggage at the boardinghouse where
John resided, the two cousins rode the trolley to the factory, where Cal
was introduced to Orville Wright (Wilbur had departed for Paris a month
earlier, to pursue lawsuits against Blériot, Farman, and nine other "in-
fringers of our French patents"), general manager Frank Russell, student
Phil Parmalee, and some of the twenty-odd mechanicians and workmen
then engaged in construction of the two Type B aircraft just ordered by
the U.S. Army Signal Corps. Cal shook hands with each, dispensing his
customary charm, not profound, not captivating, but comfortable and
subtly disarming. To the birdmen and their associates, however, he was
the "outsider," the "ground-hugger"—there was an inevitable distinction,

*Capt. Washington Irving Chambers, a veteran of 34 years in the U.S. Navy, was
assigned in Oct. 1910 to "keep the Navy informed of the progress of aeronautics with a
view to advising the department concerning the adaptability of such material for naval
use . . . and to gradually provide the Navy with suitable equipment for aerial navigation
and to instruct Navy personnel in its use."

Cal understood immediately, conferred upon those in the world of aviation.

In the afternoon Cal and John boarded the interurban electric train to the flying school at Simms Station,[3] and there it was that Cal was struck by the thunderbolt that kindled his inner workings. Confronted for the first time by the reality of a flying machine, he stood transfixed, infused with images and sounds that only he could see and hear—images of suns that burst and regrouped in radial flashes, sounds of winged music, of whisperings in foreign tongues. His genial expression melted into blankness; his bearing seemed to wilt as if under physical assault. He moved his limbs awkwardly. He worked his jaws, but no words came forth. John Rodgers was astonished to observe his cousin in the grip of his "curious happening."

When he recovered his senses, Cal remained contemplative and subdued. Whatever his thoughts, he refused to allow even John access to his private dream—as if an intruder would spoil the vision, destroying its fragile tracings. He inquired into the cost of the Wright machine, the cost of flying lessons, the number of lessons normally engaged, and he inquired if special qualifications were required for civilian students (they were not).

Cal cut short his intended stay in Dayton for his mother's home in Pittsburgh. He advised his mother that he wished to enroll in the Wright School and requested her financial support. She refused. Further, if Calbraith persisted in hazarding his life in such an irresponsible and outlandish venture, she threatened, she would discontinue his current allowance. That one member of the family had taken up an activity better reserved for birds was unfortunate. The involvement of a second Rodgers—her son Calbraith in particular—could not be countenanced.

When Mabel returned from Bennington, she perceived at once the change in her husband's demeanor—"as if the last piece of a jigsaw puzzle had dropped into place in his mind." Husband and wife conferred over their possible means of raising money. Lessons at the Wright School cost $60 per hour of direct training (in fifteen-minute units) with no charge for breakage.* After qualifying as an aviator, Cal would need his own machine in which to perform and thereby recoup his investment. The latest Wright model, the Type B, could be purchased for $5,000. Mabel was fully supportive of Cal's ambition; it held promise of grand excite-

---

*Most flying schools, except for those run by the Wrights and Curtiss, assessed the costs of aircraft damage to the student. Since these schools provided unreliable machines and inadequate instruction, breakage was virtually inevitable.

ment. Her father was less understanding. Frederick O. Graves, a conservative New England banker, urged his son-in-law toward sounder pursuits —the world of finance. Cal's cousin (once removed) August Belmont possessed wealth in abundance and headed a group of New York investors that owned 60 percent of the Wright Aeroplane Company;.* however, he was secluded at his nursery farm near Lexington, Kentucky, recuperating from his recent appendectomy. Undeterred, Cal prepared to pursue his idyllic vision at whatever cost. He wired accordingly to Orville Wright.

Cal's mother, Mrs. Sweitzer, was accustomed to indulging her two sons. John Perry Rodgers had been subsidized by family capital for more than two years in his quest for South African gold. Cal had acquired boats, automobiles, and motorcycles through his mother's largesse. Although her resources were dwindling, she could not—for long—deny him. She reluctantly consented to underwrite his essay into aviation, trusting that it was just another fever that would run its course ("Nothing but time can cure Calbraith's new fancy," she wrote to her daughter). Her sole condition was that Mabel should not accompany him to Dayton. The undertaking was hazardous enough, she asserted, without a wife to distract his concentration.

John Rodgers read with delight Cal's letter declaring his intention to master the art of flying. "In two months," he wrote back, "you will be soaring like a hawk. Just remember to go easy on us chickens." John had performed his first solo flight April 21 and was pronounced a competent aviator by Orville Wright. He had been ordered to continue at the school, practicing emergency landings and serving as official inspector of the Type B airplane (the B-1) under construction for the Navy Department. The "curious happening" of April 14 had been relegated to the dustbin of trivialities.

Cal Rodgers arrived at Dayton for the second time on June 5 and, after a restless night, proceeded directly to the Wright business office to enroll in the flying school. Financial matters and contracts were concluded with Orville Wright by midmorning. "Don't be nervous," counseled the man who first achieved powered flight. "It's just like learning to ride a bicycle." Orville duly noted the outstanding features of each newcomer: "What is unusual about this one, aside from his tree-top height, is his eyes. It's as if they were borrowed from another face—or from another time."

Cal was presented to his assigned instructor, Arthur L. ("Al") Welsh,

*Further, Belmont had served as president of the International Aviation Tournament for the first aviation meet in the East—held at Belmont Park, N.Y., Oct. 22–30, 1910.

and to the Wrights' chief mechanician, Charley ("Zach") Taylor. Both Welsh and Taylor were gruff, professional men, self-assured, with minimal tolerance for foolishness or frivolity from the students. Both were dedicated to aviation, and both soon erased any doubts in the new arrival that they expected equal dedication on his part. "You'll never make a flier," the five-foot-seven-inch Welsh growled at the student who topped him by nine inches. "Tall ships never leave the water."

Cal was now conceded his first intimate inspection of a flying machine. He maintained his composure despite an intoxicating sensation that he had just stepped over the threshold of fantasy. His eyes absorbed its form, the two forward planes spread for ready flight, behind them the twin propellers immobile but with the potential of spinning life, the chains and shafts to the empennage, the crossed tail surfaces. . . . His fingers slid over the fabric, the struts, the cold metal lips of the engine, stroking, caressing, straining for each mystical nuance. The ulterior vision, hitherto shapeless, the elusive concept of destiny, the logical consequence of his inheritance, all coalesced before him in a single form. It was the airplane, he knew— had already known—with precise instinct, that would carry him into the future.

Al Welsh tutored Cal in the Wright techniques for construction and maintenance of airplanes and in the fundamental principles of flight: the means for lifting and dropping the machine by angling the elevator surfaces and the means for turning by coordinating movements of the rudder surfaces with the wing warping.*4 Understanding was vital, Welsh insisted: "He who has imagination without knowledge has wings but no feet."

In one room of the factory building a stationary mock airplane, dubbed the "kiwi bird," had been set up for preliminary training. This machine, a Type B without engine and tail assembly, was cradled to allow lateral movement only. An electric motor driving a cam continuously changed the angle of the planes about the longitudinal axis. As the aviator manipulated the combination warp and rudder lever properly, the planes were returned to a level attitude. It was customary for a student to spend several hours over three or four days seated on the kiwi bird, practicing until correction of lateral imbalance became instinctive.

Whether through his experience in racing motorcycles or from his natural athletic prowess, Cal displayed an immediate sense of balance

*Opposite wing tips are "warped"—that is, given helicoidal twists—to present each set of tips to the wind at a greater or lesser angle than the opposing set.

control. A single fifteen-minute period convinced him that further time with the kiwi would be superfluous, and he was able to persuade Al Welsh to that effect. By noon he had been promoted from elementary class and taken to the flying field at Simms Station.

A converted cow pasture, the Simms Station field was bare except for a thorn tree at one end and a large wooden shed at the other. It measured over 300 feet in length—enough to accommodate landings by even the most inept fledgling. Al Welsh presented Cal to his other student, Henry Arnold,* a wiry (five feet eleven inches, 160 pounds) infantry lieutenant almost twenty-five years of age, and to Lieutenant Milling, a slight (five feet eight inches, 125 pounds), round-faced young man of twenty-three years, who was entrusted to the tutelage of Cliff Turpin. They accompanied Cal to the shed where the two "B's" used for instruction were sheltered, all the while disparaging the newcomer's worthiness as if he were deaf to their dialogue.

"Now this man is a true bean pole," Lieutenant Arnold began. "Just look at that long, thin shadow."

Milling agreed: "String beans, is my guess. And isn't that a head of lettuce growing from his shoulders? You ever see a bean pole that could fly?"

"Not when it's planted as deep in the ground as this one," said Arnold.

The two lieutenants helped Al Welsh to pull one of the "B's" (No. 27) from the shed, its 1,250 pounds riding on wheels and skids that had superseded the steel-track launcher used for earlier models. "This flying machine," lectured Welsh, "is the best there is. Control surfaces—elevator and rudder—are at the rear.† It has a 35-horsepower water-cooled engine that drives the two eight-foot propellers;[5] these propellers are geared through bicycle chains to turn at about 450 rpm."‡ Teacher and pupil walked around the airplane, inspecting its fitness, checking patches of fabric, testing the webwork of wires—a procedure, Welsh explained, that should precede every flight: "An ounce of precaution can save your life—or, more important, my life."

Two cane-wicker seats lined with corduroy perched on the forward edge

---

*By Army Special Order No. 95, dated 21 Apr. 1911, 2d Lt. Henry A. Arnold of the 29th Infantry and 2d Lt. Thomas deWitt Milling of the 15th Cavalry were ordered to Dayton, Ohio, to study aviation under the Wright brothers.

†Control surfaces on the Wright Type A were located forward of the planes. The "B" was referred to as a "headless biplane."

‡One chain was crossed—like a figure eight—so that the propellers would rotate in opposite directions, balancing the torque of each.

of the lower plane, and Cal and Al Welsh settled themselves side by side, Cal on the left. "Don't squirm about," Welsh advised. "We don't want you to fall off until you've paid your fees."

Between the two seats stood the wing-warping lever with a hinged upper section for independent rudder control. "It twists the planes for turning and automatically applies rudder action through a linkage,"[6] Welsh explained. "By rotating the top portion of the lever, you can add or subtract rudder action.* To change altitude, there's an elevator lever at the outside of each seat.[7] To change speed, we have this spring-loaded foot treadle you can reach from either seat; it advances or retards ignition spark and gives you a range of engine power. Now, you got all that?"

Cal removed the cigar from his mouth and regarded its cold ash. "All this talk has put out my cigar," he said. "Let's get on with it."

"All right," said Welsh, "you're in the catbird seat now. We'll see if you can hold on to that stogie without swallowing it." He turned his cap, a white checkered piece, backward and signaled to his assistants. One man primed the intake manifold from an oil can filled with gasoline. "You start the engine with compression released; otherwise, you'll need two heavy-weight wrestlers to turn the props. . . ." Two other men swung the propellers; the engine fired in a blast of smoke as they ran to grasp the wing tips. Welsh turned the compression-release lug and switched on the fuel-tank valve. "Keep it in spark-retard till it's running smooth. . . ."

Welsh looked at Cal and nodded a question mark. Cal bit down harder on his burnt-out stub. With the clatter of the chains, it was difficult to hear even the shouted word across the short space between them. He nodded back.

Welsh waved for his assistants to let loose the flying machine, then kicked at the treadle and urged forward the elevator-control lever. The craft hesitated, then bounced along, gaining speed. Its tail assembly raised, its skids left off their clawing at the ground. A few more bounces and the "B" wobbled into the air.

John Rodgers had cautioned that "there is nothing in your old, flat world that can prepare you for the experience of this new one. Some men are frightened to paralysis; others become faint with stomach sickness." Cal heeded his cousin not a whit. He had anticipated a sense of exhilaration at shedding his earthbound skin. He was fulfilled in a climax of

---

*A difficult wrist-twisting movement was required to operate this lever section; for this reason, a right-handed aeronaut was trained in the left seat so that his "better" hand was applied to the task.

unbridled zest, of soaring spirit as he perceived that anything—anything!—was now possible. Somehow he had experienced these sensations a thousand times before. He had been born and raised in a far country, a world and time beyond the age and place of man. He was elevated above his fellow creatures—not merely in altitude but in essence. He knew the language of flight. He was a sky lover—certified by the gods of Olympus.

It was customary at the Wright School for the novice student to brave his first flight strictly as observer. Cal watched Al Welsh apply himself to the unceasing task of maintaining level flight and aerodynamic turns without slipping or skidding. It seemed to Cal a task of balancing on a knife edge between land and sky; one misstep, one lapse of concentration, and they would plunge into oblivion. Hypnotized at first by the aerial perspective, he was unable to remain passive for long and placed his hands on the control levers. He rocked the planes and dipped and heaved the flying machine in expression of his emotions. Welsh signaled him to desist and reclaimed the levers. At the end of the five-minute flight, Welsh tipped the craft back toward the field. A few feet above the ground he pulled the compression-release cable. Speed decreased immediately (from the drag of the two eight-foot propellers), and the craft sank; as it met the ground it settled its weight onto the skids, which dug into the turf to brake the landing run.

As the machine was halted and silenced alongside the small wooden hangar at the field, aviators, mechanicians, and workmen filed by. In ostentatious ritual, repeated for the benefit of the new student, each ran his hand over the struts and uprights "to see if the [presumably terrified] passenger had squeezed the paint off."

"A man could become drunk with flying," Cal declared, doffing his cap and bowing rakishly to the group. He was awarded a round of applause.

Cal's exuberance at this experience was tempered only by the sharing of it with Al Welsh. He insisted that his instruction proceed straightaway into the first formal lesson. Welsh protested that learning was absorbed more efficiently with flight sessions spaced further apart. "I'm still chewing this cigar," Cal pointed out as proof of his rapid adaptability. Welsh reluctantly agreed to a schedule that entailed one fifteen-minute airborne period per day. "It's your money," he said with a shrug.

Cal chafed under this pace, pining for the next opportunity to mount the operator's seat. With successive flights over the next several days, he grew yet more assured, yet more adept at handling the controls. He readily performed turns, left and right, then figure eights. By the third flight he was participating in takeoff and landing maneuvers. By the sixth he had operated the machine under his own skills through a complete cycle.

Ninety minutes of instruction in six days, although no record,* served to reinforce the fervor—obvious to all those at Simms Station—that Cal invested in his practice. Both Al Welsh and Orville Wright had expressed disapproval of his compulsiveness, but Cal favored the notion that each success deserved an heir. On June 11, following his sixth lesson, he pressed for the consummation of his apprenticeship by a flight of his own. Al Welsh refused to countenance the prospect—protecting the machine was his responsibility, and more than once Cal had mired it in the marshy spot at the edge of the field. Cal offered to purchase the craft forthwith. Orville Wright was consulted; a document was drawn up, transferring ownership of the Wright Type B, No. 27, to C. P. Rodgers (albeit with delayed delivery). Orville then coldly disclaimed further interest; there were no rules to prevent an owner from acting as he wished with his own airplane.

To several associates, Orville had expressed his misgivings about student Calbraith P. Rodgers. Usually a taciturn man, he spoke at length of the need to observe at all times the maxims of safety; caution and concentration were bywords in his prescription for the aviator who aimed to survive. In general, he preferred activities at the flying school to business dealings at the factory in Dayton, although the latter commanded most of his attention. When he did appear at Simms Station—invariably with his derby and dark business suit—he would admonish his novice birdmen against foolhardy thoughts or acts. Often he would tell of the horse-drawn carriage waiting on the road that bounded the pasture (a carriage invisible to everyone else), its driver, a somber gentleman with tall black hat, following with keen interest each day's flights. That man, Orville confided ominously, was the local undertaker.

Although his object tales fell well short of Cal's mindfulness, Orville did not allow vexation to deter his attendance at the solo debut of the new pupil. He joined the gathering of Al Welsh, Cliff Turpin, Charley Taylor, Phil Parmalee, and others at Simms Station (Lieutenants Arnold and Milling had departed the previous day for College Park, Maryland[8]) as Cal prepared the No. 27 "B" for takeoff. Only John Rodgers expressed well-wishes—and handed Cal a "good-luck cigar."

Cal was oblivious to outsiders, well disposed or otherwise. He lit the

---

*Lt. Milling, as one example, received his first lesson on a Monday and flew solo the succeeding Friday. Generally, student flights were restricted to afternoons, and then only in still air (Orville Wright promulgated this rule—"otherwise we can't tell whether the wind or the student is knocking the machine about").

cigar and sat, puffing it furiously, as helpers dragged the "B"—his "B"—to the leeward side of the field, faced it into the wind, and spun the propellers.

People, buildings, trees faded from his vision. Engine noises, the racket of the chain drive faded from his hearing. Only the flying machine and its flying helmsman existed. Isolated from the world, Cal moved forward, accelerating in spasms, oscillating at first, then smoothing out his run. He became personally endowed with wings, with movable fins, with motive power. The airplane folded itself around him, a protective vestment, a magic carpet hanging in time. Thus embraced, man and machine rose to the air.

Immediately, the sense of consummating a unique love affair intensified, conflating with a sense of euphoria. Puffs of clouds scurried by as if to escort this newest kinsman to their realm. The high-pitched cachination of the wind echoed its own welcome through the pulsating power of the miracle machine. Earth was not a place for ordinary life and events, but a serried geometry to frame the only being of consequence that existed, that could exist. Both earth and sky were imbued with the same timelessness, the same weightlessness, the same ethereal force that sustained the flying machine and its sovereign commander. He alone could speak to the sky, could hear its answer on the wind.

For ten minutes Cal dipped and angled the "B," disporting himself with the power he controlled, watching the landscape wheel around him, filling his nostrils with the heady June air—"It smells different with altitude and with speed," he insisted.

When he returned to earth, both in body and in spirit, he was cheered, pummeled, and celebrated by the Simms Station regulars. He was now officially proclaimed an aviator, a flier, a master of airplanes, a birdman, a conqueror of the sky. He was dubbed "Uncle Cal" to commemorate his exalted status. Al Welsh and Orville Wright were less effusive than the others after having watched the wobbly takeoff and the crunching drop from ten feet above the ground—"Look at your shadow," said Welsh for the umpteenth time. "When it leaves you, you're in the air; when it clamps on to you again, you're down."

Still, Cal's ingenuous jubilation overcame all reservations. It was traditional, Cal was then apprised, that any student who flew solo after ninety minutes' instruction should stand dinner and drinks for his colleagues. That evening he was again toasted and hailed as a hearty fellow worthy of the aviation fraternity.

In his first letter to Mabel—staying with friends in New York—Cal shared as much of his feelings as he ever would: "Once you have left the ground to fly through the air, you never quite come down to earth again."

Throughout the remainder of June, Cal continued his flights around the Dayton-Simms Station area, gaining proficiency and experience (but not added confidence, said Al Welsh; he had already acquired that quality in full measure). On June 13 Welsh left for Belmont Park, New York, to establish an aviation school at that site, and Cliff Turpin assumed, for a short time, the task of polishing Cal's aeronautic skills.

Cal soon acquired a reputation as a prankster of substance. He was particularly prone to inflict his waggeries on fresh arrivals at the school. One victim of his pranks was Harry Atwood, an earnest and studious young man newly graduated from the Massachusetts Institute of Technology. Atwood immediately declared his resolve to become the world's most accomplished aviator. As a foil for practical jokes, he could not be ignored. Cal punctiliously explained to him the importance of developing a sense of balance. The prescribed course that all previous students had mastered, so Cal avowed, consisted of maintaining one's equilibrium while standing astride the axle of a two-wheeled handling truck, a long board across one's shoulders. As Atwood attempted to maintain his balance on the truck axle, Cal sat nearby, "grading" his efforts. Building on the success of this affair (Atwood's naïveté endured for days), Cal advised him that competence was judged by the ability to fly in a straight line and that therefore it was the custom for each aviator to inscribe his own line on which to practice. Atwood was soon zealously crawling over the grass field with whitewash pail and brush, trailing a daubed strip a hundred feet long. Orville Wright was finally compelled to intervene and explain to the literal-minded Atwood that these activities were not essential.

Orville Wright was less than amused by Cal's antics. Although most of his students, including John Rodgers, were invited to his Hawthorne Street residence to sup with his father, Bishop Milton Wright, his sister Katharine, and his brother Lorin,* Cal was not so honored. Katharine Wright, however, was charmed by the tallest member of all the Wright classes and introduced him to her father (who, in his diary, referred to "Calvert Rogers") and other well-known personages in the Dayton area. On one occasion Cal escorted her ("blue eyes, coal-black hair, and an unfailing smile") for an evening at the home of Frank Russell, the Wright Company's general manager.

Eighty-three-year-old Bishop Milton Wright considered Cal's charac-

*Brother Reuchlin was living in Baldwin, Kansas.

ter to be stained by a major vice: smoking. Among his and his children's close associates, only Charley Taylor was an inveterate cigar smoker. The bishop was willing to tolerate one such sinner as an example of his Christian charity, but "Calvert," he noted, carried the vice into the very heavens. "The roots of the tobacco plant," Bishop Wright had sermonized, his patriarchal beard quivering with righteousness, "reach down to the bowels of hell."

By the first of July, Cal concluded that he had absorbed all the aeronautic schooling applicable to his needs. Orville Wright praised his spirited performance but did not invite him to join the Wright Exhibition Team that flew at fairs and air meets around the country. He also reminded his erstwhile student that independent exhibitions or demonstrations with the "B" entailed a fee of $100 per day to the Wright Company in accordance with patent law.

A contract had been arranged with the National Cash Register Company in Dayton for the Rodgers cousins to secure aerial photographs of the company's grounds and buildings.* With Cal and John alternating as aviator and photographer, the contract was fulfilled within the week. Again Cal acquitted himself as a birdman whose capacities could not contain his presumptions. A single sturdy bush marred the otherwise flat landscape of the NCR field; more than once Cal tangled his machine on it.

"Why don't you have the bush removed?" Cal was asked.

"I was brought up to respect the rules of the game," he said.

Determined to perform in exhibitions, Cal convinced John that they should form a two-man aeronautic team. As their business manager, they hired R. S. Richardson, a Cincinnati businessman and aviation correspondent for the *New York Herald,* who printed and distributed notices promoting "The Rodgers Aviators." Richardson negotiated two engagements for the July 4 celebrations: at Urbana (for $500) and Springfield (for $1,000). "You can draw a crowd with a flying exhibition practically anywhere in this country," Tom Milling had said. "The Rodgers Aviators" resolved to prove him right.

When Cal had lifted up on his first solo effort on June 11, his most stalwart admirer was a thin-framed, gristly youth named Charlie Wiggin. A year earlier, as a sixteen-year-old schoolboy in Atlanta, Georgia, Wiggin

*The NCR structures, built by John Patterson in 1886, introduced the "daylight factory"—80 percent of its walls were glass—and, consequently, a new set of working standards for American laborers.

had read accounts of the Wright brothers' experiments with heavier-than-air machines and, mechanically inclined himself, determined to participate in the new enterprise. Forsaking family, friends, and education, he walked the full distance to Montgomery, Alabama,[9] where the Wrights had established an earlier instruction program, and then trailed Orville Wright back to Dayton. Known to everyone at Simms Station as "The Kid," Wiggin had installed himself as the unofficial but dedicated factotum; willing, energetic, and eager to acquire knowledge of aviation, he patterned himself after one of Horatio Alger's young heroes. He would run errands, tote machines and equipment, assist in mechanical repairs, and importune everyone for tutelage in aeronautics. Yet, neither Orville nor Wilbur Wright was willing to reward his services; to support himself he worked as an apprentice mechanician at the Stoddard-Dayton Auto Company.

More than did others at the school, Cal appreciated and admired Wiggin's mettle. He invited the young man to join his new venture as handyman and assistant to mechanician Jack Jacobs, a Dayton resident whom Cal had hired to tend the "B." Wiggin was quick to accept. He turned tail to his job and proclaimed that he was off to tour the country with "my pal, Cal."

The Urbana Chautauqua drew thousands of people from communities in western Ohio; its banner attraction was an aerial performance by the Rodgers cousins. The Wright B was towed the thirty-eight miles from Dayton, and after waiting out an early afternoon storm, Cal and John veered and dipped the big bird machine for fifteen minutes before the grandstand at the Urbana Fairgrounds. The crowning feature of the show was a race around the track between the "B," at an altitude of 200 feet, and a Buick sports car; the Buick proved an easy winner.

With clear skies to the horizon, Cal decided to aviate alone the fourteen miles southward to Springfield. As he circled over that city, his engine quit; he volplaned without mishap onto the racetrack enclosure of the Clark County Fairgrounds. Five thousand people swarmed onto the field over fences, stands, and remonstrating policemen and officials in their efforts to reach the strange machine and its driver.

Meanwhile John Rodgers, manager Richardson, and mechanician Jacobs had run their touring car off the road and suffered a broken axle in their dash for Springfield. Jacobs hailed a passing automobile and arrived at the grounds shortly after six o'clock. Repairs to the engine consumed more than an hour, and not until nearly sunset was Cal able to elevate the aircraft above the city for a brief circuit and thereby earn his fee from the Fair Committee. The "B" was then placed in a tent for close-up viewing by those who paid a twenty-five-cent admission fee.

The day's two exhibitions occasioned Cal's first exposure as the central focus of a sizable gathering. At Urbana, he stood to one side, wrapped in an envelope of silence that discouraged anyone who approached for casual conversation. Later, at Springfield, he relaxed in some measure and mingled with spectators on the field; a slouching posture betrayed a residual uneasiness.

Among the guests on the judges' stand at Springfield was Mrs. Harry Sweitzer. Her husband, although gravely ill, had undertaken a business trip to Chicago, and she had seized the opportunity to accompany him —with an excursion to Springfield for a two-day visit with her son and nephew. She clutched Calbraith to her bosom, immobilizing him with kisses, caresses, squeezes, as if the weight of her affection might render him earthbound forever. "You're alive, you're alive," she sobbed repeatedly into his chest. "My prayers have been answered."

Unable to accept Calbraith's assurances, or those of John Rodgers, that "driving an airplane is as safe as driving an automobile," Mrs. Sweitzer demanded to assess for herself the hazards of this new sporting endeavor and, to that end, traveled from Springfield to Dayton for a confrontation with the font of aeronautic wisdom, Orville Wright. That worthy personage, seasoned by commerce with kings, presidents, and premiers, proved no match for a vigilant mother, instincts aroused. Mrs. Sweitzer cut into his presence like an acetylene torch. She demanded to know how he dared to defy the laws of nature, what he hoped to gain by promoting his flying machines, why he permitted young men—her son in particular—to imperil their lives in such contraptions. Orville Wright could only stammer that he himself, alive and standing before her, the first and therefore most enduring aviator, was the best guaranty that flight entailed no extraordinary risks. Unmollified, Mrs. Sweitzer departed after vowing that she would hold him fully responsible should untoward incident befall her Calbraith.

After the Fourth of July celebrations, John Rodgers was commanded to further duties at the Wright School. In mid-July he and Captain Chambers witnessed officially the acceptance tests of the Navy B-1 (flown by Orville Wright personally).* By then R. S. Richardson had secured two

*Although the navy order called for the B-1 to be outfitted with pontoons, the airplane was delivered with wheels and skids of the standard Type B. Wilbur Wright (still in Europe) did not approve of flying from water and vetoed the pontoons.

more engagements in Ohio: a two-day exhibition at Lima and a brief show at Greenville.

More than 1,000 persons gathered at Lima's Driver Park on July 28 and 29 to witness the first heavier-than-air machine to arrive in Allen County. Demonstrations of the "death-daring spiral glide" and the "Dutch roll" were advertised. Two flights were achieved the first day. Cal flew no higher than 150 feet on each occasion, refusing to allot a free show to the frugal folk who stood outside the high board fence of the park rather than part with the admission price. The second day Cal and John alternately drove the airplane and entertained the crowd with "bomb throwing" contests, hurling oranges from a height of several hundred feet at a target set up on the field.

It was at Lima that Charlie Wiggin became the first lay passenger to accompany Cal aloft—ostensibly demonstrating to spectators that flying was safe even for youngsters. Wiggin had—without success—begged, beseeched, pleaded, and pestered every aviator who flew from the Simms Station field for the grant of a ride in the sky. He dreamed of his first flight, craved it, savored the thought of it, and never ceased his anticipation of it. Now, in its reality, he could not control himself. He shrieked and jabbered with excitement throughout the five minutes of aerial maneuvers he was treated to, pointing out recognizable objects on the ground, leaning forward and rising from his seat with such exuberance that Cal was obliged to hold him in lest he tumble from the airplane. He was surprised to experience no sense of height, no sense of hurtling through the air despite the wind rushing at his face; it was the earth spinning beneath them, not the two men who were moving. His spirits rose higher than the altitude they flew at. When Cal aimed the flying machine toward a landing at the park, Wiggin yelled in protest and strove to will it back into the air.

Thus was "The Kid" further welded in his devotion to his hero. He extracted a promise from Cal that, at some occasion not far in the future, he would be instructed in the art of flying. Wiggin, too, believed that he had found his life's calling.

Encamped in Driver Park at this time was an itinerant carnival. With attendance running below expectations, likely because of the heat and humidity then blanketing the Midwest, some of the carnival workers, among them a young man named Frank Shaffer, found time to follow the Wright biplane buzzing over the grounds. Shaffer was not an undiluted carny; he held himself apart from the gaff lads, teasers, talkers, freaks, and other denizens of the carnival world. He had worked at the Ringling

Brothers' headquarters at Baraboo, Wisconsin, until he married and settled in Lima.

Shaffer had seen airplanes before, although never at close hand. He watched the "B" skim across the field only a few feet high and turn with a wing tip almost scraping the grass ("mushroom hunting," Orville Wright called such stunts). He watched the aircraft in stalls, in steeply banked turns, and marveled as its driver "hit the cable"* and volplaned onto the field for a silent landing.

In matters of mechanics, Cal was open to anyone with an honest and energetic appearance. He learned that Shaffer was responsible for maintenance of the motors and generators that powered the rides and lit the midway. Shaffer was interested in the operation of the Wright engine, and the two men occupied themselves in discussing details of its design. As he concluded his engagement in Lima, Cal invited Shaffer to join his exhibition tour as a helper and as mechanician in the stead of Jack Jacobs, who had returned to Dayton.

The newly formed entourage of Wiggin and Shaffer towed the "B" to Greenville, Ohio, for Cal's fourth engagement (John was again recalled to Dayton). In addition to his usual aerial maneuvers, Cal dropped half a dozen baseballs from an altitude of 500 feet. The catcher, a player from the local team, missed them all.

It became apparent to Cal at this stage that sustaining himself and his assistants and providing lodging, meals, and replacement parts for the flying machine would prove a formidable task. His check from Richardson was inadequate to cover business expenses, repairs, and license fees to the Wrights. Continuing allowances from his mother still spelled the difference between profit and loss.

On August 3, John Rodgers qualified for his FAI certificate† by satisfying the requisite tests at Simms Station. He became the forty-eighth aviator thus confirmed. Cal, sparked by his cousin's example—and the natural rivalry between the two men—promptly applied for his own certificate.

---

*A cable permitted the aviator to disengage engine compression; the propellers would then rotate freely with power off although still geared to the motor. Without this capability, drag from the two eight-foot propellers could stall the machine in midair.

†The FAI (Fédération Aéronautique Internationale) was founded October 14, 1905, in Paris under the leadership of Prince Roland Bonaparte as the governing body for the issuance of licenses. Its first five licenses were awarded to Glenn Curtiss, Frank Lahm, Louis Paulhan, Orville Wright, and Wilbur Wright. No tests were required for these men. The alphabetical ordering seems arbitrary.

The FAI trials entailed the following:

Two distance tests over a closed circuit not less than five kilometers in length.

An altitude test to a minimum height of fifty meters.

A series of figure eights around two marked points situated not more than 500 meters apart.

Each landing to occur less than fifty meters from a point previously designated by the applicant, and the motor to be stopped not later than the moment the machine touches the ground.

On August 7, Cal Rodgers faced his examination. A flagpole near the Simms Station hangar and the thorn tree at the opposite end of the field were ordained as pylons. Three observers took their places, one at the center of the field and one at each "pylon" to confirm that it was properly rounded during the flight. Cal drove his "B" through the prescribed routine and forbore from any flamboyant touches. He was yet prone to "pull the cable" too soon and drop the aero from a height of ten to twenty feet; such faults, however hazardous to skids and wheels, were scarcely noted. His flight, if not surpassingly well done, was within test standards. Calbraith Perry Rodgers entered aviation annals as the forty-ninth birdman recognized by the FAI.

An added incentive for acquiring the prestige of an FAI certificate lay in the upcoming air meet at Chicago, scheduled to open Saturday, August 12. Cal had received an invitation to participate, and the prestige of certification would admit him to the meet without an entrance fee. By August 10, John Rodgers had wangled navy orders directing him "to Chicago, Illinois, to obtain information concerning aeroplanes, etc., and return." The two cousins again had the opportunity to pursue in proximity their mutual love.

With its substantial number of monetary prizes, the Chicago meet would try Cal's ability to continue as an aviator on his own merits. It would also enable reunion with Mabel; more than two months had passed without congress between husband and wife (Mabel's twenty-ninth birthday, July 19, had also passed without notice from Cal, an oversight that Mabel was slow to pardon).

Wiggin and Shaffer towed the "B" from Dayton. Cal and John drove together the 300 miles across Indiana. On the back of their auto they fastened a hand-lettered banner that read, "Chicago, Here We Come."

3

Middletown and Mother

TURNING BACK FROM his easterly heading, Cal Rodgers circled over the Sheepshead Bay field, too occupied with controlling the biplane to relish the thought that he had—at long last!—begun the climb to the upper branches of his family tree. With the planes of the flying machine leveled, he let drop a bundle of leaflets proclaiming that he was on his way to win the $50,000 Hearst prize under the sponsorship of that ideal grape drink, Vin Fiz. Resenting the commercial intrusion into his private pursuit and, even more, the impudence of Vin Fiz president Charles Davidson, Cal considered dumping the leaflets into the East River. He passed over the automobile from which his mother and sister continued to wave farewell and directed himself toward the Erie Railroad terminal in Jersey City where the Vin Fiz special train awaited.

A Hearst reporter asked Cal's mother her thoughts. "I am certain Calbraith will win," Mrs. Schweitzer insisted. "Of course, I am opposed to my boy's flying. But since he is determined, I want him to succeed. And the Wrights have told me that Calbraith is very careful."

Mrs. Pease, Cal's sister, explained that Cal was a cousin of August Belmont, who, she added, was avidly interested in the flight. "Because Cal talks so little, some people have spread a report that there is an impediment in his speech—which is entirely untrue. You should hear his words fly when he is speaking of aviation." She followed the airplane through field glasses as it closed with the horizon.

At Brooklyn's Prospect Park, the Thirteenth Regiment Band struck the final notes of Moszkowski's *Serenade* as the *Vin Fiz* flew over the bandstand. The 2,000 persons in the park cheered and waved their hats although it was not possible to identify the birdman himself at the altitude of several hundred feet. The shimmering of the propeller blades in the sharp autumn sunlight evoked a seemingly ethereal vision.

Over the Brooklyn housetops, the mammoth new Municipal Building, across the East River above the Brooklyn Bridge, Cal continued on a northerly course. Sailors on the battleship *Connecticut,* en route to the Brooklyn Navy Yard, craned to watch the *Vin Fiz* pass overhead. From 800 feet, Cal's view encompassed the profusion of pyramids, spires, ziggurats, and exotic geometries that graced the peaks of Manhattan. Left of the flight line, below City Hall Park, the rose-colored Singer Building, forty-seven stories high, stood out from the canyons of lower Manhattan. Nearby, the Woolworth Building loomed sixty stories over Broadway, a Gothic spire, turreted, gilded, intricately carved. In front of Cal lay the Metropolitan Tower of Madison Square Park; as he approached it, he could read the hour—4:45 P.M.—on its great illuminated clock, and, were it not for the deafening resonance of his engine, could have heard the booming carillon that rang out the quarter-hour. Tens of thousands peered skyward from the streets and rooftops of Manhattan, from windows and fire-escape ledges, some with spyglasses or binoculars. Beneath the *Vin Fiz,* much of the city came to a standstill, many describing the sight of the airplane as the most glorious their eyes had beheld. An excellent view was available from atop the *Journal-American* Building at Duane and Williams streets, as Cal (at the putative behest of William Randolph Hearst) had set his course directly over that edifice. News that the aviator had lifted off from Sheepshead Bay was flashed to the *American* office, and business there was precipitately suspended while everyone in the building rushed to the roof.

If those on the ground were enthralled by the sight of an aeronaut above their city, the aeronaut was more enthralled by his spectacular skyborne perspective of Manhattan. He knew the city, its wrappings and trappings, had explored its burrows and byways, mingled with its people, partaken of its diverse offerings. Now commonplace shapes and patterns deformed into novel, transcendental structures at once both known and unknown. The city and the aviator had moved out of alignment with each other. People left in the city were relics, like his former self—a self without wings—crippled, earthbound, unable to rise above their limitations. "It was as if the rules of the game had been canceled," said Cal later. "There were no goal lines, no sidelines, no umpires. I felt I could step out of the aeroplane and walk on the rooftops. If I had fallen into the streets, the machine would have swooped down and rescued me."

Ten miles into his transcontinental journey, Cal could see its end. It was a vision that had to be shared—and Cal flung out the remaining supply of Vin Fiz leaflets, looking back to watch them fluttering earthward, a paper shower to cleanse the air.

Gusts of wind swirled up the skyscraper faces to rock the planes and refocus the birdman's attention. Cal swayed sportively with the motion. Just short of the Metropolitan Tower, he turned westward over Twenty-third Street and out past the West Side docks. From the Hudson River he could discern the skein of tracks at the Jersey City Erie terminal and shortly thereafter could pick out the white-coated hangar car of the special train holding at the Pavonia Avenue sector of the station yards.

The *Vin Fiz* crossed over the train without circling. Strips of white canvas had been laid between the rails of the Erie main line at intervals for a distance of ten miles to the northwest, and Cal found no difficulty distinguishing their trace among the diverging tracks. As he flew over Passaic, he glanced backward but could not pick out the "iron guide." Engineer Charles Peeley, one of the best "hogs" on the road, had declared his determination to set a pace that would produce a world speed record for aviation. However, the late takeoff had cost the special train its scheduled clearance, and a ten-minute delay ensued while a freight train was shunted from the through track. Peeley complained that he was not allowed an equal chance from the starting gate.

The Sunday holiday afforded workers and businessmen alike opportunity to witness the airplane. Some families brought picnic baskets and camped by the Erie tracks. Mostly, people were alerted by bells and steam whistles sounded in communities along the route.

Cal and the Erie tracks passed northward across Paterson, traversing the Passaic River a second time. At P.S. 52 in Paterson, one block from the Erie line, a group of schoolboys waved energetically. The school principal, Sam Weintraub, a progressive educator who included studies of the Wright brothers in his curriculum, had gathered his charges on this Sunday afternoon to observe the passage of the flying machine. After the airplane disappeared to the north, Weintraub addressed the boys of P.S. 52. "Men," he said, "if you mind your p's and q's and keep yourselves clean in mind and deed, you may, someday, have the opportunity actually to meet a birdman such as Mr. Rodgers and to shake his hand."

At 5:30 P.M. Cal crossed from New Jersey back into New York at the town of Suffern. A pedestrian bridge straddling the tracks drew much of the local population for the occasion. In the assembly were Mr. and Mrs. Frank Pulis and their nine-year-old son, Milton. The Pulises had recently removed to Oakland, New Jersey, but their enthusiasm for aviation had brought them back by horse-drawn fringed surrey over the eight miles of rough dirt road. As the *Vin Fiz* flew by amid cheers of encouragement, Frank Pulis examined the map on which he had drawn a course for Middletown. "By George," he opined to his wife, "I think he's a bit too far to the east."

Four tracks of the Erie line passed under the Suffern pedestrian bridge, branching out to the north. Cal followed an eastern track, the Erie & Jersey Freight line, for another ten minutes before realizing his mistake. Familiar with the topography through a diligent study of pertinent maps, he recognized the town of Newburgh even before the profile of the Hudson River became visible. He veered westward along the Ontario & Western track from Crystal Run.

On the special train, Mabel Rodgers, her face flushed with exhilaration, hopped from side to side, peering out of windows to catch sight of the *Vin Fiz*. She chatted gaily with others in the aviation party without disrupting her movements to and fro. Freed from the compass of her mother-in-law and other reproving personages, she lit a Sobranny cigarette and exhaled puffs of smoke from cheek bellows satisfyingly filled.

With Mrs. deKrafft, Mrs. Shaffer, and Mrs. Wettengel (included as amanuensis for her husband's business correspondence), the female contingent on board totaled four. Mabel, as wife of the principal actor in the road show and, at twenty-nine, the youngest of the four ladies, assumed the combined roles of prima donna and queen bee ("I have more than thirty beautiful young men on the train to escort me across the country"). To Thomas Hanly of the *New York American*, she waxed effervescent: "My husband and I could not be happier or more confident. To start for the prize has been Calbraith's sole ambition since he learned to fly. He has a perfect machine and perfect control. The weather is perfect, too. A few days of this, and he will make the records fly."

Three cars composed the Vin Fiz special train and carried some forty persons, each animated with the spirit of a novel and challenging enterprise. Whenever two passengers exchanged glances, they beamed in tacit acknowledgment of the shared adventure.

Behind the Baldwin 4-4-0 engine rode the Vin Fiz hangar car, painted white and trailing long streamers for identification from the air. Black letters on its sides proclaimed the virtues of Vin Fiz carbonated grape drink, "Sold Everywhere at 5¢." Inside, mechanician Frank Shaffer, chauffeur Jimmy Dunn, and six crew members rested on their pallets, keyed up despite their night without sleep, and assured each other that the *Vin Fiz Flyer* had been rendered equal to any charge its driver might exact. Edward Sutton, overseer and dispenser of supplies, wound through the car rechecking his inventory: a disassembled Wright Type B airplane, the Palmer-Singer automobile, spare parts including four planes, rolls of rubberized-duck fabric, spools of piano wire (from Steinway & Sons), and a full machine workshop with tools and hardware.

In the day coach, coupled next in line, ten reporters from the Hearst newspapers and other publications toasted the occasion with bourbon-filled paper cups (a goodly number of pocket flasks had been sneaked aboard) and offered wagers and prognostications—heavily weighted to the negative—on the eventual outcome of the ocean-to-ocean attempt. A photographer, Victor Palumbo of the *American,* moved down the aisle, recording on film each occupant of the coach car: officers and representatives of the Armour and Vin Fiz companies, local officials accompanying the expedition for short distances along its route, and three agents of the Erie Railroad, in addition to the reporters.

The third car, a private Pullman,* *Zura,* reflected the acme of railroading luxury. Paneled in vermilion walnut with hand-carved moldings, its parlor compartment extended the forward fifteen feet. Its two staterooms were lined with red tufted velour and trimmed with scrolled-oak wainscoting. One stateroom was reserved for Cal and Mabel, the other for Mr. and Mrs. Wettengel. The Wettengels, the deKraffts, Charles Davidson, Ed Merritt, Joe Newborn, and Andre Roosevelt congregated in the dining salon to the rear of the staterooms and congratulated themselves on concocting the greatest advertising scheme in American history. Mabel, "in the right church but the wrong pew," walked through the corridor that spanned the length of the car, passing the upholstered seats behind the salon that converted to eight partitioned and curtained berths (four uppers and four lowers), alongside the rear section that contained a por-

*Also known as a "private varnish" because its interior was varnished to a high gloss, reflecting its opulence.

celain-tiled W.C., culinary and serving facilities, and narrow sleeping quarters (segregated) for chef Ed Davis and two Negro stewards, George and George.* A door at the end of the platform opened onto a cowled observation platform ringed with a cast-iron railing. Mabel mounted the few spiral steps rising from the platform; at the top step she was rewarded with a 360° view of the sky through a glass bubble mounted on the roof. Scanning left and right, up and down, her hands cupped to her eyes, she could find no trace of the *Vin Fiz.*

At 6:14 P.M., Cal hove into view of Middletown; he would recognize it, he had been told, by its numerous church steeples. Whistles of the O & W shops shrilled—the first indication to Middletowners that the aviator was approaching. Entering from the north, Cal swung around the city in a wide arc at 500 feet to afford the townspeople a full view of the machine in flight. More than 9,000 persons had gathered in the open field of the Academy Avenue Pleasure Grounds on the city's outskirts to welcome the birdman. A pack of several hundred automobiles formed an outline of the grounds. Cal dipped the airplane abruptly to less than 200 feet, traced a circle around the area, a figure eight across the grounds, and then straightened his trajectory for a landing. The excited burghers, screaming with delight, swept past the few policemen struggling to hold them back and darted beneath and ahead of the machine. Cal was forced to rise again for fear of injuring those below him. He circled through three more swoops, attempting to "shoo" away the crowd by quickly retarding and advancing the magneto spark and rocking the planes. This action and a determined effort by the policemen cleared a pathway of about 200 feet, and the *Vin Fiz* dropped into it without a jolt.

Before the machine stopped rolling, the crowd surged around it. Fire Chief Charles ("Chick") Higham, his metallic-red, sapphire-studded Gratacap helmet flashing in the sun like a beacon, Police Chief John McCoach, Mayor Rosalyn Cox, and other Middletown officials stepped forward to greet Rodgers, but were shoved aside in the rush to grabble at the airplane. Lincoln Beachey,[1] perhaps the country's most skilled aeronaut, had aviated from Newburgh especially to offer encouragement to his fellow flier; he, too, was unable to break through the tumultuous assemblage. George Kaler, manager of the Armour Company's Middletown branch, managed to reach Cal first and also to restrain a few overwrought youngsters while the machine was designated out-of-bounds by staked ropes.

---

*By command of George Pullman, all Negro porters were addressed as "George."

A goodly percentage of the throng was composed of young children and adolescent lads. Not only were they more spirited, but their eyes perceived a dimension of the flying machine unrevealed to their elders. And they could claim experience with aviation: The same youngsters, two weeks earlier, had trooped out to view the Curtiss machine driven by Beckwith Havens at the Orange County Fair.

At 6:20 P.M. the special train pulled past the Pleasure Grounds, having completed the sixty-seven-mile run from Jersey City in seventy-five minutes, with but a single brief pause to query the dispatcher at the local division office regarding the airplane's whereabouts. Shortly thereafter, mechanician Frank Shaffer, manager Stewart deKrafft, and the several crew members raced onto the field. They inspected the machine and clapped Cal on the back for his performance.

Cal, within a tight ring of policemen, waving to the hundreds of people that clustered about the escort, was bustled across the grounds and into a red Mercer runabout with Fire Chief Higham at the wheel. To a reporter from the *Middletown Times-Press,* he said that he would remain in the city during the night and arise for an early start in the morning. Chief Higham, his helmet pulled tight against the wind, then drove off to the Commercial House at West Main and Canal streets.

At the Middletown Railroad Station, Mabel Rodgers disembarked and was immediately taken to her husband's side. Unabashed at the presence of reporters, she bussed and hugged him and primped herself openly while posing for photographers. She then withdrew as Cal joined his managers for supper at the Commercial dining room.

Cal summed up the day's events in his bulletin to the Hearst newspapers:

> *I left Sheepshead Bay at 4:33 o'clock. . . . I never had the least trouble, my engine working as fine as one ever did, and the only thing that I had to contend with was the air currents over the Ramapo Mountains. Two thousand feet was the highest altitude that I attained, and this was in passing over these mountains when I had to ascend to this height in order to select a landing place in case of engine failure or some other mechanical problem.*
>
> *I was off the main line for a time. I did not know it at the time but discovered it later for I was familiar with this country.*
>
> *The only difficulty in landing was to avoid hitting somebody, but I came down smoothly. It is always a good landing when I don't knock the ashes off my cigar.*

I am in this race to win, and I intend to do so providing that I am not hindered by accidents. However, given an even break of luck, I should make the other entrants in the race know that I am after them. I expect to catch Jimmy Ward by Tuesday night and telegraphed him this afternoon to that effect.

Over his circuitous route, Cal had covered 105 miles in one hour, forty-three minutes.

Included in the supper gathering in the hotel's dining room was aviator Lincoln Beachey. He and Cal had met a month earlier at the Chicago International Air Meet, where Beachey had gained second-place money-winning honors (to Cal's third place). One of the few birdmen besides Cal to top six feet (by an inch), Beachey was a gracious competitor whose well-wishes were genuinely conferred. Attired in a natty, pinstriped suit with a two-carat diamond stickpin for his tie, he was reputed to be the most romantic of aviators, trailing a string of disappointed "fiancées" across the country. He had raced his cigar-shaped dirigible balloon at the Dominguez Meet* and there had been introduced to William Randolph Hearst. He was asked to recount his story of Hearst and the Dominguez Meet, and he responded with practiced grace:

"It was the next to last day of the meet—January of last year, I recollect. I had just finished racing my air bag against Roy Knabenshue† when Hearst came in—the grandest entrance you ever did see. He was surrounded by a retinue of more than a hundred of his people—editors, photographers, writers, what have you. Everyone in the stands and on the field stopped to watch.

"We shook hands, then he walked over to the parterre in front of the grandstand and was presented to Louie Paulhan. Now that was some sight: 'W.R.,' with his long legs and heavy stomach, talking French with Louie, who is five feet two inches and was dressed in checked breeches and wrap-around puttees. Louie was billed as 'The World's Greatest Aviator,' and to prove it he invited Hearst to 'buss the clouds,' as Louie put it.‡ 'W.R.' was not loath to accept.

*America's first air meet was held at Dominguez Hills, 20 miles south of Los Angeles, Calif. Over 11 days, from Jan. 10 to Jan. 20, 1910, it attracted 176,466 paid admissions at 50¢ each.

†Beachey won the race in a world record 4 minutes, 58 seconds over the 1.61-mile course.

‡Louis Paulhan had already, earlier that day, set a world record for passenger-carrying, having taken aloft in successive flight four newspaper correspondents, seven smart-set damsels from Los Angeles, his wife, and his French poodle, Escapette.

"Well, Hearst was so impressed with his flight that he wrote a personal account of it for his own newspapers. Every one of you should read it. Of course, he didn't stop there. 'W.R.' always backed up his 'pet diversions' with money—$50,000 in this instance. And that's why we are all here in Middletown tonight with Cal Rodgers."

"This diversion," Cal declared, "is going to cost him the fifty thousand. If you see him again, you tell him that."

After supper Jimmy Dunn drove Cal and Stewart deKrafft in the Palmer-Singer racer back to the Pleasure Grounds. His two competitors, deKrafft apprised Cal, had posted no progress that day. Jimmy Ward was stranded in Owego, his engine disabled and without the $2,000—in cash money—demanded by Glenn Curtiss for delivery of a replacement. Ward's manager, Ike Bloom, in Buffalo arranging for a landing site in that city, had vowed to raise the money but was encountering difficulties. Bob Fowler had repaired the damage to his *Cole Flyer* but was still in Colfax, California, redesigning his motor for the rarefied air of the Sierras.[2]

An impending contender for the Hearst prize, New York aviator Earle Ovington, announced that he would leave New York City on Thursday or Friday, bound for the West Coast. He would drive a Queen Blériot monoplane equipped with a powerful (70-horsepower) Gnome engine.

Cal's other concern centered on the Giants, unscheduled for play this Sunday. DeKrafft informed him that the Chicagos had twice beaten the Brooklyns, thus creeping to four games behind the New York team. With the Philadelphias ahead by eight in the American League, opponents for the World Series were clearly foretold.

At the field, mechanicians Frank Shaffer and Charlie Wiggin (who had just regained the expedition) and members of the crew were inspecting the *Vin Fiz*. The group completed its ministrations, posted two crewmen as guards, and departed for the evening. Cal and deKrafft returned to the Commercial House, the others to sleeping quarters on the special train.

During a strategy meeting at the hotel with his managers, Cal urged that train movements be better coordinated with his speed in the aircraft; when the special was needed as a pilot to Middletown, it was nowhere in sight. Still, the first lap of the transcontinental journey had been completed, and the key figures of the enterprise toasted their resourcefulness and praised themselves on their first success. Another twenty-odd hops, it was estimated, and they would cap their efforts with a victory celebration at the Pacific Ocean. DeKrafft and Andre Roosevelt then laid out the route for the next day. Lawrence Peters, the advance man, had arranged for gasoline and supplies at four sites: Callicoon, Binghamton, Elmira, and

Hornell, 264 miles distant. The mark would establish the record for a single day's flight.

Everyone in the party, it was agreed, would convene at six o'clock the following morning at the Pleasure Grounds. Cal retired to his hotel room.

Two hours later the 11:37 train pulled into the Middletown Station. Lieutenant John Rodgers, his naval uniform replaced by civilian dress, stepped off, found his way to the Commercial House, and checked into a room without encountering anyone from the Vin Fiz camp. Mabel was about, on the town with several of the more prominent ladies and gents of Middletown, the latter led by Fire Chief Chick Higham. When she returned to the hotel shortly before midnight, Cal was submerged in sleep.

The special train was shunted to a siding. Duane Wyznecki, the fireman, filled its boilers with water to build maximum pressure and "pop" the safety valve. A fire watcher was assigned to restoke the furnace as required to maintain stationary steam. Wyznecki banked the fire and stretched out on a cot in the station house.

About 300 spectators had already congregated at the Pleasure Grounds by 6:00 A.M. as mechanicians and crew prepared the *Vin Fiz* for flight. The temperature was in the low forties, and Cal had donned knee-high leggings to ward off the cold. Between his coat and shirt, he stuffed wads of newspaper sheets (a motorcyclist's device). Still, he shivered and stomped his feet to foster circulation. A young lady dashed up to present him with a medallion of Saint Gebbard. He pinned it to his lapel.

John Rodgers had risen early to greet his cousin and to contribute his own knowledge of practical aeronautics. The two men, their common ancestry evident in their bearing and lineaments, their friendship evident in their gestures to each other, strode about, assessing wind conditions and inspecting the grounds—morass on the southwest, a hollow to the southeast, the grass and dirt covering cut up by circus rings and trampling mobs. John advised that Cal aim in a line above the willow trees that fringed the Draper brook to the north.

After Shaffer tested the motor, the crew pushed the airplane toward the lower end of the field and faced it northward. The aviator settled onto his perch; Wiggin and McNally pulled through the propellers. Only the trace of a breeze could be felt. Cal stuck a cigar in his mouth, lit it, and called out, "Let her go, boys."

The machine bounced along the field for about 150 feet, barely clearing the four-foot stone wall surrounding the Pleasure Grounds, and lurched into the air directly toward the row of long-branched willows. Cal threaded the craft between two trees, the tips of the wings cutting through leaves and twigs at both sides. He pulled on the elevator-control lever and rose to a height of about forty feet. He seemed oblivious to the perilous position he had just escaped. Across his path stretched the line of telegraph wires on Fulton Street. Realizing that he could not clear the wires without extraordinary maneuvers, he dipped the biplane a few feet and then attempted a sudden swell to lift it over the obstruction. The effort proved unavailing. As it passed over a hickory tree in the rear yard of Harry van Curen's house, the machine caught its rudder on the upper limb of the tree and was deflected from its course.

Cal struggled with the levers, but the biplane was beyond his control. It dove earthward. It smashed into a chicken coop, killing several fowl, and partly buried itself in the soft ground. Cal was hurled from his seat and fell beneath the machine, its nose crumpled, its shredded tail upright, hung high on a hickory limb. The 196-pound engine tore loose from its mountings but caromed to one side and just missed crushing the aviator. Chicken feathers settled onto the scene for several seconds, while the three remaining hens squawked their outrage at this intrusion.

Harry van Curen was jolted from sleep and peered out his bedroom window at the wreckage. Two neighbors, Arthur and Eugene Conkling, rushed out ahead of Van Curen and pulled Cal from under the tangle of spars and fabric. The aviator was semiconscious, the only stirring a wisp of smoke rising from the cigar locked between his teeth. Most of those who had witnessed the start sprinted frantically to the crash site. In the forefront was Dr. Moses Stivers, who proceeded to administer first aid; Dr. Henry McBrair reached the aviator but a few seconds later, followed by John Rodgers. Cal remained supine, eyes closed, not responding to questions. John knelt down beside the body. The ash of Cal's cigar glowed, and smoke trailed from his nostrils.

"All right," said John, arising, "don't just lie there. The ship is sailing. . . ."

At the Erie Railroad Station, Fire Chief Chick Higham had posted himself as observer. He instantly ran to the train and alerted Andre Roosevelt, who grabbed a medical kit from the hangar car. The two men jumped into the chief's Mercer and raced to the scene of the accident.

Cal was sitting up, clutching the lacerations in his scalp, bleeding from a cut above his left temple, when Chief Higham braked the automobile and, with Roosevelt, leaped out to his side. The coat and trousers of his new business suit (from one of Manhattan's elite tailors, ordered and paid for by Mrs. Sweitzer) were torn through in several places and imparted the impression that the aviator was as damaged as his airplane. It was ascertained that except for a mild concussion, his injuries consisted mostly of cuts and bruises.

Chief Higham and Andre Roosevelt lifted Cal into Dr. McBrair's automobile, and the group motored quickly to the Commercial House. There Cal was examined thoroughly, bandaged, and ordered to bed. "And make sure he stays there," Dr. McBrair enjoined Mabel, who had been retrieved and delivered to the hotel by Chief Higham. Within minutes, however, Cal shook the fog from his head, shrugged off Mabel's ministrations and protests, and limped outdoors—where he commandeered an automobile, directing it to where the shambled mess of the *Vin Fiz Flyer* lay, its planes crumpled, its elevator and rudder surfaces twisted and suspended on broken longerons. "Poor, poor Betsy," sighed its human counterpart.

With John Rodgers, Frank Shaffer, and young Charlie Wiggin, who hovered solicitously near his "pal," ready to catch him should he keel over, Cal surveyed the damage. It was apparent that virtually every vital component was wrecked beyond restoration. Only the radiator and gasoline tank had survived unscathed.

Stewart deKrafft and Fred Wettengel joined the group for a brief conference. "The end of the line," muttered Wettengel, pondering the wreckage. The others nodded glumly in concurrence. Cal continued poking about disconsolately in the jumble of smashed parts. He kicked at a shard of metal—and exposed a portion of the Vin Fiz bottle. He bent down, picked it up, and found the bottle intact. For some moments he stared at it—an unpalatable product, a materialistic indignity, a token of compromise. Yet . . . it was unbroken. "Boys," said Cal, "we're going on!"

John Rodgers clapped his cousin on the back. The only sensible course, all agreed, lay in a return to New York for another start with another flying machine. The thirty-day clock for the Hearst prize would begin to tick anew. DeKrafft left to wire the Wright brothers in Dayton regarding the immediate construction and delivery of a second EX biplane. Wettengel conveyed this decision to reporters standing about the ruins. Cal, still groggy and in pain from his wounds, retired to his room at the Commercial House. The decision made, he would submit to his body's demand for recuperation.

He did not rest for long. DeKrafft returned from the telegraph office with a reply from the Wright factory at Dayton—"Price and delivery date of new EX to follow"—and a telegram from Jimmy Ward—"Will start this morning [Monday] for Detroit, 417 miles. Good luck. Good flying."

It was this second message that propelled Cal out of bed once again.

"We're in a race," he pointed out to deKrafft. "Restarting our clock doesn't restart Ward or Fowler. We're going on from here!"

DeKrafft scribbled some notes on his celluloid cuffs. They would have to salvage a few pieces of the machine, he reminded Cal, to remain in accordance with Hearst regulations. "Do it," said Cal. "I'll be ready."

DeKrafft and Wettengel, the latter with evident reluctance, conferred with officials at Middletown City Hall and gained permission for use of the asylum grounds. The *Vin Fiz* was then dismantled and carried to the asylum, where crewmen laid out the pieces like a Chinese puzzle.

Cal addressed his crew: "Boys, here we have the opportunity to do what all the king's horses and all the king's men couldn't do—put Humpty Dumpty back together again." His listeners responded with a rousing cheer.

Cal's optimistic tone proved contagious and soon replaced the initial despondency of the aviation party. DeKrafft stated to the press that Rodgers would be able to resume the race Tuesday afternoon or Wednesday morning if the mechanicians were successful in their rebuilding efforts. Meanwhile correspondence would be continued with the Wright brothers for their assistance. "I want it made as emphatic as possible," deKrafft told the *Times-Press* reporter, "that we are going through to the Coast unless something decidedly more serious than this accident happens." Cal added that he and his colleagues were far from discouraged, and promised that he would soon demonstrate some sensational flying to make up for the lost time.

Mabel, unable to capture her husband from his preoccupation with re-creating the flying machine, even to soothe him with sympathetic words, turned her efforts toward retrieving the letters and postcards scattered wildly over the crash site. She was soon surrounded by curious urchins who chanted, over and over, "Ain't it awful, Mabel? Ain't it awful, Mabel?" (a currently popular catchphrase). "If I ever catch you, you little guttersnipes," she flared back, "I'll awful *you.*"

In the afternoon the Middletown telegrapher, George Corwin, brought to the asylum grounds a second message from the Wright factory: "Advise rebuilding at Middletown. Send list of parts not with your equipment. Have complete upper and lower parts needed. Could spare two experienced men. Taylor hopes to leave tonight. Wire him instructions. Could ship another express in five days. F. G. Russell, General Manager."

To expedite communication, John Rodgers tried and succeeded in telephoning directly to Dayton. He confirmed that stock parts would arrive as an LCL (less than carload lot) shipment on Erie train No. 2 at

5:41 P.M. that evening. The engine from the *Vin Fiz* would be shipped to the factory; he would accompany it to supervise its repair and return. Meanwhile the extra engine carried in the hangar car would be installed in the rebuilt machine. A salary of $10 per day was proffered to Charley Taylor, the Wrights' chief mechanician and general superintendent; Taylor promised to board an overnight train from Dayton.

Fowler, it was learned, had also encountered adversity. He narrowly escaped death when the Colfax Hotel in which he was abiding was destroyed by fire. His mother had pounded on his door and roused him just in time to evacuate the building before it collapsed. No firefighting apparatus was available in Colfax to stay the progress of the flames.

Cal's concern over Jimmy Ward's competition was underscored when a reporter informed the aviation party that Ward had departed Owego at 10:43 that morning and, after a sky jaunt of 54 miles, had landed in Corning, 280 miles from New York City, at 11:35. The reporter added that Earle Ovington, in Boston, had rescheduled his departure from New York for September 27. There would soon be four rivals in the $50,000 air race.

Charles Davidson, the Vin Fiz Company president, took advantage of the hiatus to promote the image of his product. He instructed two crew members to letter the Palmer-Singer auto with the words *Vin Fiz Flyer* on the hood, *Official Car* on the rear, and *C. P. Rodgers* on each side. He also telegraphed the O. J. Gude Company in New York City for two sign artists.

Later in the afternoon Mrs. John Heddy, owner of the defunct chickens, accosted Fred Wettengel and demanded payment for her loss. She had been feeding her hens, she said, and had just left the spot for her porch a few steps away when the flying machine slammed down on the chicken coop. Her heart, she added dramatically, was still palpitating. Wettengel promptly settled the matter for all damages incurred.

While Cal and his crew were absorbed in the work of reconstruction, Mabel was inspecting the sights of Middletown courtesy of Fire Chief Higham and his Mercer runabout. Chick Higham, fancied as the town's leading gay blade, was inordinately proud of his automobile, and whenever a conflagration drew the Middletown fire truck, the Mercer with the chief at the wheel tootling his musical horn was close in its wake. He drove Mabel across the Walkill River trolley bridge to Midway Park between Middletown and Goshen. At the park he rented a canoe and paddled about the lake for two hours while Mabel mooned beneath a parasol. "You're a caution," she told him.

Monday evening the chief's Fife, Drum, and Bugle Corps staged its annual dance at Linden Hall. After a parade from the fire station, the corps proceeded to the hall, where Calbraith Perry and Mrs. Mabel Rodgers had been inducted as the guests of honor. Cal found himself the cynosure of the party. The light in his eye, dimmed for a time from the morning's debacle, had regained its luster; the cut of his jib was as striking as ever. Bandage strips across his forehead, he held a levee in one corner of the hall, where well-wishers lined up for a presentation. Mabel, gussied up in silk finery, drew decorous applause when she ambled through a cakewalk with Chief Higham as her partner.

Charles Davidson, a squat, boneless man in a rumpled suit and vest, whose mind marched to a one-note tune, arrived with 200 Vin Fiz pennants and distributed them to the young ladies in attendance. He also ordered several cases of Vin Fiz soda from the plentiful supply he had stowed in the Vin Fiz hangar car carried to the hall. George Kaler, the Vin Fiz Company's local manager, attempted to serve cups of the soft drink, but was unable to effect inroads against the harder spirits. At one point a news bulletin was read: A final tabulation confirmed that voters in Maine had repealed that state's dry laws by twenty votes. The announcement was received with lusty applause.

As the festivities were ending, the late-evening train from New York City chugged into the Middletown station. Out stepped Cal's mother, the formidable Mrs. Harry Sweitzer. After Cal's departure from Sheepshead Bay, she had continued her visit at her daughter's Hempstead, Long Island, home and was planning her trip back to Pittsburgh. Immediately upon learning of the accident, she had packed a suitcase and boarded the next train to Middletown. At the Commercial House she planted herself in the lobby and awaited the return of her son and daughter-in-law from the Linden Hall dance.

Mabel walked into the hotel after midnight. Cal had elected to pass the night in the private Pullman car despite her protestations. They had enjoyed no marital connection in over a week, she had warranted, and urged him to share the Commercial House's more comfortable bed. But no words could move him when his mind was set or—as in this instance —focused on other concerns. There was no argument between husband and wife since Calbraith P. Rodgers did not argue. He followed his course, and she was left to follow hers. Mabel's temper was not improved by the unexpected appearance of Mrs. Sweitzer.

From five feet nine inches, Mrs. Sweitzer looked down upon her daughter-in-law with a two-inch advantage in height and a towering preeminence in fortitude. As the late Harry Sweitzer was fond of saying, "She could have given Stonewall Jackson a few pointers in tactics." Unswayed by Mabel's assurances and reassurances that Calbraith had survived the crash without significant injury, Mrs. Sweitzer insisted upon witnessing the *corpus respirati* for herself. She strode back to the railway station and found her way to the forward stateroom of the Vin Fiz Pullman. For a few moments she stood gazing at the bandaged, sleeping form folded onto the train berth. Mollified, she then returned to the Commercial House, where she consented to share lodgings with Mabel for the evening.

Early Tuesday morning Mrs. Sweitzer confronted her son. She reproached him for his thoughtlessness in not immediately notifying her of his mishap, and demanded that he abandon his attempt at cross-country flying. She threatened to withdraw her financial support, her familial and prayerful support. She pleaded with him. She raised the image of motherhood sacrificed and the spirit of Calbraith's father, dead before the birth of his son. Mabel, when she managed to intervene in the conversation, defended her husband and upheld his resolve to continue. Her words were scarcely heard by either husband or mother-in-law.

Mrs. Sweitzer had not arrived in Middletown armed solely with a mother's emotion. She cited the increasing number of deaths in aerial accidents. Lieutenant Cannell had been killed in England the very afternoon that Cal rose from Sheepshead Bay. The French aviator Eduard Nieuport had died of internal injuries only the day previous when his airplane crashed at Verdun. Lieutenant de Grailly, John Frisbee, Kelly, Vallon, Cei, Laffort, Arch Hoxsey, et al.—Mrs. Sweitzer had compiled the list back to Lieutenant Thomas Selfridge, first to die since the inception of powered flight. For all its effect on Cal, the toll of deaths could as well have been a registry of Romans killed in the Punic Wars. His charmed life, he knew, could not be endangered by the mortality of his precursors.

"Yes, mother. Yes, mother," was the only response to defang the bite of Mrs. Sweitzer's argument.

Mother was left in the charge of Fred Wettengel while Cal and Chief Higham drove in the Mercer runabout to Port Jervis to assess the terrain between that village and Middletown. Meanwhile deKrafft announced that takeoff would occur Wednesday afternoon and that because of expenses resulting from Monday morning's accident, a fee of 25¢ would be levied for admission to the grounds. Rodgers would reach Chicago the following Monday, deKrafft promised, after stops in New York, Pennsylvania, Ohio, and Indiana.

Andre Roosevelt and Lawrence Peters boarded a train for Callicoon to prepare arrangements en route. They would remain in advance of the main party and telegraph back confirmations. A cousin of Teddy Roosevelt, albeit without his forceful personality, Andre Roosevelt found himself explaining to Callicoon officials that the former president was not aboard the special train but was closely following its progress. (Almost a year earlier "T.R." had been carried aloft for a three-minute excursion by Wright aviator Arch Hoxsey while 10,000 people at Kinloch Park, St. Louis, cheered his bravery.)

Mabel's admirers in Middletown were not limited to Chief Chick Higham. Several members of the male population attached themselves to her wake, and she was pleased to encourage their homage. Mabel was particularly partial to younger men, and when two—twenty-three-year-old Charlie Hibbard and a youth of seventeen named "Allie"—volunteered for the Vin Fiz expedition, she hired them as her "assistant mailmen." Their duties, deKrafft noted, "seemed too light to anchor a ten-inch balloon."

Middletown's public-spirited businessmen proclaimed their patronage for the city's newest, most favored guest. There was talk of a $5,000 subscription to purchase a new airplane for Cal, and the Middletown Electric Railroad contributed $1,000 to defray rebuilding costs. The armory was thrown open for use as Cal's headquarters. The birdman and his wife were inundated with social invitations. Max Gansl, the awning maker and upholsterer at 10 Union Street, gratuitously constructed a canvas cover for the flying machine, that it might be shielded from the overnight dampness. Marvin Schiffman, the tailor, had estimated Cal's measurements from afar and shortly presented the aviator with a new suit to replace that tattered in the crash. "Much obliged," said Cal.

Newspaper accounts told of Jimmy Ward's unplanned descent at Corning the day before, his new Curtiss engine spurting oil after its first hour of work. "I don't care," Ward insisted. "I'm going on to the Pacific Coast however long it takes. Even if I don't get through in 30 days to win [the Hearst prize], I am certainly going to be the first man to fly across the American continent. I am sorry to hear that Rodgers has had bad luck, but am happy to hear he wasn't hurt." Ward had been sent forth from Owego with a kiss from Mrs. Maude Ward, his bride of seven months. His projected route lay via Lockport, New York, crossing the air maelstrom above Niagara Falls, and on to Brantford, Ontario: "I can't resist a flight over the Falls, even if it does add a few miles to my path."

Robert Fowler was yet awaiting additional replacement parts, unable to rise from Colfax, California. He was disheartened to learn that owing to confusion in his telegraphed messages, a new rudder section ordered from the Wright factory had been standing unattended at the Dayton depot awaiting shipment.

Components ordered by the Vin Fiz enterprise fared better. Additional parts arrived from Dayton shortly after midnight and were immediately laid out on the fairgrounds, where Cal, Shaffer, Wiggin, and the crew members had been laboring all evening. The Palmer-Singer motorcar had been driven to the grounds, and work carried on under the light from its lamps and from lanterns furnished by the Erie Railroad Company.

Cal left the field at 3:30 A.M. after assuring himself that the EX biplane was nearing its former constitution. He folded himself onto a cot in the hangar car for the next several hours. Mrs. Sweitzer again passed the night at the Commercial House with Mabel. She could not bring herself to view the dismembered flying machine; she could not sway her son from his headstrong course; nor could she return without further ceremony to the comforts of home and friends in Pittsburgh.

Cal arose at ten o'clock Wednesday morning to stare at a gray Maltese kitten that had wandered up the auto ramp into the hangar car. The meow was given the name "Vin" and adopted as the party's mascot; Edward Sutton, the supply-keeper, was assigned to fetch cream for it from chef Davis. After sporting with the kitten for a short time, Cal walked to the field to watch the two sign artists from New York City decorate the airplane fabric with advertisements for Vin Fiz soft drink. No available space was overlooked.

Frank Shaffer advised that through some misunderstanding, the Wright factory had delivered wires for the rudder planes instead of for the warping planes as ordered. A local hardware dealer was quickly located; the proper gauge of wire purchased along with stock of bolts, wood screws, and galvanic steel strips.

DeKrafft announced takeoff for one o'clock. He informed Cal that Jimmy Ward had left Corning earlier in the morning but had advanced only thirteen miles when a leaky water pipe forced his descent. The propeller of his Curtiss biplane was smashed upon landing, and Ward was now stalled at the hamlet of Addison. Cal dictated a telegram to his rival: "Too bad, old man, sorry to hear you down again. Grit like yours is bound to kill the jinx and win. Gray kitten came into my hangar car this morning and turned the luck. Will take to air this afternoon if possible. Cal Rodgers."

At noon Shaffer concluded that he could not certify the machine for safe flight. Heated contentions ensued between mechanicians and managers. Cal sided with his mechanicians, and takeoff was postponed another day. Plaints were voiced by Armour and Vin Fiz officials sated with their sojourn in Middletown. Yet more disgruntled was the locomotive crew of the special train. After the crash of Monday morning, the engine fire had been allowed to burn out. Fireman Wyznecki had risen at five on Wednesday morning to nurse the power plant through the six hours required to increase steam pressure to the 200-pounds-per-square-inch operating level. Engineer Peeley was replaced by E. A. McAllister, and the latter now decided—with the delay estimated at twenty hours—to sustain a spot fire rather than allow the engine to cool down again.

DeKrafft released to the press the revised schedule and added that, because of the exceptional courtesy accorded the entire aviation party, no charge would be levied for admission. Within minutes he was given cause to regret his largesse. He and Wettengel were confronted by Mr. Barnes, a Wright representative in New York, who demanded settlement of an overdue bill of $1,300. Nine days of flying during the Chicago Air Meet in August plus two exhibitions in Wisconsin, Barnes computed, totalled $1,100 at the standard Wright licensing fee of $100 per day. Flights from New York on Sunday and from Middletown on Monday morning added $200 more. DeKrafft protested that Monday's flight covered all of several hundred feet and could not justify an assessment. He also challenged the legality of the Wrights' claim. Wettengel, however, placidly paid the $1,300 to Barnes, further raising deKrafft's ire.

Even before the expedition had begun Sunday afternoon, Stewart deKrafft and Fred Wettengel had discovered a natural and mutual antipathy. Resentment seethed from their overlapping roles (deKrafft as general manager and Wettengel as business manager) and erupted with the crash and subsequent delays. An hour after the meeting with Mr. Barnes, the two men encountered each other on James Street in the central section of Middletown. DeKrafft, four inches taller and thirty-five pounds heavier than his adversary, took offense at a comment casting doubt on the wisdom of persisting with the enterprise and landed his fist heavily on Wettengel's upper lip. The lip swelled up like "Pop" Smith's favorite Sunday-morning breakfast cereal—the puff ball. Wettengel immediately summoned a policeman and had his assailant haled into court, where a $25 fine was assessed. DeKrafft paid the sum, remarking that it was cheap for the value received.

In the dining room of the Commercial House that evening, the altercation was discussed among Cal, deKrafft, Wettengel, Charles Davidson,

Ed Merritt, and Joe Newborn, the latter two representing the Armour Company's interests. Early the following morning, Thursday, DeKrafft issued their conclusions to the press: "Mr. Fred Felix Wettengel of Appleton, Wisc., has returned to Mr. Calbraith P. Rodgers the power of attorney previously invested in him and will retire from all connection with the Rodgers expedition. Mr. Wettengel will accompany the party as far as Binghamton and will then proceed to his home in Appleton."

Cal slept the night in his room at the Commercial House. Nearby accommodations were found for Mrs. Sweitzer, who was expected to board a train for Pittsburgh after the expedition departed Middletown. She had passed the last two days, a Puritan among the pagan, unable to convert a single person to her persuasion and unable to monopolize her son for more than a few minutes each day. Mabel was grateful to regain her husband, but, exhausted from a full day of tinkering with the *Vin Fiz* machine, he plopped onto a separate bed and into an instant sleep. "The trouble," said Cal before retiring, "included wrong bars, wrong belts, and improper adjustments." "That's not the only trouble," Mabel complained to no one in particular.

John Rodgers arrived at the railroad station, back from Dayton, after midnight. He was accompanied by Charley Taylor, who, after some delay, had negotiated his release from the Wright brothers' organization to assist and rescue Cal Rodgers in his attempted transcontinental flight. "You'll need him," Orville Wright had wired the day before. Both Taylor and John Rodgers stretched out on pallets in the hangar boxcar to pass the night. In the morning Taylor was welcomed by Cal as a fellow member of the Vin Fiz entourage. The "world's best mechanician" was just as cantankerous as ever, Cal noted, recalling their encounters at the Simms Station flying school, and just as grudging in speech—"He treats his words like caged animals," someone had said, "letting them out only on a leash." As a fellow cigar smoker, Taylor could be counted on for a reserve of pungent, pickle-size stogies.

By nine o'clock Thursday morning a sizable crowd had gathered at the fairgrounds. The Beattie Hill School had dismissed classes that its pupils might witness the takeoff. All was in readiness except the airplane. De-Krafft issued a bulletin that Cal would depart at 11:30 A.M. At 10:00 A.M. he received and read to the crowd a telegram from Jimmy Ward: "C. P. Rodgers—Hope you are ready and have best of luck. I expect to leave here in a few minutes. Had bad luck last night. Hope it changes for both of us. Jimmy Ward."

Before his departure from Corning, Ward had splashed a bucket of

Chemung River water on his hitherto unnamed aircraft and christened it *The Hearst Pathfinder*— to no avail. "Fowler, Rodgers, and myself have sure got a jinx after us," Ward sighed, "and we certainly have paid the hoodoo all we owe it."

At noon, lift-off of the *Vin Fiz* was rescheduled for 12:30 and thence for 2:00 P.M.

To a *Times-Press* reporter, deKrafft vehemently denounced the stories circulating in Middletown concerning Cal Rodgers's alleged indiscretions. Certain citizens claimed to have observed the birdman reeling "under the influence." His departure was delayed, according to this tale, to allow recovery from his alcoholic stupor. As proof that Rodgers was a teetotaler, deKrafft offered his account that he had refused a sip of brandy even after his fall from the sky Monday morning, when a tipple would have been more than justified. If he had been observed "reeling," it was as a result of a sprained ankle suffered in that fall. Liquor, deKrafft quoted Cal as pledging, would never pass his lips.

Mabel and her two assistants, Allie and Hibbard, circulated through the crowd selling postcards imprinted with pictures of Cal and the *Vin Fiz*. Her eyes happy beneath a cloche bonnet tied to her chin by a pink grosgrain ribbon, Mabel aimed her chatter at everyone and no one. (She'll keep talking until she finds something to say," deKrafft commented; from their first meeting, he had appraised her as "relentlessly frivolous.") For 25¢, it was promised, the postcards would be carried aloft by Cal, stamped by Mabel personally, and then—if a 1¢ stamp had been included—posted into the U.S. mail system. Cards addressed and stamped could also be forwarded to Mabel, care of the Plaza Hotel, Chicago. The sender should not forget to attach the 25¢.

Every thirty minutes or so, Harry Sanger raised his megaphone to sing out his praise for the Vin Fiz blend of grape juices. A steady diet of Vin Fiz, he proclaimed, would promote a young man into an athlete of prowess, a young lass into a lady of ravishing beauty. "More likely it would turn them into frogs," muttered a crewman. With the exception of Charles Davidson, those on the train were united in the opinion that "you have to sneak up on it to get it down."

At two o'clock Cal was at the fairgrounds to direct the last touches to the rebuilt airship. Charles Davidson ascertained that the Vin Fiz bottle was again lashed to its forward brace. Charley Taylor, now officially designated the party's chief mechanician, administered a final test to the engine and pronounced it ready. Cal mounted his seat and lit a cigar— only to discover that a portion of the gasoline line was missing. A hurried search located the piece, which was quickly emplaced. The propellers were spun. Cal, natty in the suit hastily cut and sewn by Schiffman the tailor, his bandages removed, his eyes again glistening with the prospect of flight, waved his hands for the mechanicians to release their hold on the wing tips. The reborn airplane moved forward.

Official timers for the takeoff—appointed by Perry Smithers of the Aero Club of America—were Fire Chief Higham, Police Chief McCoach, and Erie agent J. M. Wright. A judges' stand had been set up for the three timers—directly astride the takeoff line. The skids of the *Vin Fiz* narrowly missed smashing into the stand. Chief Higham dived the six feet onto the fairgrounds turf. Chief McCoach and Agent Wright flattened themselves on the platform. They did not neglect to mark Cal's departure at 2:20.

The *Vin Fiz* rose to the air and headed south toward Mechanicstown. Then it turned and passed over the city westward at 2,500 feet. Cal dipped the machine, described a circle in the sky, and threw down hand-fuls of Vin Fiz leaflets. Hundreds of people below waved handkerchiefs. Youngsters scrambled to pick up the leaflets. Whistles from Middletown factories shrieked a farewell salute.

Mechanicians and crew at the fairgrounds raced for the railroad station. Hangar-car doors slid shut. Correspondents in the day coach jotted down the time and uncorked flasks of bourbon. Armour Company officials settled in their berths in the private varnish. Chef Ed Davis checked his larder and berated his Negro stewards regarding a missing bottle of milk. Mabel posted herself at the observation platform to wave farewell to Chief Higham. The Vin Fiz special train hurled long blasts from its whistle, then chugged from the Middletown station for Port Jervis.

On board was Mrs. Harry Sweitzer, her widow's veil replaced by an iron mask of resolve. If she could not deter Calbraith from continuing, she had decided at the final moment, she would accompany him to California. Family matters, suspended at her husband's funeral, were pressing for her attention. Settlement of her husband's estate awaited her return. Such concerns could be managed by others. Mrs. Sweitzer understood the obligation of her position. Her son was faced with the challenge of his life, a challenge he could not meet on his own. In such circumstance, only a mother's sustenance, a mother's insight, a mother's special instincts would suffice for the hazards ahead.

4

Big Man, Big White Bird

Sept. 21, thursday. Takeoff Middletown. Across Shawangunk Mountains at Cuddlebackville. Delaware River, Port Jervis, Lackawaxen 3:08 P.M., Callicoon. . . .

The aeroplane was working like a $100 watch, for it would take ten degrees up as easily as one. I was shooting into the sun mostly, but my glasses shaded some of the glare. The ride was really enjoyable. I was above the air currents, going faster than the wind, and the engine went on singing a sweet song. I lit a fresh cigar and let her go.

The river was my guide until I got to Lackawaxen. I had been looking out for that place because the Lackawaxen River shoots off to the left of the Delaware, and it has a branch road too.

At the Melrose farm on the east side of Callicoon, several hundred people were awaiting arrival of the second transcontinental aviator to favor the town. Jimmy Ward had preceded Cal Rodgers by precisely one week. Delayed by fog and rain, he had remained overnight to be feted by the populace. Now, with the coming of the *Vin Fiz*, the village of

64

Callicoon proclaimed itself an official way point on the Atlantic-to-Pacific air route.

George Sawyer, the hotelier, had laid out bedsheets on the field to capture the aviator's eye. As the airplane neared and lowered to an altitude of 200 feet, the two policemen on duty strove vainly to stem the rush to the marked landing spot.

> *[Approaching Callicoon], I made a quick study of my engine. Although I could tell the water was going fast, I decided to make a jump for Hancock, 25 or 26 mile away.*

Sentiment in Callicoon was benignly reflected by a painted scrawl on a wall of St. Joseph's College: "Hooray for Jimmy Ward—Boo to Rodgers —He's the bottom."

> *Just as I passed Long Eddy I heard a "pop" and out flew a defective spark plug. I cut out the cylinder and then, rather than have overheated machinery, shot down to the first field I saw ahead of me.*
> *I alighted perfectly and was slowing down when one of the skids hit a soft spot, stopped, and slewed the machine around. There was a snap of breaking timber, and my right skid was gone.*

It was 3:39. Cal had flown ninety-five miles in the astounding time of seventy-nine minutes.

Fifty feet away, two men—workers on the Busfield family acreage—were rooting out potatoes. They glanced up nonchalantly as the *Vin Fiz* floated in and spun around, then resumed their digging. Cal walked over and asked the distance to Hancock. Without disrupting their labors, they allowed as how "'twarn't fur—'bout two miles thetaway."

Fortunately for Cal, the airplane had been observed in Hancock, and, shortly, carloads and wagonloads of men bounced onto the potato field to extend a more cordial welcome.

The Vin Fiz train, meanwhile, had departed Middletown twelve minutes after its leader. The delay was by order of Chief Higham, who skidded up in his red Mercer runabout to present Mabel Rodgers with a bouquet of roses—as the other passengers stared in exasperation. Another ten minutes were lost at Port Jervis, where a stop was scheduled to pick up Conrad Diehl, manager of the Port Jervis Western

Union office.* Hitting up to sixty miles per hour, the train lost yet more ground; Fred Howard, the Erie general passenger agent, and trainmaster Michael Nolan were incredulous as they read, on successive signal towers, the chalked passage times that told of Cal's rapid progress.

Billets were reassigned in the Pullman shortly after the train settled into its run. Fred Wettengel, having been stripped of his status as business manager, was already evicted from his stateroom in favor of Mr. and Mrs. Stewart deKrafft. Mrs. Wettengel was permitted a berth on the Pullman, her husband relegated to the day coach. In deference to Mrs. Sweitzer, whose unexpected presence was accommodated without comment, the deKraffts returned to their berths and relinquished the stateroom (adjoining that occupied by Cal and Mabel) for her use. "I have to be near my son," said Mrs. Sweitzer. "If he calls out for me, I must be able to hear him."

Mabel accepted her mother-in-law aboard with an impassive facade. Others quartered in the Pullman grumbled among themselves when Mrs. Sweitzer conducted a military-style inspection and flung out every cuspidor in the car. "Expectoration is not conducive to public health," she declaimed, quoting literature of the Anti-Spitting League. No one found the temerity to oppose her.

Alerted by the Long Eddy signal tower, the special train braked to a halt at the Hancock station forty-five minutes after Cal's unplanned landing. It was 4:30 before the Palmer-Singer auto with Charley Taylor, Shaffer, and Wiggin lurched onto the potato field. Cal awaited its appearance with mounting impatience. Although the skies had been darkening with heavy clouds, he hoped to replace the skid and continue toward Binghamton. "Come on, boys," he urged, opening the doors of the Palmer-Singer and virtually pulling them out.

Almost a hundred persons were gathered around the *Vin Fiz*, most admiring its construction, but some removing bolts and wire as souvenirs. Many signed their names and addresses on the rubberized-duck planes. Smaller boys circled the craft, their arms outstretched, their voices droning, simulating the flying machine in motion.

Mr. and Mrs. Silas DeBrier and their twelve-year-old son, Alvin, stood among the onlookers, Alvin under the firm restraint of his mother's hand. Mr. DeBrier, pressed by his son to resolve a much-discussed puzzlement at the DeBrier household, moved in closer to the aviator. "What keeps

---

*Diehl was assigned to remain with the special to Chicago and to expedite wires dispatched by correspondents on board.

it up?" he asked. Cal looked at him stoically. "The air," he responded. Mr. DeBrier nodded and returned to his wife and son. "Ask a sensible question," he told them, "you get a sassy answer."

At six o'clock a drizzling rain set in, and it was decided to postpone final repairs (leaky radiator, cracked oil cup, broken struts and outriggers, and bent frames as well as the splintered skid) until the next morning. The machine was covered, and the crowd dispersed by the pleadings of Hancock city officials. Cal took the wheel of the Palmer-Singer and drove into Hancock—"just like you drive the aeroplane," said Charley Taylor as Cal bounced it over the rocky field without slowing.

Cal and Mabel were accorded the bridal suite at the Hotel Doolittle, the bill charged to the city of Hancock. Mrs. Sweitzer, Charles Davidson, John Rodgers, and the deKraffts were lodged elsewhere in the hotel; others in the party remained on the special train.

The Doolittle's bridal suite featured an inviting, canopied double bed, and Mabel set herself to turn it to best account. She unpacked her frilliest nightclothes, ordered a bottle of Champagne in an ice bucket, tucked a lavender-scented sachet into her camisole, and lit a stick of Dr. Ghose's incense and wafted its fragrance about the room. These preparations were thwarted when Mrs. Sweitzer knocked on the door of the suite to declare that, this her first night with the expedition, she was unable to sleep by herself in the foreign environment. Only her son's company could sooth her uneasiness. Besides, she added, sniffing ostentatiously, she could detect a markedly unhealthy odor in the bridal suite. Mabel was left to quaff the Champagne by herself.

"Sometimes," Mabel later confided to Mrs. Wettengel, "I suspect that Calbraith thinks showing affection to a woman would be unfaithful to his machine."

The aviator was, in this instance, out of sorts for displays of affection —either to his wife or his colleagues. He complained of bad weather ("You'd think that rain wouldn't be allowed during a cross-country air race") and bad luck and reproached train officials for their inability to maintain a proper pace.

Engineer McAllister, a veteran who had been "pulling the plug" for twenty-five years, accepted the criticism as a personal challenge and vowed to work on his locomotive all night long if necessary. "When I hit the track tomorrow," he told reporters, "I'll do a little flying myself."

It rained heavily through the night. Rain also prevented another start by Bob Fowler from Colfax, California, and a pelting hail storm grounded Jimmy Ward in Addison, New York. Members of the Vin Fiz enterprise could sleep with the consolation that their rivals had fared worse for the day's efforts.

Charley Taylor was first to awaken Friday morning; he shortly had the engine of the *Vin Fiz* tuned to peak condition. Dense cumulus clouds did not dissipate until after 10:00 A.M. Cal strode about the field impatiently, holding up his handkerchief or a moistened finger to the wind and occasionally picking up a stone to cast from his path. Wind direction had shifted, and a cold, 20-mph gale drove directly at his planned heading. He donned a leather jacket, stuffed sheets of crumpled newspapers into it, and pulled on knee-length leggings over his pants. About 400 spectators churned up the potato patch to follow his movements and those of Charley Taylor and the other mechanicians at work on the machine.

Taylor clipped an oil can onto the right side of the driver's seat—so Cal could supply additional lubrication in flight—and conferred his approval for takeoff.

> *The start was good, and I got away against the wind without any trouble. It was 11:13 o'clock. I sent her up as fast as I could—up to 2,000 feet inside of three miles, and I had to go up 500 feet higher before I could get along steadily. It wasn't the warmest day in the year, either, but I could swing my feet to keep up the circulation.*
>
> *I think I was going about 45 mph when I picked up a trestling with a railroad running underneath it. It didn't look exactly right to me, but I swung around a big hill, dropped pretty low to make sure and then let her go. The wind was quartering behind me, and I began to get along. I thought the wind had changed. I didn't see a mark on the tracks, but the way was plain.*
>
> *Pretty soon I came to a good-sized town. By my reckoning it ought to be Binghamton, so I dropped down from about 2,000 feet to about 600 feet looking for a place to land. Then I saw a couple of coal mines, and they gave me a shock. I had studied the route well enough to know coal mines didn't belong in Binghamton, so I circled and circled until I had to give it up.*

Two miles short of Deposit, New York, fourteen miles northwest of Hancock, the Delaware River folds back to the east, no longer a navigational aid for a westbound flier. One mile farther to the west, the stockyard signal tower for Deposit stands over the Erie tracks. When signalman George Hempstead, sixteen, reported for duty the morning of September 22, he was told of the planned takeoff from Hancock and instructed to chalk on the tower's side the time of Rodgers's passage. Trainmaster Nolan could thereby assure himself that Cal had not wandered from his course. Young Hempstead spotted the flying machine at 11:46 A.M.; the

Vin Fiz train roared by the tower before he could scratch his first stroke.

At Lanesboro, just north of Susquehanna, the main Erie track between New York City and Buffalo runs over a stone bridge across a viaduct. A branch of the Delaware & Hudson Railroad (known locally as the "Delay and Hesitate") passes under the viaduct and is joined to the east by the Jefferson junction of the Erie Railroad. Cal mistook the one set of tracks for the other and flew along the D&H line. Then, circling in further confusion, he landed in Carbondale, Pennsylvania.

The first two persons Cal encountered were frozen speechless by the apparition that had dropped from the skies; the third person confidently pointed to the southwest: "That's the way to Binghamton." Cal took off again, heading southwest along the Lackawanna track to Scranton. Ten miles on, realizing that he had been given the crooked finger, he landed once again, this time at Throop—at 12:30—for further directions. From Throop, news of his presence was telephoned to the *Scranton Times*. No heavier-than-air machine yet having been seen over Scranton, the *Times* editor alerted the town by telephoning schools, banks, and business offices. Thousands of people streamed onto streets and sidewalks to wave and cheer as the Wright biplane skirted Providence, west Scranton, and meandered to the north, over the large black collieries that dotted the countryside, their roofs crammed with breaker boys on the dinner hour. Shy of gasoline, and with the rudder control misbehaving, Cal selected a field near George Street, the north side of Scranton, and, although the terrain was of an undulating nature, set down the *Vin Fiz* without mishap. Within minutes it was swarmed over by frenzied burghers.

> *They went crazy. There wasn't a name on my planes when I started in the morning, but in ten minutes there wasn't an inch free from pencil marks. They didn't mind climbing on the machine to get a good spot. They worked the levers, sat on the seat, warped the planes, and fingered the engine.*

While Cal was pleading with the crowd on one side of the airplane, a woman behind him attempted to unloosen a nut with her fingers. She merely wished a keepsake, she professed, and had not imagined that taking it would cause harm since "there were so many, surely one would not make any difference." Cal retorted that "for me it might make all the difference between this world and the next." He turned from her to find another freebooter pounding at the engine with a chisel to split off a valve.

Without police protection, it required several responsible citizens in the throng to restrain their neighbors from demolishing the flying machine. Mrs. Mavis Morton rushed over from her home on North Washington Avenue with coffee and sandwiches for the aviator; her husband, Fred, hustled up a few gallons of gasoline and helped to adjust the rudder control. Of the circle of youngsters that stood gawking at the sight of a flying machine, seventh-grader Frances Higert of P.S. 39 stepped forward to plead for an autograph. Cal tore off a piece of fabric hanging from the lower plane, signed it "C. P. Rodgers," and handed it to her.

With a consensus of advice on the proper direction for Binghamton and a second sandwich from Mrs. Morton, Cal was again airborne thirty minutes after he had landed. "Someone in the crowd managed to steal the cap from the gasoline tank," he subsequently told his crew. "A few minutes more and they would have carried off the whole machine."

North through the Notch, over Clark's Summit and Dalton, Cal traced the Lackawanna tracks. At Hallstead, the Lackawanna line crosses that of the Erie. Cal circled for a few moments, then landed in a poplar-fringed oat field at Great Bend, opposite Hallstead on the Susquehanna River. The two towns, walled in by high, thickly wooded hills, constituted virtually the only level areas within his view. He had traveled fifty miles from Scranton in little more than an hour.

Meanwhile Trainmaster Nolan and Erie officials had been cast into sixes and sevens by the straying airplane. The special had chugged from the railroad station in Hancock tightly on Cal's wake, Wiggin and Frank Shaffer scrambling on board, each with a pilfered pumpkin from a neighboring farm. Engineer McAllister's orders read, "If you can't keep up with the Vin Fiz machine with the train on the track, then take to the air."

Up the Chenango Valley McAllister raced, pacing the airplane evenly. Those on the train leaned from windows for a clear view of the aviator at 600 feet. Just past Deposit, the special was halted for a brief moment while a freight train immediately to the west was shunted onto a siding.

Up to now, Erie dispatchers, by dint of extraordinary effort, had managed to provide a clear track for the special. Both freight and passenger traffic had been sidetracked, rerouted, or rescheduled to accommodate its sometimes erratic movements. Now, the offending freighter, having experienced an air-hose blowout, was slow in responding to orders.

Again under way up the grade between Deposit and Gulf Summit, the Vin Fiz entourage watched the flying machine disappear over a crest. As the special pulled into Susquehanna, people lining the track pointed southward. At the station, deKrafft and Fred Howard climbed the signal tower and learned that Cal had digressed over the stone bridge at Lanesboro junction. DeKrafft wired the Carbondale station to spread out a large canvas strip atop the train, pointing back—"That's the only way you can stop him." John Rodgers explained to Trainmaster Nolan that, to an aviator aloft, the train with its white top would be readily visible for miles against the dark-stone background of the bridge.

Accordingly, Nolan directed the special back to the bridge, where it paused, panting breaths of steam through its safety valves. He then posted his two brakemen several hundred yards ahead of and behind the train and hurried to a nearby farmhouse to telephone his dispatcher. Learning that Cal had landed in Carbondale, he arranged for the Vin Fiz special to be transferred to the D&H track. A trainmaster from the local D&H division came aboard; nearby rail traffic was diverted, and the special backed the thirty-eight miles south from Lanesboro. Stations along the line were requested to o.s.* the airplane. At Carbondale, news that Cal had departed Scranton was obtained, and, after further juggling of regular traffic, the special was granted clearance to head northward up the same D&H track to pick up the Erie main line again at Lanesboro. "On to Binghamton!" yelled the crew.

But without close knowledge of Cal's whereabouts, the possibility of further backtracking could not be discounted. DeKrafft and Nolan agreed to halt the train at the tower east of Kirkwood, New York, where the party sought further word of the errant airman. Nolan scampered up the tower to learn that Cal was passing Nicholson. He then directed the train to a siding and again knocked at a farmhouse door in search of a telephone. The farmer's wife cranked in the local hello girl and determined that Cal had just landed at Great Bend, a news item spreading like wildfire over neighboring telephone lines.

Mrs. Sweitzer bustled up and down the aisle of the Pullman, seeking reassurances from Mabel, deKrafft, her nephew John Rodgers, and whomever she could apprehend, that her son had not vanished irretrievably. As the train backed up the four miles south to Great Bend, she stood on the rear platform, straining for sight of the downed airplane.

At Carl's Flats, the Great Bend landing site, the *Vin Fiz* was again inundated by much of the local population. Schoolchildren flooded in to pencil their names on the plane fabric. Cal offered no further objection but cautioned the more ardent scribes against puncturing the cloth. He attended to the negotiation of gasoline and to confirming his location.

The owner of the oat field in which the aircraft rested appeared and

---

*O.s. ("on sheet") refers to the train report that the stationmaster would write on a "flimsy." The report would be delivered to the passing train by means of a bamboo hoop.

demanded $25 for damages to his crop. Cal stared at him for several moments without responding. Then several men stepped forward and offered to take up contributions rather than penalize their unexpected but admired guest. Hats were passed, coins dropped. A sum of nearly $4 was collected and turned over to the farmer.

A thirteen-year-old girl, Elsie Alexander, had timidly approached the machine to sign her name on one of the few spaces remaining. Four feet three inches in height, she had just finished washing her hair, never cut and normally worn in a Psyche knot, and had raced from her home three-quarters of a mile from Carl's Flats. Cal turned to her and stroked the still damp auburn strands that reached below her knees. "You have the most beautiful hair I have ever seen in my whole life," he said. Elsie could only stammer in response to the six-foot-four-inch figure from another world. Later, as a class assignment, she wrote a composition about the event: "The Big Bird that Man Made."

As the Vin Fiz train backed to a standstill at the Great Bend depot, Mabel and Mrs. Sweitzer led the others in dashing out for a brief but passionate reunion. Said Mabel: "Oh, I knew we would find you safe and sound." Said Mrs. Sweitzer, weeping from relief: "Oh, oh, oh, I feared I would never—ever—see you again."

The mechanicians inspected the airplane and assured themselves that the repairs effected in Scranton were satisfactory. Charley Taylor admonished Cal for allowing inferior grades of gasoline into the machine rather than the prescribed 64-octane fuel. "This stuff looks more like coal oil," he groused. Cal only shrugged.

> Sept. 22, Friday. Great Bend to Binghamton, 15 miles; landed Stow Park, Binghamton, 2:55 P.M. Distributed Vin Fiz leaflets. Ladies cautioned to remain on train because unruly crowd. Take-off 4:00 P.M. for Elmira, 58 miles on. . . .

At Elmira, having again outdistanced the special train, Cal could locate neither his designated landing site at the fairgrounds nor a convenient alternate field. He swung back to pick up his guide. A freight train lumbering along the single track had been switched to a siding, and the Vin Fiz special accorded right-of-way. As Cal came upon it, the special train was passing the freight, which was slowly drawing to the upper end of the siding ready to regain the main track. The freighter's crew spotted Cal and the *Vin Fiz* and was so intent upon waving at the airborne marvel that the imminent convergence of the two tracks went unnoticed. Cal swooped low and yelled a warning. The freighter, brakes screeching, sheared the last few feet of timber and railing from the rear platform of the Vin Fiz Pullman.

Those inside had also spotted the flying machine's return, but had momentarily lost sight of it as it flew over the tracks. At the sound and shock of the impact, the two Georges screamed and ran through the corridor yelling, "We's been hit. We's been hit." Both Mabel and Mrs. Sweitzer rushed to windows in a surge of panic at the thought that their loved one might indeed have collided with the Pullman. The sight of the airplane circling at low altitude restored their normal temperaments.

Cal closely followed the white-topped train from that point westward and set down at Miller's Pond on the outskirts of Elmira.

It was some day in the air. I'm about 110 miles nearer Chicago tonight. But the figures show that I wandered about 215 miles in about six hours and 37 minutes. It wasn't exactly dangerous, but when you butt into a head wind, a cloak of mountains, a new kind of an air pocket every two minutes, lose your way, wander about 105 miles out of your way, have to fight off a bunch of hysterical people who want to tear up your machine as souvenirs, have to get up with willing but unskilled assistance, and then have to go looking for your own special train toward dusk—well, I've had enough to keep my mind occupied for one day.

An exchange of views with deKrafft, John Rodgers, and Trainmaster Nolan failed to apportion blame for the day's succession of blunders. Cal suggested that the Erie Railroad should plant large white flags every mile along the track. "An impractical solution," he was told. "All right, then," said Cal, "let's get on with it."

To reporters on the train, he added: "I am now feeling as if I have just begun the first flight. I do not anticipate any more accidents as the machine is running like a piece of clockwork, and I have better country over which to fly now. I have passed the treacherous hills and mountains and am thankful I am alive, as some of the falls and accidents were enough to kill a man less fortunate."

Accommodations had been arranged at the Rathbun, Elmira's most renowned hotel. A tall, commodious brick structure at Water and Baldwin streets, it contained an eighty-foot-long bar, a billiard room with an ornamental skylight, and a cavernous lounge that rivaled a railroad station in size. Mark Twain, during his years of residence in Elmira, relaxed in the big leather-covered chairs in its marble-columned lobby and dined in its elegant, high-ceilinged banquet rooms. Elmira officials who remembered Twain's ever-present cigar suggested to Cal that he would be noted as the second-most famous cigar smoker in the city's history.

Fred Wettengel also checked into the Rathbun. Tempers having cooled, it was agreed that he would accompany the party as far as Chicago, but without official status. He was vouchsafed a berth in the Pullman, above that of his wife.

At supper, the prime topic of discussion was the news of Jimmy Ward's retirement from the transcontinental race. Ward had finally gotten clear of Addison at 7:00 A.M. after his new Curtiss OX engine had been overhauled personally by superintendent Kleckler of the Curtiss factory. "This is the best I ever seen an engine work," Ward had declared, smiling and exuberant. "I will be in Chicago in three days. From now on I'm going to cover 300 miles a day. I wish Rodgers were here. It would be some fun to race with him." Five miles after takeoff, the engine again refused to function, and he was forced to volplane onto a farm north of Rathbone. Both planes were broken against a tree, and the control mechanisms sustained irreparable damage. Ward was hurled from the machine but escaped with his life when he narrowly missed the tree, landing on a mound of soft earth.

Ward boarded the 10:25 train for Buffalo. Mrs. Ward, who had taken leave of the expedition only two days earlier, hurried back from Chicago on the brink of hysteria. A vehement conference at the Iroquois Hotel among Jimmy, his wife, manager Ike Bloom, and co-backer Harry Cavenaugh resulted in the decision to withdraw. The diminutive birdman was stubbornly determined to continue, but with $21,000 already expended, neither Bloom nor Cavenaugh would countenance additional investment. Further, Mrs. Ward was distraught to illness by the knowledge that Chicago gamblers were wagering odds of five to one that her husband would be killed before he reached Buffalo. The party left for Chicago, and Ward announced that he would instead attempt a flight from Minneapolis to New Orleans over the Mississippi River. At the railroad station he said, "I am grateful to the boys who were with me on the trip. They helped me royally. And I want to thank Mr. Hearst and the International News Service for all the aid they gave me. I hope Rodgers, Fowler, and Ovington will have better luck."

Even some on the fringes of Ward's enterprise had found themselves buffeted by ill winds. A messenger speeding his motorcycle from Addison to Hammondsport for spare parts collided with a dog, pitched into a ditch, and broke his leg. A second motorcyclist, sent to search for the first, lost his way and was not heard from until the next morning.

Cal was downhearted at learning that his plucky competitor had fared so poorly. "It was the hoodoo," he insisted. "It's been pursuing him ever since he started on the thirteenth." Mabel expressed a contrary opinion, elated that another rival had been eliminated. Several in the Vin Fiz contingent, notably deKrafft, muttered that she was "a dumb floozy who neither understood nor cared about sportsmanship." They were friends of Ward, and they, with Cal, regretted his misfortune. Jimmy Ward, Rodgers's camp concluded, had been a victim of inadequate preparations, inadequate support, and insufficient funding. Without a special train, he was dependent upon the Curtiss factory at Hammondsport for provisions and spare parts—at Addison, he was twenty-two miles from Hammondsport; as he moved westward, his supply problem would have become intractable. The transcontinental air race, it was emphasized, was not a sport for amateurs.

Mrs. Sweitzer cited Mrs. Ward's influence in saving her husband from certain death had he continued—if only, she added, Calbraith were blessed with such a concerned helpmeet. Mrs. Sweitzer contributed her own summary of the day's tidings: Frank Miller had burned to death at the Miami, Ohio, County Fair when his gasoline tank exploded in midair, and Tony ("Daredevil") Castellane became the ninety-fourth aviation fatality, fifty-sixth since the first of the year. His wife, Mrs. Sweitzer noted pointedly, was present at the tragedy. Mabel could raise neither defense nor counterattack against her granite-willed mother-in-law. Her subservience was demanded both by custom and by the imperatives of Mrs. Sweitzer's personality; her husband, as had been established long ago, was no ally in this regard.

Bob Fowler had received his long-sought rudder tail and had completed two trial flights in Colfax, California. He expected to resume his journey the next morning and vowed to alight in New York City in fifteen days.

DeKrafft noted that President Taft, on his coast-to-coast tour, had reached St. Louis, where he encountered further revolt against his leadership of the Republican party. Results of the Canadian elections were in —and "Big Bill" Taft had suffered another setback to his reelection prospects by the sweeping defeat of Liberal Prime Minister Sir Wilfred Laurier. Conservatives in Canada were adamantly opposed to the Reciprocity Act that Taft and William Randolph Hearst had shepherded through the Senate.[1] (The Conservative party had campaigned with the slogan "No truck nor trade with the Yankees.") Since Hearst had failed to annex Canada, deKrafft opined, he might now turn his gaze southward and attempt to bite off a chunk of Mexico.*

A departure time of 7:00 A.M. was scheduled. DeKrafft issued a press bulletin stating that the next day's flight was anticipated to cover 400 miles, and the group retired to its rooms in the Rathbun Hotel.

Again, Mrs. Sweitzer foreclosed her son's and daughter-in-law's privacy. A widow of but a week's duration, she lamented, bravely suppressing her tears, she was yet unable to find repose in solitude. For the remainder of her life, it was a condition that she would have to bear, but for now . . . surely her son understood. "Yes, mother," said Cal, again leaving Mabel without companionship for the night.

Through the early morning hours of Saturday, September 23, a heavy fog hung over Miller's Pond. A large crowd had gathered despite the damp, and the lone watchman struggled to restrain those who wished to tinker with the flying machine. At 9:15 A.M. the Palmer-Singer drove up, the spare Wright engine lying on its rear seat—Charley Taylor had consigned the first engine to the hangar car for further repair. Cal had appeared thirty minutes earlier and was invited for breakfast at the nearby Maple Avenue farm of A. B. Manning. Mabel and her two young helpers, Charlie Hibbard and Allie, strolled among the spectators, brandishing postcards at anyone who betokened an interest. At 25¢, few were sold.

By ten o'clock the fog had lifted. "Get back," Cal growled at the men and boys who crowded too close to the machine. He climbed onto the operator's seat and gestured for the propellers to be turned. The blast from the props removed a few hats, and black smoke from the exhaust added further warning. When a path was cleared the aviator glanced at Charlie Wiggin and Frank Shaffer holding the wing tips and yelled, "Let her go, boys!" The machine rolled across the slightly sloping field to the west, toward the Erie tracks. Beyond Miller's Pond lay an abrupt rise of ground fringed by slippery elms on the south and east and open on the north. Cal was slow in lifting the machine. To those in attendance who had witnessed Lincoln Beachey and René Simon fly from the Elmira Fairgrounds, it seemed impossible for him to escape a collision. Cal realized the danger yet more keenly, and as the biplane bounced over a small knoll and took uncertainly to the air, he whipped his elevator plane as much as he dared and skimmed over the trees by inches. But his motor had not accorded him a proper start, and he could not clear the Erie switchyard ahead with its poles and telegraph wires. He flumped back to the ground, butting on

*Hearst's Mexican holdings were reputed to be the size of Rhode Island.

a down incline toward the pond and another row of trees. The skids gouged into the dirt, sliced through several small shrubs, and halted the *Vin Fiz* three feet short of an imposing oak tree.

People watching his progress from across the field froze until they saw his lithe figure emerge from the machine. Then they swarmed to the spot where he had fallen. A score of willing hands carried the craft to a more advantageous position atop the knoll. The mechanicians made a quick survey of the damage—three broken cables and a small hole torn in the rudder surface. Charlie Wiggin scurried to the hangar car for wires, fabric, and appropriate tools. More than two hours were required to effect repairs.

Cal stood alone through this period, apart from the crowd and the flying machine. The realization that the plague of minor accidents might continue cast a pall, and he fought it off with an exercise of will.

When Charley Taylor declared the airplane ready once again, it was wheeled to an adjoining knoll—with a clear lane to the west. This time, cued by Cal's lighting a cigar, turning his cap around, and signaling with his hand, mechanicians and spectators alike shouted in unison, "Let her go, boys!"

Rising from Elmira, Cal sailed along smoothly for Hornell—under a porcelain sky that dampened his humor and seemed to presage the next, inevitable calamity.

Approaching Addison, twenty-two miles westward, the special train raced by below. On the rear platform (repaired at Elmira's Erie depot) stood Mabel Rodgers, casting out handfuls of the paper flyers with the Vin Fiz emblem.

The "jinx" that had struck Jimmy Ward at this point once again seemed to flaunt its power.

I was directly over Addison when the engine began missing. The machine began to drop. . . . I turned around and saw that the magneto plugs had slipped, shutting off the first and second cylinders. As I shot down, I reached my right hand back and pushed the plugs in. Instantly, the power came on, and I went on again with everything working perfectly. Ten minutes more. I felt her drop again, and again I pushed the plugs in. Finally, I was obliged to keep my right hand back on the plugs all the time while I tried to work the two levers with my left. But it wouldn't do. My arms got so numb with this awkward position that I couldn't hold out much longer. I picked out a field above Canisteo and sailed down. I thought the plugs would last and I took my right hand off to land.

> *The plugs stayed in until I was about to hit the ground—when they jumped out again. That stopped my engine before I was ready, and it was the furrows of the field for me. I slid down a hill, and my left plane was smashed. Lucky it wasn't any worse.*

Cal was hurled from his seat on impact but was cushioned by the soft dirt. He bumped against a brace, bruised his face, and sustained a flesh wound to his shoulder.

As the *Vin Fiz* had passed over Cameron, twelve miles east of Canisteo, news of its coming was relayed to the *Canisteo Times,* and fire bells and whistles triggered a rush for roofs, hilltops, and other points of vantage. Most of the village's population of 3,000 excitedly peered eastward for a glimpse of the flying machine. When it was observed winding its way between the twisting 1,000-foot hills that border the Canisteo River and then falling to the northwest of Canisteo toward Hornell, a general dash ensued for autos, buggies, horses, Democrat wagons, and trolley cars.

First to arrive at the fallen birdman's side was Theodore Cobb, owner of the Up-to-Date Advertising Company. Dashing up in his Buick Overland, he found Cal in a nervous state, his naturally ruddy face turned pale, pacing about the half-wrecked machine assessing the damage. "Tell the people on the train where I am and have them tell my mother and wife that I am not hurt" were Cal's first words. Cobb departed with this message and was immediately replaced by several hundred persons from Canisteo and Hornell. City officials who had been waiting at the Hornell Fairgrounds (the intended landing site) drove back to deliver their formal welcome speeches. Photographs of the event were taken by Mortimer Haring, a Canisteo pharmacist who had fought with Major Bullard in the Philippines, while scores of schoolchildren scurried in to autograph sections of plane fabric.

In consequence of a muddled message relayed by the Cameron signal tower, the special train had passed Canisteo and pulled into the Hornell Railroad Station. Mechanicians and crew members plus deKrafft, John Rodgers, Mabel, and Mrs. Sweitzer ran for the trolley of the Hornellsville Electric Railway Company, the line of which crossed close to the M. B. Flint farm where the crash occurred. Mabel was first off the trolley and rushed up carrying a quart bottle of pure cream. Cal proceeded to get himself outside the cream, replaced his cigar, embraced his mother as she came up to demand that he accept medical attention for his bleeding shoulder, then turned to his mechanicians.

Calbraith Perry Rodgers.
The indomitable spirit, the
ever-present cigar. (COURTESY
NATIONAL AIR AND SPACE
MUSEUM, SMITHSONIAN
INSTITUTION)

Ceremonies prior to takeoff. Patty and Perry Pease in driver's seat. Charles Davidson at right. (COURTESY LIBRARY OF CONGRESS)

Takeoff from Sheepshead Bay. Eddie Lynch in white shirt. (COURTESY EDWARD LYNCH)

The Vin Fiz hangar car. (COURTESY RICHARD G. LODER)

The wreck at Middletown, N.Y. (COURTESY RICHARD G. LODER)

Cal Rodgers and Charley Taylor.

Elmira, N.Y. Repositioning the machine for takeoff. (COURTESY NATIONAL AIR AND SPACE MUSEUM, SMITHSONIAN INSTITUTION)

Stow Flats Fairgrounds, Binghamton, N.Y. (COURTESY BOB BROOKS)

Dominguez Air Meet, Jan. 19, 1910. William Randolph Hearst behind Louis Paulhan.
(COURTESY FR. PATRICK MCPOLIN)

First landing aboard ship. Eugene Ely on USS Pennsylvania, *San Francisco Bay, Jan. 18, 1911.*
(COURTESY NAVAL PHOTOGRAPHIC CENTER, WASHINGTON, D.C.)

Takeoff from Olean, New York. Note trailing clump of hay. (COURTESY NATIONAL AIR AND SPACE
MUSEUM, SMITHSONIAN INSTITUTION)

Cal Rodgers adjusting wires. Note Vin Fiz bottle at left. (COURTESY BOB BROOKS)

Wright Flying School, Dayton, Ohio. Harry Atwood balancing on wheel axle. Cal Rodgers, seated, far right, "keeping score."

Examination confirmed a splintered skid, a shattered left lower wing, broken guy wires, and ripped fabric. A bent terminal in the magneto was responsible for the misfortune. The only extra plane in the hangar car (the others having been used to rebuild the machine at Middletown) was lugged to the farm, but was then identified as a right lower plane. Charley Taylor arranged to have the airplane hitched to a team of horses, whence it was towed to Alfred Slawson's carriage and blacksmith shop at Maple and Sixth streets in Canisteo.

Mrs. Sweitzer, who had disappeared from the field, now reappeared with Dr. Elkanah Smith of Hornell at her side. Neither the good doctor nor his reluctant patient could escape her vigilance, and her son's wounds were duly treated and bandaged.

As Cal was about to follow his horse-powered flying machine, he was stayed and introduced to Mrs. Alida Laine, who had arrived in Canisteo in 1830 as a young girl, crossing from Massachusetts by way of the Erie Canal. Now ninety-three years of age, her face a registry of finely webbed lines, her frame shrunken to a fragile five feet, she had experienced her first automobile ride earlier that day and wished to shake hands with the driver of this newest type of locomotion. She tamped a wad of Wigwam tobacco into her pipe. "Young man," she chirped at Cal, "are you gwina drive that machine to the moon?"

Mabel and Mrs. Sweitzer returned to Hornell to arrange for accommodations at the Sherwood Hotel. Cal remained in Canisteo to supervise repairs to the *Vin Fiz*. The Slawson brothers and their twelve employees would continue their work into the night to reconstruct the flying machine.

The shortage of major components in the hangar car was an obvious concern. It was decided that John Rodgers should again entrain for Dayton, where he would expedite the assembly and shipment of additional spare parts. He and Cal clapped each other on the back in wordless farewell. He was to rejoin the expedition somewhere in Ohio.

In the evening Cal hosted a supper party at Acker's Restaurant to reward the crew for its unflagging efforts. Complaints were sprouting over the fare of beans and ham served aboard the train to all except Cal and those few able to cultivate the chef.

Evening newspapers printed the text of Jimmy Ward's formal withdrawal from the Hearst race.* From Chicago, Ward himself expressed a

*Buffalo, N.Y., Sept. 22. "Owing to another bad spill which smashed the machine, our inability to reach Los Angeles within the time limit, and the bad run of luck which seems

resilient tone: "Hard luck did me in. I knew it was a bad omen when I flew over a funeral just west of Owego. The gravediggers stopped their work and waved their shovels at me.

"I made a mistake when I laid out my route westward through the mountains instead of along the Hudson and the Lakes. It was just one terrible mountain after another. . . . I had five falls altogether. While my machine was wrecked, I was not badly hurt myself. The last fall took me clear out of the race. I was flying so high that my carburetor froze, stopping my engine. . . . I volplaned down to an area that was a veritable mass of gullies. . . . With my machine so badly damaged, I was convinced that I could not possibly reach the Pacific Coast before the time limit. . . .

"But I'm going to try it again, though. I think a transcontinental flight is entirely feasible and believe Fowler or Rodgers may land it.

"If Mr. Hearst will consent to change the restrictions so that I can have additional time to complete the journey to the Coast, I will go right back to Addison, New York, and resume the race. . . ."

Ward's final tally showed more than 500 miles all told with 328 miles along his intended route.

Only Rodgers and Fowler now remained in the race, with Earle Ovington a promised starter four days hence.

In Omaha, Nebraska, Mayor James C. Dehlman declared: "Preparations have already been made to extend the transcontinental racers a rousing reception in Omaha. The entire West is intensely interested in the great race, and thousands of people will join in doing honor to the plucky aviators. I firmly believe that the world has never seen such a great purely sporting event. Mr. Hearst is to be congratulated for having inaugurated the world-interested contest."

Sept. 24, Sunday. Take-off from Flint farm 10:14 A.M. More than 2,000 people present (Mr. Flint threatened suit for crop damage). Cloudless sky, but puffy headwinds through corkscrew hills. 65 miles in two hours 13 minutes. Landed for gasoline Olean Fairgrounds racetrack.

Frank Close, owner of Olean's bicycle factory and garage, volunteered to hunt up a supply of fuel. Cal accepted handshakes from Mayor Foley and Chamber-of-Commerce president B. U. Taylor and a sandwich and

---

to have followed us, I herewith withdraw Mr. Ward from the contest. I thank the Hearst papers for their many kindnesses extended to Mr. Ward from the beginning of our attempt. Ike Bloom, Manager of James Ward."

glass of milk. When Close returned with a ten-gallon milk can filled with gasoline, he and Cal hoisted the can and filtered its contents through a chamois into the airplane's tank. One wheel had been wrenched off on landing but was quickly reattached. The stop at Olean consumed thirty minutes.

> *I clipped the top of a haystack in rising from Olean and took some of Olean's best hay along with me. I aimed the machine for Jamestown, 51 miles to the west. I was to land there or continue on just as I felt, but I hadn't gone more than eight or nine miles when the magnetos began to show signs of trouble. I wasn't going to repeat yesterday's experience, so I looked for a soft spot. I found one, and the landing was perfect. The next minute I saw this Indian running around the field. "Big White Bird," he shouted. "Biggest bird I ever saw."*

Cal had flown over Salamanca shortly after noting the defective magneto plugs. Shrill blasts from the Erie whistle had alerted the town to his approach, and business stopped short as nearly everyone within earshot turned his eyes skyward to watch the craft—the first in this vicinity—sail 1,000 feet over Main Street at 30 mph. Evangelist Billy Sunday was holding services in a large tent one block off Main Street; his congregation deserted him when the sounds of the *Vin Fiz* engine interrupted his sermon. Seven miles west of Salamanca, Cal landed on the Allegany Seneca Indian Reservation at Redhouse.

Several more Indians sauntered to the field to join their predecessor and to watch impassively as the airman fussed over his engine for half an hour. Cal's six-foot-four-inch height was half a foot greater than that of the tallest onlooker present. "Big man," the Indians agreed. The terrain was rough and the wind brisk, but Cal decided on a takeoff nonetheless. Several youngsters from Salamanca had augmented the growing audience, and Cal recruited two of their number to hold the wing tips as he pulled down on a propeller, blowing swells of sooty smoke over the Indians. He climbed back onto the seat, puffed at his cigar, turned the lug restoring full compression to the engine, and motioned his volunteers to release.

The airplane slewed along the ground, retarded by soft turf and long, matted grass. As a barbed-wire fence loomed ahead of him, Cal switched off the engine. A second attempt produced the same result. At three o'clock Cal prepared for another try. The band of Indians had grown to a score. One red man raised his hand: "Wait, we take fence down."

"No," insisted Cal, "I can get over it all right."

As the machine slid forward for the third time, it again seemed unable to rise. A capricious wind beat down on the planes. The matted grass snarled the wheels. Cal continued to tug at the elevator lever, then slammed headlong into the double line of high, barbed-wire fence that bounded the west end of the field. The first line of fencing was torn down, and the biplane entangled itself in the second line. Both propeller blades and both skids were smashed, wires snapped, the left wing and wheels crumpled. Two Indians stepped into the wreckage and helped the bird-man to extricate himself from the mingle-mangle of staves, fabric, and wire. Cal staggered about, shaken, bruised, but not seriously injured. His coat sleeve, ripped from shoulder to elbow, hung asunder, as if his arm had swollen to burst its skin. The Indian who had spoken walked over and gazed at him stolidly: "I said we take fence down. Big bull head."

Within minutes Cal regained his senses, but not his self-assurance. His body slumped, a portrait of despondency. His eyes could barely focus on the stricken bird-machine; reassembled and reborn only three days before, it again lay at the edge of the grave—this time, so it seemed, without hope of salvation. The Pacific Coast receded a million miles in the distance. The thirty-day time limit for the Hearst prize shrank to a few ticks of the clock.

"Poor, poor, poor Betsy," Cal muttered over and over.

After half an hour or so, the mood of gloominess still weighed on him, but he forced himself to examine the debris, assessing the cost of rebuilding. A glint of light from the buckled planes caught his eye, and he moved in to disentangle the bottle of Vin Fiz. Still whole, unscathed, its carbonated liquid frothing in its neck, the bottle took on a spirit of its own: survival. It had survived the crash at Middletown and now the smashup here at the Indian reservation. Beyond survival, it was hope, trueness, endurance. . . .

The Vin Fiz special had been detained at the Salamanca yards, a major division point where passenger and freight trains changed crews. By the time it reached Redhouse, news of the latest disaster was waiting. Ramps were pushed out the hangar-car door, and the Palmer-Singer automobile, with the three mechanicians urging on Jimmy Dunn, bounced to the site —Jimerson Field—of the downed flying machine. Taylor and Shaffer immediately affirmed that virtually the entire craft wanted reconstruction.

"Fix her up, boys," said Cal jauntily, with a brave display of poise. "I'll be ready."

Crewmen quickly reached the field and soon hauled most of the airship pieces to the hangar car. The special was then backed into Salamanca and onto a siding just north of the post office. Its locomotive was detached and assigned to duties elsewhere.

Mabel was gratified to find that the mailbag tied to a brace had not split open. After the crash at Middletown, she had enclosed all letters in moistureproof pouches and had sewn a stiffer clasp on the mailbag. She was, she insisted, taking seriously her title of postmistress; her two assistants, Allie and Hibbard, were enjoined to view their duties in a responsible light.

Mrs. Sweitzer followed the proceedings with an air of stoicism. To Calbraith, she said nothing, her message delivered loudly without words; Cal feigned obliviousness. Of Charley Taylor, whom she managed to corral briefly, she inquired if the crash had sensibly put an end to further flights; Taylor shrugged. Mrs. Sweitzer, unable to recruit an ally, retired to bide her time for a more propitious moment in which to press her case.

DeKrafft telegraphed to the Wright factory an extensive list of spare parts. Arrangements were made for an anticipated three nights of accommodations at the Dudley House, and the expedition's managers—with Cal, presentable again in his spare suit—conferred over supper at the Palace Café. It was decided to effect what repairs were practical in a local shop while awaiting shipments from Dayton. Cal attempted to telephone John Rodgers at the Wright factory, but the Salamanca hello girl was not able to complete the connection, and a wire was transmitted requesting him to expedite deKrafft's order.

A crowd had collected outside the Palace Café to stare through its window at the first birdman to alight in Salamanca. Cal left his meal to address the gathering. He delivered a few words of praise for the town and the delicious food of its restaurant and, when Jimmy Dunn arrived with the Palmer-Singer, drove up and down Main Street waving at the enthusiastic citizens and the youngsters who ran alongside and behind the auto.

A local reporter asked why the aviator had persisted in his attempts to take off from Jimerson Field. "It was a foolishness triple distilled," Cal admitted.

In the morning the body of the *Vin Fiz* was carried to the Salamanca Engine & Iron Works. Leo McNally and three other crewmen were dispatched to the Seneca Reservation to retrieve the engine and other parts abandoned overnight. McNally was accosted by one of the Indians and presented with a bill for damages to the barbed-wire fencing.

Cal passed much of the day sequestered in his room at the Dudley House. In the afternoon he held court in the lobby, fielding questions from a circle of admirers, mostly adolescent boys ("Why don't airplanes have feathers like birds?" "Don't you get burned if you fly too close to the sun?"). Later, reading the *Salamanca Republican-Press,* he learned that ill fortune was also shadowing his remaining active competitor.

Bob Fowler, the West-to-East flier, had departed Colfax, California, Saturday. Ferocious winds through the 7,080-foot pass of the Sierras battled him to a standstill twenty-five miles short of Summit and forced his return to Colfax. A more powerful Cole engine was installed, and the winds turned favorable on Sunday morning. Fowler took off again and climbed in steep circles to the upper atmosphere: "By the time I traveled twenty miles from Colfax," he reported in the local press, "I had made a height of 7,200 feet, then I spiraled again and headed toward Cisco at a height of 7,500 feet. At Cisco my barometer showed 7,800 feet. . . . I was tossed about in all directions; the aeroplane tipped nearly straight up, then sideways, and I had a very busy time of it keeping the machine from upsetting. The velocity of the wind was very near 50 mph, and I could make no headway against it. While circling in an effort to get above the treacherous currents my engine stopped, probably on account of loss of water, as it had boiled out over the top of the radiator."

In danger of being scalded first by the steam and then by boiling water as the radiator cracked open, Fowler volplaned to the ground at Emigrants Gap.* His supply train reached him later in the day and returned man and machine to Colfax, whence it was announced that he would be ready for a final attempt on Tuesday, weather permitting. Crowds that had gathered at the Reno Fairgrounds to welcome the transcontinental aviator were disappointed once again, and once again vowed to reassemble two days hence. There was expressed no lack of faith in Fowler's ultimate triumph.

The Nassau Boulevard Air Meet had opened on Saturday. Thomas Sopwith and Harriet Quimby immediately proved the most popular fliers. The lady aeronaut, known as "The Dresden China Aviatrice" (she wore knickerbockers, a mauve satin hooded jacket, and thirteen necklaces), drew groups of both admirers and detractors. On the third day Dr. C. B. Clarke, a novice aviator from Brooklyn, was fatally injured in the crash of his Queen monoplane, a fact duly noted by Mrs. Sweitzer.

Foreign news centered on Italy's threatened assault against Tripoli in

---

*Almost precisely at the spot where the ill-fated Donner party was stranded through the appalling winter of 1846–47.

its dispute with Turkey and the explosion aboard the French battleship *Liberté* in which nearly 500 sailors lost their lives (a fire had broken out in the ammunition hold). In England, newspapers printed screaming, joyful headlines over the defeat—in the Canadian elections—of reciprocity. Such phrases as "American Conspiracy Foiled," "Victory for the Empire," and "Canada Still Loyal" could be read on almost every editorial page.

Cal evinced more interest in the baseball pennant races, now virtually resolved. Philadelphia led by eleven and a half games in the American League, and the Giants by seven and a half over Chicago in the National League.

Early Tuesday Cal arose and immediately made for the Engine & Iron Works to check the progress of work on the *Vin Fiz.* Broken parts still lay in a jumble on the floor; scarcely the outline of a reemergent flying machine could be seen. Cal stormed at his mechanicians and those of the Engine & Iron Works as laggards, scoundrels, and puddingheads. How could they just stand about, lollygagging? Did they not know he was in a race? Did they not know a $50,000 purse was at stake?

Stewart deKrafft pulled the angry aviator into the Palmer-Singer auto and, with Andre Roosevelt and with Jimmy Dunn at the wheel, drove the thirty-three miles west to Jamestown. They were met by advance man Lawrence Peters, who advised on preparations for a landing in that town. The afternoon was consumed in driving about, surveying the surrounding countryside.

To a reporter from the *Jamestown Post-Journal,* Cal declared that he was considering abandoning the Hearst contest since his mechanicians were unable to repair his airplane. "I will push on westward if I can obtain a suspension of the rules providing that the flight must be made in the same machine. Then I will order a new biplane from the Wright factory. Otherwise, I just don't know. . . ." Neither deKrafft nor Andre Roosevelt allowed themselves the least emotion at this statement.

Rooms were engaged for the night at a Jamestown hotel. DeKrafft, Roosevelt, and Jimmy Dunn relaxed with a game of pinochle. Cal snubbed their invitations to join them. Instead, he sequestered himself in an adjoining room to pore over topographical charts and checklists of pertinent landmarks. "It's easier to change the course of a locomotive than the course of his mind once it's set on track," Roosevelt commented. "There's two sides to that angle," deKrafft pointed out. "On the one hand, we wouldn't be stuck in Salamanca if Cal Rodgers were a reasonable man. On the other hand, a reasonable man would have given up this effort before he started." It was agreed that aviators—especially Calbraith P. Rodgers—were different from other men, and were entitled to be.

Wednesday morning found Cal in a brighter mood. The reporter who had heard his pessimistic outlook the day before was now treated to a different story: "I plan to get away from Salamanca this afternoon and am confident I can make 100 miles before sunset. I don't think there'll be a repetition of Middletown or Redhouse. . . . There are only two of us in the race now. I'll probably pass Fowler just beyond Omaha. If we do meet there, I'll have a small American flag and wave at him. . . . He's a fine fellow, Bob Fowler, and I wouldn't feel broken up if he should win the prize. There isn't an aviator alive that I don't wish all the luck in the world. We need good wishes."

Jimmy Dunn drove the group back to Salamanca, arriving as the noon whistle sounded. New planes had been fashioned, canvas stretched over frames, and wires strung. However, several essential parts had not yet arrived from Dayton on the BR&P; they were expected shortly, said Clint Crater, the Engine & Iron Works mechanician, adding his doubt that the machine would be tuned to working order by that afternoon. Cal received this news philosophically.

Charles Yaw, who drove the fire wagon (and the fire sleigh in winter) for the Salamanca Fire Department, volunteered to escort Cal and his party around the environs of Salamanca so that a suitable starting site could be selected. Several areas were examined and found wanting. "Seeking a place of departure in this part of the country is like hunting for gold, a very uncertain thing," Cal remarked to the reporter from the *Republican-Press* who followed him about.

Midafternoon saw a heavily overcast sky; thoughts of continuing the flight that day were dismissed. The press was informed that Cal would depart Salamanca on the morrow from a yet undesignated location.

Cal drove up and down Main Street waving at the natives, who now spoke of him in awed but possessive terms—Salamanca's own birdman. Elgar Noyes, president of the town council, invited him and Mabel for supper. Charles Gibson and Frank Prescott, two businessmen, indulged him with shoes and a new coat (the sleeve lacerated on the barbed-wire fence at the Seneca Reservation had been mended by the Negro stewards but was ruled unbecoming by Mrs. Sweitzer). Scores of Salamancans called him friend.

Charles Davidson had arranged for additional supplies of the Vin Fiz grape drink to be shipped in, and huge quantities of the soda pop were consumed by the Salamanca populace, largely out of deference to Cal—few words of praise and many of distaste were heard for the drink itself ("a fine blend of river sludge and horse slop").

Three hundred and twenty-five miles to the southwest, in Dayton, Ohio, John Rodgers had flown from Dayton to Marion at the behest of Wilbur Wright and had thereby missed Cal's telegram. Learning of the further delay, he had boarded an Erie train and arrived in Salamanca Wednesday evening in time to join the aviation party at dinner. "At least, when you are hung up on a barbed-wire fence," he told Cal, "you can't get lost and wander from one state to another."

After dinner the Vin Fiz entourage heard a discourse from Thomas Hanly, the *New York American* correspondent aboard the coach car. Hanly had listened to Lincoln Beachey's account the previous Sunday of the 1910 Dominguez Air Meet and of William Randolph Hearst's first airplane experience.[2] He had observed Hearst on several occasions and thought him a character whom Shakespeare might have invented, "particularly if Shakespeare were writing a part for a forty-eight-year-old bear with the presumption of an elephant." From his New York office, Hanly had obtained Hearst's personal record of the flight with Louis Paulhan, and he presented it to Cal. It read (in part):

> *No one could watch an aeroplane skimming swiftly and gracefully through the air without wanting to fly. I got aboard [the frail machine] and managed to fold myself into a little space back of M. Paulhan. . . .*
>
> *For a few minutes M. Paulhan busied himself with preliminary adjustments of the machine, then he gave a signal. The big propeller behind us swished through the air; the engine gave musketry fire of successive reports, like a racing automobile with its throttle wide open. We started and skimmed along the ground at a constantly increasing speed. The men who were running alongside the machine let go, with a shout of good-bye, and we rose majestically into space.*
>
> *We left the commonplaces of this worn-out world behind us and lifted into a new life, a new era.*
>
> *The sensations of flying are difficult to describe, for the human mind operates through analogy and is convinced with comparisons, and there is nothing with which to compare the sensation of flying. I felt that great sense of exhilaration which all aviators describe, and, in addition, a deep serenity —a calm enjoyment of what seemed to be the perfect condition of a new and better state. . . .*
>
> *Rising steadily, we were soon several hundred feet above the earth and our former associates thereon. . . . We were now sailing far above a road to the*

city. Many automobiles were rolling through the dust of this road, for the day was nearly over and the people were beginning to go home. Some automobiles stopped, and the people in them waved veils and handkerchiefs at us. We waved in return and then swept on past them, over the fields where the green grass lay in great square patches on the brown sod. . . .

We swept on, higher and higher, farther and farther. . . .

There was wind, and there was cold in the upper air, as M. Paulhan had said, but oh! there was a glorious view. The sun was just sinking in the Pacific, and the clouds were red with its last rays. In the distance was San Pedro harbor, and between it and ourselves were some inlets of the sea that lay like mirrors and reflected the rose-red of the heavens among the greens and grays of the marshes. Then we turned, [back] towards the enclosure. . . .

M. Paulhan pulled a little cord in front, lowered the front of the aeroplane a trifle, and we tipped down towards the earth. We came down very fast. It was like shooting the chutes for hundreds of yards, without a splash at the finish. For, as we neared the earth, M. Paulhan tipped up the forward plane again, and we settled as calmly and gently as a lighting bird.

Hanly was impressed: "There's the hint of a Wagnerian overture that seems to accompany him whatever he does."

"Maybe I have misjudged him," said Cal. "He does seem to have a feeling for the sport. I think he could learn to drive an aeroplane. If he did, he would give us more than thirty days to make this trip."

Thursday the twenty-eighth dawned with flawless weather. Final touches to the *Vin Fiz* were applied. A reworked engine was installed, and the propellers were joined. The bottle of Vin Fiz grape juice was trussed to the forward brace. "The repairs used about all the spare parts we carried with us," Cal informed the *Republican-Press* reporter. "However, new supplies have been ordered from Dayton—that is, all except a new aviator. The old one has learned his lesson, he hopes, and will take better care of his 'irreplaceable parts.' "

The Eckhart farm at Great Valley was fixed upon as the departure point, despite its location five miles to the northeast of Salamanca. Its level space from the base of the hills and its adjacency to the highway were deciding factors in its selection. Bulletins to that effect were posted in shop windows under deKrafft's direction, and virtually the entire population of Salamanca flocked from the village to Great Valley. Most wore their Sunday go-to-meeting clothes out of respect for their celebrated guest and the momentous occasion. Peanut butchers and lemonade vendors transacted a brisk trade. Mabel and her helpers sold a record number of postcards.

The *Vin Fiz* was wheeled from its shed on Rochester Street and towed behind the Palmer-Singer to the Eckhart farm, trailing a long wake of gleeful schoolchildren. At the farm, the planes, rudder, and elevator were attached under the supervision of Charley Taylor. The machine was pronounced ready for flight shortly after 10:00 A.M., but before Cal could mount the seat, swarms of youngsters converged on the reassembled craft to inscribe their names on the clean white fabric.

Several Indians from the Seneca Reservation appeared, one holding in his hand another bill for the damaged fence; he could find no one to accept it. The brave who had cautioned Cal four days earlier conferred his benediction despite the unpaid debt: "May you fly on wings that never tire until you reach the great ocean of the West. And remember," he added, "only birds can land on barbed-wire fences."

Cal estimated the wind to be 15 mph in his favor and anticipated a smooth flight: "If everything is working well, I shall not stop until I reach Meadville and perhaps I won't land there."

The propellers were pulled through, and the engine was operated for several minutes. Cal and Charley Taylor agreed that it sounded perfect and that no trial flights were necessary.

A file of cigars lined the pockets of Cal's leather vest—like condemned men at a firing wall, Cal described them. He extracted one, lit it, and signaled his readiness. Charley Taylor matched his action with an equally stout cigar and mimed his concurrence.

Again Cal felt the emotional surge that came with every takeoff. Two fresh lads were holding the wing tips at either side of him—Douglas Arrowsmith, thirteen, and Charles Dickson, sixteen. He nodded to them and advanced the magneto spark.

Three thousand spectators on the field, on barn roofs, woodsheds, tree limbs, and hanging from telegraph poles cheered on the *Vin Fiz*. It rose majestically, turning first across the town. Cal sowed leaflets over the area and circled in birdlike evolutions for ten minutes, allowing his crew and mechanicians to scramble for the special train. Mabel and Mrs. Sweitzer perched on the observation platform, competing in the vigor of their arm waves at the aviator overhead. At 2,000 feet the machine leveled off and aimed westward. Whistles of the BR&P and of the Erie shops swallowed up the farewell salute of Salamanca's Christian Men's Marching Band.

With classes canceled, almost every youngster in the vicinity was at the

Eckhart farm. One exception was Mabel Noyes, thirteen, daughter of the council president, whose parents had forbidden her to approach the flying machine. Her teacher at the West Salamanca School, Ora Winshop, had set up a telescope in the schoolyard. Through the scope, Mabel Noyes watched the *Vin Fiz* sail up the valley, across the Allegheny River, until it shrank to a speck on the glass and disappeared.

5

O, Hi, Ohio and
Windy Indiana

OVER KENNEDY, HIS motor humming like bees in a hive, the steady clacking of the propeller chains assuring him of the airship's well-being, Cal elected to bypass Jamestown. As he flew over that city—at 11:09 A.M. —he flung out handfuls of Vin Fiz leaflets. Hundreds of schoolchildren —all schools had been dismissed for the morning—scrambled to collect them.

Mr. John Lee, superintendent of streets, wrote, "I was driving my horse and buggy along Fluvanna Avenue when the flying machine went by. The horse cocked its head so as to look upward several times and apparently wondered what the noisy bird overhead might be."

Sept. 28, Thursday. Corry, Pa., 11:31 A.M. Cambridge Springs, Meadville 12:25 o'clock. . . .

With the weather as nearly perfect for the machine as it can be—though a little chilly for the driver—I at last succeeded in getting past the hills which had been my constant companion since I left New York and into the level country where if you miss a swamp you get a good landing place. I didn't have to go much higher than 1,200 feet for the wind was pretty steady. I made the turns and got into a few little pockets and eddys. The engine was working, the radiator was doing its job, and the magneto had all its plugs and was holding on to them. . . . Presently I was up to 2,500 feet and the panorama of little villages spread out ahead of me, looking like a set of black checkers on a monster board. . . . a flock of birds that looked like pigeons started toward me [near Jamestown] and then turned and flew off as hard as they could. They must have thought me a new kind of hawk.

Cal circled Meadville at 1,000 feet, searching for the country-club golf links. The site was to be outlined in white canvas—so Lawrence Peters had telegraphed—but the markings were not apparent to the aviator. Instead, he spotted the horse barns, grandstand, and hotel of the Kite Racetrack on Rogers Ferry Road and alighted nearby on the bank of French Creek. He had gained 102 miles in 110 minutes.

A steady stream of citizens headed for the Kite racing grounds by foot, trolley, and automobile.* Among the first to reach the airplane were pupils of the First District School on North Main Street. They milled about and gawked at the lanky figure clad in leather jacket and breeches and darted in to sign their names whenever he looked away.

The Vin Fiz train stopped a short distance from the grounds; its occupants raced out, fording the small creek intervening, to check the condition of airman and airplane. Mabel bore a chicken sandwich and, at Charles Davidson's behest, a bottle of Vin Fiz that Cal downed ostentatiously while Harry Sanger called the crowd's attention to the act. Charley Taylor decreed a test of the motor—despite Cal's assurances that it had been functioning perfectly. A rope was passed around a post and then connected to the rear structure of the airplane through a large set of "fish tail" scales. With the engine engaged, the scales registered its effective pull. Taylor was satisfied with the readings, but still voiced a vague concern over the engine's appearance. (Observing the procedure, many young lads of Meadville instantly acquired *soi-disant* expertise in aeronautics; their newfound knowledge resulted in numerous model airplanes, none of which performed to its owner's expectations.)

Sept. 28. Take-off Meadville 2:27 P.M. Greenville, Shenango. . . .

*Rodgers was Meadville's first skyborne visitor except for Alex Thurston the year before in his balloon, *Meadville*.

Several youths lounged at the Main Street crossing of the Erie line through Greenville. First they saw the Vin Fiz special roar by "like a pay train passing the hoboes," an animated blond lady in a wide-brimmed hat on the rear platform dispensing leaflets into its wake. Then, a moment later, they saw directly overhead the magnificent sight of a flying machine. Each claimed to have observed some unusual detail. One noted that the aviator wore his cap backward like a catcher's. Another noted the cigar. Lastly, Ed Zurer drawled, "I saw the polky dots on his necktie."

The *Vin Fiz* crossed into Ohio over Orangeville; at Burghill, three miles on, the Wright engine began overheating. As Cal complained to Charley Taylor, "We had done everything else for the machine at Meadville, but had forgotten to put in a new supply of oil."

Increasingly ominous noises rose from the engine as the flying machine approached Warren, a town of 11,000 inhabitants, spread out along a stretch of bottomland beside the winding Mahoning River. Cal spotted the fifty-yard strip of white gunny that had been staked out on the W. H. Loveless farm and dipped the aircraft toward it.

> *A little of the hoodoo apparently still clung around, for in the field was a little ditch carefully concealed by weeds. In this ditch I broke a skid. The train was only about five minutes behind me, however, and the men went at it without a minute's delay.*

The Loveless farm at Warren had been chosen and marked by Andre Roosevelt and Lawrence Peters a week earlier. Roosevelt had placed a notice in the *Warren Daily Tribune* requesting that spectators remain on the banks of the canal and not crowd the field. In response to the announcement that the coast-to-coast flier would reach Warren on Sunday, September 24, 2,000 people trampled across the farm, only to learn that the birdman had wrecked his machine at Salamanca. Again alerted on Thursday by telegraph from Salamanca and Meadville, they flocked back to the Loveless farm to witness Cal's descent at 2:43 in the afternoon. While the machine was under repair, the crowd grew to 5,000.

Those present watched as the towering, leather-coated birdman, his long legs rising from Hessian boots, his cap reversed, directed and assisted his three mechanicians with a concentrated intensity. A gentleman from the board of trade brought up a glass of water and delivered it to the birdman along with the knowledge that Warren, incorporated only six years earlier, was the site where J. Ward Packard had built his first automobile; in further distinction, last year Warren had become the first city in America to install Mazda tungsten lamps on its streets. Cal thanked the gentleman for the water.

After nearly two hours of work, Charley Taylor certified the *Vin Fiz* again ready for flight. More than thirty youngsters who had vaulted the canal bank to write their names on the planes assisted in dragging the machine across the soft ground to the south end of the farm.

Cal stated that he would pass up his scheduled stop at Akron and strive for Mansfield, 107 miles away. He mounted the seat, beckoned for Shaffer and Charlie Wiggin to turn the propellers, and bounced along the ground for almost 100 yards before becoming airborne. He described a wide arc over the city and, at 4:45 P.M., turned westward along the Erie tracks.

> *There was a pretty good crowd at Warren. They offered to do everything for me. I could have eaten a bale of pies and cakes, and they did not try to pick the machine to pieces. Having my machine wrecked by souvenir hunters is becoming one of the dreads of this trip. Women are the worst offenders, and I can see that they do it without thinking. Sometimes they crawl right onto the planes to write their names and they cannot understand why I try to prevent them. The weight of a good-sized woman on one of the planes would mean disaster.*

Sept. 28. Windham, Freedom, Ravenna, Kent, 30 miles in 30 minutes.

Every engine and shop whistle in the Kent yards shrilled, raising a din that roused all but the cemetery inmates. Hundreds stood on the Main Street Bridge and cheered, waving hats and handkerchiefs at the first airplane in Portage County. Ohio was friendly territory, the aviator noted, both in the welcome of its citizens and the soft contours of its terrain. The cheers and waves would increase, he decided, as the length of his course increased, as more and more of the country acknowledged his destiny.

At the west side of Kent, Cal circled at 1,000 feet, dispensed a load of Vin Fiz leaflets, and continued on toward Akron. Five miles farther, eight miles short of Akron, faced with a setting sun and the risk of a landing at dusk or later, he turned back to an expedient field noted several minutes earlier. Spectators on the Main Street Bridge were still watching his movements as he swooped down on the Alonso Johnson farm two miles to the northwest in Franklin Township. The *Vin Fiz* flopped onto ground newly mown, skittered over a layer of chaff, and nosed into a haystack across the road from the house of O. M. Gooch. Cal brushed stalks of hay from his head and backed out over the lower plane. The day's flight had spanned 204 miles.

People in the vicinity hurried to the Johnson farm to welcome the unexpected birdman. Within a few minutes the special train, which had passed through Kent, backtracked to the bridge crossing. The auto ramp was extended and the Palmer-Singer driven out Hudson Road carrying Mabel, deKrafft, John Rodgers, and Charley Taylor to the scene. They found Cal, shivering with cold despite his suit, leather vest, sweater, and leggings, accepting a glass of milk from Farmer Gooch, while a ring of solemn-eyed cows looked on. When crewmen arrived on foot, the airplane was tugged from the haystack, enveloped with its light canvas shroud, and entrusted to the custody of a guard.

A record run had been achieved by the train, now pulled by Erie engine 802 under the control of engineer A. A. Stearns and fireman H. B. McGruder. The new locomotive had been attached at Salamanca, where a fresh crew, including conductor John Eckhart and brakemen Johnson and Walters, had boarded the special determined to improve on its earlier performance.

After supper Cal and John Rodgers proceeded to the Revere Barber Shop, where Clyde Lighton shaved and trimmed the aviator before an audience of awestruck boys who snatched up the hair-cuttings as they fell to the floor. At 8:15 P.M. Cal collected his wife and mother and drove the Palmer-Singer to Akron—"the rubber capital of the world"—to meet the welcoming committee in that city and to pass the night in Akron's Buchtel Hotel. Although Mabel was yet unable to reclaim her husband for the purpose of conjugality, her accommodations at the Buchtel afforded a sense of relief. No sooner had the train departed Middletown, one week before, than Mrs. Sweitzer had assumed charge of maintaining her son's (and daughter-in-law's) stateroom. She had rearranged the furnishings, refolded Calbraith's smallcothes and stockings, sniffed at Mabel's wardrobe, and—somehow—had immediately stamped the room with her own cachet. "You can't just leave it to George—or anyone else without the proper background," she said pointedly.

In Akron, the Rodgers family was entertained by C. W. Seiberling, vice-president of Goodyear Tire & Rubber Company. Seiberling reminded Cal that the *Vin Fiz* was covered with Goodyear's rubber-impregnated airplane fabric and apprised him of Goodyear's new "No-Rim-Cut" airplane tire, a wire-base construction that was lighter and more durable than the Wing tire used on the EX. He later told reporters, "I asked Rodgers what he thought was the reason of so many deaths in aviation, and he replied that it was due to foolhardy feats, and that if aviators would confine themselves to straight flying, the death list would be cut down considerably."

Rain poured down on northeastern Ohio throughout the night. A gale sprang up about midnight and tossed the *Vin Fiz* about; lying in an open space with a canvas cover, it presented a large surface. The storm awakened Charley Taylor, who roused Shaffer and Charlie Wiggin. The three mechanicians, clad in slickers and sou'westers, stumbled along a dark country lane to the Johnson farm. For four hours they wrestled with buffeting forces, struggling to protect the engine from the pelting rain, maneuvering the airplane to avoid ripping its fabric as they checked each blast of the wind.

Cal awoke at 4:00 A.M.—central time,[1] an hour earlier than the clocks of New York—and squinted through the window of the hotel room he shared with Mrs. Sweitzer to observe that "it was raining hard and blowing at a grand rate." It was no better at six o'clock, and at nine o'clock, while the downpour abated, a 40-mph gale persisted directly out of the northwest, straight into the projected path of the *Vin Fiz*.

"It is only 389 miles from Kent to Chicago," mused Cal, "and I had hoped to see the roofs of Chicago beneath me before sundown tonight. I don't know who is responsible for this wind, but whoever it is should have more consideration for us aviators. . . . Mother Nature? Well, I'd like to get my hands on Mother Nature. . . ."

With no possibility of flying in such weather, Cal put Mabel and Mrs. Sweitzer on the trolley car to Kent, then drove the twenty miles to Canton for a concourse with several of the aviators participating in that city's air meet (now suspended because of the wind). Walter Brookins, Harry Atwood, and Andrew Drew were colleagues from the Wright Flying School and the Chicago Meet. Andrew Drew insisted that Cal relay "a special kiss to my good buddy, Mabel."

During the afternoon, schools in the area showed markedly decreased attendance as pupils played hookey to visit the Johnson farm and examine the aircraft. They were rewarded in late afternoon by the presence of the birdman himself, who appeared on the scene to tinker with the craft for more than an hour before quitting the field. Frank Lawrence, a seventeen-year-old high-school senior in Tallmadge, had hiked the seven miles to Kent. With his Brownie box camera, he snapped several pictures of the aviator and his machine. Cal asked Lawrence to send him copies of the prints.

"Vin," the party's mascot, was joined at this time by another kitten, a white feline of uncertain ancestry that stared at the crew through one blue eye and one brown eye. The newcomer was promptly named "Fiz," and since it showed no inclination to wander off, it too was afforded a blanket in one corner of the hangar car.

At the Commercial Hotel, deKrafft informed Cal that Bob Fowler was still at Emigrants Gap, on the verge of yet another effort to vault the Sierras to Reno. Earle Ovington had not taken off Wednesday as previously announced, and with Cal now 460 miles along, it seemed unlikely that he could overcome such a lead. On Tuesday Ovington, appointed by Postmaster General Frank Hitchcock as "special mail messenger # 1," had flown a sack of mail from the Nassau Boulevard Aviation Field (where the air meet continued) to Mineola, Long Island, ten miles distant.* With the sack perched on his lap (he had to balance it with his knees and peep over it to see ahead), he was unable to land his Blériot monoplane. The Mineola postmaster stood in the center of a field, waving a red flag. From 500 feet, Ovington aimed at him and dropped the sack. It broke on impact and scattered its contents over the field.†

Mabel had earlier petitioned the postmaster general for official recognition of her "aerial mail" postcards but had been spurned. It was of little consolation to read that her husband's efforts in the transcontinental race had gained such renown as to be commemorated in "Mutt and Jeff." Jeff (the small one), who was planning to enter the race, had procured huge quantities of equipment, but had overlooked the need for one essential item: an airplane.

William Randolph Hearst, it was noted, had sailed into New York Harbor Thursday evening. He had volunteered no comment on the coast-to-coast race. A reporter asked if Hearst had not changed the rules in midstream by imposing a deadline of October 10 for the conclusion of the contest. Hearst merely scowled. Earle Ovington, on the other hand, told the press that Hearst's own regulations unequivocally allowed thirty days for the journey as long as it was begun before October 10 and threatened to sue Hearst personally over the matter.

From Kitty Hawk, North Carolina, came reports that Wilbur, Orville, and Lorin Wright were conducting secret trials of their new "buzzard" machine, "designed to emulate the buzzard in its minimal use of artificial power." The Wrights' concept seemed to be based on their observation

---

*The route was designated by general order as Mail Route No. 607001.
†In the sack were 640 letters and 1,280 postcards, each canceled with a special stamp, "Aeroplane Station No. 1," and marked with the cachet "Aerial Special Dispatch."

that "some huge birds are able to soar for long periods almost without effort—because of their ability to change the position of their wings as a whole as well as individual parts separately." Charley Taylor had assisted with sections of the new aircraft but did not believe the principle a sound one. John Rodgers had heard of the new machine during his recent trip to Dayton and also expressed skepticism. Added Stewart deKrafft: "The Wrights have been ingenious in their studies of aeronautic principles. But it is a misguided notion to imitate the birds. Birds, if they knew how, would imitate aeroplanes."

A contract had been signed earlier for Cal to perform aerial exhibitions at Canton in the Wright Type B carried in the hangar car. The Aviation Committee of the Canton meet announced earlier in the day that C. P. Rodgers would appear from two to four o'clock Saturday afternoon. However, with thirteen days of the allotted thirty already consumed, it was decided to cancel this engagement and proceed to Chicago. "Even if Fowler is stuck," said deKrafft, "time isn't. You can't win a race by not moving."

Sept. 30, Saturday. Take-off Kent 8:55 A.M. Akron, Pavonia . . .

In the morning air, washed clean by the rain of yesterday, rivers and lakes were etched so sharply on the landscape that an aviator could feel he was staring down at a life-size map. To the north, Cal could see the Cuyahoga River carving a giant horseshoe through the rock walls of a deep gorge. To the south, the Tuscarawas River connected the Portage Lakes and merged itself with the Muskingum. Rivers, thought Cal, run their courses in preordained channels, each surge of water following its predecessor precisely . . . until . . . until there comes a flood. . . . Over Akron, Cal crossed the Ohio and Erie Canal, its banks lined with marketplaces —like piglets along a feeding trough.

Lookouts at the Ohio State Reformatory were first to sight the *Vin Fiz Flyer* as it approached Mansfield; Dr. J. A. Leonard, superintendent of the penal institution, triggered the giant whistle atop the guard tower to alert the nearby town, where fire bells and the Erie shop whistles took up the cry. Factory workers on the industrial North Side abandoned their jobs, and hundreds of persons scampered to roofs and fire-escape ledges to witness the spectacle.

At Kent, Cal had been handed a telegram from Lawrence Peters describing the landing site, provision for which had been concluded with the Mansfield Reception Committee only moments earlier. Now he removed one gauntlet, fished the telegram from his pocket, and read it again—while airborne. With the description fresh in mind, he circled twice before spying the 200-foot-long strips of white bunting staked down on the William Isley dairy farm along North Main Street Road. The rectangle between the strips had been cleared of twigs and stones that might impair his landing, and cows removed to a nearby pasture. The *Vin Fiz* bumped down at 10:43 A.M., having spanned 77 miles in 108 minutes.

Cal jumped from the machine to be greeted by Joe Newborn and his assistant, Virgil Howey, both of whom had been pressed into duty as surrogate advance men. Cal remanded the aircraft to their charge and repaired to the Isley home about 500 feet away, where he refreshed himself with a drink of milk and warmed himself at the Isley hearth. He appeared to be suffering from the cold and hugged his arms to his chest, puffing furiously on his stogie. His face was pale, and he moved stiffly. After about twenty minutes he emerged from the house, still not fully thawed. Two thousand persons had gathered about the *Vin Fiz.* Automobiles, carts, and wagons had been pressed into service and were parked on the farm. The *Mansfield News* of the previous day had requested onlookers not to autograph the planes. The request was, as usual, ignored, and the few remaining white spaces on the fabric were soon darkened with penciled inscriptions. Cal shook hands with Mayor Huntington Brown (enlisted as the official timer); conveyed his recollections of Lieutenant Frank Lahm, a native of Mansfield with whom he had trained at the Wright Flying School; and halfheartedly shooed a few youngsters away from the machine.

Charley Taylor, Frank Shaffer, and Charlie Wiggin had arrived from the special train, replenished the gasoline supply, and effected some bits of minor mending.

R. B. ("Mud") Gardner, an eighteen-year-old Mansfield racing enthusiast, was at the fairgrounds across town testing his motorcycle; he had jumped into an automobile and sped to the Isley farm to observe his first airplane and to speak with its driver. "That's a nice-looking machine you got there," said Mud Gardner. "Yup," said Cal. "Where you going in it?" asked Mud. "California," said Cal. Mud shook his head, jumped back in his auto, and returned to the fairgrounds.

Another visitor to the Isley farm was " 'A' No. 1," the world's most famous hobo, who had arrived incognito in Mansfield earlier in the day. Dressed in clean white collar, clean shirt, and a suit, sporting a shine on his shoes, flashing a gold watch, and holding a small bundle under his arm, he joined the procession to admire the "aeroplanist" and the contraption that carried him aloft. " 'A' No. 1" had, to date, compiled a travel record of over 400,000 miles without paying a single railroad fare. He politely asked if he could hitch a ride aboard the *Vin Fiz* to the next town. Cal only stared at him.

At 11:52 A.M. Cal rose into the air, his teeth clamped over an unlit stogie (in the cold he had difficulty working his jaw muscles). Three long blasts from the Vin Fiz train whistle signaled that those on the special were prepared to take up the chase. The crowd at the Isley farm drifted back to homes and businesses; with the hundreds of autos, wagons, and horses returning to Mansfield, North Main Street Road was blocked for an hour after the flying machine had vanished to the west.

Forty-two minutes and thirty-eight miles beyond the Mansfield takeoff, the last foothills of the Appalachians now behind him, open tracts of Ohio farmland below him, Cal sighted the next town slated for a touch-and-run: Marion, Ohio. At the Roberts farm northeast of the central district, 5,000 people, including the "Buckeye Song Birds" of the Marion High School, were assembled to welcome the coast-to-coast flier, summoned by blasts from the whistle of the Marion Steam Shovel Company. Prepared to extend words of welcome was Warren G. Harding, Marion's leading citizen and publisher of the *Marion Star.* *

Cal tilted the *Vin Fiz* toward the Roberts farm, but found the terrain not to his liking. The masses of people scattered about the field left no space to alight safely. He veered and drove the machine into a meadow a mile south of the city and far removed from road or path.

Marion Maxwell, thirteen, and a companion were at the edge of the meadow, gathering black walnuts. Barefoot, "nigger-killers" dangling from the pockets of their dusty overalls, they observed and conversed with the redoubtable birdman for fifteen minutes without interruption. They autographed the planes and gawked openmouthed as the aviator detached a worn propeller drive chain.

Two policemen arrived and consented to guard the machine. Ezra Weltfish, owner of a nearby apple orchard, drove up in his Stanhope buggy. Cal climbed in beside him and was carried into town, where he took lunch at the Pilgrim Inn, the propeller chain deposited beneath his table. The inn's waitress, regarding the chain as if it were a coiled snake,

*Harding—a former state senator, lieutenant-governor, and defeated candidate for governor—had just returned from several weeks' holiday in Scotland and Ireland.

served her curious customer apprehensively. Within minutes, members of the *Vin Fiz* crew, having inquired of the whereabouts of their leader, discovered him at the inn.

Charlie Wiggin was dispatched to the hangar car for another chain; the others joined Cal in an unexpected repast (made doubly welcome as a respite from chef Ed Davis's monotonous servings), their rough dress and manners giving further alarm to the waitress. When Wiggin returned shortly, lugging a drive chain, the waitress fled the inn for safer quarters.

After lunch—the bill for which went unpaid—Jimmy Dunn wound the Palmer-Singer into the meadow with Cal, Taylor, and Shaffer aboard; the new drive chain was quickly attached.

At 2:40 Cal seated himself in the *Vin Fiz Flyer* and signaled for the propellers to be pulled. Less than 300 persons had managed to tramp through the shrubs and thick grass from the Roberts farm to the meadow. Not among them were the "Buckeye Song Birds." Garbed in long white skirts, white high-buttoned shoes, white bolero jackets, and white frilled bonnets, the four young ladies of that group did not dare risk their finery in the brush. For days they had practiced the lyrics and music recently composed by one of their number and had anticipated parading their talents to the headline-making skyborne visitor. Disappointed, they retreated to a room at the high school and performed the song for a circle of their friends:

> *O, hi, Ohio—*
> *O, me, o my-o.*
> *We are the Buckeye gals.*
> *We fly on high-o.*
> *O, how we sigh-o*
> *Over our Buckeye pals. . . .*

By the final note and the final buck-and-wing, Cal was miles to the west, the rails of the Erie line glimmering in the red-hued western sun as he headed for Huntington, Indiana, his next scheduled stop.

Sept. 30. Kenton, Lima, averaging 40 mph. [Exhibition at Lima two months earlier.] Ohio City . . .

> *An airman cannot tell too much about the country he goes over. There are no signs up where he is, and the little towns come so fast that a new one seems to begin before an old one ends.*

Precisely at the Ohio-Indiana state line, the motor of the *Vin Fiz*, ticking like a frenzied metronome, began missing its beat. Cal assumed that he was running short of fuel. Four miles into Indiana, he dipped the airplane onto "Red" Hilpert's pasture near the village of Bobo. It was 4:39 P.M.

By that moment the flying machine had well outraced the sight of its guide train. Just west of Lima, the Vin Fiz special had been halted by a hot journal on the forward truck of the locomotive; it did not reach Bobo until 5:34 P.M., when it was flagged down and its occupants advised of the landing.

Cal pranced about for some minutes in vigorous exercise to increase his circulation, impatient for his mechanicians to bring up a supply of gasoline. The cool breeze carried pungent odors of damp hay, of manure, of poppies in the meadow. The bucolic scene momentarily tempered his restiveness.

Noises from behind the *Vin Fiz* diverted Cal's mood; he turned to see a sizable and unfriendly-seeming bull—Red Hilpert's prized Holstein—trotting directly toward the airplane. Cal yelled and waved his arms, but without effect. He then stripped off his jacket and ran toward the beast, flagging the jacket before its eyes. That maneuver succeeded—all too well. The bull swerved and galloped directly toward the would-be matador. Confronted by the prospect of a head-on collision, Cal flung down his "cape" and spun about for a quick reversal. His athletic prowess deserted him at this moment, and he tripped over his legs, sprawling onto the damp turf. The bull paused to paw at the jacket, and Cal fled to the safety of a nearby copse of sycamore trees.

One of the Hilpert farmhands appeared within moments, absorbed the situation of the strange machine, the esteemed Hilpert bull, the tall, oddly garbed stranger yelling at it from behind a tree, and shook his head. "Well, thar," he said, "this is a pretty how-de-do." He inquired as to how the machine had scaled the trees and fences onto private property.

"Never mind that," said Cal, "just keep that animal away from my aeroplane."

The farmhand squinted with suspicion, but walked over to the bull, grasped the ring through its nose, and led it away.

Several other farm folk materialized to gawk at the contraption before Charley Taylor and Frank Shaffer arrived from the train. Taylor quickly diagnosed the engine problem as a clogged fuel line. With dusk approaching, Cal asked that a wire be sent to Huntington requesting illumination of the designated landing site. Perry Smithers, the Aero Club representative, telegraphed accordingly to C. D. Williams, secretary of the Boom Fund Committee and the Commercial Club,[2] in charge of Huntington arrangements. Bonfires were quickly lit. Cal and deKrafft then deemed it "foolhardy" to attempt the remaining thirty-six miles to Huntington in darkening skies, and the flight was postponed until the morrow. A total of 205 miles had been advanced in 258 minutes of flying time, the best progress to date.

C. D. Williams wired that 8,000 people had been awaiting the transcontinental flier and were keenly disappointed; he added that a banquet at the Huntington Hotel was prepared and suggested that the Vin Fiz train proceed with the aviator to Huntington Station.

Cal felt undisposed toward a formal appearance, but deKrafft persuaded him that the Huntington committee deserved better treatment for its efforts. The machine was covered with its protective canvas, a guard was posted—already several horses and buggies clogged nearby lanes, their drivers clambering over Red Hilpert's palings—and the train pushed on to Huntington.

That evening the Vin Fiz party attended an informal dinner hosted by the Huntington Commercial Club at Sheller's Café. Cal pledged that if he did not alight in Huntington the next day, he would execute three circles above the city to allow its inhabitants an unsparing view of the aircraft. C. D. Williams, in turn, conveyed his committee's tender of $300 for a landing, the offer to expire at 4:00 P.M.

In Chicago, Armour & Company officials were planning a gala reception for the birdman who had written the name of their 5¢ purple product across the skies. An Armour representative informed the press that the flight was ultimately to cost the company $150,000—"the most gigantic advertising scheme ever undertaken by an American corporation."

Saturday night, the close of the second week of the journey, found the entire entourage sleeping aboard the special train—to the disgruntlement of some. Cal and Mabel occupied the first stateroom in the private Pullman, with Mrs. Sweitzer partitioned to the adjoining compartment. At the least sound of human activity—or the suspicion of such a sound —to reach her ears, Mrs. Sweitzer would pound on the intervening bulkhead and call out, "Is everything all right there?" "Yes, mother," Cal would answer. "We might as well go to sleep," he whispered to Mabel. "Anything else will keep her up all night."

Mrs. deKrafft, Mrs. Shaffer, and Mrs. Wettengel qualified for Pullman berths, as did Charles Davidson, Ed Merritt, Stewart deKrafft, and Fred Wettengel. Other officials and reporters curled up on seats of the day coach or stretched out on mats laid in the aisle. Crew members and mechanicians slept in the hangar car as per their usual custom. At 6:00 A.M. the train backed out of Huntington to Bobo.

Sunday, October 1, confronted the expedition with cold, rain, and blustery winds. Conditions much less severe ordinarily pinned even the most intrepid aviator to the ground. Cal was driven to the Hilpert field at 9:00 A.M. The rain offered no hint of abatement—"At least it keeps the bulls in the barn," said Cal. The engine of the *Vin Fiz* was tested and pronounced in perfect shape. At 10:30 A.M. Cal concluded that if he were to retain a reasonable probability of reaching the Pacific Coast by the allotted time, he would have to pioneer where all others had stayed. Moreover, the $300 premium offered by the Huntington Commercial Club was not an inconsequential consideration. Charley Taylor protested vehemently: "In this weather, even the birds are walking." Cal insisted: "I'm going. I'm going over those clouds, around them, or through them. If I have to, I'll plow a furrow and go under them."

Light-headed in the heavy air, Cal hopped onto the driver's seat. The demons nipping at his heels goaded him on; the powers on high that judged him had collaborated—conspired—to confront him with this supreme test. He could not reject the challenge. The sullen mists before him held the key to his passage westward, to his ultimate deliverance.

With considerable misgivings, Shaffer and Wiggin spun the propellers as Taylor shouted over the roar of the chain drives and the wind, "You'll never keep your cigar lit in this kind of rain!"

Rising over Bobo (Rivare on railroad maps), Cal was unable to discern either the train or the Palmer-Singer auto along the road. At 500 feet he was faced with a 45-mph tempest and a biting downpour. Thickset cumulus clouds above and on all sides promised further gales and torrents of rain. The compass on his wrist was swinging wildly. He pushed the airplane down to 100 feet, located the railroad track, and pursued its heading for some twenty minutes, flying so low that "if the earth had whiskers, my machine would have given it a shave." He was tracing not the Erie track, however, but that of the southbound Rennsylvania Railroad, which crossed the Erie line west of Bobo. The *Vin Fiz* passed over Berne, directly over the Noah Wulliman barn. Sunday worshipers at Berne's Mennonite Church wondered at the sound from above—from a source no one could identify.

With a solid black thunderhead beating down on him, Cal swung due east in an effort to skirt the centric turbulence. He spied a rift in the woolpack and shot through it. Then the clouds closed in again, and the *Vin Fiz* was buffeted about in a double storm. Raindrops battered at his goggles; the very air turned metallic.

> *It was like flying through milky water. It was impossible to see a foot ahead of me.*

Bolts of lightning flashed close by. Thunder cracked and rumbled over the clatter of the machine, over the pain threshold of Cal's impaired hearing, jarring his brain, smothering his thoughts. Struggling to contain the tossing and twisting of the craft, he was too preoccupied with the control levers to become fearful of the lightning.

> *I was riding through an electric gridiron. I didn't know what lightning might do to an aeroplane, but I didn't like the idea. So I swung her and streaked it for the east only to run bang up against a big rain cloud in active operation. I seemed to have run into a cloud convention.*
>
> *If you have ever been out in a hail storm, you know how that rain cut my face. I had taken off my goggles for fear that I might be blinded by the water, and I took off my gloves and covered what I could of the vital points of the magneto. It was a cold and painful situation.*
>
> *I looked for my engine to stop on me any minute and began searching for a place to alight. I couldn't find one because a big cloud had quickly rolled in under me, and the earth had disappeared. It was lonesome. I might be a million miles up in space. I might be a hundred feet from earth. I breathed better when I sailed over the edge of the cloud and saw the misty land beneath me.*

The brief clearing found Cal over Portland, twenty-five miles south of Bobo. Again he pursued the Rennsylvania rails, now northwest against a quartering wind as the gale increased. He crossed back over the Wabash River at Geneva, where he quickly sought the security of terra firma. He had chosen a field surrounded on three sides by trees and bumped down roughly but without damage. He jumped from the driver's seat and knelt under the machine, using it as shelter from the punishing deluge.

Braving the elements, almost 200 of Geneva's 1,500 citizens materialized within minutes. The field was on the farm of Charles Mann, and Mrs. Mann invited Cal to dinner at their nearby house. While he was dining and drying his soaked clothes, yet more persons trekked out to the landing site to autograph the *Vin Fiz*. Clarence ("Punk") Shepherd, twenty, brought a pencil of indelible lead so that his signature would not wash off. Others scratched their names into the cloth and wood with wire nails.

After dinner Cal recruited several men to carry the machine to a pasture a half-mile away on the John Kelly farm, where he could gain an open run for takeoff. Meanwhile he walked into the center of Geneva and, at the telephone station, was connected with Fred Wettengel in Linn Grove. "Tell everyone not to worry," he ordered. "It's only drizzling now. And it can't get worse than what I've already lived through."

Wettengel, spurred by the opportunity to demonstrate his worth, had borrowed an automobile when the special stopped at Preble and, in company with Shaffer, Wiggin, and Leo McNally, had driven in the direction last reported for the missing airman. At Honduras, he had stopped at the general store, where, via telephone, he alerted villages to the south and southwest to watch for C. P. Rodgers and his airplane. He then headed for Linn Grove, where his telephone search was rewarded.

The mechanicians soon reached the Kelly farm. They found one propeller of the machine in poor condition. On the planes, dampness had softened the glue, and strips of fabric had been pulled loose by overzealous pencil wielders. "We'll have to tow it back to the train," Cal was informed.

"There is more than glue holding this machine together," said the aviator. "I flew it in, and I'll fly it out."

A bystander advised that he could follow the course of the Bluffton, Geneva, & Celina traction line or the narrow channel of the Wabash River and be led directly into Huntington. The *Vin Fiz* took off from Geneva at 3:40 P.M., leaving its mechanicians in a state of trepidation.

No sooner was Cal airborne than the forces pitted against him rallied for renewed attack. A cold, buffeting wind bruised the sky and rocked the flying machine as he strove to get his bearings. The sound of his engine seemed almost visible in the sodden sky; the wobbling of the misbehaving propeller added a rhythmic wail. To the east, the mantle of clouds and rain that covered everything within view congealed to a black maelstrom. He shifted his course westward to give it a wide berth.

At Bluffton he picked up the trolley line—and began to lose altitude. Gaps opened in the lifting planes as bits of fabric flapped wildly in the wind and tore into long strips. At Uniondale, where Cal regained the Erie track, he was down to 200 feet and unable to avoid further sinking. He was under 100 feet when he came into view of the Gorman farm just north of Saint Mary's Church in Huntington, where he flumped to a landing at 4:36, exhausted, drenched, thoroughly relieved, and exquisitely triumphant.

Never in the history of aviation had a flier performed under such hazards as Cal had faced. Nor had any birdman lived through such grueling adversities. His valiant feat, agreed those who witnessed it firsthand and those who later heard its recounting or read of it in newspapers, was not likely to be repeated throughout the future of aeronautics.

More than six hours had elapsed since the takeoff from Bobo. The *Vin Fiz* had meandered eighty-five miles in advancing thirty-five, arriving in Huntington thirty-six minutes beyond the forfeiture time for the $300 reward. Tattered and drooping, with rifts in its fabric that a man could fall through, it had survived an assault on its structure never intended by its designers.

The mailbag, affixed at Bobo to the gasoline tank, had vanished, prey to the Indiana storm.

Mrs. Sweitzer was at a point of near collapse. Mabel, John Rodgers, deKrafft, and others of the Vin Fiz contingent fretted as they waited in the Huntington Station without word of Cal's whereabouts. DeKrafft berated Charley Taylor for allowing Cal to take off and issued a continual flow of directions to Erie officials in telegraphing surrounding communities. A telephone rang—its caller yelled at deKrafft that Calbraith Rodgers was safely down on the Gorman farm. Within seconds the station was empty.

Two miles north of the station, Cal staggered from the machine, pale and shivering, shreds of soaked newspaper dangling below his vest. He lightly touched the bottle of Vin Fiz grape soda and turned to receive the adulation of about 500 persons who had sloshed out Jefferson Street to Pat Gorman's property, alerted by the Huntington Light & Fuel Company whistle. They milled about in the mud and probed at the flying machine, its frazzled driver beyond protest.

The Palmer-Singer and other automobiles with members of the aviation party soon sped onto the field. Mabel led the scramble to reach the aviator. Mrs. Sweitzer, lugged along by Mrs. deKrafft and Mrs. Wettengel at either elbow, could only gasp incoherently. Cal embraced each and every one—wife, mechanicians, crew members, reporters, train officials; he hugged his mother and bussed her cheek, ignoring her dithers and whimpers. Reunion with colleagues on the ground engendered as much emotion as had his harrowing experience in the skies. Leaning on his cousin John and Stewart deKrafft for support, he downed a glass of milk and mustered enough breath to tell reporters that he would resume his flight at seven o'clock in the morning.

DeKrafft added that Rodgers would alight at Grant Park, Chicago, between 3:00 and 4:30 the next afternoon. Fifteen days would remain in which to reach the Pacific Coast—a virtual certainty. Even if the new—and patently unfair—deadline of October 10 was upheld, he would have eight days, a time that still admitted a high probability of success.

Jack Brumbaugh, the locomotive engineer who had replaced A. A. Stearns at Lima for the run to Chicago, was a Huntington man, as was the new fireman, Frank Wolverton. Brumbaugh came onto Gorman's farm and was quickly surrounded by friends, who solicited his story of the train journey. Erie dispatchers, he said, had cleared the track to Huntington of all passenger and freight traffic, and "I was ready to highball it through. But I've never seen such a blinding storm. If it warn't for the ol' iron harness, the train would've gotten lost too."

Cal was escorted to C. D. Williams's open Marmon motorcar and hauled away to the Hotel Huntington. Mabel and Mrs. Sweitzer (quickly recovered) commandeered the automobile and chauffeur hired by traffic manager Howard Benell and sped off in pursuit of their loved one.

In his hotel room, Cal pulled off his rain-soaked, mud-plastered suit, which was turned over to the Negro stewards on the train for "dry cleaning," and flopped onto a bed, where Mabel kneaded his face with Vaseline Jelly (obtained from the mechanicians, who used it to coat spark plugs against dampness and wires against corrosion). A physician was summoned; Cal was examined and ordered to remain abed for the evening.

Mabel had been invited for an outing about the city with the distaff membership of the Huntington Club, and, eager to be lionized "at the nod of a head," she left for that engagement. Mrs. Sweitzer took charge of nursing her son. Propping his back with two fluffed-up pillows, she fed him spoonfuls of soup made by the hotel's chef, threatening all the while to take her leave of the expedition should he ever again attempt to aviate in such horrific weather. "Oh, mother," said Cal in an even tone, "I can always rely on you."

The enforced bed rest afforded Cal his first opportunity in several days to read accounts of his flight and to note other news of front-page caliber. With Mrs. Sweitzer rising periodically from her bedside chair to draw a heavy quilt higher up his chest, he scanned through the columns of the *Huntington Times-Democrat*.

Much space was occupied by reports of the dam disaster at Austin,

Pennsylvania. A thousand men, women, and children, one-quarter of the town's population, had been drowned, a tragedy comparable to that at Johnstown in '89.

President Taft's train had been delayed ten hours by a flood in Omaha as storms continued to plague the prairie states.

Warfare between Italy and Turkey had broken out as the Italian Navy, under Admiral Abruzzi, first bottled up and then sank the sultan's fleet in the Dardanelle Straits. Tripoli and Prevesa fell to Italian troops. "Victory for Italy would be civilization's gain," newspapers editorialized, "a victory for Christianity over the Muslim hordes."

News items from England still belabored the reciprocity measure as a "scurvy trick" to deliver Canada into U.S. hands. William Randolph Hearst was excoriated for his freebooting practices and denounced as "that Devil in Printer's garb who prowled the halls of Congress."

Bob Fowler had abandoned his game fight to breast the Sierra mountain chain, defeated by the rarefied atmosphere. He announced his withdrawal from the transcontinental contest, noting that while he was willing in unreserved measure, his Wright machine was not equal to the task. Saturday he had flown two attempts, one to within fourteen miles of Summit; in each instance his engine sputtered to futility and he was again compelled to descend. "It can't be done," said Fowler, "at least not at this time of year when the equinoxial storms are due and the weather in the mountains is unsettled." He had managed but three flying days in the fifteen since he left San Francisco, traversing 173 miles over some of the most cragged terrain in the United States. Cal Rodgers now stood as the sole remaining contender in the coast-to-coast run, left to race against the clock alone.

While Cal lay abed at the Hotel Huntington, the Negro stewards, George-1 and George-2, were tending to his soiled garments and the jacket trampled by the Hilpert bull. A plunger bucket was half-filled with petroleum naphtha; first the trousers were immersed. But as George-1 was pumping the plunger, he scraped the metal bucket—plumes of fire flashed up, burning his hands and face. He jerked away, upsetting the bucket. Rivulets of flaming naphtha coursed over the W.C. floor, into the corridor and the galley. George-1 howled with pain. George-2 quickly drew water from the faucet into a washbowl and poured it onto the flames. Repeated efforts with bowls of water succeeded in dousing the fire.

The two stewards surveyed the damage: walls and floor of the Pullman singed, Cal's trousers destroyed, his coat charred in several spots. They considered fleeing the train, but, with no apparent refuge in Huntington,

Indiana, loyalty to the Pullman Company prevailed. George-1 bandaged himself and tried to scrub away the patches of scorched wood, while George-2 delivered Cal's spare suit to the doorman at the Hotel Huntington. When their crime was discovered some hours later, they were tongue-lashed for clumsiness, incompetence, and stupidity. Charles Davidson swore that their wages would be docked—for the next ten years if necessary—to cover costs of the suit and repairs to the Pullman car. Chef Ed Davis added his own vilifications when he found that George-1 had spread the ice locker's meager supply of butter on his wounds. Stewart deKrafft explained that petroleum naphtha has a low flash point and can be easily ignited by static electricity; he advised extreme caution with further dry-cleaning work. When informed of the vestiary disaster, Cal accepted it philosophically: "One suit is all I need," he said, and asked that the two disfigured coats—the one charred and the one mended at Salamanca—be given to the stewards to ease their distress.

Cal and his mechanicians were on hand at the Gorman farm early Monday morning to adjust the propellers and to stitch new sections of fabric on the planes of the *Vin Fiz.* The anger had drained from the sky, but a brisk wind still swept the field and, although unable to inhibit a crowd of 8,000 persons from gathering, kept the airplane firmly anchored to the ground. "When the wind is up, the machines are down," Orville Wright had said often, and Charley Taylor repeated it once again. Chief of Police Philip Baker had assigned a special force of fifteen officers to patrol the boundary fences and to exclude all spectators. Printed cards had been delivered to Chief Baker by Lawrence Peters and had been posted on nearby trees and stakes; they warned of the danger in interfering with a moving airplane and cautioned that "owing to the great speed with which a flying machine travels, it continues for fully 100 feet after alighting on the ground. If anyone is injured by disregarding this warning, both the Vin Fiz Co. and Mr. Rodgers disclaim all blame for the accident."

At 11:30 A.M. Cal announced that he would test the currents aloft with a circuit of the city and would return to the field before starting his 150-mile trip to Chicago. "Better not," counseled Charley Taylor. "That's too much wind for a flying machine."

"It's not too much for this machine," said Cal with some braggadocio, "not with this driver. After yesterday, nothing is too much. . . . Pull the propellers. . . ."

The *Vin Fiz* took to the air sluggishly, aimed to the southwest across a northwest wind. It was driven off the cleared pathway. Fearful of injuring spectators if he continued only a few feet over the heads of the dense crowd, Cal swerved sharply to the south. Still beaten toward the ground by the wind, he dodged between two sycamore trees, the tips of his wings cutting leaves on either side. He banked the machine at a steep angle and turned back to the west along a wheat field. Now directly across his path stretched the string of telephone wires along Flax Mill Road. Cal had risen no more than fifteen feet against the objecting winds. Reacting with remarkable quickness, he dipped below the wires (which scraped the upper plane) to gain momentum, projecting to rise into the air once more. Ahead at this critical moment lay an upward slope of ground. He was no more than ten feet high when an angling gust of wind careened the machine to the right. Cal applied warping to the fullest extent, but a tip of the lower plane scooped into the earth, and the aircraft spun into a vertical cartwheel. The left lower wing tip snagged and buried itself; the *Vin Fiz* tilted over and crumpled onto its nose.

Cal leaped from his seat, bleeding from cuts, his legs bruised painfully, the trousers of his last suit shredded below the knees. The flying machine sustained the substance of the damage; its wheels, skids, and left wings were fully demolished, its longerons twisted. Of the entire front of the craft, only the bottle of Vin Fiz escaped intact. Cal gazed at it and sighed —the bottle was whole, the airplane again smashed into impotence after four days of soaring spirits. Was it to be thus every four days? The bottle whole, the airplane smashed, the bottle whole . . .

Hundreds of spectators hurried over the quarter-mile that Cal had traversed to ascertain that the birdman had not, as they had at first feared, paid with his life for his daring act. No one moved to help him as he stood mumbling to himself, shaking his head.

Charley Taylor walked up. "Damn it!" he said, shocking several ladies nearby. "Don't you know enough to take off into the wind?"

Cal broke from his musings to look up at Taylor and the others in his crew. He perked up his shoulders, threw them a forced smile, and called out, "Fix her up, boys. I'll be ready.

Taylor appraised the damage at $3,000 and estimated that two or three days of around-the-clock labor would be necessary to revitalize the stricken bird-machine to its prime condition.

Mabel and Mrs. Sweitzer, already settled into their respective state-rooms aboard the special train, were driven to the Gorman farm to assure themselves that the object of their affections had survived with life and limb. Mrs. Sweitzer, poised to strike at the world should her son lie wounded, was unable to raise her emotional pitch above that of the day before. She and Mabel repacked their clothes and small articles—packed and unpacked early that morning—and again booked rooms at the Hotel Huntington.

Stewart deKrafft, meanwhile, had struck a contract for use of the Frazier Auto Inn at Cherry and Washington streets, and the Palmer-Singer was again hitched to the airplane for a tow to the garage. William Frazier, owner of the establishment, personally guaranteed that the citizens of Huntington would gladly defer care of their own vehicles while his team of mechanicians helped to reconstruct the *Vin Fiz.*

After conferring further with Frazier, Cal informed reporters that he would depart Huntington for Chicago Wednesday morning, October 4. A telegram was sent to Dayton requesting immediate dispatch of additional planes, wires, and other components in short supply.

Police Chief Baker annulled all speed laws for the Palmer-Singer and alerted people to be on the lookout for it along the route between the Erie Station and the Cherry Street garage.

When Cal returned to the hotel, he was seized by Mrs. Sweitzer. She washed and bandaged his head, dabbed at his legs, inspected the rest of his body, and impelled him to the nearest haberdashery. There he was fitted for a brown business suit ("Brown is the color that favors his sea-blue eyes") and successfully withstood attempts to include a second pair of pants. Mrs. Sweitzer pressed the dubious store owner to assign the bill to her bankers in Pittsburgh.

By midafternoon several hundred persons had gathered before the expansive entrance to Frazier's garage (formerly a livery stable) to peer at the "pile of junk" that had been a high-flying machine. People from outlying communities—Markle, Zanesville, Majinica—were drawn to the Cherry Street attraction. From Fort Wayne, twenty-five miles away, twenty-one-year-old Art Smith, the "Indiana Bird Boy," drove in to offer his support and condolences. Smith, small of stature with a winning, boyish smile, resembled Jimmy Ward in age, appearance, and enthusiasm for aviation.[3] He had constructed his own flying machine two years earlier and had flown it successfully around Fort Wayne's Driving Park.

So large grew the crowd at the garage and so presumptuous some of its members that Lewis Schenkel, owner of the building, strung a "hot" wire across the entrance. It inhibited only the timorous.

Mabel, meanwhile, had surpassed her previous sales of Vin Fiz postcards. These sales were achieved through her own efforts. Both Charlie Hibbard and Allie, her "assistant mailmen," were summoned to their homes in Middletown, as the latest interlude raised the prospect of further, and unbargained-for, delays. Mabel kissed each lad farewell and turned to the task of sorting the cards and letters lost during Cal's horrendous flight from Bobo and thence returned, deposited anonymously in the lobby of the Hotel Huntington (the mailbag was evidently retained as a souvenir by its finder).

"I'll miss them," Mabel told her husband of her two young friends. "At least they know how to treat a lady. I suppose I'll have to look elsewhere now for some proper attention."

"Oh, tell me if you need help with the mail," said Cal with his characteristic parry. "I'll find someone for you."

"I can do it myself," huffed Mabel. "I'm not just a spare part on this trip."

The concept of an "aerial mail" service had been broached by Cal and his managers since the Post Office Department had conferred its blessings on Earle Ovington. Mabel was already billing herself as "the world's first aerial-mail postmistress," and the group was seeking some scheme to counter Ovington's official status. It was suggested by John Rodgers that the Vin Fiz expedition design and print its own aerial-mail stamp. Affixed to each postcard or letter to be carried aloft, it would constitute a voucher, as it were, for the purchaser and could reap additional revenue now pressingly needed. The idea of competing with the U.S. postal system appealed to Cal. A letter to his uncle Robert S. Rodgers, an attorney and amateur philatelist in Kansas City, solicited his advice for the stamp's design and requested him to commission a qualified lithographer to produce the stamp.

Soda fountains in the city reported booming sales of the Vin Fiz carbonated drink, and Charles Davidson distributed Vin Fiz advertising placards for every store window in town that had not already been serviced by advance man Lawrence Peters. A large billboard with the patented grape cluster was erected across Cherry Street from Frazier's Auto Inn.

Monday evening Cal, Stewart deKrafft, and Vin Fiz and Armour Company representatives hosted a banquet at the Hotel Huntington in honor of C. D. Williams and other members of the Commercial Club, in appreciation of the aid provided the transcontinental expedition in its adversities at Huntington. Mayor Milo Feightner spoke at length, reciting the history of his hometown. Originally called Wepecheange ("the Place of Flints"), the name was changed in 1831 in tribute to Samuel Huntington, a member of the First Continental Congress. He was pleased, the mayor declared, to present their distinguished guest, Calbraith P. Rodgers, with the key to the city. Further testimonials to the bravery of the first birdman to cross the borders of Huntington County rang out for over an hour. Cal listened to it all with apparent stoicism.

The banquet menu included Vin Fiz Pot Luck, Vin Fiz Steamed Rice with sliced tomatoes, broiled Vin Fiz Steak, Vin Fiz Sundae, and Rodgers Cup à la Vin Fiz.

In addition to Charles Davidson and Ed Merritt, three other officials of Armour & Company were present, delegated by J. Ogden Armour to convey his greetings to Calbraith P. Rodgers and to prepare for welcoming ceremonies in Chicago. Employees of all Armour companies and subsidiaries in the Chicago area would be granted a half-day from work (with pay) to attend the landing at Grant Park. "The idea that Rodgers will abandon his attempt to reach the Pacific Coast," said an Armour spokesman at the banquet, "is absolutely without foundation. We vehemently deny any rumors to that effect." While the source of these rumors was unidentified, suspicion centered on "a woman in her mid-fifties, dressed in black, who circulated among those witnessing the morning's crash, telling anyone who would listen that 'Calbraith Perry Rodgers would not be so foolish as to continue to jeopardize his life and the peace of mind of his family —especially his loving mother.' "

This sentiment was further buttressed by Orville Wright, who, in response to a reporter's question at a St. Louis press conference, declared, "It is a suicidal project. . . . The aeroplane is not yet ready for such an undertaking."

Before midnight, parts ordered from Dayton—skids, wheels, spars, etc. —arrived on Erie train No. 8 and were immediately removed to the Frazier garage. Taylor, Shaffer, and Wiggin pulled themselves from their pallets in the hangar car and began a period of work that stretched through all of Tuesday and into Wednesday.

Cal contributed to the reconstruction by running the Palmer-Singer about the town, securing wire, hardware, and sundries from local stores. On one of these trips, Tuesday afternoon, he twisted a wheel in a rut along a dirt road, rendering the automobile *hors de combat.* The accident left him fuming with frustration, and for much of the day he snapped curtly at those townspeople who came to offer their aid.

C. D. Williams repaid the homage of Monday's banquet by entertaining principal members of the aviation party in his home on Warren Street Tuesday evening. His wife and son Chester (who plied the aviator with questions) stood as cohosts in demonstrating the quality of Hoosier hospitality. Mrs. Stewart deKrafft sang "In the Shade of the Old Apple Tree" and a favorite song composed the year before, "The End of a Perfect Day" (tears flowed from every eye). Thomas Hanly contributed his impersonation of Lillian Russell. Joseph Newborn, known to those on the train as "Laughing Joe," performed his card tricks. The ladies retired to enjoy "500," while the men indulged in a smoker. Mabel protested that "the ladies of the Huntington Club treated me as if I were visiting royalty—and I ate so much that I gained three pounds." (Over the past two weeks, Mabel's weight had dropped from 130 to 120 pounds, possibly in response to chef Ed Davis's culinary skills.)

Mr. Williams, an ardent aviation enthusiast, had written a letter of praise (unacknowledged) to William Randolph Hearst for encouraging—with $50,000—the continental air crossing. His brother was employed by the Hearst organization and was familiar with the thoughts that had led the publisher to the prize offering.

After Hearst had experienced his flight with Louis Paulhan at the Dominguez Air Meet in January 1910, so Williams recited for his guests, he had returned to his New York mansion on Riverside Drive, where he discussed with close associates his views on aviation. He knew that Lord Northcliffe, owner/publisher of the *London Daily Mail*, had posted £1,000 ($5,000) for the first air crossing of the English Channel (achieved by Louis Blériot the previous July) and that James Gordon Bennett of the *New York Herald* was planning to award his trophy and cash prize (for the speediest airplane) on an annual basis.* Another publishing competitor, Joseph Pulitzer, owner of the *New York World,* had recently offered $10,000 for the first air voyage between New York City and Albany. Hearst resolved to devise an aerial challenge worthy of his sponsorship.

On April 27, 1910, his friend Louis Paulhan flew the 185 miles—with but a single interruption—from London to Manchester for a $10,000 prize. Reading accounts of this race, Hearst was struck by the thought that Paulhan had completed the first authentic cross-country air passage between two major cities. Why not, he asked, an air race across the only country that mattered—the United States?

"One measure of a great man," Williams declared, "is his ability to rise above the views of his subordinates." Hearst's associates, more knowledgeable of aeronautic capabilities, remonstrated with him that such a feat lay well beyond the realm of practicality. Suitable engines were low in horsepower and yet lower in reliability. Even if lightweight engines of greater

---

*The first Gordon Bennett Trophy was won by Glenn Curtiss at the Reims Air Meet (the world's first) in Aug. 1909. Curtiss averaged 49 mph twice around a 10-kilometer course.

horsepower could be developed, a man's face and body could not withstand the assaults of air currents at greater speeds. Controls were of uncertain effectiveness. Safety measures were nonexistent. The list of obstacles to a transcontinental flight stretched interminably. It would raise cries of ridicule and foolishness, Hearst was advised, to publicize such a proposal.

Known for his bullheadedness, Hearst was undeterred. "All that is needed to open the door to a new world," he pontificated, "is the right man to turn the key." He solicited opinions from Louis Paulhan, from the Wright brothers, from other prominent aviators. "Impossible," he was told by each. Accordingly, Hearst proceeded to enumerate for himself the details of a transcontinental air race, and on October 9 in New York City he announced his $50,000 prize.* The successful contestant could fly, in either direction, between New York or Boston on the East Coast and Los Angeles or San Francisco on the West Coast; a stop at Chicago was mandatory. The contest was open to all for the year from October 10, 1910, to October 10, 1911.

That closing date, it was agreed by those at Williams's house, could only refer to the start of the journey—otherwise the offer would be valid for only eleven months.

From aviation, the talk turned to politics. Despite his admiration for William Randolph Hearst, C. D. Williams was a confirmed Republican. An erstwhile supporter of President Taft, he had switched his allegiance to LaFollette. "While Taft is in the White House, the whole country tilts to the East," said Williams, repeating a popular reference to the president's elephantine girth and his presumed bias toward East Coast financial interests. Tuesday Taft had spent an uninspired fifteen hours in Denver addressing small audiences, then departed for Rawline, Wyoming, where his talk on wool drew hoots of derision.

The Giants that day had cinched the National League pennant by defeating the Brooklyns. McGraw's men would contend with Connie Mack's A's in the eighth World Series a week from Saturday at the Polo Grounds. Most of the men at C. D. Williams's gathering believed the 1911 A's superior to the 1905 club that had lost to the Giants. Cal stuck with the New York team.

*Hearst had offered the same sum after the sinking of the battleship *Maine* (Feb. 15, 1898) for information "that will convict the person, persons, or governments criminally responsible for the destruction of the American battleship and the death of 258 of its crew." (The death toll was finally fixed at 266.) The money was never paid.

It had been reported that Earle Ovington was again resolved upon a cross-country venture and would depart New York City Wednesday morning for Utica carrying a special sack of mail. Other reports, vague, suggested that Bob Fowler might reenter the transcontinental air race, leaving from Los Angeles on a southern route.

By Wednesday, work at Frazier's garage had progressed to where an entire left lower wing had been attached, new skids and wheels emplaced, and every wire and chain tested and replaced if suspected of weakness. The bottle of Vin Fiz drink was reaffixed to its brace. DeKrafft issued a bulletin that takeoff would occur Thursday morning. An elaborate reception would be awaiting the aviator in Chicago, the site of his previous aeronautic triumph, where he would remain for a full day.

With few crew members tending the train, the Maltese pussycat, Vin, wandered from the hangar car and disappeared. A reward of $25 was posted for her recovery, but no trace of the meow was found. Fiz, now assigned full mascot duties, acquired a tidy colony of fleas and was doused in a chemical bath.

Mabel, after two days of diluted spirits, regained her rosy-hued outlook: "Of course I realize that flying is a dangerous profession, but Calbraith is careful not to take unnecessary risks and understands the operation of his machine perfectly. His flight Sunday should convince anyone that he is fully competent to drive his racer. . . . [But] I am only human to be devoutly thankful that another day has passed and my husband is still alive." As another contribution to her husband's success, Mabel relinquished her ladies' watch and sewed it onto the back of Cal's gauntlet. That it was difficult to extract a pocket watch while flying she understood (the significance of a time measure was explained to her by members of the crew), and she was proud to have struck upon a solution.[4]

Teas and levees with the elite of Huntington's socialites claimed the focus of Mabel's eyes and ears. Mrs. Sweitzer applied her social faculties toward engaging a suitable young feminine companion for her son, one who could supplement her own efforts in furnishing solace during this period of dormancy. Charley Taylor, who often vied with Mabel and Mrs. Sweitzer as the guardian of Cal's welfare, thwarted Mrs. Sweitzer's tempting gambit. He shooed Cal from the garage, bundled him into a borrowed automobile, and packed him off to Fort Wayne "for a vacation from the whole lot of us." Cal spent the evening at the Anthony Hotel and was escorted about by Art Smith.

Virtually every member of the aviation party was accosted by the

Huntington press. Charles Davidson and Ed Merritt lauded the gustatory qualities of the Vin Fiz drink and the generosity of the Armour Meat-Packing Company. Chef Ed Davis gave out recipes for his favorite European cuisine (recipes unknown to the Vin Fiz passengers) and bemoaned the problems of feeding upwards of forty persons with only the inept help of his "two sticks of licorice."

(The two Georges, invisible to the citizens of Huntington, ineligible for accommodations in the city, were left to fend for themselves. Each draped with a patched-up, hand-me-down suit coat that hung to the knees, they extended their domain throughout the private Pullman, sleeping in lower berths, lolling about the staterooms, and setting ham-and-beans suppers for themselves with the finest napery, china, and silver service. George-1, puffing on a stogie he had found in the pocket lining of his coat, rendered his verdict of the cross-country attempt: "Dat Mr. Calbraith am a true gent'eman. Howsomeber, ain' no flyin' machine what can fly across dese United States. Jes' ain' no point 'n tryin'.")

Edward Sutton, supply-keeper on the hangar car, was solicited for his perspective on the expedition. "Three smashups are fierce," he complained. "It's guard the *Vin Fiz Flyer* every night to keep souvenir hunters from cutting the flying machine to pieces and leaving us nothing, not even the prints of the skids on the sod, to tell where the EX stood. . . . During the day I have to answer a lot of damfule questions. I try to hand out the same bunk that the press agent deals to the reporters. It's just as classy, for it gets away with the goods. That's what we are all tryin' to do, ain't it?"

Howard Benell, traffic manager for the Vin Fiz Company, was not overlooked. He, too, belabored reporters' ears with the mandates of his job: "I have nothing to do but see that shipments meet the train as it flashes through the towns, see that the supplies are waiting at every stop, see that the passengers are furnished with the things they need and the things they think they need, see that the delicate machine parts aboard are safeguarded, see that the passengers in their eagerness to follow the flight of the racing birdman above do not stroll off the rear to an untimely end, see that the luggage connects with the taxi at every stop and start, and lots of other things. When that is done, there is nothing to do at all —just make out reports on what had been doing at every stop in the day. . . . And besides, the traffic man is the one with whom all the kicks are filed."

Mrs. Sweitzer was interviewed but once. "Do you know how many young men have lost their lives flying?" she asked the reporter. "Let me tell you. First, there was Lieutenant Selfridge . . . and only yesterday, poor Cromwell Dixon,* only nineteen years old. . . ."

For his part, Cal again relayed his unflagging confidence and determination: "The model EX has been rebuilt entirely except for the engine, and everything is in tip-top shape. If I can get any kind of wind back of me, I can cover the 142 miles in short order. The program is to get into Grant Park about three o'clock. That will make a stop necessary—probably at North Judson, seventy miles from Huntington. The stop at Chicago will be as brief as possible. I hope to leave Friday morning for Kansas City, and the Rock Island has already arranged a special train for me. We will keep on, and we will get to Los Angeles first of all the transcontinental aviators, no matter how long it will take."

Thursday morning a light drizzle persisted through the early hours and, although seeming to wane, hung on until after eleven o'clock. Farmers, townspeople, and visitors trooped out to churn up the muddy field at Gorman's farm in numbers greater than the 8,000 that had assembled the previous Sunday.

The *Vin Fiz,* now fully restored for the third time, was towed to the farm at 7:30 A.M. and, under a tarpaulin, awaited the moment for takeoff. That moment came when, the drizzle abated, a final round of hands shaken, and a final session of airplane autographing concluded, Cal mounted the seat at 11:30. This time, as Charley Taylor took pains to assure, he was pointed into the northwest wind.

As the engine was ignited, William Frazier ran up with a four-leaf clover and fastened it to the Vin Fiz bottle on the lower plane. Cal thanked him and opined that the "jinx" that had bedeviled him since New York was now surely vanquished.

Slipping across the surface of the Gorman field, the *Vin Fiz* lifted slowly to the air, swinging in a great arc—so that, after almost disappearing from view, it returned to swoop across the field at an altitude of 500 feet. Cheers from the monster crowd competed with the droning noise of the engine. Cal turned directly over the Erie depot and received a series of whistle blasts from engineer Brumbaugh's locomotive as the Vin Fiz train moved forward.

Oct. 5, Thursday. Rochester, 40 miles from Huntington and 100 miles North of population center of U.S. Hands stiff with cold; can't grasp

*Dixon, a member of the Curtiss camp, died when his machine crashed at Spokane, Wash., Oct. 2.

control levers. 25 miles farther on, landed Aldine 12:55 o'clock on farm of William Milne and walked to nearby farmhouse.

Mrs. Della Milne revived the aviator with hot coffee and sandwiches, while the nine Milne children stood about her kitchen, gawking at the strange visitor. The Milne property was bisected by the Erie track, and crew members spreading out from the special train soon found their quarry.

By 2:30 Cal felt his circulation sufficiently recovered to attempt a takeoff. However, because of the three-foot tickle grass on the field, the aircraft was unable to take the air properly. It slithered into a swampy area, breaking a skid.

Farmer Milne was requested to clear a fairway through the tickle grass while Taylor, Shaffer, and the crew replaced the skid. Milne, a short, stocky Scotsman, made three cuts about fifteen rods long, then stopped. Cal asked for a fourth. Milne declined to proceed with the final cut until his promised $2 was forthcoming. "If he'd been rowing George Washington across the Delaware," deKrafft said as he paid the farmer, "he'd have stopped in midstream to collect his toll."

Oct. 5. Take-off from Aldine 4:44 P.M. North Judson, dropped Vin Fiz leaflets on large crowd. Flour mills and canning factories along route. Crown Point. Landed Hammond.

West of Crown Point, Cal looked down on two section hands pumping a handcar along the Erie rails. As they waved at him, he spotted a train speeding toward them, but hidden from their view by a curve in the track. He swooped down, rocked his planes, and yelled a warning. The two men only waved more vigorously. To direct their attention, he then dipped to within a few feet of the track and drove the *Vin Fiz* toward the onrushing locomotive. He peered back to note the men scrambling to derail the handcar.

Skies were dimming as Cal searched for the prearranged landing site at Hammond. He identified the Grand Calumet River traversing the town from east to west and Wolf Lake at the town's edge, but then became confused by the lights of an immense steel mill. He circled twice in wide loops, then picked out a small field on the Jarnecke farm a mile and a half south of the Erie depot, and bumped down safely by the lights of the steel-mill foundry.

Twenty miles short of Chicago, the expedition had traversed 1,173 miles since Sheepshead Bay; a total of twenty-three hours flying time had been realized over the nineteen-day passage.

The corps of newsmen, functionaries, and Vin Fiz and Armour Company officials checked into Hammond's Majestic Hotel, where the press was notified that Cal Rodgers would lift off for Chicago early the following morning.

In New York, Earle Ovington announced that he would not announce the departure date of his transcontinental flight to Los Angeles. A special forty-gallon fuel tank had been installed on his Blériot machine, and further adjustments for balance were indicated.

In San Francisco, Bob Fowler withdrew his withdrawal from competition and prepared to ship his Wright biplane to Los Angeles for a start eastward on October 10, the last eligible day—according to the original interpretation of the rules—for beginning the Hearst ocean-to-ocean race. Fowler insisted that he would hold Hearst accountable for the $50,000 if and when his flight was completed in thirty days.

Harry Atwood confirmed to reporters that the deadline would pass without his entry. The mission was an impossible one, Atwood declared, adding that, as holder of the world record for air-distance spanned, he was the aviator best qualified to assess its feasibility.

Most of the Vin Fiz principals gathered for supper in the dining room of the Majestic Hotel. Not present was Mabel Rodgers. Nettled at losing her marital prerogatives to the nightly claims of her mother-in-law, she had accepted an invitation to dine privately with Count Jacques Alexander Von Mourick De Beaufort, a member of the fourth estate from the *Chicago American.* Of the various correspondents who traveled with the aviation party for short distances, the count was assuredly the most charming and suave. He had been dispatched to Huntington and was to remain on board the special train as far as Kansas City. He had entertained the ladies with tales of his European and American escapades, flattered each in turn, and ensured that no female hand went unkissed for long. Mrs. Sweitzer dryly remarked on her daughter-in-law's absence.

Friday, high winds in the morning and rain squalls in the afternoon prevented departure from Hammond. Charley Taylor turned the delay to advantage and ordered a complete overhaul and grooming of the machinery preparatory to its Chicago debut. In late afternoon the aircraft was towed from the Jarnecke farm in south Hammond to the more level expanse of Douglas Park.

Erie officials also took advantage of the delay and replaced crew and locomotive engine on the Vin Fiz train. Erie General Agent J. B. Dickens, in charge of the Chicago terminal, would control the train to Chicago. Trainmaster J. H. Kline fretted that his men, although appreciative of their special assignment, were becoming exhausted by the constant anxiety. Scheduling was a dispatcher's nightmare, and, of all railroad officials involved, the dispatchers had suffered most. They had been ordered to maintain almost continual contact with the special train and to anticipate its movements to guarantee a clear track. In one instance the train would be held for several hours owing to an accident with the airplane, and in another instance it would be charging over the rails at a mile-a-minute pace. Schedules of passenger trains had been disrupted, and freight trains were fearful of moving between sidings lest they be caught in the open by the special; some slow-moving freights were rescheduled for the nighttime hours. "For a business that runs by the clock," said Kline, "it's as if someone unwound our mainspring."

Cal passed Friday in ill humor, cussing the weather, the conditions of the Hearst contest, Hearst himself, and the state of aeronautic development that held him prisoner of the elements ("Someday they'll learn to fly in these conditions. . . . Having nothing to do is worse than having to repair a wrecked machine"). Everyone in the party except Mrs. Sweitzer —who engaged him periodically with milk, sandwiches, and maternal guidance—deliberately steered themselves to dodge his path.

Blizzards, floods, and rain squalls pounded the Midwest. Three dams in Wisconsin ruptured, inundating several small towns. Kansas City was raked with gales. In Hammond, strong winds persisted through Saturday. Charley Taylor substituted for Cal (secluded in his hotel room) in confronting the press. "If the wind declines this afternoon so that Rodgers can have enough time to make the flight to Chicago before dark," he said, "then he will start. But it seems improbable. Rodgers has had enough night flying and has never attempted it but what he got into trouble. When he alighted in Hammond, he got into such a bad place that we had to move the machine. . . ."

Saturday night, members of the Commercial Club hosted an informal dinner at the Majestic Hotel. Club president E. G. Jenner told his audience that the fair town in which they found themselves was incorporated twenty-seven years earlier and named for George H. Hammond, a Detroit butcher who built the local slaughterhouse. Cal did not attend. "If I hear another official tell me about his town and its name," he said in anticipation, "I'll drop a ripe tomato on his head."

Charley Taylor's weather prognostication proved an accurate one. Sunday morning, October 8, arrived before Cal was able to take leave of

Hammond. It was the first day in a week that the expedition had been greeted by mercifully clear skies. Taylor and the other mechanicians had awakened well before sunup to prepare the *Vin Fiz* for its next trial. The machine was moved again, this time to the William Norman farm, the merits of Douglas Park having been devaluated. Shortly, Mr. Norman concluded that his cow pasture would be ravaged were he to allow the trespass of large numbers of people. He refused the use of his property. Cal was piqued, and pointed out that many other cities were offering substantial sums of money for the privilege of his presence. Mr. Norman, thumbs hooked in his galluses, was unimpressed. Hammond police remonstrated with the farmer. Mr. Norman was obdurate. The entire Vin Fiz entourage swore to spread the bad name of Hammond from coast to coast. Mr. Norman was unconcerned. Ultimately, a team of horses was procured and hitched to the flying machine. It was then dragged across the Illinois state line some 200 yards onto a field in the village of Lansing.

Two hundred persons followed the horse-drawn aircraft to the Lansing field. They were soon joined by others who arrived in wagons, in carriages, and on foot from the Hammond business district, a mile and a half to the north. Still muttering his indignation over Mr. Norman's obstinacy, Cal rose from the site at 11:31 A.M. He first turned back over the Jarnecke field to ensure against a gap in his flight line, then flew across Hammond, where people in the streets waved and cheered him on his way.

At a height of 500 feet, Lake Michigan could be seen, cold-blue, shimmering through the dense smoke of factories in East Chicago. Cal flew due north and then followed the lake shore until he recognized the topography of Grant Park, where 5,000 persons watched as the *Vin Fiz* grew from a black dot in the south to a magnificent mechanical bird overhead. He veered away from the open lakefront and floated above the Michigan Avenue skyscrapers. He swung over the Loop, over the fifteen-story Home Insurance Building ("the world's first skyscraper"). A series of spiraled dips drew gasps of apprehension from those below. Once he plunged precipitously and, with the crowd fearing a crash onto the street, tilted his lateral planes at the final moment and rose to safety. Turning back toward Grant Park, he descended for a landing and, at 11:57, switched off his engine, fifty feet from the hangar where he had sheltered his Wright B, "Old No. 27," during the Great International Air Meet and Exhibition of August.

6

The Great Chicago
Air Show

CHICAGOANS WERE ACCORDED their first opportunity to observe a flying machine in October 1909. Glenn Curtiss, shortly after he captured the Gordon Bennett Cup in August of that year, received a telegram proposing a $1,000 guaranty for a week of aerial exhibitions in "the windy city." The telegram was dispatched by Stewart I. deKrafft, a civil engineer representing a party of Chicago promoters.

Chicago lived up to its sobriquet—only once during the week's schedule did winds subside below the 10 mph specified as safe for flight. Curtiss seized the moment to aviate his biplane a quarter-mile in forty seconds over the Hawthorne racetrack in Cicero. The promoters lost $26,000 on the event.

Early in 1911 Harold F. McCormick,* president of International Harvester Company, undertook to uplift the level of Chicago's enlightenment

*Son of Cyrus H. McCormick, the "reaper king." The McCormicks (he was married to the former Edith Rockefeller) dominated Chicago society. In 1913, Harold made news by flying from his home to his office, landing on the Grant Park lakeside in his "aeroyacht."

by persuading the Illinois Aero Club, of which he was treasurer, to sponsor an aviation show that would draw the world's top birdmen. Chicago newspapers were to call it "the Greatest Aviation Meet Ever Held."

An association to organize the meet was founded, with James Plew as president. Nine days of exhibitions were scheduled from August 12 to 20 at Grant Park. McCormick, Plew, and their associates began fund-raising efforts, striving for a minimum $100,000 guaranty in prize money and operating expenses. Their initial endeavors met with small success; few would subscribe to the cause of an amusing but impractical toy such as the airplane. A more concrete obstacle materialized early in the summer: A letter from Dayton, Ohio, conveyed the Wright brothers' claim of patent jurisdiction over virtually every aspect of aeronautics. To permit their own airplanes and aviators under contract to them to enter competition, the Wrights demanded payment of $20,000 in license fees and royalties; otherwise, they threatened, they would sue to block the meet.

McCormick declared his determination to proceed, if necessary, without the Wrights' approval. "Not a cent for tribute," insisted James Plew, and the Meet Association volunteered to join "in common cause" with any aviators harassed by litigation. Public opinion shifted in opposition to the Wright brothers. Letters denounced them as "a grifting bunch" . . . "greedy" . . . "monopolistic" . . . "opposed to free competition." McCormick's defiance grew yet more unyielding. To bolster his promotional staff, he engaged the services of Stewart deKrafft.

Although the Curtiss exhibition had stumbled into a financial pit, deKrafft remained in touch with aeronautic progress. He had organized automobile races for a time and had served as map-maker for the 1910 Glidden tour.* To ensure the participation of crackajack aeroplanists at the Chicago meet as well as to parry the Wrights' legal threats, deKrafft concentrated on procuring graduates of the Wright Flying School. Among those he courted was Calbraith P. Rodgers.

Cal received deKrafft's proposal with keenness. Both the prize money and the prospect of wider acclaim were alluring. (He was, however, as a flier without established repute, required to post $1,000 bond against his appearance.) Mrs. Sweitzer conferred her approval. A sojourn in Chicago offered an opportunity to advance her son's position with people of dis-

---

*Since 1905, wealthy sportsman Charles J. Glidden had donated a cup each year for the winner of a long-distance (1,000 miles) automobile tour designed to promote automotive reliability.

tinction and influence. With his mother's patronage, his cousin in attendance, and a letter from Mabel assuring her presence, Cal adjusted his focus to the specific events of the Chicago meet.

The Illinois Aero Club had devised a novel method of dispensing monetary rewards. Aviators were guaranteed $2 for each minute actually airborne. No more than $500 was allotted for travel and lodging expenses; the preponderant proportion of the $100,000 purse was to be awarded on the basis of performance. Studying the contests and conditions listed in the program, Cal decided that flights for overall duration offered favorable chances. His Wright Type B was not powered to compete for speed or altitude.

Cal and John Rodgers arrived in Chicago late Thursday evening, August 10, and registered at the Plaza Hotel—which Mrs. Sweitzer had selected and into which she had moved two days earlier. (Her husband, Harry Sweitzer, had been removed to a hospital in Pittsburgh.)

Friday, Charlie Wiggin and Frank Shaffer drove into town towing the "B." They arranged for space in one of the airplane sheds set up in Grant Park and proceeded to reattach the planes and ready the machine for flight.

The first airman to sign the Meet Association's entry book was F. E. Post, a wealthy amateur flier from Milwaukee, who arrived Monday, August 7. He was followed by John B. Moisant, René Barrier, and Captain Thomas Baldwin with his *Red Devil No. 1.* The Curtiss group was headed by Lincoln Beachey and included Eugene Ely and Jimmy Ward (whose aircraft was dubbed the *Shooting Star*). The Moisant International Aviators included René Simon, John Frisbie, and St. Croix Johnstone flying Moisant monoplanes. Charles Willard, J. A. D. McCurdy, and Earle Ovington entered as independents flying Curtiss machines. Tom Sopwith, George Beatty, Andrew Drew, and Cal Rodgers filed as independents using Wright biplanes. Among the entries from abroad, Ladis Lewkowicz, the "sensational flying Pole," gained attention with his Wellington boots and flowing cape. In all, thirty-eight aviators vied for the grand-prize money.

Lincoln Beachey undoubtedly ranked as the preeminent aviator at the meet and in the country. A "daredevil flier," he had—in June—maneuvered his Curtiss airplane into the spray over Niagara Falls, under the suspension bridge, and through the winding gorge below. Thomas Sopwith, twenty-three, "His Majesty's Own Airman," was celebrated as the winner of the $20,000 Baron de Forest purse for the longest continuous flight across the English Channel by an Englishman in an all-English-made machine. Eugene Ely's fame derived from his landing and subsequent takeoff from the deck of the *Pennsylvania.* Andrew Drew and Calbraith Rodgers were probably least noted of the American aviators.

On Thursday a telegram to the *Chicago Tribune* from Roy Knabenshue (representing the Wright aviators) deplored the dissension between two groups dedicated to the advancement of aeronautics. Plew and McCormick immediately conveyed through the *Tribune* a sincere invitation for the Wright fliers to participate. A seven-man team including Walter Brookins and Al Welsh was thence entered into the competitions.

Public interest mounted as the gathering of birdmen certified the forthcoming meet. One Chicagoan, a would-be entrant, appeared at Meet Association headquarters wearing a harness of home-built feathered wings. Several couples proposed airborne nuptials ("marriages made in heaven") in exchange for suitable dowries. Billboards proclaiming the grand occasion were plastered to every inviting wall. Marshall Field & Company exhibited a Curtiss biplane on its main floor and distributed to customers a pocket-size daily schedule of events. Harold McCormick, in an interview printed in the *Tribune,* emphasized his faith in the potential of the heavier-than-air machine and predicted that "in five years, today's machines will be on view only in museums." The *Tribune* also furnished its analysis of aerial mechanics. "An aeroplane," it explained to its readers, "is nothing but a huge kite using a motor and a propeller to push it instead of a rope or string to pull it."

At three o'clock Saturday afternoon a ten-gun salute officially raised the curtain on the Great Chicago Air Show. Flags of the U.S., Great Britain, Canada, France, Ireland, and Russia were hoisted over the Grant Park grounds. More than 250,000 persons had streamed into the area. Grandstand seats at 50¢, $1, and $1.50 were sold out. Temperatures hovered in the seventies; moderate 10- to 15-mph northeast winds swept across a cloudless sky. At 3:30 a flotilla of flying machines ascended, and the nine-day contest for aerial supremacy was under way.

Those competing for the duration prize were first, each afternoon, to take the air. An hour later an over-water race began around a three-and-a-half-mile course (two revolutions were required). Passenger-carrying races were scheduled for 5:30 with altitude competition at 6:00. Speed contests, monoplane trials, and other events followed, with the final event of the day, the cross-country flying, concluding at 7:00 P.M.

Jimmy Ward, a native-born Chicagoan and protégé of James Plew, gained popular honors the first day, achieving two flights of half-hour duration describing figure eights over Michigan Avenue. In celebration, he welcomed to his room at the Hotel Wellington anyone who wished to converse with him or with his wife (whom he often carried aloft as a passenger). Only the day before Ward had passed his FAI examination at the Cicero field and received Certificate No. 52. Earle Ovington won the speed competition over Tom Sopwith, covering a twenty-mile course in slightly less than twenty-four minutes. Howard Gill won the altitude climb—to 4,980 feet—exceeding Lincoln Beachey's peak by almost 1,500 feet. Cal Rodgers triumphed in the duration contest, remaining aloft two hours, fifty-six minutes. Altogether, twenty-five airplanes participated the first day; at one instance, nine were airborne simultaneously.

Not every flight was successful. Arthur Stone, executing a steep, low-altitude turn, scraped the ground with a wing tip of his Queen Blériot monoplane, flipping the craft onto its back and demolishing it. Frank Coffyn, carrying two passengers, foundered his Wright biplane onto a parked Moisant monoplane, wrecking both machines. René Simon toppled into a tree on takeoff, and James Martin crashed his Bristol-Farman through a fence. All involved in these accidents emerged without disabling injuries.

Mabel arrived in Chicago late Saturday afternoon—as the meet was in progress. Cal dispatched Wiggin to the railroad station to convey her to the hotel: "She's blonde and she bubbles, kid—you can't miss her." Wiggin, up to then, had been unaware that Cal was married. When he found Mabel, she sniffed at him, "Where's my husband?" "He's in the air," Wiggin told her. "Then take me to him," said Mabel. "Just hold your horses, lady," said Wiggin. "He's only got enough gasoline for another fifteen minutes. Then he'll have to come down to you—whether he wants to or not."

At the Plaza Hotel, Mabel induced the desk clerk to change the Rodgerses' room from that adjoining Mrs. Sweitzer's quarters to another wing of the hotel. Sparked by two months of singleness, she maneuvered with fixity of purpose to enjoy her husband without the intrusion of her mother-in-law. For an hour she succeeded. Only the mysteries of the air were kept from her. Despite entreaties that he recount for her his experiences at the Wright Flying School and the exhibitions in Ohio, Cal would reveal but little. "It's a feeling impossible to express with one's feet on the ground," he insisted.

Later that evening John Rodgers's fiancée, Ethel Greiner, arrived at the train station and was accommodated at the Plaza Hotel. Mrs. Sweitzer invited her to supper along with Calbraith, John, and Mabel. "Isn't it nice that we are all together again," said Mrs. Sweitzer, smiling pointedly at

Miss Greiner, with whom she shared the view that aviation was too dubious and hazardous a profession for the respectable social classes. "It is so comforting to dine with a person of breeding." Cal and Mabel retired shortly after supper.

Spectators at Grant Park had quickly spread word of the aerial extravaganza. The next day, Sunday, August 13, over 600,000 persons packed themselves into the park area. Officials estimated the throng as the largest since Chicago Day of the 1893 World's Fair. Chief of Police John McWeeny called out the entire reserve of 125 officers from Central Station and augmented that force with 175 men in blue from other stations. Traffic on nearby streets stalled with abandoned vehicles as drivers scurried for better vantage points to view the flying machines. People perched on signs and tree limbs, strapped themselves to lampposts, and stood on benches, viaducts, and railings. The two-mile aerodrome area was so blanketed with humanity that those on the lakeside could not have quit the premises had they so desired.

Society ladies were excited over the prospect of experiencing personally the thrill of flying. Aviators with passenger-carrying machines were importuned by the most attractive and influential Chicago belles. Cal Rodgers was a special target of the ladies, and he obliged several each morning in his "B." Mabel Rodgers was not among them. Cal deflected her repeated requests for an aerial excursion—"After the meet," he promised.

The most sensational accident of the meet occurred when John Frisbie scraped his airplane against a statue atop the 250-foot tower of the Montgomery Ward Building. The machine plunged nose-first toward the ground. Frisbie, one hand injured, struggled with his other hand to regain control, pulled his machine from the dive, and landed in front of the judges' stand to tumultuous applause.

Lincoln Beachey quickly proved his claim to the title of "Daredevil." He thrilled the masses on the field and in the city by skimming low over Michigan Avenue, his wheels grazing the tops of automobiles.

Walter Brookins created a stir when he announced his resignation from the Wright Exhibition Team. He, not his employers, would pocket his prize money, he declared; he would relinquish his Wright salary of $15 weekly and continue as an independent flier.

Several incidents marred Monday's competitions. René Simon's Moisant monoplane lost engine power and fell into Lake Michigan beyond the Government Pier; Simon was picked up by a launch and taken ashore. Lee Hammond also plunged into the lake and was rescued by a fire tug as his airplane sank from view. J. A. D. McCurdy crashed on the beachfront when he snagged a wing tip on a high-tension wire. McCurdy was thrown clear, but his machine burned to a charred ruin. Earle Ovington, rounding a pylon at low altitude, lost power and dipped until one wing of his aircraft smashed into the ground, cartwheeling and wrecking the machine.

The schedule of events on Monday was capped by the arrival of Harry Atwood. En route from St. Louis to New York (for a world record and a $10,000 prize posted by Victor Evans, a Washington, D.C., patent attorney), Atwood had guided his Burgess-Wright biplane over the 283 miles from St. Louis along the track of the Chicago & Alton Railroad, while the crowd at the Chicago airfield attended his progress through telegraphed dispatches. When he swooped into Grant Park and climbed from his airplane, enthusiastic demonstrators swept aside police guards to swarm over him, hoist him onto their shoulders, and thusly deliver him to the judges' stand. Some in the crowd had greeted him at his two earlier stops (Springfield and Pontiac) and had traveled to Chicago specifically to repeat their salutations.

Monday evening Cal and other graduates of the Wright Flying School held a dinner at the Hotel LaSalle in honor of Harry Atwood. It was agreed that Atwood had well matured from the naïve schoolboy enrolled at Simms Station two months earlier (he had, in fact, become the first of his class to gain his FAI certificate—July 3 as Aviator No. 33). Atwood delivered a short speech detailing the special equipment he carried on his airplane during the long, taxing flight: a suitcase holding a change of clothes, ligatures, surgical bandages and other medical supplies for the injured, a flask of brandy (included on all flights), a box of compressed food tablets, and an American flag. "If I complete the St. Louis-to-New York passage safely," Atwood resolved, "I will probably try next for the Hearst prize."

Atwood's managers, George Stevens and C. C. Meyer, were more definite. Said Stevens: "We are going after the Hearst prize as soon as practical, perhaps in October. There are a couple of Frenchmen in this country who will be hot after this prize, but I feel sure that the American with his coolness and calm judgment will triumph." Added Meyer: "The cross-continent feat would be the world's greatest aeroplane achievement along practical lines. Atwood is the man who can accomplish it."

Although Cal had previously heard vague references to the Hearst prize, this was the first time he had heard the specific declaration of an attempt to fly from one ocean to the other. The aviator who succeeded, he thought, would surely fly into the history books as well.

Early Tuesday afternoon Atwood ascended from Grant Park toward Elkhart, Indiana, escorted by "Bud" Mars in his Red Devil Baldwin and Al Welsh in his Wright machine. It was shortly after this takeoff that the inevitable casualties of the meet occurred. First, the wealthy novice William Badger died, trying to emulate Lincoln Beachey's stunt of flying through a sunken, hollow section of Grant Park. He was unable to rise with sufficient acceleration; his Red Devil machine burst into pieces on impact, and he was crushed by the engine. An hour later St. Croix Johnstone and his Moisant monoplane dove steeply into Lake Michigan; Johnstone became entangled in the twisted structures and drowned as the craft sank less than a mile offshore.

The two deaths were described by meet officials as "part of the sacrifice necessary to the advancement of aviation. . . . Postponement or cancellation of the meet would effect nothing." McCormick and Plew issued orders to eliminate henceforth all recklessness in flying activities: "No further exhibition of bravery will be tolerated."

Some of the participants agreed with the demands for greater caution. "I would rather be the oldest living aviator in America than the best," said Walter Brookins. Cal Rodgers appeared somewhat insouciant. "I suppose there is always a risk in flying," he said. "You just can't let it affect you."

A protest against continuation of the air show was mounted by a score of the aviators' wives and mothers. Spectators jeered the women and pelted them with overripe fruit. A group of religious votaries marched through Grant Park bearing placards denouncing manned flight as a violation of God's law. "These two deaths," proclaimed the group's leader, "are a sign. Aviation is unnatural. Mark my words, no good will come of it."

No further fatalities plagued the remainder of the meet. Wednesday Arthur Stone dropped his Queen airplane into Lake Michigan but survived without injury. Howard Gill's Baby Wright pitched over and was crumpled. Friday Earle Ovington dumped himself and his craft into the lake. A cylinder blew out in Jimmy Ward's Curtiss machine (his first failure in more than a year of flying); metal fragments struck the propeller, smashing it to smithereens. Cal Rodgers suffered a break in a rudder support but volplaned safely to the field. On his next landing he shattered a propeller blade against a rock.

With the duration prize assured if the "B's" engine could withstand the prolonged strain, Cal and his mechanicians devised an airborne tuning procedure. Both Wiggin and Shaffer wedged themselves against the spars, and Cal drove the airplane aloft. The plan called for the two mechanicians to adjust their respective sides of the engine. However, the "B" could not sustain itself with the weight of three men, and it lurched back to earth in sinking swoops. Wiggin regurgitated his dinner over sections of the lower plane.

John J. Frisbie won the $1,000 bomb-throwing contest—wherein the aviators dropped bags of flour onto a "ship" outlined in whitewash, a five-foot bull's-eye painted on its "deck." Although Frisbie's flour bag exploded less than four feet from its mark, experts agreed that real ships were in no danger—a sharpshooter in the crow's nest would have put the airplane out of commission before it could do any damage.

On Saturday word was received that Harry Atwood, after stops at Toledo and Cleveland, Ohio, was downed in a cornfield near Swanville, Pennsylvania. Subsequent messages indicated that he had repaired the damage and was en route to Buffalo.

On the final day of the meet, Sunday, the twentieth, Lincoln Beachey reached a world-record altitude of 11,578 feet.[1] Two other world records were established: Tom Sopwith climbed his Blériot 1,634 feet in three minutes, twenty-five seconds, and George W. Beatty carried a passenger in his Wright machine for three hours and thirty-eight minutes.

Troubles outside the domain of flight continued to harass officials and participants. On Thursday the Wright brothers filed an injunction in a U.S. circuit court against officers of the International Meet Association, charging patent infringements. The Wrights declared that they had no wish to interfere with the Chicago meet but sought to bar all future meets until the issues of patent rights were resolved.

Jimmy Ward was beset by another form of legal action. In Chicago's court of domestic relations, Mrs. Margaret Ward accused him of abandoning her and their child for the pursuit of aeronautical pleasures. An arrest warrant was issued by Judge Edmund Walker. At five o'clock, as a deputy sought to execute the warrant, Jimmy Ward spied his approach, promptly ran for his machine, and took off, not alighting until seven o'clock. Said Ward: "I ought to have stayed up another hour." He was taken to the Harrison Street Police Station, where he was released on bond. "Jimmy's been getting entirely too many nice names in the paper to suit me," grumped Mrs. Ward. "I think it's about time he was doing something to take care of his wife and child." Said Ward: "We have been divorced for more than a year. She [Margaret Ward] is a thorn in the tail section both for me and my present wife, Maude."

By the conclusion of the nine-day international air meet, Tom Sopwith had accumulated the greatest sum of prize money, winning $14,020 for seven firsts, two seconds, and one third-place award in the speed contests. Lincoln Beachey finished second with $11,667 from prizes in the racing, climbing, altitude, and duration events. Third place in the money stakes went to Cal P. Rodgers with $11,285, mostly as winner of the duration contest. "Lolling in his seat each afternoon, legs crossed and dangling, a cigar in the long holder he held in his mouth," Cal had remained aloft for a nine-day total of twenty-seven hours and sixteen seconds of a possible thirty-one and a half hours.

Thirty other airmen were awarded a range of purses for an aggregate of $101,120. The Pole, Laddie Lewkowicz, found no close competition for the booby prize. His Queen machine encountered mechanical problems throughout the meet, and he compiled a total air time of eighteen seconds. He received a check for 60¢.

The Great Chicago Air Show, the most extensive aviation gathering yet held in the United States, convinced millions in Chicago and throughout the country that the airplane not only could fly but could sustain itself aloft for more than three hours at a time. "This city now knows . . . the wonders of air navigation and the practical use of heavier-than-air craft," said James Plew. Harold McCormick predicted that the air show would "provide the greatest stimulation to aviation progress since the invention of powered flight."

Almost 3 million spectators witnessed events at the meet. Nonetheless, the promoters sustained a $50,000 loss. It did not deter them. The Aero Club of Illinois immediately set about preparing a more elaborate and varied program for the following year.

Bonuses from Cal's winnings went to Frank Shaffer and Charlie Wiggin, who had labored throughout the meet to maintain the "B" in flying condition. The aviator and his two mechanicians congratulated each other on their accomplishment and awarded themselves a week's rest in Chicago before seeking additional engagements. Rest, however, did not mean confinement to the ground. Cal had lost none of his initial ardor for flight; several times each day he rose to circle above the lakefront, often with a trembling but exhilarated young lady gripping the passenger seat beside him. Aloft, he was alive. If he never came down, he told himself, he would never die.

Through his mother, Cal had met many of Chicago's wealthiest and most influential families. He was besieged by scores of society folk— Charles ("Pop") Dickinson and Joseph Medill Patterson, among them— seeking a turn in his airplane. Only a small fraction of the requests could be accommodated.

Wednesday afternoon, August 23, at the invitation of Chicago's Saddle and Cycle Club (prompted by Mrs. Sweitzer), Cal flew from Grant Park to the Cicero Aviation Field. There he carried aloft, in succession, Mrs. Hobart Chatfield Chatfield-Taylor, wife of the prominent clubman, and Mrs. Redmond Stephens, the well-known promoter of charitable functions. These flights, conducted *en tapinois,* were soon made public by an item in the society columns of the *American.* Mabel was particularly furious since Cal did not return to the Plaza Hotel until the following day. Disinclined to pass the evening in solitude, she toured several Chicago nightclubs with Andrew Drew, the Wright aviator and young (twenty-six) bachelor from a socially prominent St. Louis family.

Mabel's social contacts could not compare with those of Mrs. Sweitzer. Mabel had enjoyed little of her husband's company since arriving in Chicago. She had persisted in her pleadings to be initiated into the romance of flight, but it was not until Friday the twenty-fifth that her entreaties broke through Cal's resistance. When, on that date, she climbed onto the passenger seat of the "B," circled a strip of cloth below her knees to fasten down her skirts, and nodded to her husband, Cal was nervous for the first time since his aviation career began two and a half months before. Rising from the field of the Chicago Aero Club, Cal drove cautiously at low altitude for about ten minutes and landed. For his obligingness, he received only a scolding from his wife.

"You mean boy—why haven't you taken me up before?" she was heard to exclaim as the aircraft alighted. "Think of all the fun I have missed! I'll want to go up every day hereafter."

On Wednesday Harry Atwood reached Fort Plain, New York, where his financial backers declared the dissolution of their contract since he was earning insufficient side moneys throughout his flight. He was—perhaps —compensated by an announcement from Miss Alice Williams of New York City of her formal engagement to the aviator; Miss Williams had been following in his wake by train. Before departing for Castleton, New York, Atwood disclosed his firm intention to start for the Hearst prize on October 1.

Two days later, after a dangerous landing at Nyack with a broken connecting rod, Atwood took off for the final leg of his trip, aiming for Sheepshead Bay, Long Island. At 2:36 P.M. on August 25, he descended onto Governors Island ("Sheepshead Bay has crosscurrents and holes, and there was eight inches of mud on the field"), completing a world-record distance of 1,265 miles in twenty-eight hours, fifty-three minutes of actual air time in twelve days and twenty hops since departing St. Louis. The following day, August 26, attorney Victor Evans handed him a $10,000 check for his achievement. Said Atwood: "Now it is definite. I am going to fly from San Francisco to New York for the $50,000 prize. I shall try that flight before October 1. I will be in New York twenty or twenty-five days after leaving 'Frisco.'"

Cal reacted to Atwood's triumph with mixed emotions. The exclusive brotherhood of birdmen engendered pride in every member when one excelled, a sentiment amplified among graduates of the Wright Flying School. On the other hand, Cal was senior to Atwood in age (by ten years) and in enrollment at the school (by one week). If Atwood could fly from St. Louis to New York City, logic suggested that he, Cal, could surpass that feat.

At the same time, similar thoughts were simmering in the mind of Stewart deKrafft. Although he had held only brief conversations with Cal Rodgers throughout the air meet, deKrafft was impressed by "the only aviator I can look up to" (by two inches; most birdmen were of short stature). "His is a strangely shadowed face," deKrafft described Cal, "at one minute waggish and the next so profound you know you are in the presence of an historical figure." DeKrafft had been aware of Hearst's $50,000 purse since it was posted and, sensitive to the pulse of aviation affairs, knew that Robert Fowler had filed his entry and that Jimmy Ward, Harry Atwood, and Lincoln Beachey were potential contenders. Cal Rodgers, by winning the prize for total time aloft, had proven his endurance if not his aviating skill. DeKrafft met with Cal to sound his interest in a transcontinental flight.

Listening to deKrafft's recital, Cal became more and more enthralled by the Hearst proposal.

When Hearst held court, it was said, people lined up like iron filings near a magnet. The announcement of his proposition, blazoned in headlines across the country in October 1910, had triggered an outburst of emotional praise and tributes that flooded Hearst offices with telephone calls, newspaper editors with letters, and potential contestants with advice. The offer was hailed as generous, inspirational, and practical by virtually every aeronaut in the land—not excluding those who shortly before had scoffed at it as buffoonery—and by leaders in science, industry, and the military. With this single, magnificent gesture, most people agreed, William Randolph Hearst had regained for America the lead in the world's aeronautic endeavors.

Wilbur Wright commended the prize donor: "What impresses me most about the Hearst offer is its perfect fairness. It is one of the few prizes an aviator can reasonably hope to win. The transcontinental flight can be made. Aeroplanes can fly from 50 to 500 miles in one day, but . . . a motor sometimes develops cranky streaks lasting over several days. Then you must stop to repair it. . . . I think 60 days ought to be allowed for this reason."

Glenn Curtiss, too, was fired by the fascination of a coast-to-coast flight: "It is a magnificent conception and a magnificent prize. . . . It will be tremendously stimulating to aviators and will make all other cross-country competitions look insignificant. . . . I have not the slightest doubt that it will be done."

Similar encomiums were recorded by other aviators in the United States and abroad. Claude Graham-White expressed the admiration and envy of the British: "Only America could conceive and execute such a daring project. . . . I wish we had your Mr. Hearst in Europe."

Enthusiasm and optimism at the prospect of the transcontinental flight were endemic. The entire nation, the Hearst papers asserted, stood ready to speed the daring fliers across the country.

Experienced aviators, amateur birdmen, and many who immediately signed up for flying lessons announced their intentions to compete in the monumental enterprise. Seven fliers filed formal applications with the *Examiner.*

For several days newspaper commentary on the rich prize and Hearst's sublime courage in posting it continued to command front-page space. Unmentioned was the fact that not a single aviator had moved to convert intent into reality. A rare, cynical voice was heard denouncing the offer as wildly impractical and self-serving (the five cities specified in the rules were homes to the five Hearst newspapers).

By the beginning of the new year, 1911, the fervor, the plans, the concept of the race itself had faded into dim memories. Aviators devoted themselves to more sensible goals. Hearst was otherwise engaged in pursuing his divers schemes of grandeur, foremost among them the annexation of Canada. His proposal briefly recaptured attention on April 27, 1911, when, at the Hotel Astor, he was the honored guest of the New York Aeronautical Society at its first annual dinner. He was awarded a gold medal for "the greatest service rendered the science of aeronautics during the past year" and eulogized by President Taft and other dignitaries present for his "most conspicuous act in donating the princely prize of $50,000 for a transcontinental flight."

On May 24 W. R. and Mrs. Hearst sailed for Europe on the *Maure-*

tania. If Hearst held further reflections on his benefaction to aeronautics or on the vagaries of the response to it, he did not reveal them.

The Chicago Air Meet, deKrafft pointed out, was principally responsible for revitalizing speculations of the cross-country race. Flying machines, if not yet as reliable as might be desired, had been demonstrated worthy of serious regard. Harry Atwood's St. Louis-to-New York flight had demonstrated what a determined and persevering aviator could achieve.

No one weighed these considerations with greater presumption than did Calbraith Perry Rodgers. He prided himself that whenever a challenge appeared, he had risen to the game. And if magic had touched him at first view of a flying machine, that magic could now be woven into a carpet that stretched from sea to sea. He shook hands with Stewart deKrafft, agreeing that they should join forces toward the organization of a venture to cross the nation by air.

Mabel, when Cal broached the subject to her, was fully supportive. Frank Shaffer and Charlie Wiggin were instantly enthusiastic. Lieutenant John Rodgers, before returning to Washington, D.C., offered his encouragement: "Give it a go. No horse ever won a race it didn't enter." Mrs. Sweitzer registered grave reservations: There were obvious dangers inherent in such a trip; it would separate Calbraith from his mother for another prolonged interval; it might prove an expense that his winnings at the Chicago meet could not cover; etc. On the other hand, Mrs. Sweitzer, who sometimes moved with an eye to history, recognized the opportunity for her son to make his mark on a world that had not learned to appreciate him.

Mrs. Sweitzer and Stewart deKrafft discovered a territory they held in common: the belief that Calbraith P. Rodgers could will heroism upon himself. DeKrafft confided to Mrs. Sweitzer his conviction that only her son had both the physical and mental qualities to achieve a transcontinental flight. "Why does one man fail and another succeed?" he asked, and suggested that Cal's self-assurance and quicksilver perceptions promised an explicit answer. Mrs. Sweitzer concurred. "Calbraith was born to an aristocracy of heroes," she said. "If it is not this endeavor that proves his spirit, it will—inevitably—be another."

DeKrafft issued a release to the press: "Mr. Rodgers will begin his flight for the Hearst prize on Sept. 15. He will leave from New York City. His final destination will be either Los Angeles or San Francisco." DeKrafft then handed a formal statement of intent to the publisher of the *Chicago*

American * and departed for Dayton to confer with the Wright brothers regarding a machine suitably modified for a 4,000-mile odyssey. Before leaving he told reporters, "At the recent aviation meet here, Orville Wright watched Mr. Rodgers and declared that he was, with one exception, the best operator of a Wright biplane in the world. He did not name the man he considered superior to Mr. Rodgers."

Jimmy Ward's managers, I. K. ("Ike") Bloom and Harry Cavenaugh, filed their notice of intent with the *New York American.* Cavenaugh, a Chicago businessman, provided financial support; Bloom, a former manager of prizefighters, would serve as general manager en route. Ward himself was occupied in a Chicago courtroom with wife number one, Mrs. Margaret Warner Ward. He emerged with a valid divorce decree in hand, having conceded a divorce settlement of $250.

Both Cal Rodgers and Jimmy Ward were preceded by Robert Fowler,† who had negotiated financing with the Cole Motor Car Company of Indianapolis and with C. Fred Grundy, a multimillionaire California sportsman. Grundy personally filed the required fourteen-day notice at the New York office of the *Journal-American* and immediately left for the Pacific Coast. He would back Fowler to the extent of $35,000, he stated to the press. Named the *Cole Flyer,* Fowler's machine, a modified Wright Type B, would be tended by a special train with crew and spare parts. Fowler thus became the first entry in the transcontinental race since the rush of overzealous aviators in October 1910. In Dayton, Fowler estimated that he would require no more than twenty-six—twenty with favorable weather—of the thirty days allowed to win the Hearst $50,000 prize. After testing his new machine at Simms Station, Fowler said, "It is one of the most beautiful specimens the Wrighf factory has ever produced." Concurred Orville Wright: "It is the best." A greater plane expanse and a greater warping area at each wing tip endowed the craft

*Dated Aug. 30, 1911, the statement read: "Publisher of *Chicago Evening American,* Chicago, Ill. Sir: On behalf of C. P. Rodgers I desire to make formal entry for the William Randolph Hearst $50,000 prize for a transcontinental aeroplane flight which Mr. Hearst has so generously contributed to the science of aviation.

"Mr. Rodgers will start his flight and will attempt to end it at Los Angeles, Cal., stopping at Chicago. He will fly a Model B Wright biplane, the same type of machine which he used during the recent International Aviation Meet at Grant Park and with which he won the endurance prize of $5,000. [Signed] S. I. deKrafft, Manager for C. P. Rodgers."

†Fowler had already acquired some measure of renown as a motorcar racer. Promoted as "the fastest man on wheels," he had, a year earlier, set the automobile speed record between Los Angeles and San Francisco: 14 hours, 49 minutes.

with more sustaining power than the conventional Type B; it could fly higher, perform more acute turns, and better battle the gusts anticipated over the rugged mountains of the West.

Cal summarized for Chicago reporters his preparations to date: "I am going into this race for the Hearst trophy convinced of my ability to win against any obstacles. The only obstacle that I fear is the destruction of my aeroplane by a storm while it is not flying. I have brought this feature of the race to the attention of Mr. Hearst's representatives, and I believe that Mr. Hearst, who is a splendid sportsman, will see the justice of my claim. In the wilds which we shall have to cross on the way there will be no possibility of protecting the aeroplane from sudden storms. It is impossible to dismember it and put it together again in so short a time, because it takes nearly a day to assemble the various parts and a day to tune the machine up after it is put together. What I want is to be allowed to substitute another machine in case of a sudden storm coming up when the aeroplane is moored for the night or pending the passing of bad weather and carrying off the machine and destroying it. I believe this condition will be met in the spirit of fair play in which it is made. . . .

"I have planned an itinerary that calls for about 150 miles a day, but I shall not be bound by that because I shall take advantage of every good flying hour. . . . Mind you, I am not planning to wear myself out. I shall have a surgeon with me on my special train. He will watch my condition closely, and if he considers that I am overstraining my vitality or nerve force, I shall rest for a day. . . .

"I am confident of my ability, stamina, and resourcefulness to overcome the strain and accidents of the voyage, and I firmly believe that I shall be the first airman to fly from coast to coast."

On September 2 Cal towed the "B" 175 miles north to Neenah, Wisconsin. Mabel had preceded him to that town to visit her sister Bess and brother-in-law Frank Whiting. From the Neenah aviation field, Cal whisked aloft first Bess Whiting, then other family friends and relatives in his flying carriage—thus cementing Mabel's reputation as the wife of a dashing, romantic, and almost Olympian figure.

Also in Neenah, he conferred with Fred Felix Wettengel, a businessman Cal had met in Chicago. Wettengel was on hand to pursue his acquaintance with the aviator. He encouraged Cal to attempt the cross-country flight and offered his own services as business manager. To aid in financing the enterprise, Wettengel suggested that the National Cash Register Company in Dayton, Ohio, be sounded as a potential sponsor.

Cal telephoned Edward Deeds at NCR headquarters; Deeds offered to consider the proposition—to the extent of $20,000—if Cal would carry an NCR machine with him throughout the trip. Wettengel added that his own observations of the Chicago Air Show proved to him that the Curtiss machines had outperformed the Wright machines. Both Beachey and Ward drove Curtiss airplanes at Grant Park and would use them in their transcontinental flights.

To reporters who approached him at the Neenah field, Cal declared: "I will start within two weeks from San Francisco in a Curtiss biplane and will end in New York City. I expect that Harry Atwood will be my main competition. I have agreed to carry a register from the NCR Company with me, as NCR is providing the financial backing."

Over the telephone wires from Dayton to Neenah, deKrafft blistered Cal's ears: "Who in the name of Holy Moley is Fred Felix Wettengel? What does he know about Curtiss or Wright machines? A register on the aeroplane? Is it filled with cash? If so, you can throw out dollar bills all across the country—to the millions of people below who will be laughing at you!"

Wettengel, unintimidated, continued to advance his influence. His hometown, Appleton, Wisconsin, six miles from Neenah, had scheduled an aviation meet in his honor—the meet was titled "Ask Wettengel"— for Sunday, September 3, and Labor Day, September 4. Wettengel engaged Cal for an aerial performance each of the two days. Then, when arrangements with the NCR Company stalled, he telephoned another prospective backer: J. Ogden Armour, president of the Armour Meat Packing Company. A meeting was scheduled for Tuesday, September 5, in Armour & Company's Chicago headquarters.

DeKrafft, meanwhile, was present in Dayton to watch Bob Fowler test his modified Type B ("Every spar and rib glistens," said Fowler) and then pack it into an express train for San Francisco. Enough additional parts were included to construct three more such machines.

Both Orville Wright and Al Welsh were present at the loading. Both congratulated Fowler on the aviating prowess he had demonstrated (during a brief period of instruction at the end of July) and expressed hopes for his success. Orville advised Fowler to cross the western mountains by a southerly course. But his erstwhile student was obdurate. "The greater elevation [over Donner Summit]," he said, "will enable me to volplane to a safe landing if the engine stalls." Orville had become fond of Fowler, the only aviator who indulged in neither liquor nor cigars (vices epidemic among aviators). At age twenty-six, six feet tall and 180 pounds, blue-eyed

Bob Fowler was personable, well educated, and with a distaste for self-aggrandizement. Al Welsh described him as the best airman he had ever taught.

Fowler planned to fly from San Francisco directly eastward across the Sierra Nevada range. His transcontinental air route then led by way of Reno, over the Great Salt Lake to Utah, across the Rocky Mountains (between Laramie and Cheyenne), via Omaha, Des Moines, Chicago, thence toward Pittsburgh, and finally north into the Mohawk Valley and upper New York.

Possibly the most elaborate campaign ever to assist an airman had been devised on Fowler's behalf. His special train* would carry, in addition to two mechanicians and supporting personnel, a physical-culture expert to supervise the aviator's diet and to direct a masseur and a trainer in their ministrations to his body. Every convenience that money could procure would be committed to this stupendous undertaking. It was planned to use automobiles as a moving chain of observation posts so that the flying machine, if downed, could be reached within five minutes. The Grundy/Cole organization promised to establish along the route fuel stations, lubricating-oil depots, water tanks, and all other necessary first aids.

Fowler scheduled his departure from San Francisco's Golden Gate Park for September 10.

DeKrafft was duly impressed with Fowler's character and his detailed planning. Fowler had much in common with Cal Rodgers, he decided, and would likely provide Rodgers's toughest competition.

In consultation with Orville Wright and chief mechanician Charley ("Zach") Taylor, deKrafft concluded that, for the optimum combination of speed and durability demanded by sustained long-distance flying, the Model EX, whose design had only recently been sketched, offered greater promise than the Type B. Equipped with blinkers for turning stability, the EX, said Orville Wright, "would move in the direction it is headed and head in the direction it is moving."[2] Orville was not encouraging a transcontinental flight, he emphasized to deKrafft—developments in flying machines simply had not reached the state to warrant such a venture, nor would they through the foreseeable future.

To Mrs. Sweitzer, who had insisted upon traveling to Dayton with deKrafft to ascertain for herself the probable perils and rewards of the proposed undertaking, he was more sanguine. Thoroughly cowed by his

---

*A baggage car, a Pullman Palace Sleeper, a dining car, and coaches—at regular ticket prices—for anyone who wished to accompany Fowler on his journey.

encounter with her two months earlier, Orville Wright quickly assured the *grande dame* before him that if any aviator in the world could successfully fly across the country, that man was her son; if any flying machine in the world could endure such a journey, that machine was the EX.

DeKrafft assumed general command of the enterprise. He realized that while gasoline supplies and some spare parts could be stocked in advance in towns along the projected route, dependence upon specific stops would not admit the flexibility to exploit favorable conditions. Further, a major component of the flying machine might require replacement at a town not convenient to rapid transport from the Dayton factory. These considerations, combined with his skepticism that Cal could follow the proper railroad track from coast to coast, led him to the conclusion that a pilot train would be vital. The train could carry duplicate parts, a machine shop, the special tools, and a full crew complement. It could also contain Cal's "B," in which he might perform exhibitions in small towns en route, thereby helping to defray what deKrafft foresaw with increasing apprehension as the forbidding expenses of the journey. He telephoned Cal in Appleton to apprise the aviator of his concerns.

After the exhibit at Appleton, Cal flew the "B" to Kaukauna, to Sheboygan, and thence to Milwaukee over the track of the Northwestern Railroad. As an aviator whose feats at the Chicago Air Meet were celebrated in newspaper headlines and whose movements still commanded column leads, he was welcomed by crowds of several hundred enthusiasts at each stop. He reported no difficulty in tracing the line and could fare as well, he maintained, with tracks across the country (skeptics pointed out that, flying along the Michigan lakefront, he could scarcely go astray).

Present in J. Ogden Armour's office early Tuesday morning were, in addition to President Armour, Wettengel; Stewart deKrafft; E. B. Merritt, Armour's advertising manager; Charles H. Davidson, an Armour department manager; and Andre Roosevelt, representative-at-large from the Wright Aeroplane Company.

Charles Davidson had acquired the presidency of a subsidiary company recently formed for the manufacture of a grape-flavored soft drink. He and J. Ogden Armour agreed that the proposed flight by C. P. Rodgers might provide an expeditious means of advertising the new beverage. At meeting's end, J. Ogden Armour retained reservations. "It is true that such negotiations are pending," he admitted to the press, "but they are being attended to by our advertising manager Mr. Merritt and by our Mr. Davidson. I am not acquainted with any of the details."

Before offering his imprimatur, Mr. Armour wished a conference with the principal actor in this airborne drama. The following day, September 6, Cal returned to Chicago and was introduced to J. Ogden Armour and Charles Davidson. The aviator and the packinghouse executive entered the meeting room with one obvious habit in common: Both smoked large, expensive cigars. Both also were "tall sycamores"; both stood straight and self-assured. They shook hands, eyed one another squarely, and signed the agreement. Charles Davidson reflected that it might be inappropriate for an "imbiber" to sponsor a soft drink. "Liquor," said Cal, "has never passed my lips."

After a telephone call to Orville Wright, Cal departed immediately for Dayton accompanied by Andre Roosevelt. Stewart deKrafft left for New York. Charles Davidson announced: "The deal was consummated today whereby C. P. Rodgers is to fly from New York to Los Angeles. It is an advertising proposition. The machine in which Rodgers is to fly will be named after our new drink that we are making, and the name will be printed on the biplane where it can be seen by everyone witnessing the flight across the continent."

"How much money is involved?" Davidson was asked.

"We are financially backing the trip," he replied. "We signed contracts with Mr. Roosevelt to that effect today."

"The drink," Davidson volunteered when no one asked, "is called Vin Fiz. . . . My wife Mary named it. She likes Gin Fizz . . . and, you see, she thought that Vin Fiz sounds like . . . uh . . . so!"

Financial details of the contract, although withheld by Davidson at the news conference, were soon ferreted out by reporters. Armour & Company was to underwrite the cost of the Model EX airplane, the renting of locomotives, a private Pullman car, a day coach, and a boxcar converted into a hangar car for transporting the aeronautic support equipment and crew. On board the train would be representatives of Armour & Company and its Vin Fiz subsidiary. Armour was also to pay $5 for every mile flown from New York. Armour's commitment was to extend up to $40,000.

In return, Cal was obligated to support his own crew and to shoulder the cost of repairs and parts for the flying machine. He was obliged to paint the name *Vin Fiz* on the machine and on the train accompanying it and to drop advertising leaflets at such times and places designated by the Vin Fiz representatives.

Davidson and Ed Merritt made contact with John S. Runnells, president of the Pullman Company. Runnells had succeeded former president Robert T. Lincoln less than four months before and was quite willing to pledge his company's cooperation. Pullman agents were directed to exercise their influence with railroad officials—particularly those of the Erie line—to obtain compliance in subordinating normal traffic in favor of the special train.

The Erie Railroad Company was not pleased at the prospect of disrupting its scheduled services. However, Armour & Company was a prized customer, and relations with the Pullman Company were manifold and remunerative. Further, association with a project sponsored by the politically weighty William Randolph Hearst could reap dividends, if only through favorable mention in the Hearst newspapers. It was arranged that the special train would be afforded superior status from the Jersey City railroad yards all the way to Chicago. Three top officials of the Erie Company would accompany the train throughout, facilitating whatever business and executive matters might arise.

President Runnells personally selected the private Pullman *Zura* for the transcontinental run. The car featured hot and cold water, an ice locker for vegetables and meats, and was supplied with its own stylish china, glassware, silverware, and linen supplies. Services of a chef and two Negro porters were included. Expense for this apotheosis of luxurious travel ran $50 per day if rented for thirty days or less. For longer periods, reduced rates applied. Armour chose the thirty-day charge.

In Dayton, Cal discussed details of his plans with the Wright brothers and studied components of the Model EX as they were assembled. Wilbur Wright had returned from Europe August 10.

A smaller, speedier version of the Wright Type B, the EX spanned thirty-one and a half feet in width and twenty-one feet five inches in length. It boasted spruce framing trussed with solid steel piano wire and planes covered with rubberized duck fabric. Its propellers (laminated spruce wrapped with linen) extended eight feet four inches in diameter.

A conventional four-cylinder, four-cycle engine was installed—developing about 30 horsepower at 1,325 rpm and enabling a speed of 55 mph. Eleven sprockets on the engine drive and 34 on the roller chains turned the propellers at 429 rpm. Wright engines excluded carburation; Charley Taylor, a major contributor to their design, preferred the reliability of direct fuel insertion, fearing the "flashback" potential of a carburetor. Gasoline to the engine flowed by gravity from a tank beneath the upper plane. Ignition was provided by a French-made "Mea" high-tension magneto. Water for cooling was circulated from a three-foot-high radiator by a centrifugal pump attached directly to the end of the crankshaft. Taylor described it as a typical Wright engine: "temperamental, unforgiving, no sense of humor."

To eliminate the need for a man to prime the intake manifold, the engine was designed for only partial release of compression (push rod collars held open the exhaust valves upon rotation of a face cam) and the flow of fuel was not shut off during this phase. Consequently, the Vin Fiz engine started with bursts of dense black smoke as excess fuel burned off. "Don't leave it in low compression any longer than necessary," warned Taylor. "You're cooking the exhaust valves."

For an additional $2 per wheel (because of special rims), Cal requested that the standard Wright tire be replaced with the lightweight twenty-by-two-inch Wing Tire in accordance with Harry Atwood's recommendation (not a single blowout during his St. Louis-to-New York flight).

Total weight of the flying machine, including 196 pounds for the engine and with a full load of gasoline and oil, was estimated at 903 pounds. "Six good men," said Orville Wright slyly, "could carry it across the country."

The airplane was dubbed "Betsy," a private appellation, the inspiration for which Cal refused to divulge.

Orville had warranted that the EX airplane—the first ordered—would, upon payment of $5,000, be delivered within a week. Nevertheless, he emphasized to Cal, "there isn't a machine in existence that can be relied on for 1,000 miles, and here you want to go over 4,000. It will vibrate itself to death before you get to Chicago. But if you're going to try it, we might as well profit by selling you the machine."

With the resurgence of interest in the Hearst contest, cities—particularly in the West—vied to participate. Small towns posted sums of several hundred dollars for any competing aviator who would choose to include them in his itinerary. The *Kansas City Star* offered $1,000 for the aviator passing through Kansas City, and the *Denver Post* offered the same sum for Denver's inclusion in a transcontinental route. Sacramento businessmen anted up $2,500, the Reno Chamber of Commerce $500. In Los Angeles, a committee was formed to raise funds for those aviators who elected to start or finish the Hearst Air Race in the City of the Angels. The *Los Angeles Examiner* editorialized the need for the city to secure for itself distinction as a major flight terminal. Civic pride was aroused. Total bonuses from Los Angeles reached $6,000. The supplemental purse from all the interested towns, clubs, organizations, and individuals exceeded $33,000.

Governor Carroll of Iowa declared that "the traversing of the country by airship is of such historical and educational value that it should be fittingly observed by proclamation wherever the airman flies."

Newspaper columns detailing the plans of Fowler, Ward, and Cal Rodgers stirred the thoughts of other aviators. Lincoln Beachey and Arthur Stone issued statements of intent. Beachey tentatively adopted Fowler's route with a departure from San Francisco September 22. Harry Atwood had just signed a $50,000, twenty-five-week contract for a vaudeville theater tour. When several Los Angeles businessmen espoused his candidacy and wired him accordingly, he announced his acceptance in spite of this prior commitment. He filed his papers on September 1 and promised a takeoff from New York on September 15, a date soon changed to October 1.

Phil Parmalee entered the Hearst contest September 1 with a predicted takeoff date from Los Angeles as soon after the fourteenth as the condition of his airplane would permit. The Wright brothers indicated that they would advise Parmalee on the preparation and execution of his undertaking but would not participate actively in the Hearst contest because of the Sunday flying to which they objected strenuously. "Those trying East to West," said Parmalee, "have virtually no chance. . . . The winds are against them. I have studied all this in mapping out my route." Parmalee was less optimistic than his competitors: "If just one of us makes it across the continent, it will be an achievement for the world to remember."

Earle Ovington joined the ranks of announced contestants. Immediately after his first-place finish in the 160-mile cross-country race to Boston on Labor Day, he telephoned the *New York American* that he had mailed in his notice of participation. "The winning of the New England race was child's play," he said. "With my equipment I am certain I can get to New York first." Ovington specified departure from Los Angeles September 18 in a Blériot monoplane that reportedly could exceed 70 mph.

René Simons and Bud Mars each promised to enter the race; Simons claimed probable backing from Alfred Moisant. Formal entries were also recorded from James V. Martin of Nassau Boulevard, Long Island, and Amandee J. Reyburn, Jr., of St. Louis. Reyburn would fly a Blériot monoplane with a 60-horsepower Emerson motor.

Jimmy Ward announced that he would operate a Wright machine rather than his Curtiss biplane and would soon visit the Burgess-Wright manufactory in Marblehead, Massachusetts. Glenn Curtiss threatened a lawsuit if Ward attempted to sever his contract with the Hammondsport company. Ward answered that he had taken the matter up with his Chicago attorneys and would file countersuits, if necessary, to free himself from the Curtiss connection. On September 5, in Olean, New York, for an exhibition flight, Ward declared that his point of departure had definitely been fixed at Boston in a Burgess-Wright aircraft and that he and the Curtiss camp had reached an amicable settlement. On September 8 he declared that he would definitely start from New York in a Curtiss machine.

Altogether, some twelve entrants and would-be entrants continued to jockey about behind the starting gate. Ardent feminists protested that all contestants were male. Both the Wright and Curtiss schools had steadfastly refused to enroll female pupils at any price. Only two aviatrixes were licensed by the American branch of the FAI: the Misses Mathilde Moisant and Harriet Quimby. An article by Claude Graham-White in the Hearst newspapers found particular offense. Wrote the eminent British aviator: "Women do not belong in the air. When calamity overtakes them, they cannot react. . . . [They] do not have qualities which make for safety in aviation. They are temperamentally unfitted for the sport. Bravery and courage are not essential in aviation. But supreme confidence is. Women possess the former, but they generally lack the latter."

In New York City, Stewart deKrafft registered at the Hotel Martinique and began investigating aviation locations and logistics for a takeoff site. In consultation with Erie engineers, he laid out a route to Middletown, thence along the lower edge of New York State, across Ohio and Indiana into the Chicago terminal (canceling a previous plan to trace Jimmy Ward's course through Buffalo, skirting the Canadian border)—a northern circuit that flanked the Allegheny Mountains. A telegram arrived from the Los Angeles committee reiterating the financial advantage were the expedition to choose Los Angeles over San Francisco as its destination. That consideration seemed decisive.

To assist deKrafft, Lieutenant John Rodgers journeyed to New York on September 10. Three days earlier he had flown the navy's Wright biplane from Annapolis to Washington, D.C., where, after circling the Washington Monument, he had landed near the White House. Consequently, upon his arrival in New York, he was sought out by a *Times* correspondent for a statement regarding the transcontinental flight: "I went to the Weather Bureau in Washington a few days ago and made a study of the maps showing the average winds that have prevailed during September and October for the last ten years. These maps indicated that the most feasible route was East to West. . . . The aviator who can accomplish a flight across the continent must be a man of strong constitution, great patience and sticking powers, in addition to strong financial backing and a strong, substantial machine. . . . I think the flight can be done, but it might take more than a month."

DeKrafft had clarified with Hearst representatives the matter of repairs en route—except for a "complete and total" wreck, it was resolved, a machine could be rebuilt without penalty. This decision was rendered by a committee newly formed to arbitrate points of dispute that might arise during the progress of the coast-to-coast air race. Ten of the most notable captains of industry, the military, and science served on the committee (two from each of the cities named by Hearst). New York City was represented by B. F. Yoakum, chairman of the St. Louis and San Francisco lines, and Hudson Maxim, past president of the Aeronautical Society and inventor of maximite and other high explosives.

Following a suggestion by Will Menger, a close friend of Cal Rodgers's and owner of the Menger Hotel in New York,[3] deKrafft had met with controllers of the Sheepshead Bay Racetrack in south Brooklyn. A contract was signed for use of the grounds as Rodgers's starting point in the transcontinental race. DeKrafft also purchased a six-cylinder, 60-horsepower 1911 Palmer-Singer touring car* for toting luggage, maps, and members of the aviation party about New York City. The auto, he realized, might prove of benefit at the many stops projected for the trip; he arranged for it to be carried in the hangar car and ordered a suitable ramp for its loading and unloading.

During these several days both Fowler and Ward were suffering setbacks and misfortunes. Fowler had passed an entire day on the observation platform of a train running from San Francisco to Reno, recording contours of the countryside, nearby mountain peaks, and possible emergency landing sites. He returned to San Francisco to learn that C. Fred Grundy had switched his starting point to Los Angeles. The sweeter financial plum dangled by that city, the failure of the San Francisco Rotary Club to fulfill its offer of $10,000, and Grundy's serious reservations regarding Fowler's (or anyone's) ability to surmount the Sierras all favored the southern route. Bob Fowler protested that he had spent four months gathering data pertinent to the northern route, that he was a native San Franciscan, and that he anticipated no difficulty in crossing the 7,017-foot pass through the Sierras. Grundy cited the recent death of George Chavez in attempting to fly over the Alps and reiterated that finances were the deciding factor. He wired the Wright factory to divert ordered parts and engines

---

*Built in New York City by the Palmer & Singer Mfg. Co. (1620 Broadway), the automobile cost $3,000 with parts guaranteed for one year.

to Los Angeles and boarded the *Owl* train southward to negotiate with the Salt Lake Railroad for a special car and locomotive. Ascot Park was selected as the departure site. Fowler was instructed to ship his airplane to Los Angeles and prepare for takeoff on September 11, Monday morning, at nine o'clock.

At 6:00 P.M. Friday, as Fowler's machine was being loaded into a railroad car at the Santa Fe freight yards, it was dropped and severely damaged. Fowler telegraphed Grundy, still en route south, that a Monday start would be impossible if repairs were to be made in Los Angeles and urged Grundy to return to San Francisco and the original plan. Grundy telegraphed back to ship the damaged biplane and to keep the mechanicians working on it en route. Fowler allowed that he would obey orders.

Grundy's efforts, meanwhile, with the Salt Lake Railroad proved unavailing; further, the Los Angeles Citizen's Committee announced that its prize money had been specified for the aviator finishing—not starting—in Los Angeles. Grundy wired Fowler to hold in San Francisco and boarded the *Owl* train northward.

Upon arrival he spoke with C. C. Moore, president of the Panama-Pacific Exposition Company, and James Rolph, Jr., official timekeepers representing San Francisco for the Hearst Committee, requesting a waiver of the rules to authorize a start from Oakland (where, Grundy believed, he could raise a $15,000 purse). When permission was denied, Grundy attempted to communicate directly with William Randolph Hearst. When this final strategy failed, takeoff was reaffirmed for Golden Gate Park, eleven o'clock Monday morning the eleventh.

Ten thousand people flowed into Golden Gate Stadium to cheer Fowler on his way. In a white shirt open at the throat, corduroy knickerbockers and puttees, face bronzed a deep tan, he presented a picturesque figure of an airman. He had had not a moment to shave, and a day's growth of fuzz covered his chin. Still, he was the target for many a lady's flashing eye. One young lass dashed up to kiss him, and while he was thus engaged, another pinned a "Votes for Women" badge on the breast of his leather jacket. The aviator blushed and took refuge among his mechanicians, although he did not remove the suffragette emblem.

After ceremonies with army, navy, and city officials, Fowler was handed a letter of appreciation from C. C. Moore addressed to Mr. Hearst in New York City. Mrs. Frances Fowler clasped her son in a farewell embrace: "Take care of yourself. Don't forget your warm coat. It may be cold up there." She turned to a reporter and said, "I didn't want Bobby to see me cry. Later, I'll sit down somewhere and let the tears flow."

James Rolph, candidate for mayor of San Francisco, presented Fowler with a miniature of the Bear Flag of the California Republic; it was attached, along with a small version of the Stars and Stripes, to a halyard strung between the upper and lower planes. "I'd rather be in your shoes," Fowler offered. "Your race is nearly over. Mine is just starting." To christen the aircraft, Rolph splashed a container of Pacific Ocean water on the forward skid panels and wished the aviator "Godspeed."

Over his white shirt Fowler pulled a sweater and over that a heavy coat. He hauled his hat down around his ears and slipped his goggles into place. A battalion of photographers snapped final pictures. The propellers were pulled through and whirled into motion. Fowler sat for a moment, his ear cocked to the engine sounds. He signaled to policemen, who cleared a wider path before the machine. His left hand went up. . . . His mother came charging through the crowd. "Bobby," she called out, "you mustn't leave until you've had something to eat." "I'll get a sandwich in Sacramento," he yelled back. His hand dropped; the mechanicians at the wing tips released their grips. The first round in the great transcontinental air race was under way.

Two days later, Wednesday morning, September 13, Jimmy Ward, Mrs. Maude Ward, mechanicians J. J. Horton and J. L. Swain, and 100 other dedicated aviation enthusiasts gathered at Governors Island for the second attempt to span the continent by air. The young aviator, scarcely twenty years of age, arrived wearing a gray sack suit buttoned over a red and green sweater, his head encased in a padded football helmet. Two reporters and a photographer bustled about to record the event. Ward regretted that he was unable to underwrite the expense of a special train to support his enterprise; his wife, mechanicians, and manager would have to abide with regular passenger-train service. "But the Erie Railroad," he said, "has agreed to place signal flags along the course over the Hackensack meadows and to send out a pilot locomotive with a flag." He voiced full confidence in his Curtiss machine: "I put it together in two hours by lantern light, and it has just been thoroughly re-braced with extra wires. If any machine can withstand a transcontinental flight, this is it."

Mrs. Ward invested her confidence in her husband: "I know Jimmy will win. There is no man who can fly across the country as well. . . . He can handle a machine in all kinds of circumstances. I have seen him get out of tight pinches no other man could have escaped from. . . . I am sorry we did not get our special train. I wanted the chance to cook Jimmy's meals for him to ensure that he keeps to a good diet."

Just as Ward was seating himself in the Curtiss machine, General

Frederick Grant was driven up in a Peerless automobile to hand him a letter to the commander of the port at Los Angeles. Hudson Maxim, the only other official present, signaled for the takeoff. Not a cloud marred the clear air over New York. Ward said he expected no difficulty in picking out landmarks and that he would fly at 2,000 feet, aiming the first day for Middletown, Callicoon, and Susquehanna. Maxim and General Grant formally certified his starting time as 9:08 A.M.

The Curtiss biplane rose over Castle William to the cheers of thousands of people lining the harborfront at the Battery and thousands more on ferryboats in the bay. It passed directly over the liner *Tuscania,* outward-bound for Europe; the ship's whistle saluted Ward with a gigantic blast, and the passengers on board shrieked and shouted.

After crossing the Hudson River, Ward became hopelessly confused by the vast maze of railroad tracks leading out of Jersey City. He circled for a time, chose one track and then another, searching for the Erie main line to Middletown. Neither choice proved correct, and he landed on the front lawn of a house on the outskirts of Newark. The two elderly spinster ladies of the house were delighted to entertain him at lunch and listen to his tales of driving airplanes and horses; they pointed him in the direction of Middletown and, with a crowd of neighbors who had gathered, wished him *bon voyage.* After this second takeoff, Ward soon became lost again and landed, in sequence, at Ashbrook, Rutherford, and Orange. At Ashbrook, while the airplane rested on the Robinson farm, he asked for a map. He was told that no maps were available in Ashbrook, and a boy was dispatched to the nearest school, at Picton, four miles away, to borrow an Atlas from the schoolmaster. At 6:25 in the evening, Ward performed his final landing of the day in Lambert's Lane on the extreme western edge of Paterson, New Jersey. By his estimate he had flown close to 200 miles. He was twenty-two miles northwest of Governors Island. From the Manhattan Hotel in Paterson, he announced that he would begin his second day's flight at dawn and, set at last upon the proper path, would cover at least 225 miles.

While Ward was tracing a tangled web about New Jersey, Fowler's *Cole Flyer* lay shredded in the gloom of the Sierra Madres, thirty miles east of Auburn, California. With the exception of its engine, the machine was virtually demolished* from a 900-foot somersaulting plunge, precipi-

---

*The crew of a passing freight train added further demolition by pilfering parts as souvenirs. A broken propeller was displayed in a Truckee, Nev., store window with a card reading, "From Bob Fowler's Cole Flyer."

Kent, Ohio. Charlie Wiggin (with cap) at left. (COURTESY FRANK LAWRENCE)

The Vin Fiz train passing through Kent, Ohio. (COURTESY FRANK LAWRENCE)

epairing Ward's Curtiss machine. Jimmy Ward (in sweater) at left. (COURTESY CURTISS MUSEUM, *MMONDSPORT, N.Y.*)

arle Ovington accepting the first sack of "aerial mail" from U.S. Postmaster General Frank Hitchcock. COURTESY EARLE K. OVINGTON)

The crash at Huntington, Ind.

Huntington, Ind. Charlie Wiggin and Cal Rodgers survey the damage. (COURTESY NATIONAL AIR AND SPACE MUSEUM, SMITHSONIAN INSTITUTION)

Cal Rodgers flying the Wright "B" No. 27 above the Chicago lakefront. International Aviation Meet, Aug. 1911. (COURTESY CHICAGO HISTORICAL SOCIETY).

Mabel Rodgers's first flight. The Wright B. Chicago. (COURTESY NASM)

Cal Rodgers and sister-in-law Bess Whiting. Neenah, Wis., Sept. 2, 1911. (COURTESY FRANK WHITING II)

Harry Atwood lifting off from Chicago en route St. Louis to New York, 15, 1911.

Harry Atwood.

The Vin Fiz *at the Dallas State Fair.*

Protecting Cal Rodgers against the cold.

Mastodon, N.M. Bob Fowler readying for takeoff from railroad handcar. (COURTESY BOB BROOKS)

Circling the Amicable Building, Waco, Texas.
(COURTESY THE TEXAS COLLECTION, BAYLOR UNIVERSITY)   *Robert G. Fowler.*

tated when the vertical rudder failed to answer to its control. Fowler escaped with a wrenched back and severe bruises. He insisted that he would continue the journey upon receipt of a second Wright biplane from the Dayton factory. "I'll cross the Sierras," he vowed, "if I have to work with pick and shovel to get the money I need."

From San Francisco, Fowler's first landing had been at Sacramento, after an airborne arc of ninety miles traversed in one hour and fifty-one minutes. While Fowler was the guest of Governor Johnson for luncheon at the state capitol, his special train was just leaving Oakland, having awaited the arrival by ferryboat of the fifteen-person traveling party.* He departed Sacramento late in the afternoon. As he climbed onto the driver's seat of the *Cole Flyer,* a man walked up and handed him a printed ticket to heaven.

Thirty-five miles and forty-one minutes later Fowler descended to a stubble field a half-mile from the Auburn depot. He was greeted by Auburn's Mayor Walsh and domiciled at Freeman's Hotel. His special train did not reach Auburn until 11:00 P.M. Trainer Tim McGrath found the airman asleep at the hotel and awakened him with the intelligence that his crew had arrived to support him.

Through the night, by lantern light, mechanicians worked to repair the *Cole Flyer*—split skids, clogged oil feeds, and rips in the plane fabric. In the morning Fowler announced, "Everything is fine for my flight. I am confident that I will land in Reno with colors flying. My only concern is for the cold." He bathed his face with glycerin to ward off the bitter winds, strapped a Thermos of coffee and a canteen of water to his seat, and rose from the Auburn stubble field. Forty-five minutes later he crashed at Alta, just east of Colfax.

Cal Rodgers, meanwhile, performed his single test flight of the Model EX at Dayton on September 12. He drove the machine in circles above Simms Station for five minutes and landed. Because of its similarity to the Type B, the EX required no additional skills. Despite Orville Wright's prediction, it offered no greater stability than the "B"; full-time application of the controls was demanded. "Better not to get an itch," said Cal. "You can't scratch it."

---

*Mrs. Frances Fowler, C. Fred Grundy, Mrs. Grundy, Harold Grundy, Alma Grundy, chief mechanician Ralph Newcombe, mechanicians Earl Cummings and Frank Murray, crewmen Earl Cooper and John Kierulf, Mrs. Cooper, Tim McGrath (Fowler's trainer), a correspondent and a photographer from the *Chicago American,* and telegraph operator George Jessop.

As the EX took the ground to conclude its test flight, a cable to the rudder snapped. "We'll need a stronger link there," said Orville Wright. He asked an assistant to fetch the pull chain from the Simms Station bathroom, then supervised its installation in the flying machine.

Orville had guaranteed the worthiness of the EX, but Cal suggested that another mechanician might provide needed insurance. Cal and Charley Taylor had previously discussed the possibility of the latter joining the transcontinental expedition. The forty-three-year-old Taylor, as chief mechanician of the Wright factory, was earning $25 per week. Cal offered him $10 a day plus expenses. Taylor was tempted. His wife had given birth a month earlier and remained in ill health; his financial status was critical. Although he thought Rodgers a mediocre flier, Taylor could foresee no advantage by continuing with the Wrights (for whom he had worked since 1901, managing the bicycle shop when the brothers were away from Dayton). He promised to ponder the offer.

Taylor was not alone in his appraisal of Cal's prowess as an aviator. Al Welsh noted that "Rodgers is particularly ill-suited for long-distance flying because of his inability to hear if the engine is running properly." Cliff Turpin had instructed Cal at Simms Station and observed him at Chicago. "His sense of equilibrium is not fully developed," he said. "When it is cloudy or misty, and he can't see the horizon clearly, he can't keep his machine level. Imagine flying across the country at a tilt!"

Tuesday night, September 12, Cal telegraphed deKrafft at the Martinique to confirm a new starting date of September 16. DeKrafft released this information to the press and also informed Hearst reporters that Cal Rodgers would be sped on his journey by Thomas Sopwith and by his cousin, Lieutenant John Rodgers of the navy. These gentlemen in their own machines would escort the transcontinental flier across the Hudson River and until he was safely over the Erie Railroad tracks that he would follow to Chicago.

The special hangar car, prepared by the Armour Company under the supervision of Andre Roosevelt, was dispatched from Chicago's Polk Street Station at 4:45 P.M. Tuesday. On Wednesday, in Dayton, it was loaded with supplies and with the crated Model EX. Cal then departed for New York, leaving Charlie Wiggin to safeguard the packaged aircraft —and to sleep alongside it—on its train journey from Dayton to Jersey City. "Remember," Cal told him, "you and the aeroplane are one and the same. Don't open the doors when you go through small towns." He again telegraphed to deKrafft to re-reschedule takeoff from Sheepshead Bay for Sunday afternoon, September 17.

Lieutenant John Rodgers boarded a train for Washington, D.C., where, with the advocacy of his father, Rear Admiral (ret.) John A. Rodgers, he succeeded in wringing a month's leave and permission from the Navy Department to accompany his cousin on the cross-country expedition. Saturday he flew the navy's Wright machine from College Park, Maryland, to the lawn of his parents' home outside Havre de Grace (where his brother Robert welcomed him with a drum-and-fife display). He announced that he would fly on the following day from Havre de Grace to the racetrack at Sheepshead Bay.

In New York, as he reached Grand Central Station Friday night, Cal enthused over his imminent adventure: "My machine can go fifty miles per hour. I have tested it out, and it is in perfect shape. . . . I have mapped out the flight completely with the assistance of my cousin, Lieutenant John Rodgers of the navy. [Each day] I will leave at dawn and fly till I am exhausted. I expect to do more than three hundred miles some days. I do not fear any physical or mental strain on the flight. . . . I will be disappointed if it takes more than four days for me to reach Chicago. . . . I have already engaged two of the most expert mechanicians in the country to travel with me [and] I was informed [this evening] that the Wright brothers of Dayton have given Charles Taylor a leave of absence to accompany me. Taylor is perhaps the greatest aeroplane mechanician in the country." Cal expressed confidence that he would soon overtake Ward and would subsequently outdistance Robert Fowler. The first day of his journey, he predicted, he would pause for refueling at Middletown and stop for the evening at Susquehanna, Pennsylvania, 193 miles from New York City.

At the Martinique Hotel, a waiting message informed Cal that his stepfather, Harry Sweitzer, had died the day before; the funeral would take place Saturday in Pittsburgh's Allegheny Cemetery. Cal telegraphed to his mother in Pittsburgh his expression of sympathy. He would be unable to attend Mr. Sweitzer's obsequies owing to pressing matters in connection with the imminent transcontinental journey.

Saturday morning at eleven o'clock, the boxcar with Charlie Wiggin and the EX arrived at the Jersey City trainyard. Following instructions "to the dotted eye," Wiggie, almost fainting from lack of oxygen, steadfastly forbore from opening the car door until he heard Cal's voice. Cal took the young man to the Martinique for an obviously needed bath. Saturday afternoon they drove back to Jersey City to supervise transfer of the airplane parts from the boxcar onto the truck that would furnish transport to Sheepshead Bay in south Brooklyn.

As Cal Rodgers was checking through his final preparations, as Robert Fowler and Jimmy Ward were struggling along their respective paths, the Hearst Committee announced that to qualify for the $50,000 prize, the successful aviator must reach his cross-country destination by October 10.

Managers of the three competing aviators and others protested. The committee's decision, they said, clearly contravened the only sensible interpretation of the Hearst conditions: that the winning aviator must begin—not end—on or before October 10. The Hearst Committee remained adamant. The participants promised to sue if one of them was deprived of the prize by this reprehensible ruling.

With imprecations against Hearst and the Hearst Committee, and with the support of public opinion, which (futilely) condemned the decision as unjust and un-American, the great transcontinental air race proceeded.

7

A New World Record

FOUR HOURS AND five minutes elapsed on the ground at Grant Park. A continual stream of city and business officials, social personages, aspiring aviators, and friends from the Chicago Air Meet lined up for a few words and a handshake from the man hailed by Chicago newspapers as "the Aerial Forty-Niner." Harold McCormick and James Plew were among the first to greet him. "I'm pleased to be back in Chicago," he told them. "Everything looks just the same, except that I miss the pylons and the hundreds of thousands of people." Cal was subdued, preoccupied with impending flight problems. To reporters he admitted, ten minutes after landing, that if the Hearst Committee stood by its October 10 deadline —two days away—he would have no hope of winning the $50,000 prize.* But Cal had not flagged in his confidence of completing the trip by October 17. "I am bound for Los Angeles and the Pacific Ocean," he said, "prize or no prize. . . . Whether I get fifty thousand dollars or fifty cents,

*The two Chicago members of the committee—Brig. Gen. Ramsey Potts and Rear Adm. Albert Ross—were not present. They sent a message requesting a meeting with the aviator or his managers; the request was ignored.

I am going to be the first to cross the country in an aeroplane."

Politicians lined up to be seen with the intrepid birdman, while photographers recorded the moment for posterity and for the next municipal election. Mayor Carter Harrison II offered him the services of the city, and, next in line, Alderman "Hinky Dink" Mike Kinna and his colleague, "Bathhouse" John Coughlin of the First Ward, made it clear that Chicago's "services" knew no conventional bounds. Behind the politicians, operators of "establishments" along the Levee—most notably, the Everleigh sisters—strove to appraise the man responsible for the Sunday afternoon lull in their business.

Several youngsters hired by Charles Davidson and Ed Merritt circulated through the crowd distributing Vin Fiz leaflets. Harry Sanger, he of the black-and-white-checked suit and vest, bellowed through his megaphone that "the famous and sensational birdman C. P. Rodgers gets his cool head, quick eye, and steady nerve through drinking this ideal blend of fruit juices. For only five cents, one-twentieth of a dollar . . . Vin Fiz . . . Vin Fiz . . . Vin Fiz!"

At Union Station, all but those in the hangar car disembarked; the locomotive, private Pullman, and day coach were changed for the journey west (Armour & Company duly received a bill from the Pullman Company for damages to the private varnish: the rear platform splintered in the collision with a freight train east of Elmira, New York, and the burnt flooring and walls from the stewards' flaming bucket of petroleum naphtha at Huntington, Indiana). Mr. and Mrs. Fred Wettengel expressed their regrets over the brawl with Stewart deKrafft and departed for their home in Appleton. Andre Roosevelt found a message from Orville Wright recalling him to Dayton since "the expense of your continued participation is no longer warranted." The portly Charles Davidson, dewlaps drooping down his chin, had taken abrupt leave five minutes after the train came to a halt. He offered no well-wishes for the expedition's future; his absence, it was agreed unanimously, could only improve the climate (and the quality of drinks) aboard the Pullman.

Mrs. deKrafft and Mrs. Shaffer bade their farewells, accommodations through the western states being inadequate for ladies. It was deemed forthrightly that Mrs. Sweitzer, too, would be more comfortable returning to her home. There had been letters from her attorney, both Cal and Mabel reminded her, urgently requesting her presence in Pittsburgh to settle her late husband's estate.

"I would never allow my comfort or legal matters to interfere with my duties as a mother," said Mrs. Sweitzer.

At Hammond, Cal had told her that "I couldn't have gotten this far without you, but the hard part is over. From Chicago on, it will be smooth sailing."

Mabel added that with no other ladies of her generation on the train, Mrs. Sweitzer would be lacking suitable companionship.

"I am shocked to hear that I am not wanted," Mrs. Sweitzer declared, to protestations of misunderstanding. With an air of self-sacrifice, she agreed to remain in Chicago for further reflection.

Officials of the Chicago & Alton line took command of the special train and promised new records on their run to Kansas City. Several reporters were recalled to their homegrounds and were replaced by colleagues from newspapers to the west. The Vin Fiz aviation party now totalled twenty-one persons—"Twenty lovely men and me," said Mabel.

After an automobile ride to Grant Park, Mabel and Mrs. Sweitzer pushed through the crowd of 5,000 people that surrounded the celebrated birdman and his flying machine. "Why, hello, dear," Cal was heard to exclaim to his wife. "You see I'm here. It won't be so hard now. We'll be going southwest, and it will be warmer." Mabel had brought an extra sweater and insisted that her husband add it to his already heavy raiment. "I don't feel right when I am bundled up," said Cal, but proceeded to don the sweater.

Precisely three weeks earlier, as Cal prepared to rise from Sheepshead Bay, he had told reporters, "Chicago in four days." Now, more reticent than usual, he declined to predict specific goals. He pulled from his mailbag letters for J. Ogden Armour and for Frank Whiting of Neenah, Wisconsin, who was present at Grant Park. With his wife, mother, and Armour & Company officials, he then repaired to the La Salle Hotel for luncheon.

After a hasty meal, Mabel took leave of her husband with a kiss, pecked dutifully and with well-concealed emotions at her mother-in-law, then collected her mail at the Plaza Hotel and managed a hurried shopping tour (boots, riding breeches, a full riding habit for "out West," and several packs of Sobranny cigarettes). Accompanied by Lawrence Armour, who joined the expedition as Armour & Company's personal representative in the stead of Ed Merritt, she was driven to the newly formed special train, which was scheduled to depart Union Station at three o'clock. In the forward stateroom of the new private Pullman, *Orkney,* she strewed clothes and cigarettes about and leaped joyfully onto the panel bed.

The two Georges, after transferring all personal belongings from the Pullman *Zura,* welcomed returning passengers with toothy smiles and whisk brooms flicking off imaginary dust particles acquired in Chicago. They received no gratuities for their efforts.

Cal was taken for a brief tour of the Loop, Mrs. Sweitzer at his side, and thence back to Grant Park at 3:30. Fully 8,000 persons were awaiting his return. Policemen found it necessary to use force to clear a space sufficient for him to approach and ready the machine. Thirty minutes were spent tinkering with the engine.

Lolita Armour, fourteen-year-old daughter of J. Ogden Armour, hammered the aviator with questions as he worked: "How much had the venture cost thus far? How much had Armour paid? Had sales for the Vin Fiz drink risen since he started? . . ."

"Normal children," said Cal, shaking his head, "ask about the control levers and what makes the aeroplane go up and down."

At 4:02 P.M. Cal lit a fresh cigar, suffered his pockets to be stuffed with fresh supplies of leaflets, mounted the seat, and, with a final wave to his tearful mother, lifted the *Vin Fiz* from a knoll at the north end of the park.

A reporter from the *Chicago American* approached Mrs. Sweitzer to record her thoughts on this occasion: "When Calbraith would start on one of the laps of his journey, he would always kiss me goodbye. I would say, 'Be careful, Calbraith,' and he would reply, 'Don't worry, mother.' His words were always comforting to me because I knew that he was thinking more of me than of himself. Now, I won't be there. . . ." Here, Mrs. Sweitzer dabbed at a tear.

Just prior to taking the air, Cal had been given a navigational "tip" by a fellow aeronaut. "Head toward Hammond," he was told, "and pick up the Drainage Canal—that way you can't get confused by the maze of tracks leaving the railroad yards." Cal circled once over Grant Park, turned south, and sighted a meandering creek that he mistook for the canal. He followed it for fifteen miles, then, becoming apprehensive, retraced his path back to Chicago and circled over the Illinois Central depot. Unable to locate the white-topped train, he again flew south along the lakefront and turned in over Jackson Park in the general direction of Joliet.

The Vin Fiz train, having pulled away from Union Station an hour earlier, waited at Argo, thirteen miles on, for sight of the airplane. Mabel, puffing heavily on a succession of cigarettes, discussed the tardy aviator with trainmaster Harry McEvoy and conductor H. C. Oliver. She left the Pullman, bantered with crewmen standing at the open door of the hangar car, then chatted lightly with engineer George Stuart and fireman H.

Bolonski, who told her that their locomotive, No. 147, was one of the fastest on the C&A road. At 4:55 P.M. McEvoy spied the flying machine through the smoke from a nearby factory, and engineer Stuart tooted his whistle. Other engines in the vicinity joined in the railway symphony to attract the aviator's attention. Ruffled by the mix-up, Cal passed over the train without rocking his planes.

> Oct. 8, Sunday. Finally got clear of Chicago after much confusion, but sun nearing horizon. Canvas markers placed along Alton rails . . . easy navigation after Argo. Lockport. Short of Joliet, over Dellwood Park, tried to land, but crowd swarming over field. Landed nearby Daniel O'Connor farm 5:20 P.M. Cracked skid, twisted wheel on soggy ground.

About 200 people from Dellwood Park poured over the countryside to surround and examine the flying machine. Cal was thoroughly chilled, and witnesses reported that he seemed dazed and trembled considerably. He did not venture to warm himself at a nearby farmhouse lest the crowd despoil his unattended aircraft.

Meanwhile those on the Vin Fiz train were unaware of their leader's descent. The special rode into Joliet, where no sign of Cal's passage was posted. The local dispatcher was alerted by trainmaster McEvoy, and the train backed to Lockport and onto a siding. Dirt roads (Illinois's highway system was notoriously antiquated) had been churned to quagmires by recent rains, and it seemed pointless to crank up the Palmer-Singer. Instead, search parties spread out on foot to seek word of the missing aviator. Crewmen Leo McNally and Edward Upton, guided by a local newsman, located him well after sunset. "Where's the train—I'm weak with hunger" were Cal's first words. The two men guarded the airplane while George Woodruff, a Joliet businessman, carried Cal to the Lockport siding in his Reo automobile.

Vehement arguments ensued among Cal, deKrafft, train officials, and crew members regarding responsibility for the missed connections at Chicago and at Dellwood Park and for failure to send out the Palmer-Singer auto. "OK, boys," said Cal shortly. "That's some pretty kettle of fish, but there's no point in overcooking it."

The flight of seventy-seven miles from Grant Park had gained but thirty-two miles of progress.

Supper was taken aboard the special train. Chef Ed Davis prepared steak for Cal and for those in the party who had thoughtfully motivated his special attention. The others were served the invariant meal of ham and beans with a side order of eggs. Cal and Mabel retired to their stateroom; Stewart deKrafft and Lawrence Armour shared the adjoining compartment. Reporters and lesser officials again curled up on day-coach seats or stretched out in the aisle. The realization that three weeks of strenuous effort had reached only to Chicago settled over the group and cast a gloomy atmosphere. The usual jokes and optimistic predictions for the next day's travel were quickly extinguished. For once, no poker games were organized among the reporters.

No mood of depression, of indifference, no excuse of weariness, of preoccupation could sidetrack Mabel from her goal. Freed from her mother-in-law's pervading presence, she left no doubt in her husband's mind that he was committed—after almost a month without connubial bliss—to the inevitable.

"Calbraith," she declared, "I don't care who hears what. I don't care where we are. I do care when. And that when is now!"

The darkness in the Pullman compartment was no obstacle to the personal, inward flight that Mabel had set her mind upon; indeed, darkness encouraged its own geographic ranging—over unseen peaks and canyons. Mabel knew the power that sustained her husband aloft, that penetrated her consciousness. She felt herself rising, descending, gliding over steps, dizzyingly, along a tightening spiral. All flights of fancy were possible. All feelings settled into a dimension of order and serenity.

Cal awoke at sunrise Monday morning to a chorus of crickets and katydids. Since the takeoff from Sheepshead Bay (when he overslept in the Hotel Martinique), he was awakened each day by an inner timepiece more insistent than any alarm bell. After scrutinizing the sky and the course of the wind, he pronounced conditions ideal for flying. With his mechanicians and assistants, he was driven to the O'Connor pasture at seven o'clock. It was ascertained that the *Vin Fiz* had incurred no appreciable damage from the citizens of Dellwood Park. "A great day!" Cal exclaimed. "Nothing will stop me this side of Kansas City except brief pauses for fuel and one overnight stay." For half an hour the flight was delayed, awaiting the signal that a coal train blocking the special had been switched to another track. At 8:10 A.M. Cal took the air, spiraled to gain altitude, and at 2,000 feet passed over Joliet. Crowds in the streets, atop roofs of the wallpaper mills, and along the Alton tracks, could scarcely hear the whir of his propellers. Vin Fiz leaflets dropped from the airplane glistened in the October sun as they fluttered to earth.

Over the thick, corbeled walls of the Joliet State Penitentiary, Cal put his machine through a series of figure eights, Dutch rolls, and volplanes for the entertainment of the inmates. Warden Murphy had granted all 1,800 convicts a thirty-minute reprieve from work, and they pressed into the prison yard to observe the spectacular show.

At Dwight, thirty-eight miles beyond Joliet, the expedition, according to its own log, exceeded the 1,265 miles flown by Harry Atwood from St. Louis to New York. Cal was now owner of the world record for long-distance air travel. The moment was commemorated with extended blasts from the train whistle. Inmates at the Keeley Institute (for treatment of alcoholism) poured from their building to join their voices to the din. Another 3,000 persons had gathered at the Dwight depot; they applauded members of the aviation party who stepped out onto the railway platform while locomotives were changed on the Vin Fiz special.

Cal circled above the scene and rocked and dipped the *Vin Fiz* in acknowledgment of his number-one ranking. He was no pretender, no trespasser on a private domain. He had earned his right to inhabit the sky, to join the guild of eagles, to flaunt the laurels of his conquest.

Thus entranced with his thoughts, and with his guide train behind him, Cal headed westward along the tracks of the Peoria branch of the C&A as it diverged from the main C&A line just below Dwight. As his concentration returned, he realized that he had strayed off-course, and twenty-two miles on, he landed at a race track on the north side of Streator.

Engineer George Stuart had not lost sight of the *Vin Fiz* as it veered from the main C&A track. A freight train to the west was quickly signaled to a siding, trainmaster McEvoy given clearance to transfer to the Peoria branch, and the special charged full-throttle in pursuit of its leader.

At the Streator racetrack, it was decided that Cal should proceed along the branch line to Peoria and then to Springfield, where he would regain the main C&A line. The airplane was refueled and broke ground at 11:45 A.M.

> Oct. 9, Monday. Left Streator after 40 minutes. Wenona, Varna, Lacon, along Illinois River. Landed Peoria Fairgrounds in time for dinner.

Volplaning onto the Peoria Fairgrounds, Cal spotted a Type B biplane roosting at one side of the open field. For the first time since its journey began, the *Vin Fiz* shared residence with another mechanical bird. The "B's" driver, Cliff Turpin, immediately appeared with a bottle of scotch to toast the new world-record holder (Turpin offered to substitute his scotch for the Vin Fiz soda on the EX, but was dissuaded). Saturday Turpin had attempted a flight from Chicago to Springfield, also along the C&A rails, but had failed to complete the journey. He and Cal dined together, and he presented Cal with a map of the Springfield State Fairgrounds, detailing the location of prominent trees and buildings around that locale. At 3:10, when the EX rose for the seventy-five miles to Springfield, it was escorted over the Illinois River by Turpin's Wright "B."

> *[From Peoria] people along the way came out in crowds and watched as I went by. Most of them evidently had never seen an aeroplane before. When I found my supply of oil was running low, I stopped at a little town which I later learned was Middletown.*

Cal dipped the *Vin Fiz* over Salt Creek and swooped down at Hink's Field just north of Middletown. During his forty-minute stay, virtually the entire local population (nearly 1,000 persons) ran out to the field across the railroad tracks to examine the heavier-than-air contrivance. Those who wished to autograph the fabric were cautioned by Cal that a small pencil-point puncture could soak up oil sprayed out by the engine or, under tension, could expand to the size of a half-dollar. Grant Heatherwick, thirty-one-year-old editor of the *Middletown Weekly*, asked the advantage of flying over traveling by train. "The biggest advantage," said Cal, turning away, "is that I don't have to listen to foolish questions when I'm in the air."

"Rodgers is a bit of a swell," Heatherwick reported. "He looks as if he has skinned his nose on a clothesline."

John Rodgers suggested that a telegram be transmitted to the Reception Committee at Springfield, requesting that bonfires be lit. Cal insisted that sufficient daylight remained. At precisely five o'clock the machine, refueled and rechecked, ascended from Hink's Field.

A mist and light clouds hung over Springfield, eighteen miles on, as the *Vin Fiz* sailed across its boundary at 200 feet. Witnesses described the flying machine at a marked inclination to the horizon (confirming Turpin's earlier observation of Cal's inability to maintain level flight). Cal sighted the lofty Dome Building of the capital while still some distance north of the Sangamon River and, with approaching darkness, quickly selected an open space to the northwest between the fairgrounds' half-mile and mile racetracks. Except for a leaky radiator, the flight was uneventful. The detour between Dwight and Springfield accounted for 26 of the day's log of 175 miles.

At the Springfield Hotel, Cal retired for a nap, while Mabel was escorted out Monument Avenue to Oak Ridge Cemetery for a tour of the Lincoln Tomb. Returning to the hotel, she was handed a telegram from Postmaster General Hitchcock stating that he had relented from his previous opposition and confirmed her as the official "aerial postmistress." In celebration of her now legitimate title, Mabel purchased several boxes of cigars and distributed their contents to everyone on board the train from the engineer to the chef (excepting the two Negro stewards). With each cigar, she bestowed a kiss.

The private stamps ordered to promote sales of "aerial mail" were not yet printed. Sales of souvenir postcards continued in modest numbers, but few chose to spend 25¢ on a letter or card to be carried on the *Vin Fiz Flyer.*

Earle Ovington had scheduled yet another departure that morning from New York City to Utica, and Bob Fowler was, ostensibly, to leave Los Angeles at about the same time. News of neither event could be obtained by the Vin Fiz aviation party in Springfield. At the Nassau Boulevard Aviation Field, Sunday, Ovington, along with Miss Mathilde Moisant, had provoked riots and semi–martial law. Although the air meet had been canceled—following a State Supreme Court decree that forbade charging admission to such events on the sabbath—Ovington and Miss Moisant decided to participate in flights on their own account. Sheriff De Mott of Nassau County, twenty-three deputy sheriffs in uniform, and numerous plainclothesmen patrolled the field to enforce the edict. Nevertheless, both aviators ascended. Miss Moisant flew to Mineola, where deputy sheriffs immediately sought to arrest her. Onlookers protested, and several deputies were pitched from the field. Miss Moisant charged that she was brutally dragged away. Her wrist was cut and she was bruised and shaken. Meanwhile Ovington had launched his proposed flight to the Pacific Coast and consequently escaped the harassment that befell Miss Moisant. He was forced to descend a short time later near Belmont Park when his monoplane nearly capsized in a squall. He announced that he would start again the next day from Governors Island and fly directly up the Hudson River.

Cal and Earle Ovington had first met more than three years earlier when both were racing motorcycles in East Coast meets. In direct competition, "Ovie" usually prevailed. "But not this time," said Cal. "He couldn't catch me now if he tied a flock of trained eagles to his planes."

DeKrafft had received word from the St. Louis Businessmen's Association that its offer of $1,000 to the first of the transcontinental aviators to reach that city had been withdrawn. Consequently, he announced, C. P. Rodgers would bypass St. Louis and, furthermore, would be compensated by yet greater emoluments from organizations in Roodhouse, Illinois; Louisiana, Missouri; and other towns that deemed it a privilege to host the celebrated birdman. The flight to Kansas City, said deKrafft, would commence at 7:00 the next morning.

Oct. 10, Tuesday. Take-off Springfield 8:35 A.M. Roodhouse, Pearl, over flat Illinois prairie. Reckoned gasoline low. Landed Hunter Cemetery, Nebo.

The noise of the *Vin Fiz* engine—the first such airborne sounds heard in Pike County—drew every man, woman, and child in town racing to the cemetery. Ed Franklin, co-owner of Franklin Brothers International Harvester agency, ran from his washbasin, his face lathered with shaving soap; his wife, Fannie, grabbed their three-year-old son, Evans, and chased after him. Dr. R. R. Pollock abandoned the patient he was examining; the patient hobbled behind, pulling on his trousers. At the William Nevius Bank (a structure with the audacity to protrude four feet onto Union Street), tellers and bank officers rushed out, leaving the vault unlocked and money in open drawers.

Students in Miss Cromwell's upper-grades class at the Nebo School were lined up along open windows performing, under Miss Cromwell's guidance, their daily breathing exercises: "In, two, three, four. Out, two, three, four." When the flying machine sailed into view, the scramble to evacuate the school tore the classroom door from its hinges.

R. T. Dinsmore, twenty-five-year-old editor and printer of the local paper, was first to engage Cal in conversation. "Damn," said the gangling birdman, who towered over everyone else at the cemetery, "I lost that train again!" (Mr. Dinsmore wrote "Consarn it" when he published the story.)

While Cal and Dinsmore were talking, the name of every literate soul in Nebo was inscribed on the fabric of the *Vin Fiz.*

When the special train arrived fifteen minutes later at the Nebo depot, Mabel rushed out with a pitcher of cream. The mechanicians refueled the machine and poured a packet of laundry soap into the leaky radiator. From the depot, John Rodgers wired to the Commercial Club of Louisiana questioning its $100 guaranty for a landing and brief aerial exhibition. A return telegram acknowledged that the money had not been raised. DeKrafft deemed that Louisiana would be bypassed in favor of Mexico, Missouri.

Ninety minutes after the descent at Nebo, Frank Shaffer spun one of the propellers, Archie Scranton, a local lad, pulled the other, and Cal took the air from Hunter Cemetery at 11:25. Behind him, he left the greatest commotion since the town was laid out forty years before.

Climbing as steeply as his machine would allow, Cal exceeded an altitude of 6,000 feet—the greatest height ever scaled by the *Vin Fiz*— as he crossed the Mississippi River at 11:40 A.M. Twenty-five miles below Hannibal, it lay like a smooth silver ribbon across the checkered landscape of green farmland that it nourished, too serene from 6,000 feet to provoke floods, boatwrecks, or even the turbulent adventures of Tom Sawyer.

Cal had once before traveled west of the Mississippi. Yet he was struck with the sense of passing into new territory. "It is the descendants of pioneers who will pioneer the next unknown," his mother had told him. Explorers, cavalry, railroad men had preceded him, he thought, but not at almost sixty miles an hour. He could cover in a day distances that had wearied them for weeks. The Mississippi was a milestone on his journey. Beyond it lay the end of the rainbow.

> *From 6,000 feet there is an awesomeness of distance and depth that is overwhelming. Wherever the eye turns, it falls upon a pageantry of colors, shifting like a giant chameleon. From this height one can read a message on the land: Manifest Destiny. America had claimed the frontier beyond this river. Now it can claim the frontier above it. And there will be frontiers not yet dreamt of. . . .*
>
> *There is a sense of isolation. The world passes idly below you. By merely pulling on the warping levers you can take the world in your hands and twist it around.*
>
> *There is a sense of detachment. I watch myself fly. Far, far below stands the rest of humanity. Have I really walked with them—slow, ant-like creatures? Will I walk among them again?*

Sailing over the village of Louisiana on the river's west bank with scarcely a glance downward—"I'll fly over that town so damned high, no one will be able to see if I'm on an aeroplane or a bird," he had sworn when informed that Louisiana had reneged on its $100 offer—Cal dogged the C&A line as it turned southwest, coasting down the skies to an altitude of several hundred feet. The only view of the Vin Fiz enterprise available to the indignant Louisianans was that of the special train during a hurried stop for water. Two correspondents from the *Springfield State Journal-Register* disembarked for the return to Springfield and were met with glances of hostility.

At Bowling Green, ten miles on, a group of schoolchildren—Miss Frances Frey's fifth- and sixth-graders at the Bowling Green Public School —alerted by the whistle of the Hume Flour Mill, had raced to "the hill" (a rise overlooking the railroad station) to semaphore excitedly at the figure whose legs dangled below the incredible flying machine. Cal waved back at them. "I had read about aeroplanes," said Miss Frey, "but I never thought I'd actually see one."

The wind, which had turned against him across the Mississippi, shifted in Cal's favor. He sped along the C&A track over Vandalia ("at a tremendous height—at least four times as high as the town's new water tower," reported one resident), Farber, and Mexico at 12:53. Several hundred persons had collected on the Mexico Fairgrounds, announcements of the aviator's advent having been posted by Lawrence Peters in the town's store windows. Cal decided that there were too many wire fences in the fairgrounds area and, with the aircraft functioning flawlessly, maintained his course west. Seven miles beyond Mexico, the engine sputtering from a dirty spark plug, he took the ground in an open pasture at the hamlet of Thompson. Residents of the region had been alerted that morning by Frank Cawthorn, the Alton Railroad agent, to the passage of the transcontinental airplane. Its unexpected landing quickly drew the entire population to poke at and autograph the machine. Cal offered no objection when some of the younger children climbed onto the driver's seat of the *Vin Fiz*.

Charley Taylor replaced the offending spark plug, Shaffer and Wiggin refueled the machine from two five-gallon containers of gasoline, and Mabel set up a table next to the special train, from which she sold several postcards and Vin Fiz pennants to those who tarried at the railroad station. Meanwhile telegraphed entreaties from the Mexico Committee persuaded Cal to retrace his path. C. M. Clay, the committee head, wired that the Vin Fiz group could retain the tendered $100 in exchange for an aerial demonstration alone.

Oct. 10. Back eastward to turn capers over Mexico Courthouse and cluster of steel and corregated-iron buildings (the A. F. Green Brick Co.).

Westward again at 3:00 P.M. Centralia, Yates, Glascow, across the Missouri River, Slater. Landed Marshall* 4:23 P.M.

From the ring of people that quickly surrounded the flying machine at the Marshall Fairgrounds, a young man stepped forward, holding out a ham sandwich. "I read that flying makes you hungry," he said. Cal accepted the offering, took one bite, and handed it back. "Never put mustard on my sandwiches," he groused.

Previous computation of mileage traversed by the *Vin Fiz* had led the aviation party to acclaim Cal holder of the world distance record as he reached Dwight, Illinois. A retally, using "railroad mileage," now indicated that the record was established just west of the Mississippi River. At Marshall, the total distance spanned was certified as 1,399 miles, surpassing Harry Atwood's flight by 134 miles. Cal Rodgers, without question whatsoever, was now the longest-distance flier in the world.

What did the aviator think about his world record?

Cal paused to light a fresh cigar. "Wait till I'm through. I'll set a record no one can beat unless they fly out over the ocean. . . . There is one problem with these long flights. I ran out of cigars and had to suck on a pencil for the last few miles."

In view of the gathering darkness, it was announced that the expedition would remain in Marshall overnight and continue the eighty-five miles to Kansas City at eight or nine o'clock the next morning.

The *Vin Fiz* had spanned 234 miles in the air, an astounding distance for a single day's flight. It was difficult to credit that Cal had departed Springfield, Illinois, only that morning and had crossed two major rivers of the United States.

> *It was a bully day for a flight. If I had started earlier this morning, I certainly would have been in Kansas City tonight. . . .*
>
> *I met the Missouri Mule for the first time today and for gentleness I pass them up for an aeroplane. Near Mexico I saw several of them in a pasture, I thought I'd scare them and swooped down. Instead of running, they laid back their ears and kicked at me. I was up bout 20 feet, but I swear their heels almost touched me. I expect some of the farmers are sore at me tonight. Pigs and cattle everywhere ran from me—sometimes through the pasture fences. I'll have to admit I chased the fat off some of them just for sport.*

*Named for John Marshall, chief justice of the U.S. Supreme Court.

At the Marshall Hotel, Mabel declared that "my husband could not be happier than he is tonight. The weather was perfect. A few days like this, and he will be in sight of Los Angeles."

The entire aviation party was invited for supper at the Elks Club, where several pleasing recitations were offered by hosting members of the Marshall Commercial Club, and where "Laughing Joe" Newborn responded on behalf of the Vin Fiz group with a series of sleight-of-hand tricks and his "calling on the telephone" act. Mayor Ed Page lauded the world-record holder, offered a toast in his honor and another to "the next president of the United States, Champ Clark" ("We may vote dry," said the mayor, "but we drink a lot to make up for it"). Commercial Club president G. A. Radford presented the aviator with a check for the $100 raised by local businessmen for his landing in Marshall.

"My machine really wanted to fly today," Cal told the supper group. "I couldn't hold it back. It may reach Los Angeles before I do."

Later that evening many in the Vin Fiz party joined townfolk in attending a scheduled Chautauqua;[1] further entertainment was provided by a sizable band that had traveled in by tallyho. Cal rested in his hotel room, weary from almost five hours in the air. Earlier he had telegraphed to the Hotel Montague in Kansas City, where his uncle Robert S. Rodgers resided. Mr. Rodgers boarded the next train for Marshall. At the Kansas City station, he told a reporter from the *Star,* "My nephew wired me to meet him in Marshall tonight because he would have no chance for a visit here tomorrow. If the weather is good, he will be here only a short time. I shall be greatly relieved when the boy gets to the coast. He has been in the game only four months and has had three bad spills. No matter how clever and experienced an aviator may be, he is liable to have trouble at any time on account of the treacherous holes in the air. They are the uncharted reefs of the air sea." At the Marshall Hotel, he greeted his nephews, passed two hours discussing family matters, philately (imminent delivery of the Vin Fiz aerial stamps was promised), Cal's and John's prospects in aviation, and arranged for overnight accommodations. He would return to Kansas City aboard the Vin Fiz special.

This date in the transcontinental journey marked the passing of the deadline as redefined by the Hearst Committee. An announcement printed in the *New York American* read, "The Hearst prize was offered one year ago today [October 10, 1910]. The time limit within which the flight must be made to win the prize therefore expires today. Messrs. Fowler, Ward and Rogers [sic] have tried and failed."

Stewart deKrafft had ordered reprints of the contest rules as originally promulgated by William Randolph Hearst himself. He distributed the sheets to local reporters and to correspondents traveling with the expedition. The conditions for the $50,000 award, Hearst had written, were as follows:

> *The distance, approximately 3,000 miles, must be made in 720 continuous hours, or 30 days. Start must be made either from Boston or New York City, finish made at Los Angeles or San Francisco, or vice versa, from West to East. A landing must be made in Chicago on the way. It is optional with the contestant whether East or West. Any route may be chosen, stopping as often as wanted, and as long as desired in any town. It is permissible to make flights of any distance or duration providing entire distance is traversed in consecutive town to town flights within the time limit of 720 hours or 30 days. Aeroplane may be repaired as often as desired. Any broken, damaged or defective parts may be repaired or replaced at the option of contestant at any stage of the flight, and as frequently as the judgment of the contestant may dictate. To all intents and purposes, the contestant may rebuild the aeroplane on the way by substituting all the damaged or broken parts, or any other similar machine, but the prize winner must use the same machine throughout. Any type of self-propelled aeroplane or a heavier-than-air flying machine capable of carrying the contestant may be used. Any person, regardless of sex, nationality, race or residence, is eligible to compete. Fourteen days before attempting the flight, contestants must deliver in writing to the New York* American *approximate time and place of start, route and point of finish. There are no other conditions.*

"Although no time limit for the prize was specified in this particular document," deKrafft told the reporters, "the Hearst newspapers of October 10, 1910, had printed the statement: '[The winning contestant] must start on the flight within one year from today.' Note the word 'start.' If October 10 were the finishing date, the Hearst Committee should have informed those filing entries after September 10 that they had less than thirty days to win the contest. Without a flyspeck of doubt, Rodgers has seven days left to reach the Pacific Coast. We are not going to allow Mr. Hearst to renege on his offer."

In New York, Hearst declined comment. Not once in his life had he permitted himself to doubt his own infallibility, and he was not to draw an exception for this occasion.

South of Marshall that evening, on a small farm tenanted by a Negro family, Mrs. Mary Johnson gave birth to her seventh son. The boy was named Calbraith Rodgers Johnson. The following day, a son born to Mr. and Mrs. Grover C. Lyle, owners of Marshall's principal hardware store, was also christened with the aviator's name: Howard Rodgers Lyle.

Cal took the air from the Marshall Fairgrounds at 8:45 A.M. The clatter of his engine straining for takeoff frightened several horses tethered too close to the field. One horse pulled free and galloped wildly across the grounds, dragging a driverless buckboard. A young woman, Mrs. Hilda Matthews, was struck and her leg broken.

Taylor, Shaffer, and Wiggin, ignoring the accident, scurried into the Palmer-Singer racer and sped the quarter-mile to the C&A depot, where the auto was quickly driven up the ramp into the hangar car. Cal was cutting spirals to gain altitude, and the train led the airplane westward out of Marshall. Mabel leaned from a window of the Pullman and clapped her hands as the *Vin Fiz*, at 1,000 feet, passed overhead.

"I don't worry when Calbraith is in the air," she said. "The danger is in landing and starting, and as long as I see him away up high, I never fear."

Oct. 11, Wednesday, Higginsville, Odessa. Magneto plug trouble; landed Blue Springs 9:55 A.M. Taken by Mayor and Police Chief to Elks Club for breakfast. Taylor repaired engine by 10:50 A.M., but unable to take off from small field. Local citizens lifted machine over barbed-wire fence to open pasture. Took off for Kansas City.

From Blue Springs, Cal followed along the course of the Missouri River at an altitude of 700 feet, braving the treacherous air currents that eddy about its bluffs. At the mouth of the Kaw River,[2] he dipped to less than 200 feet to slip under a bank of clouds and angled over the stockyards, turning southwest over the new Union Station site and the tall buildings of Kansas City. His machine, rocking like a boat on choppy water, paralyzed the business of the city, for every worker stopped and gazed Rodgersward as long as he was in sight. On the Kansas side of the city, the shrieking of every packinghouse whistle sent thousands to nearby roofs to scan the skies for the aerial spectacular.

Heretofore, aviators had avoided direct flights over the city because its air was reputedly pocked with holes and because no safe landing was available in the event of a suddenly disabled engine. Cal, too, had been advised to avoid the Kansas City business district. "However," he said, "when I got over the river and saw the city's smoke, I couldn't resist. I didn't intend to go over. I just wanted to see. So I came up over the bluff —then just decided to keep going." He continued circling over the city and the two rivers, thrilling the populace with his daring, at one point banking his planes over 45°. He straightened over Rockhurst College and the Evanston Golf Club and, before 10,000 excited citizens of Kansas City, slewed to a landing at Swope Park at 11:30 A.M.

Near the Swope Park shelter house, an immense white canvas (used in the christening of the balloon *Kansas City II* the previous week) had been spread on the ground. Cal rolled the *Vin Fiz* onto the canvas and switched off his engine. Mounted patrolmen and motorcyclemen proved unable to restrain the crowd, and the aviator was mobbed by spectators who swept aside all barriers. For thirty minutes Cal could not escape the swarm of humanity around him. Finally, after he had lost his cigars to frenzied souvenir hunters (who even plucked the stub from his mouth), he was rescued by a squad of policemen and escorted from the field.

As he entered the shelter house, Cal was grabbed and smothered in a familiar embrace. "Mother!" he gasped, with less astonishment than the event might have warranted.

Mrs. Sweitzer, left to her own thoughts in Chicago, had determined that her son could not and should not continue without her support. Further, she concluded, it would be unseemly for her daughter-in-law to travel as the only woman aboard the Vin Fiz special. She had wired her attorney regarding her further absence, booked train passage from Chicago to Kansas City, registered at the Hotel Baltimore upon her arrival, and, rather than passively await the aviation party, hired a taxi to Swope Park. "I am with you all the way," she exclaimed to her son.

The Vin Fiz train had stopped at Independence, where Mabel, John Rodgers, Stewart deKrafft, and virtually the entire contingent except for railway officials boarded a special streetcar for Swope Park. They had observed Cal's steep bank over the city, and Charley Taylor scolded him: "A man has about three times to do that stunt, and then they lay him away in a box."

After a joyous reunion with his wife (momentarily transfixed by the sight of Mrs. Sweitzer) and colleagues, and handshakes with Mayor Crewdson and George Meyers, president of the Kansas City Aero Club, Cal was tugged into Meyers's Peerless automobile for an excursion through the streets of Kansas City. Thousands of people shouted, applauded, waved hats, handkerchiefs, and newspapers, and screamed their acclamation of the aviator perched on the auto's rear ledge. At one point on Minnesota Avenue, Cal asked that the automobile be stopped so that he could run into a tobacco shop and replace the cigars lost at Swope Park. He lit one in public view and drew a prolonged round of applause for the act.

At three o'clock Cal was deposited back at Swope Park. Remaining spectators milling about the field were surprised when he signaled that he wished to relocate the flying machine to Overland Park, the site selected to begin his next lap on the transcontinental journey. The decision also surprised deKrafft, who had scheduled an exhibition at Swope Park for the following morning. Cal donned a heavy sweater and a coat and drove the airplane down a runway cleared for him by policemen. He flew westward along the Strang Electric Line at a height of 200 feet, cutting occasional wide loops in his flight path. Below, W. B. Strang,* president of the line, sat beside Mabel in the rear seat of the Palmer-Singer and directed the way to Overland Park. He was trailed by a motorcar train of forty automobiles packed with Kansas City dignitaries. Mrs. Sweitzer rode in the second car.

Some 300 persons, the entire suburban population of Overland Park Station, were on hand as Cal landed. They were soon joined by the caravan from Swope Park. For more than an hour, the crowd clustered about the machine and hampered efforts to attend it. When police arrived to open its path, the *Vin Fiz* was pushed to a hangar at the aviation field; one of the three airplanes stationed there was displaced to accommodate the famous craft.

It was past sunset before the Vin Fiz party checked in at the Hotel Baltimore. After supper at the Kansas City Club, deKrafft decided that the Swope Park exhibition would be canceled and that Cal, instead, would perform a series of aerial maneuvers from Overland Park at three o'clock Thursday afternoon. The coast-to-coast journey, consequently, would not be resumed until Friday, October 13.

Cal protested: "There are only six days left before the time limit expires. I can't afford to waste even a minute." DeKrafft pointed out that the aviator needed a rest and the flying machine an overhaul. Cal was adamant: "Absolutely not!"

Cal retired early to his hotel room and left his companions to fend off reporters, laymen, and would-be emulators. To all who asked, Mabel praised her husband and admitted that she encouraged his hazardous

---

*As representative of the Overland Park Athletic Club, Strang had been responsible for arranging the first flight seen in Kansas City—an exhibition by Charles K. Hamilton in 1909, at Overland Park (founded by Strang in 1904).

undertaking. Mrs. Sweitzer confessed that she was filled with fear lest her six-foot-four-inch "boy" meet the fate of so many followers of his game. Joe Newborn and Lawrence Peters opined that Rodgers might yet complete the cross-country trip within thirty days. They admitted, however, that doubt had largely eroded their hopes. Newborn added that "Rodgers won't stop in any event. He said he is going to the Pacific Coast, and he means it."

Count Von Mourick De Beaufort appeared at the hotel for a farewell gesture before returning to his desk at the *Chicago American*. He kissed Mabel and presented her with a bouquet of long-stemmed roses. A second bouquet was addressed to Mrs. Sweitzer. Mabel accepted the gift for her mother-in-law (who was in attendance at her son's bedside) and, promptly upon the count's departure, dropped it into the nearest trashbin.

Thursday morning was consumed in answering congratulatory letters and telephone calls. Then, with Mabel, deKrafft, and Lawrence Armour, Cal took luncheon at the University Club. The club president commented on the appropriateness of his presence on Columbus Day and compared the aviator with the Italian navigator in their common courage and accomplishments. A second speaker likened him to Saint George, and William Randolph Hearst to the dragon. He was, as those present knew, the only competitor with a chance for the Hearst prize. Earle Ovington had risen from Governors Island on Tuesday, the final day of eligibility, but had crashed within seconds; details were unavailable. Bob Fowler had been conducting trial flights about the Los Angeles area and expected to leave on his cross-country attempt next Sunday, five days beyond the deadline. Were Cal to reach the Pacific Coast by the seventeenth, he was assured, Kansas City would demand that Hearst pay the $50,000.

Other speakers related the history of Kansas City—its beginnings as a departure point for early explorations of the West (such as that of Lewis and Clark) and its founding as Wyandotte in 1843 by Wyandotte Indians from Ohio. One speechmaker recalled in detail his experiences during the great flood of "aught-three," when twelve of the thirteen bridges over the Kaw River were swept away by raging waters. Lawrence Armour presented the history of Armour & Company's meat-packing plant that had been built in Kansas City exactly forty years earlier. Cal managed a catnap during most of the speeches.

The afternoon's exhibition at Overland Park began with ruffled feelings. A disappointed and irritated throng was left to kick its heels for ninety minutes after the billed three o'clock start. The ground underfoot was soggy from rain, and the Strang cars to the field were overpacked.

"The advertised service of one car every fifteen minutes from the state line was a joke," the *Star* complained. When Cal arrived, the event swiftly got under way. His mechanicians prepared the airplane, and within a few minutes he was circling the field. His flight was a remarkably clever one. He dipped, turned at steep angles, "rode the ocean wave," and made sudden shoots downward. A dog at one end of the field ran out and barked at the machine, and the aviator amused the crowd by flying above the animal several times. He remained aloft fifteen minutes.

Before he left the field, Cal was introduced to William Eisengart, an elderly blind man who had been taken to Overland Park to "see" the machine that could perform like a bird. Mr. Eisengart listened to the motor and the chain drives of the *Vin Fiz* as it maneuvered overhead. Later, he was encouraged to touch its fabric and structure. "Will it help me to see?" he inquired. His startled companion explained that it was not that kind of a machine. "Well, then," said Mr. Eisengart, "What good is it?"

Throughout the day deKrafft, Taylor, and others close to the airman forbore from the mention of a takeoff time. To their surprise, Cal did not raise the subject. His only comment—to a solitary reporter from the *Kansas City Star*—was "If the weather remains favorable, I will make short work of the remainder of the ocean-to-ocean flight." DeKrafft intervened before the reporter could pose specific questions.

Thursday night found most of the aviation group at the Orpheum Theatre, invited without charge by manager Martin Lehman to view film of the ascent from Sheepshead Bay. Cal and Mabel had attended nickelodeons in New York, but Mrs. Sweitzer was innocent of such experience. Picture shows (or "galloping tintypes," as they were called by legitimate artists), she maintained, were disdained by people of taste and breeding. Nevertheless, she was pleased at recognizing her son and herself on the screen.

Before attending the Orpheum Theatre, Mrs. Sweitzer had dined with her brother-in-law Robert Rodgers at the Hotel Montague. A successful attorney such as himself, Mrs. Sweitzer supposed, surely had occasion to encounter numerous young ladies of high character. Perhaps he could advance the name of one such who could—far better than Mabel—match Calbraith's standing. Mr. Rodgers demurred. He had no wish to interfere in his nephew's affairs. "Is the boy not fully occupied in planning his flight?" he asked Mrs. Sweitzer.

A conference among Cal, Stewart deKrafft, and Vin Fiz and Armour & Company officials had weighed alternative routes westward. Larger bonuses and more county-fair exhibitions were tendered in Colorado and Utah, but the mountainous terrain in that direction seemed forbidding.* A path southward through the Mississippi Valley and then westward along the Rio Grande Valley held greater promise of safe passage. Accordingly, arrangements between the Armour Company and the MK&T Railroad were initiated. Takeoff was reaffirmed for the morning of Friday the thirteenth.

Lawrence Armour personally negotiated the contracts with railroad representatives and issued a statement to the press that Armour & Company would stand by its commitments regardless of deadlines for the Hearst prize. To deKrafft he reiterated his pledge but suggested that if Rodgers and his entourage should wish to abandon the enterprise, Armour & Company would accede to that wish with understanding. In either event, he insisted, it was impossible for the company to continue its payment of $5 per mile. Between Kansas City and the West Coast, Lawrence Armour lectured, the population consisted largely of jackrabbits —and jackrabbits were not likely to prove paying customers for the Vin Fiz drink. After discussions of some fervor (wherein deKrafft threatened legal action), a compromise figure of $4 per mile was accepted. Lawrence Armour returned to Chicago, and Ed Merritt replaced him aboard the special train.

The third car of that train, the day coach, was uncoupled and returned to the C&A. Its occupants had dwindled in number to less than six—one reporter and the photographer from the *New York American* plus an average of three or four correspondents from other midwestern newspapers traveling limited distances with the expedition. DeKrafft was notified that the Vin Fiz Company could no longer justify the expense of the coach car. Those few journalists still interested in accompanying Mr. Rodgers would be accommodated in the private Pullman.

Some in the Vin Fiz crew were opposed to a takeoff on Friday the thirteenth. Cal maintained that he should not defer to superstition and that to stay the flight for such reason would constitute tacit admission that he had despaired of reaching the coast by the seventeenth. Further, thousands were expecting his arrival in Vinita and Muskogee, and he should not disappoint his admirers. Charley Taylor advised against the

*DeKrafft recalled to the others that a year before (Oct. 1, 1910) J. C. ("Bud") Mars had essayed a flight across the main range of the Rocky Mountains (near Helena, Mont.) and had smashed his machine against a mountainside. (Mars was trying for a prize posted by John Ringling, the circus entrepreneur.)

fantasy of finishing the passage in five days and favored the delay as an opportunity to complete a thorough overhaul of the machine. Cal would listen to no further talk of delay. "I'm ready. Get the machine ready," he commanded, and disappeared into his hotel room.

Mrs. Sweitzer swept across the hotel lobby ("She seems to float two inches off the ground," commented the *Star* reporter). "I'll speak with him," she volunteered, and swept after her son. Thirty minutes later she descended to the lobby and addressed waiting reporters. "The influence of a mother's love," she proclaimed, "can move mountains. Calbraith has consented to defer his departure until Saturday morning at eight o'clock."

"Of course I am going along on the special train," Mrs. Sweitzer said in response to a question. "Young man, would you leave your mother behind when your future is at stake?"

It was on Friday the thirteenth that Charley Taylor received a telegram stating that his wife (removed to California when he transferred from the Wright Company) had been hospitalized in critical condition in Los Angeles's Good Samaritan Hospital. His presence was required to attend her and to care for their two adolescent children and infant daughter. At first Taylor planned to leave immediately for the Coast. With second thoughts he decided to accompany the aviation party as far as San Antonio, since little time would be lost thereby over a direct train route to Los Angeles.

Owing to conflicting reports regarding the takeoff site, 200 persons gathered at Overland Park Saturday morning, while nearly 1,000 appeared at Swope Park under the impression that the flight would be renewed from that point. Cal arrived at Overland Park at 11:40 A.M. and squandered no time on preliminaries. He was accompanied by Mabel and his mechanicians. Mabel helped him into his leather clothing while the mechanicians afforded the airplane a fleeting inspection. Fifteen minutes after he reached the field, Cal was seated in the *Vin Fiz Flyer*, a cigar stub between his teeth. "Now, keep her on an even keel," Charley Taylor carped at him. Cal nodded and gave the sign to spin the propellers. The great blades cut the air with a whir. The machine trembled. "Let her go, boys," he called out. To himself he murmured, "Come on, Betsy—we're halfway home." The *Vin Fiz* bounced over the turf and took the air to a sky tinted with a pale yellow haze.

To set himself right with the crowd at Swope Park, Cal flew back to the east, through the slippery, wallowy air over Kansas City, and performed a few stunts for those assembled at that field. Twenty-three minutes after takeoff, he again flew across Overland Park, where his official start was registered at 12:18. Less than a score of persons had remained to watch as the *Vin Fiz* disappeared into a bank of cream-colored clouds on the horizon, heading toward its next scheduled stop at Parsons, Kansas, 136 miles to the south.

In the three days since the expedition reached Kansas City, a substantial decline was apparent in the size and enthusiasm of the crowds that attended the transcontinental aviator. Reasons advanced for this circumstance included the passing of the Hearst deadline, the protracted duration of the flight, and the general fickleness of the public. "People are like Sancho Panza," deKrafft philosophized. "They see only windmills and can't understand the man who sees wicked giants." Mabel could see neither; she denied that the demonstrators had turned lukewarm ("Her postcard perspective," muttered deKrafft in private). Cal was too practical to accept comparison to Don Quixote. "It's not cheers and big crowds that keep the machine going," he shrugged. "It's oil and gasoline—and the driver."

After the airplane had lifted from Overland Park, Mabel, Charley Taylor, Frank Shaffer, and Charlie Wiggin boarded a Strang Electric Car. Its conductor applied full throttle, and the car raced forward, sparks of electricity flashing from its pantograph. At the Lenexa MK&T depot, Mabel and the three mechanicians sprang off the trolley and onto the special train that would carry the aviation party across Kansas, Oklahoma, and into the great state of Texas.

8

Katy All the Way

THE FIRST RAILS to enter Texas from the north were those of the Missouri, Kansas & Texas Railroad Company. Known from its inception in 1870 as the "Katy,"* it became one of the most influential factors in the development of the great Southwest. Its first years were plagued by the remnants of Quantrill's guerrillas, renegade bands of Creeks, Chocktaws, Cherokees, and Chickasaws, and battles with rival railroads. There followed a period of organized train robberies. Nevertheless, it proved an immediate bonanza for its backers: August Belmont,† J. Pierpont Morgan, Levi P. Morton, John D. Rockefeller, Levi Parsons, and George Denison. By 1889, through acquisitions and building, the line extended north to Kansas City, and by 1903 its southern terminal lay in the mission city of San Antonio. With its track to Houston and Galveston, the company realized its visionary goal of through rail service from Junction City, Kansas City, and St. Louis to

*Its stock exchange symbol was "K-T."
†August Belmont (the first) married Caroline Perry, Calbraith Perry Rodgers's great aunt, the daughter of Commodore Matthew Calbraith Perry.

the Gulf. MK&T directors jubilantly proclaimed, "Katy all the way."

From Lenexa, the two-car Vin Fiz special idled southward, those on board peering back for evidence of the flying machine. Just south of Olathe, the airplane, bucking an 18-mph headwind, sailed directly over the train. Weather conditions aloft, except for the brisk wind, were ideal, and Cal droned over the monotonous terrain without untoward incident. At Paola, white strips of muslin enabled him to distinguish the Katy track from those of the Frisco and of the Missouri-Pacific, both of which also ran southward from the town.

> Oct. 14, Saturday, Paola, Parker, Kinkaid. Landed Moran 2:10 P.M. Great hunger.

Rural telephones notified farmers from miles around of the unexpected arrival of a cross-country flying machine. People appeared on horseback, in motorcars and buggies, and on foot. Women, some carrying babies, rushed from their Saturday housework to the Alfred Johnson cow pasture, where the airplane had alighted. The editor of the *Moran Herald* approached the aviator but was rebuffed. "Rodgers is a man of great physical strength and endurance, large-boned and a giant in height," wrote the editor, "but without humor or imagination. He is abrupt in speech and inclined to be shy when interviewed. In fact, he has a way of quickly dismissing the interviewer. He holds himself aloof, as if his real life were carried on in some private, interior sphere."

The Vin Fiz train arrived thirty minutes behind its pacesetter. Mechanicians and crewmen appeared with their red, green, and gray containers* and ministered to the machine. Mabel stoked the aviator with two sandwiches and a quart of milk.

Mrs. Sweitzer held to the confines of her compartment. Regaining her place aboard the Pullman had obliged a reshuffling of sleeping assignments, and chewing tobacco and cuspidors had been whisked from view lest her intimidating eye be provoked by such abominations. At Moran she busied herself unpacking the suitcase of clothes, reading material, and other articles mailed by her daughter to Chicago.

At 3:13 Cal again put to the air, heading south to Parsons. Advance man Lawrence Peters had remained in Parsons all of Wednesday, inspecting the grounds for Cal's scheduled Thursday landing. He chose a field on the edge of Calvary Cemetery, and it was duly marked with white

---

*A red container was used for gasoline, green for oil, and gray for water.

canvas. Approach of the birdman was to be signaled by switch engines in the Katy yards, by factory whistles and fire bells.

Thursday both telephones in the *Parsons Sun* office rang continually through the day with inquiries as to aviator C. P. Rodgers's whereabouts. Friday anticipation mounted; the subject of the transcontinental flight monopolized virtually every conversation.

Saturday 10,000 persons—of the population of 18,000—assembled at the state asylum grounds on North Twenty-sixth Street adjoining the cemetery and patiently awaited the great event. Many had arrived at ten o'clock in the morning. Others waited on rooftops, fire escapes, and water towers. Even the faro and keno joints were bereft of customers. At 4:15 P.M. the *Vin Fiz* flew directly over Parsons, not deigning to circle; not a leaflet fluttered to earth to acknowledge that the town was anything more than a whistle-stop on its path.

When the special train paused for water at the Parsons depot, members of the expedition indicated their surprise that the birdman had ignored the scheduled landing. DeKrafft told the *Sun* reporter that "Rodgers is the most bullheaded man I have ever known. No one can do anything with him." Train conductor J. J. Koch, a resident of Parsons, also voiced his complaint that Rodgers, "a dad-blamed ornery cuss," would leave the railroad right-of-way and cut across the track curves—so that even doing sixty on the straight stretches, the train could not pace him.

"So far as Parsons is concerned," editorialized the next issue of the *Sun*, "Cal P. Rodgers is a frost. He is the whole frigid zone. If he ever flies over Parsons again, he will have to take protection of the game laws protecting song birds."

Not everyone in Parsons was disillusioned. A short distance from the crowd at the asylum grounds, bundled in an overcoat to shield himself from the chill Kansas autumn, thirteen-year-old Tubal Claude Ryan stared in awe at the skyborne wonder that passed over his head at 700 feet. A delivery boy for the *Parsons Sun*, Ryan promised himself that he would one day learn the makings of such a machine.[1]

South of Parsons, over a cornfield near Bartlett, Cal spied a message spelled out with white rocks in a clearing on the field. It read, "God Bless You, Cal." The farmer who had so painstakingly arrayed the rocks stood to one side waving his arms. Cal rocked his planes at the man and waved back.

The *Vin Fiz Flyer* crossed the Oklahoma state line at 5:22 P.M. Almost immediately its engine began sputtering, and Cal was forced to descend, touching the ground four minutes later at Russell Creek, a switch-track hamlet of six homes. With the airplane hammered head-on by 20-mph headwinds, the special train had gained the lead and was already at a standstill only yards from the landing point (albeit separated by several rows of six-foot-tall cornstalks). Charley Taylor replaced a balky spark plug, directed refueling of the machine, and performed minor adjustments to the engine, while Cal downed a glass of milk and consumed half a cigar. The machine took the air after seventeen minutes, the briefest interruption yet logged.

News of Rodgers's coming was flashed to the office of the *Vinita Chieftain* by the Katy telegrapher at Parsons ("Keep a sharp eye out," read the wire. "He may fly over without looking down"). The various steam plants of the city were notified, and their whistles sent 10,000 persons rushing pell-mell to the College Heights Addition to witness the landing. For an hour and a half, the crowd scanned the northern skies for a glimpse of the predicted biplane. A telephoned report that the birdman was downed at Russell Creek circulated swiftly, and, with twilight dwindling, the disappointed group dispersed. Those reaching town, however, learned that the aviator had resumed his flight and was passing Welch toward Blue Jacket. Another stampede for the marked landing place ensued. The sun had settled behind a bank of clouds on the horizon, hastening the dusk. At 6:30 only a dim speck could be described by the most keen-eyed, but everyone at the field heard the clatter of the *Vin Fiz* engine, and a great shout rent the air.

Cal had been flying at an altitude of 100 feet for thirty minutes in semidarkness. Not one of the onlookers dreamed of lighting a signal fire, and the aviator swooped down to scarcely twenty feet over their heads peering at the shadowy outlines of the field. Circling once to his right, he bounced onto the ground adjoining the Willie Halsell College for the first airplane landing in Vinita.

As soon as the machine stopped, Cal jumped from the seat and turned his back to the crowd that surged toward him. His face a starched shroud, eyes frozen and withdrawn, he refused even to acknowledge questions, lit a cigar, and looked about for members of his party. When they were not soon forthcoming, he accepted a carriage ride to the Katy station, where he waited, still uncommunicative, for the special train. When it arrived several minutes later, he boarded the Pullman and vanished into the seclusion of his stateroom. "These people must think there are roads in the sky," he muttered. Stewart deKrafft appeared on the Pullman-car steps to announce that the birdman was indisposed and that the transcontinental flight would resume the next morning, Sunday, at seven o'clock.

Within an hour Cal's curdled temper had loosened. He was officially welcomed by J. C. Starr, the part-Cherokee attorney who served as mayor of Vinita. Mayor Starr delivered a brief history of the city, the largest hay-shipping center in the Territories, named for Vinita Ream.* Cal, Mabel, Mrs. Sweitzer, deKrafft, and John Rodgers repaired to the Cobb Hotel for supper and an overnight rest.

Cal and Mabel were lodged in one room; Mrs. Sweitzer occupied another. Her three-day absence from the expedition had somehow blunted her claim to her son's company.

A Tulsa newspaper delivered to the hotel told of the opening game of the World Series, won by the Giants 2–1 over the Athletics. Before a crowd of 38,000 patrons, Christy Mathewson had triumphed over "Chief" Albert Bender, a Chippewa Indian with a large following in Oklahoma. Giants manager Tug McGraw had ordered for his team the black uniforms worn in the 1905 series, also against the Philadelphias, which New York had won, four games to one. "A superstitious lot, these baseball players," said deKrafft. "Well, it worked," said Cal.

Political news raised little interest in the Vin Fiz party, although columns reporting the activities of Cal P. Rodgers and other aviators were read avidly. President Taft, after receiving the first warm reception of his tour from Utah Mormons led by Reed Smoot, had traveled through Idaho and on to the Pacific Coast, where sentiment for his renomination remained cool. In the war between Italy and Turkey, an Italian expeditionary force had landed at Tripoli to accept the Turkish capitulation there. William Randolph Hearst, in his Columbus Day speech, had toasted Italians as the agents chosen to drive the "Unspeakable Turk" out of Europe. Italy threatened an aerial bombardment of the Turkish camps (an item John Rodgers noted to Cal) and assembled eleven airplanes and two dirigibles for shipment to Tripoli.

Earle Ovington, after his fiascos at Nassau Boulevard and Governors Island, conceded defeat in his attempt to launch a transcontinental flight. The previous Tuesday he had kissed his wife goodbye (she had strapped a sack of sandwiches and a Thermos of soup to a brace) and begun his takeoff run. His engine died before he could quit the ground. Several times he again kissed his wife and ignited the machine into motion, each time with the same result. On the final trial he took the air and rose to twenty feet; the engine again failed him, and his machine dropped to earth

*The renowned American sculptress commissioned by Congress to create a statue of President Lincoln.

tail-first. The frame of the Queen monoplane was crushed, its propeller broken, and its right wings smashed. He was shaken but uninjured; his good-luck mascot, a French gendarme doll, "Treize," tied to a longeron, survived intact. Said Ovie philosophically, "Well, I've done all I can to make this combination fly. But the Lord never meant it to stay in the air, and far be it from me to dispute the matter any longer."

The remaining contender, Bob Fowler—so his manager, C. Fred Grundy, announced—would depart from Los Angeles on Sunday, the fifteenth, in his second start of the great coast-to-coast race.

Wilbur Wright, in an interview in New York City, discussed the "secret" trials that he and his brothers, Orville and Lorin, were conducting at Kitty Hawk, North Carolina. "Anybody who has seen the buzzard fly," he said, "knows that there is a method by which man may sustain himself in the air once he gets there. What a bird can do, a man can do, as Darius Green said. . . . There seems to be a great curiosity about whether we expect to use a motor or not. Well, at the start we don't expect to use one. The problem is to find out whether once we are in the air we can stay there for an indefinite period. . . . It may take years for man to fly like the birds fly, but there isn't the slightest doubt in the world that ultimately he will achieve it."

Sunday morning in Vinita dawned on puffy winds with velocities up to 40 mph. Better to delay another day, it was decided, than to risk the neck of the aviator and the possible destruction of the *Vin Fiz* in such a stiff blow. Charley Taylor seized the time to tinker with the machine. His concern centered on the roller bearings in the drive chains—they had shown an inclination to overheat, vibrate violently, and eventually break. A local "fix-it man," Charlie Schneider, advised the mechanicians to mix a quantity of oil into their graphite lubrication. Taylor subsequently confirmed the benefits of Schneider's advice.

In the afternoon, a band of full-blooded Cherokees traveled in from the hills to inspect the big white bird. Attired for the occasion in their regalia of buckskin and feathered bonnets, their faces daubed in bright colors, the Indians surrounded the Pullman car—a tableau caught for an instant in the frame of an earlier time. "Them's Indians!" screeched one of the Georges, leading those on board to fear for their scalps. Chief Buffington, distinguished as the band's leader by his Prince Albert coat and derby hat, found Mabel in her stateroom and flashed his filed canines at her: "I have come to present this token of friendship to the squaw of the human bird, Mr. Rodgers."

"Oh, you speak English" was all that Mabel could extemporize.

"Yes, ma'am," said the chief. "I go to college. I speak good English." He looped a beaded necklace over her head and proclaimed that she would henceforth be known among the Cherokees as "White Wings." He then bowed low, kissed her hand with a flourish that would have shamed Count De Beaufort, and left the train in search of her husband.

Mabel recovered her composure and attempted to market her postcards and "aerial mail" among the chief's tribesmen. "Send an aerial message for your sister White Wings," she urged. The Indians stared at her without expression.

Engaging Cal in laconic conversation, Chief Buffington asked if an Indian might learn to drive such a complex machine—several of his braves had demonstrated the ability to direct an automobile (the Cherokees had recently purchased a Thomas Flyer). Cal assured him that if an Indian could pitch in the World Series, an Indian could fly an airplane.

One Indian and a cowboy had raced forty miles into town for the spectacle. The puncher offered to bet Cal $100 that the aviator couldn't ride his horse. Cal protested that the *Vin Fiz* bucked enough to suit him, and he did not wish to break the pony's back.

Not until 5:00 P.M. did the wind abate. Cal was driven in the Palmer-Singer to the field where the *Vin Fiz* stood beneath its canvas tarpaulin. A quick hop to Pryor, thirty-six miles to the south, seemed feasible. However, flashes of lightning and a towering black cloud rapidly swept in to discourage any notion of flight. The *Vin Fiz* was sheltered in the courtyard of the college buildings* (four stories of brick and stone) and there staked down. At 6:30 heavy rain began falling and soaked the area for three hours. Cal announced his start for daybreak, weather permitting; a fast time would be made for Forth Worth with one or two stops en route.

Oct. 16, Monday. Clear air, gentle southwest breeze, cold temperatures. 2,000 people at College grounds. Take-off Vinita 7:55 a.m.

This is good flying country—fairly level, although there are some places with odd patches which caused me to fly higher so as to plan for a landing. Passing a field with four or five cows in it, I noticed that even they began to stare at me. It seemed funny, for it is usually hard to attract a cow's attention with anything.

*The Willie Halsell College was known for the two-year attendance of one of its students, Will Rogers, currently on tour through the Midwest with his roping and "joshing" act.

Over Muskogee, sixty-five miles south of Vinita, Cal looked down on a scene of apparent confusion and panic. Earlier that morning Fire Chief John Templeton had explained to School Superintendent E. S. Monroe that he had arranged to switch on the fire whistle at the moment C. P. Rodgers was sighted. "That's a bully time to have a fire drill," thought Mr. Monroe, and kept the information to himself. Thus, when the whistle blew, the school's fire alarm was sounded. Students at the high school rushed from the building, then milled about, searching for smoke and flames. They were soon joined by three hose companies, two steamers, and a fire truck. Moments later the crowd saw the flying machine and learned that Cal P. Rodgers was the cause of the alarm.

The *Vin Fiz* touched down at the Muskogee Fairgrounds at 9:14 A.M. —precisely on the spot where aviators Beckwith Havens and Leonard Bonney had held forth during the Great Muskogee Fair of the previous week. First to greet the cross-country flier as he stepped from his seat was Tams Bixby, president of the fair. Cal was stiff with cold, and he massaged his numb fingers before shaking hands.

"What city is this?" he asked.

"Muskogee," Mr. Bixby replied.

"I wish it was Los Angeles," said Cal.

In less than thirty minutes the EX biplane was refueled and prepared for takeoff. Then the engine misfired immediately upon ignition. Charley Taylor found two broken plugs and water in the magneto. Two hours of repair work were conferred on the machine while Cal nervously paced about, puffing his cigars. He would break his single-day record, he had promised the crew, reaching Fort Worth by nightfall. Taylor indicated his preference for an engine overhaul before hazarding further flight. Cal overruled him.

Reporters from the *Phoenix* and the *Times-Democrat* addressed the skittish aviator, posing the usual requests for explanations. Cal stared at them with the steel-edged, tempered-in-history look that gave them pause: "An aeroplane can't be explained in terms of structure and horsepower or of lift and drag forces. An aeroplane has a soul—as demanding as that of its driver. It is a soul that gives itself to a man like a woman in love gives herself. That's why I keep flying. Not for money or fame." The reporters inscribed the names of their newspapers on the plane fabric and turned to their subject's wife and mother. "Calbraith is going to take the Pacific Coast," said Mabel, beaming as she talked of her husband's achievements, "but I never tell him, 'Be careful.' He's got enough to worry about without worrying about my worry." Mrs. Sweitzer's view was less ebullient: "These winds here are terrible. If they keep up, I am not going to let him fly at all. I am going to make him give up his flight."

Mayor D. H. Middleton pulled the birdman into an automobile, drove him on a short tour of the city, and introduced him to other prominent citizens, including nineteen-year-old Miss Katherine Hull, who two days earlier had become the first woman in Oklahoma to be taken aloft (courtesy of Leonard Bonney). Muskogee, now grown to some 26,000 souls (largely owing to nearby oil developments), had been a typical frontier town where, for its first few years, "the graveyard held more customers than the saloons."

"You should have been here in the rough old days," puffed the mayor, "when the Dalton boys rode through on one of their train holdups. Why, I was out at Coffeeville in '92 when the Daltons were undone. Why, we still have an occasional stickup along the Katy."

> Oct. 16. Take-off Muskogee 11:26 A.M. over Taylor's objections. Puffy winds quartering at 25 mph. Forced to fly at 3,000 feet over woods and low hills.

Seventy miles along, still short of McAlester, the *Vin Fiz* engine coughed, labored, and exuded spurts of steam. Cal dropped abruptly into the only field available to him—a fenced-in meadow of the King Dairy. He was observed by but one person: ten-year-old Clarence Sittel, who had been working in the barnyard of his parents' farm in Northtown and looked up to see the airplane just clear the height of Mount Moriah to the north and then dip from view. Young Sittel threw a hackamore on the family's bay mare, grabbed a quirt, and rode out to the landing spot. Forging over a rise, he saw the machine squatting in the meadow, a tall, peculiarly garbed figure standing beside it. Clarence asked if the man was hurt.

"Nope," said Cal. "How far is it to the railroad?"

" 'Bout a mile, mile and a half, I reckon," said Clarence.

Cal explained that he had a special train following him. "I've got to get over and stop it. Can you take me there?"

"Get on," Sittel offered.

Cal straddled the horse behind the young man and they trotted west to the Katy track. Within two minutes they heard a whistle from the north as the Vin Fiz train blustered around a curve. They flagged it down, and Cal apprised his mechanicians of the predicament. Since no automobile could negotiate the rough terrain and fenced pastures, Cal again mounted the rear of Sittel's bay mare and asked to be carried back to the airplane. The horse was followed on foot by an entourage of nine crew members and mechanicians plus deKrafft and John Rodgers. Examination of the engine disclosed that water had leaked into the firing chamber and mixed with oil in the well. The water was siphoned out and it was deemed that Cal should chance the few miles to McAlester, where the motor could be repaired more conveniently.

After the *Vin Fiz* had lifted from the Northtown meadow, Charlie Wiggin, mimicking "my pal, Cal," climbed on the horse behind Clarence Sittel, and the procession trudged back to the waiting train. "It was," reflected Sittel, "the first bareback taxi service in Pittsburg County."

A thousand people were awaiting the transcontinental flier at McAlester's baseball park, where a game was in progress. But as Cal flew over the town, his engine exhaling puffs of vapor, he picked out a level area closer to the railroad track and more accessible to his mechanicians. He landed, accordingly, in Sans Souci Park at the McAlester Fairgrounds.

It soon was determined that a cracked cylinder was to blame for the trouble. Charley Taylor opined that before the cylinder could be rebuilt, the sky would be too dark for further flying. The day's travel totaled a disappointing 127 miles.

Cal, Mabel, Mrs. Sweitzer, and John Rodgers took lunch at the McFarland Hotel, where they booked rooms for the night. Cal was then invited to the ball park to greet the people who had been deprived of the spectacle of an airplane landing. Although repairs had just begun on the *Vin Fiz*, Cal interrupted his mechanicians and flew to the McAlester baseball diamond, where the machine was displayed for the patient crowd.

Charley Taylor followed in the Palmer-Singer, its rear seat laden with tools and spare parts. After further examination, he decided to change engines again and shooed Cal away for a rest. Taylor himself needed a rest. Exhausted by the continual demands of the engine, he stretched out on a bench by the grandstand. Charlie Wiggin, passing by, decided that such an opportunity to remove Taylor's moustache might never again arise. He approached stealthily and with a pair of shears attempted to clip the moustache. Taylor stirred, and the shears gashed the tip of his nose; it bled furiously. Taylor chased Wiggin around the field but was unable to overtake the lubricious seventeen-year-old. When Cal returned, Taylor insisted that Wiggin be dismissed from the aviation party.

Cal grabbed Wiggin, called the crew together, and demanded an apology. Wiggin refused. "Kid, apologize—or you're out," said Cal, twisting Wiggin's ear. The Kid squirmed—more from the lash of Cal's tongue than the punishment to his ear—and then surrendered without much grace, mumbling, "I'm sorry."

"He's still uncooked," Cal told Taylor. "He needs another hour in the oven. But that's it. The kid stays."

A wire at the dispatcher's station imparted the news that the Philadelphia Athletics had evened the World Series contest with a 3–1 win over the Giants on the strength of Frank Baker's homer in the sixth inning. "A bad day all around," Cal grumbled to his cousin. John Rodgers only offered to increase their wager on the series.

John was afforded another reason for elation. At Kansas City he had requested a two-week extension of his leave from naval service, and a telegram to McAlester conveyed his superiors' endorsement of that request. He would, he vowed to Cal, be waiting at the water's edge when the *Vin Fiz* crossed the Pacific shore.

Tuesday morning the *Vin Fiz* machine was judged to be in fine shape by Charley Taylor, Cal was judged to be in fine fettle by Mable, and the weather was judged to be in fine condition by all. With no reason for delay, the birdman, rigged out in top boots, goggles, and cap, tanned by the winds of more than 2,000 miles, took the air at 7:30 A.M. He circled the Union depot at low altitude and quickened his speed to the south as virtually the entire population of McAlester waved him on his journey. The special train, now pulled by Engine No. 354, the "best hog on the Katy," was delayed twenty minutes awaiting the Palmer-Singer's dash from the ball park and up the ramp into the hangar car.

On board the Pullman for the leg to Denison was Mr. Jasper Allen, the eminent editor and publisher of the *Hartshorne* [Oklahoma] *Sun.* Mabel promptly charmed him into purchasing a Vin Fiz stamp, her first such sale. The sheets of Vin Fiz stamps sent by Robert Rodgers from Kansas City had arrived the night before at the McFarland Hotel. Twenty-five cents entitled the purchaser to an oversize label, an uninspired drawing of the Model EX in an oval frame.[2] A letter or card with the stamp affixed would be carried on the succeeding leg of the transcontinental passage and then (with conventional postage) deposited in the U.S. mail system. The recipient would, Mabel pointed out, retain the privately issued stamp as a souvenir and as proof that the letter had indeed been delivered through the air.*

---

*Allen placed his stamp on a postcard addressed to his wife in Hartshorne. The card was flown from Fort Worth to Dallas and canceled Oct. 19, 7:30 P.M. A second card and Vin Fiz stamp was purchased by Allen and delivered to his mother in Hartshorne.

Thirty days had passed since the send-off from Sheepshead Bay. Forfeiture of the $50,000 purse dangled tantalizingly by William Randolph Hearst was now a *fait accompli,* regardless of interpretation of the rules. Almost to the thirtieth day, Mabel and Wiggin—more than others on the train, more than Cal himself—had borne the pretense that the prize could yet be gained. "We're not doing this for the money" was now the consensual rationale to any black sheep insensitive enough to broach the subject.

Cal assumed an attitude of nonchalance: "The thirty-day limit is not important. This is not a race against time. It's not against a competitor. This is a demonstration that man is not held down by the dead hand of the past."

"Somehow, when the prize was gone, a second wind blew up," wrote Jasper Allen. "The crowds grew bigger, and the cheers louder. There was something about the tall, cigar-smoking man struggling against gravity, bad luck, vagaries of weather, and critical mechanical failures that presented a time-piercing vision."

More often than before, those on the special train noted, signal towers along the track were chalked with the appeal "Help that man Rodgers fly across America."

Still, aside from Mabel, most passengers in the private varnish found it difficult to shake the air of pessimism that hung over them—a realization of the true size of the dragon their knight-errant had agreed to dispatch. Mrs. Sweitzer rarely left her stateroom and seemed strangely indifferent to her son's activities. Stewart deKrafft directed operations and business matters with mechanical mien. The "second wind" did not easily penetrate the Pullman walls.

Oct. 17, Tuesday. Kiowa, Chockie, Tushka. Engine misfire; landed Durant 9:07 A.M.

I had never before seen a cotton field. From the air it looked so beautiful that when my engine began misfiring, I ventured to alight in it. I was fortunate in escaping without damage to my machine.

Scores of people rushed to the downed airplane, two miles south of the Durant depot. Cal was in good humor, spoke freely with those who addressed him, and invited spectators to write their names on the fabric of his machine. He adjusted the engine himself in twenty minutes and, just as the special train was passing Durant, again took the air to his next scheduled stop—just south of the state line at Denison, Texas.

Across the Red River, Cal flew over tracts of fertile black-wax land ("It needs only a tickle with a plow to sprout a bountiful harvest") and over business and residential areas. He drifted from the north-south (short) branch of the Katy and alighted in an open pasture in Pottsboro, seven miles to the west of Denison, at 9:30.

Thousands had lined the main track into Denison to await the bird-man's coming. Fred Sisson, an employee in the Katy shop, climbed to the roof of his building, as did most of his fellow workers. When foremen couldn't persuade the men to descend, they, too, climbed up to witness the passage of the *Vin Fiz.* A strip of white canvas three feet wide marked the track through Sugarbottom; Sisson and his colleagues were therefore surprised to observe the airplane angling westward over the Katy reservoir and in the direction of Pottsboro.

From the crowd that soon ran onto the pasture where he landed, Cal learned of his location. J. Frank Bennett, president of the Citizen's Bank, had, with his fifteen-year-old daughter, Beulah Belle, driven up in his red 1909 Buick Overland. Cal asked if Bennett would take him to the train depot in Denison, and the banker was pleased to oblige.

At the depot, deKrafft was particularly unsettled to find that Cal had disappeared. Fenwick Auto Sales had offered to furnish free oil and gasoline for the landing at Denison. Joe Fenwick confronted deKrafft to threaten withdrawal of the offer unless there was more to the Vin Fiz enterprise than immediately met the eye. Fenwick also wished to view the coffin carried on the train "just in case." DeKrafft informed him that there was no coffin. Fenwick was skeptical; he had heard of it from good authority.

Further compounding deKrafft's anxiety was an agreement just concluded with officials of the Dallas State Fair for a Rodgers aerial exhibition; failure to begin the exhibition by 2:00 P.M. Wednesday would forfeit a $500 guaranty. When Cal, in banker Bennett's auto, arrived at the train siding, Fenwick demanded that the flying machine be produced for a performance over Denison. DeKrafft demanded, in return, sufficient inducements to warrant annulment of the Dallas contract. Fenwick thereupon refused to dispense his gasoline, with or without remuneration.

Fuel supplies in the hangar car had been reduced to little more than ten gallons, and Bennett confirmed that it would be difficult if not impossible to locate that amount in Pottsboro—his was one of only six or seven automobiles in the town. Two five-gallon containers of gasoline were loaded into the Buick, and Cal was driven back to the Pottsboro pasture. He accepted a handful of cigars from Mr. Bennett, autographed a slip of paper for Beulah Belle, found two volunteers to help strain the gasoline into the tank, and, with the assistance of two young ladies recruited to turn the propellers, effected a lift-off toward Fort Worth.

At 11:30 A.M. the Vin Fiz special quit the Denison depot westward for Whitesboro and thence southward along the Texas & Pacific line to Denton and Fort Worth. A half-mile below the Whitesboro junction, the train was slowed and then brought to a standstill as it was realized that the airplane was either delayed, downed, or astray. Katy dispatchers were alerted to halt nearby rail traffic and to inquire at adjoining stations regarding the whereabouts of the *Vin Fiz Flyer.*

After rising from the Pottsboro pasture shortly before noon, Cal had quickly picked up the Katy track. At Whitesboro, white canvas markers had been duly laid along the T&P turnoff, and the special remained within view of that point. Unaccountably—and subsequent discussion failed to solve the mystery—Cal missed the train and the canvas strips, while observers on the train missed the airplane.

It was not missed, however, by the inhabitants of Whitesboro, virtually all of whom gathered at the depot and cheered as the *Vin Fiz* flew by along the Katy long branch toward Wichita Falls. News of Cal's mischance was relayed to the Vin Fiz train by the Whitesboro telegrapher. A message to flag down the aviator was transmitted to the Gainesville station, fourteen miles to the west. With only moments to react, the Gainesville agent quickly mustered his several waiting passengers to the tracks by the depot. They waved frantically to the aviator passing overhead at 500 feet. He waved back.

Word was flashed to Bonita, twenty-eight miles farther west. Telegrapher Duane Masterson, following instructions, assembled a pile of straw and lit a bonfire just as the *Vin Fiz* sailed by. His wife, Felicity, viewed this signaling effort with little confidence. She dashed into the yard of the Masterson home, pulled down the bedsheets hanging from the clothesline, and spread them out in the form of an "X" by the railroad track. She stood on the sheets and waved her arms. Cal turned his machine and took the ground alongside the Bonita depot. Apprised of his location, he nodded and walked back to the airplane without an outward trace of emotion.

Cal had learned earlier a method for starting the EX without assistance. Since both propellers were coupled to the same drive shaft, pulling on the one would turn the other. (This procedure, however, placed a strenuous load on the already troublesome drive-chain mechanism and was to be reserved for strict emergencies.) To restrain the airplane with the engine running, a rope (stowed behind the radiator for just such purpose) was tied to a tree or fencepost from the tail structure and then released via a slipknot. Cal, in no mood to court favors, was thus able to ignite the machine, rise from Bonita, and head back to the east.

At Gainesville, the three Sapp children—Rudolph, Queenie, and Aubrey—were celebrating younger brother Aubrey's fourteenth birthday. At 12:30 next-door neighbor Mrs. Will Bradley shouted excitedly, "Look out, look out, an airplane is going over!" The children rushed out for a glimpse of the first flying machine to pass over Gainesville. Believing they had seen the last of it, they drove their horse and carriage to the hardware store for needed supplies. Two hours after its passage came word that the machine had returned to Gainesville and was landing on a lot near the Santa Fe roundhouse.

In the general excitement, several horses panicked and bolted along the street, their rigs caroming into storefronts and hitching posts. By the time the Sapps scrambled to the landing site, dozens of buggies, wagons, and horses encircled the intruder as if to ward off Indian attack. The sheriff and his deputies were vainly struggling to hold back the crowd, and Cal was tugging at rambunctious youngsters climbing spars and crawling over the lower plane. The Gainesville High School had been dismissed, and virtually every student contrived to autograph the fabric of the flying machine.

After thirty minutes of tumult, a deputy was dispatched to locate a stock of gasoline. Ten gallons were discovered at a nearby farmhouse, but the owner demanded a premium price—$2 for his supply. Cal could root out from his pockets only $1.22. The farmer proved unable or unwilling to grasp the concept of billing the Vin Fiz expedition, as Cal suggested. Six gallons were negotiated (at 20¢ per gallon plus a 2¢ bounty) and strained into the fuel tank. "It was more like coal oil than gasoline," said Cal. He resolved to depart Gainesville through his own efforts and rudely disdained offers of assistance. The restraining rope having been abandoned to a tree in Bonita, he wedged a clump of wood beneath each skid forward of the wheels. However, when he pulled down on a propeller and the engine ignited, the machine lurched over the chocks and snaked across the field. Cal chased after it as the gathering watched from a distance. Some cheered for the airplane, a few for the aviator pursuing it. Cal caught it by the tail, swung it into the wind, and raced around to the driver's seat. He stepped on the spark-advance treadle and escaped into the air. "A bunch of animals," he described the Gainesville citizenry.

Flying east to Whitesboro, Cal was carried along on a favorable breeze.

This time the canvas strips and white-topped train stood out prominently in his vision. He picked up the Elm Fork of the Trinity River and covered the sixty miles south to Fort Worth in one hour without mishap. Crossing the packinghouse district, he dipped down, threaded a line between two water towers on the military reservation (measurement showed a forty-two-foot space between them), and tilted toward his designated landing site at the Ryan Addition, southwest of the business district.

Since October 12, five days earlier, when the *Star-Telegram* printed a front-page headline that "Daredevil Cal" Rodgers had placed Fort Worth on his itinerary, excitement over the airman's coming had built to a volcanic pitch. Before the Vin Fiz train pulled from Denison, the *Star-Telegram* correspondent on board had wired an alert, and over 8,000 of Fort Worth's 75,000 citizens streamed out to the Ryan pasture.

For more than four hours they waited in vain, scanning the northern sky. At 4:15 P.M. the *Vin Fiz* was spotted, and factory whistles took up the cry in deafening extravagance. Patrolmen and a squad of mounted police were unable to restrain the impatient throng, and men and boys swarmed over the pasture, racing along beneath the airplane, flinging caps and hats into the air. To negotiate a landing, Cal feigned a descent at one edge of the field. As the entire crowd flocked to his alignment, he swerved to the opposite side of the field, and plopped heavily onto the ground.

Begrimed and perspiring, Cal stumbled stiffly from the the operator's seat and stretched his cramped muscles. First official greeters to shake his hand were Amon Carter,[3]* publisher of the *Star-Telegram,* and J. M. North, Jr.,† editor of that newspaper. In response to their questions concerning his delay, Cal would only comment, "It was a mite cold up there today."

By railroad mileage, the expedition had now passed the 2,000-mile mark; distance traversed through the air, it was estimated, measured 2,685 miles. The day's flight had covered more than 315 miles in advancing 225 from McAlester.

Cal's bent of mind was not smoothed out by a squabble with deKrafft and others about the missed connection at Whitesboro. Both Mabel and Mrs. Sweitzer fussed over him, lamenting his haggard condition. He had,

---

*Carter was responsible for staging Fort Worth's only aerial exhibition to date—that of the "International Aviators" (Garros, Frisbee, Audemars, and René Simon), Jan. 12 and 13, 1911. Since this group and its mechanicians toured by train, Cal Rodgers was first to fly into Fort Worth.

†North received from Cal the first piece of aerial mail delivered to Fort Worth, a letter from McAlester, Okla.

as a scale in the hangar car confirmed, lost fifteen pounds in the month since departing Sheepshead Bay. John Rodgers mollified him somewhat by emphasizing that the end of the journey could now be scheduled with accuracy. A telegram was dispatched to George B. Harrison of the Aero Club of California, forecasting arrival in Los Angeles November 1. Harrison, in turn, promised a hearty welcome promoted by his group. It was decided that John Rodgers would leave the aviation party for Los Angeles to conclude arrangements in that city and would then rejoin the expedition in New Mexico or Arizona for the final laps.

Lieutenant Rodgers also voiced his confidence that he would, at that time, collect his wager with Cal regarding the outcome of the World Series. The Philadelphias had just won the third game of the series 3–2 in eleven innings over the Giants at the Polo Grounds and now enjoyed the home-field advantage for the fourth game. Third baseman J. Franklin Baker again acquitted himself as the A's hero, tying the game with a homer in the ninth.

In Los Angeles, it was announced that Bob Fowler would lift off at 10:30 the next morning toward the East Coast, his first stop scheduled for Pasadena. He would be accompanied by a special baggage car carrying full aeronautical equipment and spare parts under the charge of Ralph Newcombe, his head mechanician. His planned route lay along the Southern Pacific track to El Paso and the Rock Island line to Kansas City, from where it would probably cleave to the course that Cal Rodgers had pioneered. Presumably, over the deserts of New Mexico or Arizona, one of the greatest events in aviation history would take place when the two transcontinental airmen would cross paths.

Fowler was preceded out of Los Angeles by President Taft (who refused all comment on the LaFollette boom and also shrugged off the alleged plot to dynamite the El Capitan Bridge at Santa Barbara as the train bearing him and his party passed over it en route to Los Angeles). Stewart deKrafft, who had initially hypothesized for reporters a "race" between Taft and Cal Rodgers, now predicted that Cal would win the "revised race" —reaching Los Angeles before the presidential train returned to Washington.

DeKrafft was handed a telegraphed message stating that the aeroplanist was responsible for a shooting in Pottsboro. After C. P. Rodgers had departed that morning, the message read, a husband and wife had engaged in a vociferous argument over which direction the *Vin Fiz* was taking. The argument ended when the wife fired a shot into her husband's chest. DeKrafft suggested that the incident deserved no further publicity.

Cal and Mabel were driven over Fort Worth's vitrified-brick streets to the Westbrook Hotel, where a supper sponsored by the Southwest Aeronautical Association awaited them. The *Vin Fiz* crew remained at the field to tune the flying machine for the hop to Dallas the next day.

The agenda for the 1911 Texas State Fair at Dallas ran from October 14 to October 29. Every industry and every product of the Lone Star State were on display. A range of political speakers was invited, beginning with Champ Clark and ending October 28 with New Jersey governor Woodrow Wilson. Daily aerial performances by aviator J. A. D. McCurdy in an airplane of his own design were scheduled (weather permitting), and after protracted negotiations, the fair management announced the appearance of the most celebrated birdman in America, the transcontinental flier, that most daring and redoubtable pathfinder of the air, Calbraith Perry Rodgers.

At 12:15 P.M. Wednesday, after two ineffectual efforts to rise into a stiff southwest breeze, Cal gained the air for the thirty miles from Fort Worth to Dallas. Just east of Forth Worth, at 500 feet, a full-grown eagle appeared off his right wing tips.

> *It looked larger than the biplane I was driving. I am not well versed in the ways of eagles, but this one evidently thought I was another bird invading his territory and started towards me, coming up. There was danger that he would attack the planes, which might mean instant death, and of course I was a bit trembly. On he came, as swiftly as the machine was going toward him, and all at once I saw him swerve and dart downward. In another minute he was lost to sight. I figured that he had caught sight of the rapidly whirling propeller blades and couldn't figure out what kind of an attack this strange bird might make on him. Fortunately, the big bird was frightened by the bigger "bird."*

Cal sailed on by Oak Cliff and its surrounding cotton fields, over the Dallas Courthouse, the tall Adolphus Hotel building, the jumble of flat roofs and narrow streets, and, after a low pass by the grandstand as thousands of spectators raised a mighty cheer, spiraled onto the oval enclosure of the Dallas Fairgrounds racetrack. He was welcomed to the state fair by the crashing strains of music from the Thurber Band (a group of professional miners). After a circuit of the racetrack in a Duryea motor wagon (featured by the fair's management as an "old-time auto"), Cal was driven to the Southland Hotel. His record-breaking flying machine was rolled into a shed near the steel grandstand to rest on its journey from the

Atlantic Coast and gather strength, as it were, for the final laps to the Pacific Ocean. Visitors to the state fair were invited to view the amazing Wright EX biplane, and over 1,000 accepted the invitation.

The entire aviation party, except for the chef and the two Negro stewards, George and George, was escorted to the Southland Hotel for the pleasures of a warm bath.

An announcement in the *Dallas Times-Herald* welcomed the populace to inspect both the hangar car and the magnificent private varnish car. Hundreds of people lined up at the Katy depot to board the train and stare curiously at the array of aircraft components and at the dismembered "B," its planes stacked in sections against a wall of the hangar car. Most lingered in the private varnish, agog at its plush paneling and opulent appointments. Rarely seen by the public, such cars were the ultimate hallmark of financial success, the mansions on rails of legendary barons of industry: J. Pierpont Morgan, Harry Payne Whitney, the Vanderbilts, the Rockefellers. They were beyond even the dreams of the common man.

To reporters at the Southland Hotel, Cal declared that the "hoodoo" that had dogged his flight earlier had been shaken for the final time. He would take off promptly at noon Thursday and fly into San Antonio before darkness overtook him. The 190 miles to Austin, he vowed, would be put behind him in 190 minutes. What was his most fearful experience to-date? "Without doubt," said Cal, "it was flying through an electrical storm between Kent and Akron.* I feared the lightning would strike the wires of the machine and I would be lit up like one of Mr. Edison's glow bulbs." Reporters described the famous birdman as "ruddy of face, big of bone, prognathous of jaw, a man who speaks tersely and with a peculiar reticent manner."

For a rare occasion Cal and his mechanicians arrived at the takeoff point in advance of their forecast departure time. They found, to their annoyance, that two ribs had been broken on a lower warping plane by one or more of the inquisitive visitors who had probed the machine for its secrets. Ninety minutes of repair work were required to mend the damage. Cal rose from the racetrack oval at 1:50 P.M. to an accompanying salute of three guns fired by Battery A of the Dallas Artillery. For fifteen minutes he drove the *Vin Fiz* through the series of aerial maneuvers contracted for with the State Fair Committee. Promptly at 2:05 P.M. he worked the machine to 1,000 feet and, without coursing over the Dallas business district (as the press had been advised), flew directly south from

*Cal's memory was faulty; the storm was between Bobo and Huntington.

the fairgrounds to pick up the long strips of white canvas placed along the Katy rails by order of W. G. Crush, general passenger agent of the Katy. The Vin Fiz train followed closely behind.

Oct. 19, Thursday. Starrett, Waxahachie, Hillsboro. Landed Waco 4:10 P.M. 85 miles in 125 minutes.

Lookouts on the roof of Waco's twenty-two-story Amicable Building ("Texas's tallest") could command an unobstructed view of the Katy road across the Brazos River. They saw the airplane first over Paul Quinn College, then watched it wing across Elm Street and over the river. The big siren whistle sounded. The city's thirty-foot star-spangled banner was hoisted up the Amicable's flagpole as Cal swung over the skyscraper in a great loop around the business district at 800 feet and descended into Gurley Park.

Some forty automobiles and as many buggies brought 200 people to the park, which had been tendered free of charge by its proprietor, Davis Gurley. (Attendance was depressed by a rumor that an admission charge was to be levied.) Half a dozen times someone had cried out, "Here he comes," mistaking a real air fowl for the birdman. As the machine took the ground—precisely on the bedsheet laid out to mark the field's center—people ran alongside, pulling on the planes and then overwhelming the aviator with outbursts of enthusiasm. Thirty minutes passed before officials of the Young Men's Business League could secure a police cordon about the airplane and protection for its driver. Cal refused to leave the park until his mechanicians and crew arrived from the special train (delayed at Hillsboro by rail traffic). He shook hands with every spectator, answered a hundred witless questions, and posed for pictures by the eminent photographer F. A. Gildersleeve (who had lugged in his black Graflex camera, tripod, glass plates, and flashpowder tray) and a score of amateur shutterbugs with their Kodaks. Meanwhile the crowd grew from 200 to 500 persons, and a solid line of automobiles stretched from town to the park, the length of South Third Street.

"I rode the north wind into Waco," said Cal to a journalist from the *Times-Herald*. "I could look far back and see the engine of my special train pouring out smoke. It was going lickety-split, but it was no match for my flying machine. . . . It's a shame people have to walk when they could fly." Someone in the crowd yelled out, "If the good Lord wanted me to fly, he would have grown wings on my shoulders." The crowd laughed, and Cal smiled thinly, having heard the remark innumerable

times over. ("If God had meant man to fly," deKrafft remarked in mim-
icry, "He'd have made us with hollow bones—as hollow as the heads of
the bumpkins who talk like that.")

"Clad in a dark suit with a large cap set backward on his head, wearing
a leather vest, big gauntlets with the daintiest of ladies' watches worked
on the back of one wrist, and leggings, with grease, perspiration, and dust
on his face, he could hardly have passed for the hero in an aviation novel,"
so the silver-penned reporter described the birdman for his readers. "But
when he got in several minutes work with his handkerchief and water,
turned the cap right, removed his vest and lighted a cigar, he began to
look like the gentleman in books who would fly across a hundred miles
to see his lady love and elope with her by the light of the silvery moon."

After Cal was escorted to the Metropole Hotel, where he was greeted
by Mabel and Mrs. Sweitzer, the crowd at Gurley Park continued to peer
and poke at the flying curiosity. "Lookee at the bicycle wheels"—"I'm
gonna build me one" were exclamations heard again and again. "You see,
it works this way," explained half a hundred encyclopedias of the male
persuasion to as many seemingly ignorant creatures of the opposite sex.
The rubberized-duck fabric, once white and again smudged with the
inscriptions of previous witnesses, was darkened further with another
hundred signatures.

In view of the ardent reception and sincere hospitality on the part of
Waco citizens, at the insistence of the Young Men's Business League,
because it was already past sunset, and because the YMBL pledged a $250
bonus for an exhibition flight, the expedition remained overnight in
Waco.

Supper for principals of the Vin Fiz party was hosted at the Huaco
Club by S. M. McAshen and Dr. A. F. Sonntag of the YMBL. In response
to Cal's inquiry, McAshen informed him that the fourth game of the
World Series had again been postponed, owing to inclement weather in
Philadelphia. Bob Fowler's takeoff from Los Angeles, Cal was told, had
also suffered another delay—a shift of wind during a trial flight had tipped
over his *Cole Flyer*, breaking a skid and an upright and tearing the fabric.

As guests and members of the Huaco Club were beginning their meal,
word arrived that Eugene Ely had been killed that afternoon in Macon,
Georgia. With 10,000 persons looking on at the Georgia State Fair, the
aviator had maneuvered a spectacular earthward dip of great velocity. He
was unable to level his direction, and his machine shattered against the
ground, sending wood and metal fragments flying hundreds of feet. He
made a desperate leap to quit the airplane before it struck, but was caught

under the framework and mangled. He died eleven minutes after the fall, regaining consciousness just before the end to mutter, "I lost control. I know I'm going to die." His body was shipped to Mrs. Ely in Davenport, Iowa.

A gruesome feature of the tragedy was the scramble by spectators to obtain souvenirs. Constables were overwhelmed by the crowd, and in a few minutes every piece of the wreckage had been carried away. Ely's cap and tie disappeared. The collar was stripped from his neck.

Cal was shaken by the news. He had become friendly with Ely and his wife at the Chicago meet and had received letters of encouragement from the flier. From Ely's landing on the *Pennsylvania* sprang the tree of events that begat Cal's affiance with flying and his transcontinental venture. "That's what gets them all, if they stay at it long enough," he told McAshen. "That's why I'd like to get out of it—before it gets me. Just missed jumping clear? Well, inches will do it sometimes."

After supper, to bolster Cal's spirits, McAshen and his colleagues staged for their guest a traditional entertainment for a stranger to the Lone Star State: a badger fight. At the St. Charles Hotel, where the fight was held, Cal examined the badger ("a ferocious-looking animal") and the bulldog ("a fine animal—it's unfortunate the badger should have a chance to injure him") and declined to participate in the wagering. Reluctantly ("I really don't cotton to it"), Cal was induced to "pull the badger" (release it from its cage). He watched the gory combat without emotion and immediately afterward declared that he was exhausted and retired for the night.

Mrs. Sweitzer was waiting for her son at the Hotel Metropole, but he had no appetite for further discussion of Eugene Ely's death and excused himself firmly.

Mabel was under escort about town by the wives of Waco businessmen and a reporter from the *Waco Tribune.* "Do you ever get frightened at seeing your husband so high in the air?" she was asked for probably the hundredth time.

"Why, flying is so easy—I have made short flights with Calbraith, and the sensation was delightful. . . . It is like motoring real fast except that it is so much smoother. The only drawback to aeroplaning is that you can't talk for the noise of the motor."

"Eugene Ely's crack-up obviously affected Mr. Rodgers. Is there any chance he will quit the flight?"

"No, no. We are both very sad about Mr. Ely. And we are sending a telegram of sympathy to his wife. But that sort of accident couldn't happen to Calbraith."

Plans for an early-morning takeoff were postponed when Jimmy Dunn, driving the Palmer-Singer auto, collided with another vehicle on Bosque Boulevard. Matters of responsibility were not settled until eleven o'clock. The damaged auto was loaded into the hangar car to be repaired en route by the aircraft mechanicians. Mabel, during the morning hours, attempted to market her postcards and "aerial mail." Whether her salesmanship was unpersuasive or the stamp too expensive, few sales were consummated. However, Mabel was not disheartened; she hovered close by when W. H. Hoffman, the Waco postmaster, swore in her husband as an official United States postman and tied a small mailbag onto the airplane for delivery in Austin.

Cal, still unsettled by the news of Ely's fatal crash, turned the extra hours to purpose and inspected the *Vin Fiz* machine with meticulous care. He discovered elevator- and rudder-control wires worn so thin that they could not have been expected to outlast the day's flight.

Measured lengths were clipped from the two-foot-high spool of piano wire in the hangar car and secured between the lever controls and the rear plane surfaces. At 11:05 A.M. Cal prepared to rise from Gurley Park for San Antonio, with a scheduled stop at Austin, 100 miles distant. As the propellers were spun, deKrafft ran up with a telegram from the city council of Granger, fifty-eight miles to the south. A sum of $100 had been raised for a landing and ten-minute demonstration in that town. Cal nodded, lit his cigar, and called out, "Let her go, boys."

> Oct. 20, Friday. Take-off Waco. Temple (two circles and dropped leaflets). Landed Granger 12:20 o'clock on downhill slope of Granger School playground. Side-slipped and cracked skid. Shook hands with Mayor Sheffield and took off. Circled for ten minutes (at $10 per minute). A 37-mile sky jaunt to Austin in 40 minutes. Landed Ridgetop Annex 1:55 P.M.

A small provincial capital of 25,000 people, Austin lay astride the Colorado River, almost at the edge of a 250-mile plateau of prairie blacklands. The pride of its architecture was the gigantic pink dome of the State Capitol Building, modeled on, but even larger than, the great dome in Washington, D.C. From the air, it stood out from the dun-brown plains and hills of the Texas hill country, attracting Cal's eye moments after the *Vin Fiz* had risen from Granger.

Promoters of Austin's new suburban Addition had hung a $200 purse to associate their project with the transcontinental flight. A thousand persons had turned out for the celebrated birdman's appearance, although the site was a mile from the Hyde Park Station of the Austin electric streetcar line. Cal was welcomed by Will T. Caswell, president of the land-development firm, who lauded the aviator's accomplishments to the crowd. His attention straying, Cal noticed a bird circling overhead.

"What a lovely, beautiful bird," he remarked. "Is it a hawk or a falcon?"

"It's a buzzard," someone rejoined.

Conversations in the crowd were equally edifying. "How does the thing turn?" asked one sweet young lass. Her escort explained that one of the propellers was made to revolve faster than the other. A man whose enormous girth marked his weight well in excess of 300 pounds waddled up to the lanky aviator and asked, "How can that gimcrack contraption fly with a man of your size?"

Cal and his managers were escorted into downtown Austin for lunch at the Driskill. Lawrence Peters explained to reporters that "a keen competition exists as to which city on the Pacific Coast will have the honor of receiving Cal Rodgers at the end of his epic, history-making journey. One has offered $15,000, and another has gone it better and offered $20,000. You may be able to guess which will scoop the stakes."

Cal ascended from the Ridgetop Annex at 3:29. He looped over the suburban area to gain height, so as not to be subject to the air currents swirling above the Austin business district, then worked straight for the 111-foot dome of the State Capitol Building (where, it was reported, Governor Colquitt toasted the flier with hard liquor). Wrote one observer, "With spectacular dips and glides, he danced a quadrille with the 21-foot lady who holds the sword and five-pointed star atop the dome and chassied her back and forth three times." Thousands in the streets and on the Capitol grounds saw him depart, with a light wave of his hand, across the Colorado River, southward to San Antonio.

Below Austin, a moody, light-stitched sky thickened quickly; clouds lowered and formed bruise-blue underbellies. A slight drizzle spat at the aviator, but with steady winds and open, rolling prairie encompassing his field of view to the horizon, he felt no concern. Twenty miles en route, at an altitude of 1,500 feet, a sharp explosion jolted the *Vin Fiz*. The ensuing jarring clatter bespoke a broken piston. The engine thrashed on its mount, pounding at the ribs and spars of the planes. The explosion assaulted man as well as machine, shattering Cal's confidence and command and leaving him with nerves exposed. He yanked at the compression-release cable. The airplane immediately dropped, and the aviator pushed forward the elevator control to orient the machine at a steep angle, lest it stall. Though the heavy concussions stopped, the racket of the chain drives prolonged its memory in his ears; through it, he could hear the humming of the bracing wires.

Sluggish controls demanded that the driver replace the engine's power with his own. He shoved forward the warping lever; the aero responded reluctantly and banked to the left in a steeply descending spiral. Warped to the right—lever pulled back—it straightened its path, then volplaned down in dizzying undulations. Cal clung desperately to the sky, feeling it slip from his grasp. He watched the ground rush up relentlessly as the *Vin Fiz* skimmed over a cedar brake, sliced across rows of cornstalks, and slammed with a crunching impact onto a patch of shrubs.

Damage to the airplane was moderate. The aeroplanist fell from his seat, seemingly on the verge of collapse. Those who reached him first described him as "ghastly pale and trembling from fright."

Within minutes most of the 500 inhabitants of the village of Kyle dashed out to the Whisenant farm, where the flying contraption had been observed to descend. They were able to probe and examine the "wounded bird" at their pleasure. Its driver was oblivious to his property. In a daze, he accepted a tumbler of water from Will Groos, a farmer who lived nearby, and awaited the coming of the Palmer-Singer.

The Vin Fiz train was alerted to the accident by a signal from the Kyle station agent; it was quickly shunted onto a nearby siding, and crewmen hurried out to retrieve the fallen birdman. Mabel and Mrs. Sweitzer were shocked by Cal's appearance—palsied, his skin ashen, his features creased with weariness, the verve drained from his body. Mabel massaged his face with Vaseline Jelly. Together the two women undressed him, forced a glass of warm milk down his throat, and tucked him under an extra layer of blankets. Cal passed the remainder of the afternoon and the evening curled up in his stateroom berth (inadequate to his full six feet four inches). He was disinclined toward food or drink, and his steak was auctioned off by chef Ed Davis. Mrs. Sweitzer patrolled the aisle to ensure that he would not be disturbed.

Through the night Taylor, Shaffer, and Wiggin labored with the flying machine, replacing pistons and other broken parts. The subject of Cal's affliction was not discussed by his mechanicians, but it was apparent to them that the aviator was as much in need of mending as was his airplane.

The Negro stewards again faced the task of cleaning Cal's rain-drenched, mud-caked business suit. This time the suit was gingerly dunked into the bucket of petroleum naphtha, and George-1 exercised the plunger with exaggerated caution.

Saturday morning found Cal improved but pallid, his hands still trembling at intervals. His sense of mortality, suppressed since his first meeting with a flying machine four and a half months before, now seeped to the surface and lay upon his countenance for all to see. Belatedly, he inquired if the bottle of Vin Fiz had survived the rough landing. Assured that not a drop of the soda drink had spilled, he nodded indifferently.

The drizzle of Friday had intensified to a full Texas norther sweeping down off the Great Plains, and Cal seemed relieved at the excuse to remain grounded: "I don't know which is wearing out faster, me or the machine." When correspondents in the Pullman asked if he would start for San Antonio that day, he snapped, "There is a driving rain, a high wind, and the temperature is dropping rapidly, all of which makes a flight extremely uncomfortable if not downright unsafe. Now, what do you want me to do?"

Mrs. Sweitzer lambasted the reporters: "Do let him be! He has a plate full of problems. It is you people who keep pushing him, pushing him. Because of you, he keeps on when he should stop. You will be the death of him!"

DeKrafft denied emphatically that the cross-country aviator had shown signs of losing his nerve after falling from a great height. "Rodgers did not fall," deKrafft averred, "but volplaned to earth. The transcontinental journey will resume as soon as weather conditions permit."

Cal turned back for a baleful glance and the final word: "If I falter, it will be through accident or mechanical imperfection, not through decline of purpose or desire." With that, he encased himself in his cylinder of silence and disappeared into his stateroom.

The airplane passed the day under a tarpaulin on the Whisenant farm. Its engine, removed to the hangar car, stoutly resisted repair (fractured pistons, twisted shaft, etc.); the mechanicians reluctantly installed the spare engine. Cal moped through the morning, hunkered up on a passenger seat, staring out the window. In midafternoon he climbed into the hangar car to deliver some sharp words to his crew. Those on the train had come to believe in a man with limitless resolve, unflinching in the face of every setback. They were taken aback by that man now out-of-sorts, morose, apparently possessed by prickly-skinned hobgoblins. No one spoke to him or looked at him directly. "There is a worm in his apple," said Charley Taylor, "and he will have to work it out."

A contagion of melancholy infected most of the aviation contingent. Few mustered the energy to explore the town or socialize with its citizens. Mrs. Sweitzer wrote letters, read through the books sent to her by her daughter (Edna Ferber's *Dawn O'Hara,* Gene Stratton-Porter's *Harvester,* and, her favorite, Margaret Deland's *The Iron Woman*), and pressed Mabel into an unsatisfying game of cribbage. Lawrence Peters left for San Marcos and San Antonio to attempt to raise further cash bonuses now desperately needed for spare parts.

San Antonio newspapers, delivered to Kyle by train, carried the latest intelligence from the Fowler camp. The West-to-East flier had finally escaped Los Angeles Thursday, but immediately found himself enveloped in a heavy fog. After losing his bearings and spiraling about well into the twilight hour, he descended at Tournament Park in Pasadena. He was saved from a certain crash and probable death by his intrepid mother, Mrs. Frances Fowler, who, while others in the waiting crowd stood by doltishly, grabbed a lantern, ran to the center of the polo field, and waved it back and forth as a landing beacon. Mrs. Fowler announced that henceforth she would accompany her son on the private train throughout his journey across the continent. "See, see, see," said Mrs. Sweitzer, "what a mother can do."

Friday, as Fowler was preparing for takeoff from Pasadena to Banning, he was diverted to a telephone call from manager C. Fred Grundy, who ordered the aviator to remain in Los Angeles until Sunday and depart thence from Venice. Fowler returned to the clubhouse in a rage, telling reporters that he had broken relations with Grundy. "I refuse to make myself into a hippodrome. . . . I won't return to Los Angeles after the good start I have made, and there is nothing that can make me do it. I am off for the cross-country jaunt or I stop right here."

"Maybe Fowler can make a race of it, after all," said Cal. "That would add some interest for both of us."

In Damon Runyon's column, Cal read of the scandal brewing over distribution of gate receipts from the first and third games of the World Series (those played at the Polo Grounds). Another postponement of the fourth game was ordered by the baseball commission on account of wet grounds at Shibe Park.

Several members of the Kyle town council visited the Vin Fiz train and invited everyone on board to Martin's Saloon. Cal glumly informed them that he never touched alcoholic spirits. Ed Merritt advised that they switch their drinking allegiance to Vin Fiz grape juice. A group of young men (unaffiliated with the town council) offered Cal an automobile ride to La Grange for a "blowout" at the infamous Chicken Ranch.[4] "It ain't eggs that get laid there," cackled one youth with a leering grin. Cal declined.

Three boys found the courage to approach the human skyscraper to ask how a heavier-than-air machine could fly with nothing to hold it up. "The air isn't a nothing," Cal told them. "It has substance and mass and, when it is stiffened by speed, it pushes and pulls and has the power to lift great weight."

Saturday night, the end of the fifth week of the journey, the special train again provided housing (cramped) and meals (mostly ham and beans) for its occupants. The correspondents on board proposed a scheme to hurl chef Ed Davis from the train as it crossed the next high bridge.

Whether from Davis's tedious cuisine, from the forced landing and subsequent delay in the hinterlands, or from five weeks of effort without fulfillment, a sense of frustration hung over the Vin Fiz party. Three young, unmarried men—Jimmy Dunn, Charlie Wiggin, and Leo McNally—were particularly restless. Mention of the Chicken Ranch stirred them to action.[4]

At 9:30 P.M., as a heavy stillness settled over all sections of the train, the trio, straining to muffle their sounds, slowly slid back the doors of the hangar car and eased out the rails of the loading ramp. The Palmer-Singer was maneuvered into its exit position (on a platform extended out the opposite door) and rolled onto the train yard. It was pushed for a hundred yards, whence Jimmy Dunn cranked the motor and sped over the seventy-seven miles to La Grange.

Seven hours later the Palmer-Singer sailed back into Kyle, its occupants "three sheets to the wind." Two additional passengers had been acquired: a pair of painted ladies from the Chicken Ranch. With Jimmy Dunn at the wheel, and with Charlie Wiggin and Leo McNally each draped over a *poule,* five voices shrieked in revelry. "There it is!" shouted Charlie Wiggin. "There's the greatest train, the greatest flying machine, and the greatest little ol' flying man in the whole little ol' world—my pal, Cal." He was loudly shushed by the other two men.

Wiggie, McNally, and the two ladies staggered from the automobile, shushing each other in unison. Jimmy Dunn squared up the Palmer-Singer with the hangar car, drove it up the skidways, into the boxcar—and across the extended platform through the opposite door, plopping the auto onto the main track of the Katy.

Crewmen in the hangar car were jolted from their sleep. In the Pullman, the commotion apparently went unnoticed; no official called out or came to investigate.

"C'mon," said Wiggie to his lady, ignoring the crash. "You've got to meet my pal, Cal." He tugged her up the steps of the Pullman and pounded on the forward stateroom. Cal, barefoot and clad only in nightshirt and tasseled nightcap, slid back the door. "This one's for you," Wiggie announced proudly, pointing to his grinning companion.

"What is it? What's happening?" asked Mabel and, from the adjoining compartment, Mrs. Sweitzer almost simultaneously. Cal assured them that all was well and pushed Wiggie and the *fille de joie* out of the Pullman and along the siding.

By this time every member of the crew was engaged in lifting the Palmer-Singer from the main track up to the floor of the hangar car. Cal groaned at the sight, then lent his own strength to the task, distressing his feet on the graveled roadbed. "Get those two chippies out of here," he barked at Wiggie and McNally, who stood abashed at their hero's lack of appreciation. "What would mother think—or Mabel? . . . Now I want everybody—and I mean everybody!—to cease this tomfoolery." He glowered at each man in turn, then gingerly walked away on his scraped feet.

As soon as Cal disappeared back into the Pullman, everyone in the hangar car gathered around the five besotted sinners, demanding a full accounting of their frolic at the Chicken Ranch. It was by then almost five o'clock of a Sunday morning.

The dawn of Sunday, October 22, conferred on Kyle a sky free of rain, but with stiff winds and a thin cover of clouds. At seven o'clock it was decided that Cal should test the air currents aloft with a short flight. The "B" machine was unloaded and assembled near the depot.

Events of the preceding night evidently had served to dissipate Cal's dour mood. Spectators who soon materialized were asked if any among them would pay $5 for a flight in the Wright "B." There were no takers. "One dollar?" said Cal in exasperation. "Fifty cents? . . . Twenty-five cents!" An eleven-year-old boy stepped forward, holding out a two-bit piece.

Issac Newton ("Newt") Millhollon was lifted onto the passenger seat and instructed to "hold tight." Cal handed the lad his 25¢. "This one is a gift," he said, "a gift of flight—the sky and the wind. You will see your whole town, the fields around it. You will know a different world. Now that is a gift to remember." The "B" took to the air and circled for several minutes over the village of Kyle. For months thereafter young Millhollon was the envy of his classmates, and adults who knew of his deed never ceased in their admiration for his courage.

Charley Taylor demanded yet another hour to tinker with the spare engine now powering the EX. Fidgety, Cal borrowed the Pope-Toledo runabout owned by the mayor (all four wheel spindles on the Palmer-Singer were bent from its belly flop onto the tracks) and drove the ten miles to San Marcos to appraise the landing site selected by Lawrence Peters. He returned to Kyle at ten o'clock.

Early-morning winds had abated, and the aircraft was pronounced in acceptable, though not faultless, condition. The bottle of Vin Fiz, Cal ascertained, was wired in its accustomed place. "Let her go, boys," he called out. The machine rose splendidly from the Whisenant farm, trailing globs of mud from the field made boggy by recent rains.

Wrote Cal in a dispatch to the *New York Times:* *

> *The black loam clung to my wheels and made it hard for me to get up speed. I felt as if I had taken half the field with me on my wheels.*

A freight train blocking the Vin Fiz special had been directed to a siding before Cal mounted the driver's seat. However, an air-hose blowout arrested its movement, and he circled about, awaiting clearance of the track. Twelve minutes of direct flight carried him over the Blanco River, over a heavily wooded area of Spanish oaks, elms, and cedars interspersed with splashes of goldenrod and golden evening primrose, to the edge of the San Marcos River. He banked above the normal school that perched atop College Hill and descended alongside Porter Street on the Armstrong Flat, the west side of San Marcos.

> *I made an altitude of 2,000 feet and found that the air, although very warm below, was almost frigid at that height. Still, it was a good flying day with a wild quartering to beam.*
>
> *Just as I was coming down [at San Marcos], and about 50 feet from the ground, a bunch of negroes ran right under the machine, seemingly without a particle of fear. They acted as though they were impelled to run somewhere, anywhere, just so they could run.*

*Still in a pet over the equivocation of the Hearst deadline, deKrafft, at Cal's urging, had canceled the agreement to dispatch personal bulletins to the *New York American* and signed another with the *Times*.

Many of the town's residents were at church when the noise of the engine was heard. A series of blasts from the Old Mill whistle confirmed the arrival. At the First United Methodist Church, the Reverend Collum H. Booth and Presiding Elder W. H. Biggs were conducting a "love feast." The two pastors looked up to find themselves addressing empty pews. Methodists and Baptists were soon gathered about the first flying machine in Hays County. They were treated to a sermon by Harry Sanger on the nonalcoholic morality and salubrious virtues of the Vin Fiz grape drink.

Eighty-year-old Rebecca Diefendorfer was in the forefront of those deserting church services for a more immediate reward. "It has come. It has come!" screamed Miss Diefendorfer with some fervor as she beheld the flying machine. "It has come to take me to heaven!" She was led away.

"They told me," said Cal, "that I was the first attraction that had come to San Marcos that had ever broken up their regular church attendance. San Marcos is, I believe, a very religious town. I wish religion lent them more courtesy and understanding—when I was ready to start, I was annoyed greatly by people who persisted in standing in my way. It worried me more because it was a small field and very soft soil, and I was forced to start with a leading wind as that was the only practical manner to ʳet out of there." (Charley Taylor was unsympathetic. "How many times do I have to tell you," he yelled, "don't take off with the wind behind you!")

The stop at San Marcos enabled those in the hangar car to separate themselves from the two Chicken Ranch ladies, who, ensconced behind a stack of crated aircraft parts, had entertained mechanicians and crew members in a fashion unexpected and long remembered. Passing the hat had not collected sufficient funds to provide transportation for their return to La Grange. Stewart deKrafft was petitioned for additional moneys. DeKrafft discreetly concluded the transaction. "Maybe we should have kept one of them," he said, "instead of the pussycat. We certainly could use a luckier mascot."

Cal gained the air at 11:45. Just short of the Guadalupe River, eleven miles south of San Marcos, over a stretch of sparse cropland, a skyrocket sizzled across his path, trailing sparks and tendrils of red smoke. Cal looked down along its wake—about thirty-five men, women, and children waved animatedly from the roof of a two-story brick mercantile store. Cal dipped his planes in response.

The mercantile store was owned by Ernst Gruene, who had founded the surrounding town that bore his name after emigrating from Adenstedt, Germany, in 1865. Townspeople, Mexican vaqueros, and ranchers from outlying sections had congregated at the saloon and dance hall—also owned by Ernst Gruene—awaiting with some skepticism the coming of the flying machine. Mr. Gruene invited patrons of his saloon to possess themselves of a supply of ale or bourbon and thence join him on the roof of his store. He then arranged a stepladder to the trapdoor of the roof and braced it against a stack of coffins in the second-floor storage room.

People, many inebriated, filed up the stairs, up the ladder amid the coffins, and through the trapdoor. They found precarious perches on coamings of the high-pitched corrugated-tin roof. Ernst Gruene followed them and hoisted Old Glory up the gablepole. He then unpacked his supply of fireworks and prepared for the launching of his most spectacular skyrocket.

For an hour the group clung to the roof, spirits flowing liberally. Non-believers laid wagers that the alleged airplane was a hoax—it was ridiculous to think that a man could fly in some sort of machine. No bet went uncovered.

A few moments after noon, a cowpoke, waving his bottle of bourbon, whooped, "There he is!" Another cowboy emptied his .45 revolver in the air and triggered a fusillade as others followed his lead. Ernst Gruene signaled for the giant skyrocket to be lit. . . .

Afterward Gruene addressed the crowd: "Boys, listen to me. Today we have seen a wonderful thing, and it's been a glorious day. In our lifetime, we may never again see another flying machine with a man in it. So I'm setting up drinks on the house for everyone."

Across the Guadalupe, the landscape regained its checkered viridescence. At New Braunfels, workers near the Katy depot watched the train and airplane whiz by in partnership, both trailing showers of leaflets.

From above the Cibolo River, at an altitude of 2,500 feet, Cal could discern the outlying buildings of San Antonio. The Polo Grounds of Fort Sam Houston was easily identifiable by the 10,000 persons eagerly hopping up and down at the sight of his machine. He sailed over the army post at a height of 200 feet. At the far end of the Polo Grounds, he turned and lit smoothly on the center of the field.

The Vin Fiz special rode into the Katy terminal. It would be switched onto the Southern Pacific track with a new engineer, conductor, and train crew. Westward ran the SP rails, ending where the sun set, where the course of empire met its destiny, where the greatest welcoming crowd in the history of aviation would no doubt await them: the Pacific edge of the North American continent.

9

Down by the Rio Grande

FORT SAM HOUSTON, a complex of stone barracks, vast parade grounds, and a Quartermaster Depot (known as the "Quadrangle"), was built on 1,000 acres of land donated by the city of San Antonio in the 1870s. It was an army post that might have been designed by Rudyard Kipling and set in the hill country of India. Both infantry and cavalry troops were garrisoned at the post through Indian campaigns and the "splendid little war" with Spain. In February, because of unsettled conditions along the U.S.–Mexican border, President Taft had ordered mobilization of a provisional division under the command of Major General W. H. Carter. Virtually every man in the division joined the crowd of civilians lining the lower post field (the Polo Grounds) to witness the arrival of Calbraith Perry Rodgers, the ocean-to-ocean flier.

They assembled first on Friday, October 20, with Secretary of War Stimson and Major General Wood as special welcoming officials. Several hours passed before word was received that Rodgers had crashed at the village of Kyle. The second gathering began at ten o'clock Sunday morning. Discomfort and suspicions of another disappointment were forgotten when the *Vin Fiz* flying machine touched down on the lower post field at 12:40 P.M.

This field, an open parade ground, extended some 300 yards long and 100 yards wide. At its west end (a short side of the rectangle) stood three houses of white stucco and red tiled roofs (occupied by General Duncan, the post commander, and his two aides) fronted by two dirt tennis courts and a small gazebo from which the review of troops took place. At the east end rose the Quadrangle with its commanding observation tower.

B.B. Hunter, a thirteen-year-old lad with a passionate interest in fliers and flying machines, had taken up a position in the observation tower. As soon as he spied the *Vin Fiz* approaching from the northeast, he raced down the tower steps, across the Quadrangle grounds, and along the south side of the parade-ground rectangle. He sensed instinctively the landing course and ran onto the field toward the airship. Observing that the aviator had noticed him and might fear a collision, he veered parallel to the line of motion. At the instant the airplane stopped rolling, "B.B." was present to doff his cap and murmur, "How do you do, Mr. Rodgers."

Cal ignored the boy, who, hurt and disappointed, was quickly submerged in the wave of people that engulfed the machine.

The military guard assigned to protect the aviator and his machine proved inadequate to restrain the headstrong, boisterous crowd. Cal fended off several youths who pulled at his scarf and jacket. He searched about frantically for deliverance as the *Vin Fiz* was rocked and slewed about. A group of mounted cavalrymen rode into the melee to reinforce the foot soldiers. Under the direction of a corporal, who ordered his men to "cut off the toes of anyone who gets too close," the cavalry pressed back the crowd and formed a twenty-five-foot "moat" around the airplane.

Cal was shivering from the freezing temperatures aloft. His speech impediment showed markedly as he told a reporter from the *San Antonio Express*, "I had a splendid trip. Flying conditions were ideal. Why many aviators don't come here for training is a mystery to me. I never saw the air better." He glanced at the small timepiece sewn to his gauntlet and declared that he had measured the fifty miles from San Marcos in fifty minutes. Since departing Sheepshead Bay, he had traversed more than 2,700 miles of railroad track.

Dr. George Fairfield, representing the Aero Club of San Antonio, was passed through the defense line to extend official greetings and was followed closely by senior military officials. Flanked by a detail of dignitaries, behind a cordon of mounted cavalrymen, paying no heed to the cheering thousands who could only catch a glimpse of his cigar smoke, Cal was taken to the Officers Club and offered an alcoholic beverage for obviously needed warmth. Instead, he calmly called for a glass of milk.

After responding to a score of questions about aviation and inquiring about the nature of the terrain west of San Antonio ("Rugged country, with few spots clear enough for landing an airplane"), Cal was driven to the St. Anthony Hotel, the most modern and luxurious hostelry in Texas, where the aviation party would locate and where Mabel and Mrs. Sweitzer already awaited him.

Lawrence Peters had been unable to secure financial guaranties for an aerial exhibition by the transcontinental flier. Airplanes were so common in the skies of San Antonio, he was told, that an exhibition would not recoup its expenses. A $50 payment for a landing at the resort suburb of Harlandale, just south of the city, proved the only offer forthcoming. At 4:30 Cal returned to the Polo Grounds and flew to the Harlandale Addition, where a thousand people collected to witness his landing and five minutes of aerial maneuvers. The *Vin Fiz* was consigned for the night under guard at the Harlandale field. Cal was delivered back to the St. Anthony Hotel for a sumptuous supper as guest of J. H. Redfern of the Texas Central Railroad. Later the party was treated to an evening's entertainment at the Plaza Theatre.

Charley Taylor had, since Kansas City, planned to quit the expedition upon its arrival in San Antonio. His wife's condition had not improved, and his three children were tended by the mercy of strangers. But Taylor, like his employer, was loath to abandon an undertaking short of success. He had never once failed the Wrights in more than a decade. He would, he told Cal, continue with the aviation party a short time further.

No firm plans had been established for the length of the respite in San Antonio or for the ensuing itinerary. The Sunset route favored by Cal—he had traveled its rails ten years earlier—ran due west via the Southern Pacific track (the "Soup Line"). An alternative course lay to the northwest along the line of the Texas & Pacific Railroad. Either passage encompassed miles of mesquite without clearings for emergency landings. "A third choice," said Cal, "is to stay here—give it up." DeKrafft, Charley Taylor, and the others stared at him. Cal walked away. "He is still down the rabbit hole," deKrafft remarked. "And even when he's out, you can never tell what's going on inside of him."

With the aviator evidently stung by a bee in his bonnet, resumption of the journey was postponed until Tuesday morning. Charley Taylor decreed a complete retuning of the *Vin Fiz* and, following Cal's suggestion, a complete rewiring as well. (The last-moment discovery of the worn wires—at Waco—still haunted Cal's thoughts.) The entire supply of wire from Steinway & Sons Piano Company was thereby depleted; additional wire was purchased in San Antonio hardware stores.

While the mechanicians worked on his airplane at Harlandale Monday morning, Cal drove the repaired Palmer-Singer to the post to inspect Army Airplane No. 1, the subject of numerous news bulletins during his days at the flying school in Dayton. When Captain Joseph E. Myers of the Third Field Artillery heard of Cal's presence, he was quick to suggest that the famous birdman act as instructor for student Myers. Cal agreed, and Captain Myers made application to General Duncan. "Suppose you get killed," said the general. Captain Myers replied, "Well, I have my life insured." General Duncan declared that it was not within his province to grant this authority, but consented to relay the request to Brigadier General Allen, chief of the Signal Corps.

Awaiting the telegraphed response, Captain Myers escorted Cal to an inspection of "No. 1," a Collier-Wright machine, and introduced him to the several other officers at the post with leanings toward aviation. Cal entertained them with anecdotes of his flying and of the Wright brothers. Captain Myers recited the story of Jacob Brodbeck of New Braunfels (just north of San Antonio), who was credited locally with having preceded the Wrights in heavier-than-air flight (in his spring-powered machine) by thirty-eight years. Cal allowed that such claims should be swallowed with large grains of salt.

DeKrafft had joined Cal at the fort and spread the word that the aviator would soon fly the Collier-Wright "B" with a passenger. A sizable crowd collected. At four o'clock a telegram arrived at General Duncan's office. It read, "Chief Signal Officer objects to use of Wright machine." "Now," said the general, "wouldn't it have been the dickens if I had let him use it?" There would be no flying on washday, he told Captain Myers, and politely suggested to Cal that his presence on the post could only have a disquieting effect. The ghost of Lieutenant George Kelly,* opined the junior officers, still haunted the army brass.

When Cal returned to the St. Anthony Hotel, he found that Mrs. Sweitzer had received a telegram from her attorney warning that her further absence risked serious financial forfeitures. Familial obligation—

---

*On May 10 Kelly, a Curtiss-trained student, took off for his qualifying flight in Army Airplane No. 2 (a Curtiss LV Model D). Upon landing, the forward plane assembly collapsed. Kelly was thrown from the machine and killed. All aviation activities at Fort Sam Houston were thereupon discontinued. Kelly Air Force Base, on the outskirts of San Antonio, is named in honor of Lt. Kelly.

to his brother, his sister, and himself, as well as in respect of the late Harry Sweitzer—Cal declared, dictated his mother's attendance in Pittsburgh. Mrs. Sweitzer protested that the living needed her attention more than the dead. Mabel interjected that in the wilderness west of San Antonio, women of full years were sometimes brutally attacked and subjected to unspeakable mortifications. "No cross is too heavy to bear for my son," rejoined Mrs. Sweitzer. Cal emphasized that with the final misfortune— at Kyle—behind him, henceforth only smooth sailing could be anticipated. Mrs. Sweitzer grudgingly consented to quit the expedition for the period necessary: "I might as well go home. If I can't comfort my own son, there is little else I can contribute."

At midevening, her bags hastily packed (by Mabel, who forwent her supper for the task), Mrs. Sweitzer was put aboard a Katy train for St. Louis, with transfers to Chicago and Pittsburgh. Cal and Mabel promised a card or letter from every stop.

Social engagements and other activities for the sought-after visitor to San Antonio were canceled, and Cal relaxed in his hotel room while Mabel substituted for him with reporters, business groups, and inquiring citizens.

Bob Fowler, he read in the *San Antonio Light,* was holding at Stewart's Ranch near Banning, California—after an overnight stop at Riverside, fifty-five miles from Pasadena—where he and his mechanicians were installing a new engine; a local humorist predicted that Fowler would reach the East Coast by 1921. Rising from Tournament Park Sunday afternoon, he had circled the Maryland Hotel to drop a tennis ball containing three letters—to his mother; to D. M. Linnard, owner of the hotel; and the third to Mae Sutton, the champion tennis player. (Miss Sutton, racket in hand, stood below on the Maryland's tennis court. The ball missed its target and fell upon the grounds of the Franklin School.) Fowler carried with him another letter, this one from Pasadena's mayor William Thum ("The Flypaper King of America") to Mayor Gaynor of New York. In other news of aviation, Orville Wright had crashed his buzzard machine at Kitty Hawk, dropping from fifteen feet and tumbling through a crumpling somersault; he escaped without injury. Eugene Ely, a small notice reported, was buried in Davenport, Iowa.

Tuesday morning Cal was driven to the Harlandale suburb, where Charley Taylor displayed the *Vin Fiz*—overhauled, rewired, retuned, and again gleaming white with new or scrubbed fabric on its planes. Cal worked the machine for a test flight over the Alamo, the "cradle of Texas independence," and returned, pleased with its performance. It was suggested that the aviator, still looking gaunt and haggard ("I strongly recommend cross-country flying as a weight reducer to anyone who is interested," said Cal), soak for half an hour at one of the famous Harlandale hot-water mineral baths. The invitation was accepted—and soon regretted. Cal's suit plus his leather jacket, leggings, gauntlets, goggles, and cap —his aviation apparel—were stolen from the dressing room of the bathhouse. This theft struck Cal as the final straw on the camel. "That tears it," he stormed. "I'm not going on. I can't drive an aeroplane bare as a plucked duck."

Leaving Mabel to soothe her outraged husband, deKrafft and several others in the party scurried about to purchase suitable new garments, a difficult task in view of Cal's exceptional height, and one that drained the last dollar from the expedition's coffers (deKrafft was unable to send the $100 payment due the Wrights for the Sunday flight from Kyle). Rumors meanwhile circulated that the cross-country flier had abandoned his attempt to reach the Pacific Coast. The crowd of 2,000 that had assembled at the Harlandale Addition field at nine o'clock dwindled to several hundred.

Those who inquired at the special train were told by supply-keeper Edward Sutton, "It makes me sick to hear a bunch of know-it-alls bettin' that Mr. Rodgers won't fly *Vin Fiz* to the Coast. He'll get there. You can see it in his eyes, no matter what his mouth may say. That man has real sand in his craw."

Rumors were given the lie when, at 11:45 A.M., the aviator appeared at the field (wearing trousers that stopped three inches short of his shoe tops). As the Palmer-Singer touring car bore him onto the grounds, it suffered a punctured tire. Cal jumped out and aided the crew in changing the wheel—despite the hazard to his spanking-new (and ill-fitting) ready-to-wears.

Stewart deKrafft engaged reporters from the San Antonio newspapers: "This is not just a flight from one coast to the other. There is a broader meaning to what Calbraith Rodgers is doing. It is a flight of the human spirit. . . . That is why, when he seems to have exhausted his strength, he is able to reach within himself and find yet more resources."

Why does he keep on with it? "C. P. Rodgers is a public figure. He must play out the role assigned to him on the stage of life. . . ."

Harry Sanger's orotund voice invaded deKrafft's interview. Praise of the elixir known as Vin Fiz rang out over the field—"at only five cents, five cents, five cents a bottle." "It's not milk for babies," deKrafft grumbled back in response.

Cal announced that he would follow the Sunset route, with as few stops as possible because of the stretches of mesquite brush and the turbulent air currents along the Rio Grande Valley. He bade his goodbyes to Dr. Fairfield and to members of the Aero Club, accepted apologies and a box of cigars from the manager of the Harlandale bathhouse, stuffed the stogies into the pockets of his new jacket, lit one, and climbed onto the seat of the *Vin Fiz*. The propellers were spun; the engine coughed into life. "Let her go, boys," Cal called out once again and at 12:30 P.M. drove the Wright EX biplane into the skies of Texas, fanning the air for the western shore.

The Pullman car of the special train had been painted, groomed, and aired for the trip west. A new mascot rode with the train. "Fiz," the mongrel kitten, proved to be a copycat of its predecessor, "Vin," and abandoned its keepers after having been left unattended for two days. Crew members quickly replaced the pussycat with a jackrabbit snared on the outskirts of San Antonio. The reluctant guest was housed in the hangar car. "We'll get more luck out of the rabbit than out of the two cats together," it was predicted.

The Vin Fiz train had been switched to the South Flores Street crossing of the Southern Pacific Railroad, convenient to the Harlandale field. Less than two wide circles of the airplane were required before mechanicians and crew raced to the crossing, drove the Palmer-Singer into the hangar car, and drew in the ramp.

As the special moved westward from San Antonio, an impromptu spiritual session was held in the private Pullman (where cuspidors had magically reappeared in the aisle). Mabel led deKrafft, Ed Merritt, Perry Smithers, and train officials in offering a prayer for the safety of the man they followed. "He may need it," deKrafft murmured. "It can't hurt," Cal had said when Mabel informed him of her intentions. (Words were also spoken for Mrs. Sweitzer's welfare: "May she remain safe and sound in Pittsburgh.")

Whatever their value for the aviator, the prayers did not sustain the airplane. Twenty miles to the west, the engine of the *Vin Fiz*, newly installed and certified by Charley Taylor, began sputtering once again.

Oct. 24, Tuesday. Volplaned more than three miles to land Lacoste 1:05 P.M. in cotton field. Repaired magneto. Hired boys to pull up cotton plants to clear space. Take-off 2:25 P.M. Landed Sabinal 3:10 P.M. on table cloth, fenced-in field. Ten-minute demonstration. Collected $50 purse. Take-off 4:07 P.M.

Most of the time I was winging along at about 3,500 feet. This would give me about five miles of volplaning before reaching the earth and a chance to pick my landing space. This caution, a benefit of my experience at Kyle, proved its worth when my engine went back on me near Lacoste.

Just short of 5:00 P.M. Cal crossed the Leona River at "Two Mile Hole" (a popular swimming area), sailed over groves of pecan trees and across the track of the recently constructed Crystal City & Uvalde Railroad, and landed on a level grassy field of the Loma Vista Addition near Sansom, two miles from the center of Uvalde. The waterworks whistle had sounded when word of the takeoff from Lacoste was telegraphed, and Uvalde's entire population of 4,000, including tuberculosis patients from its tent encampment, raced out Getty Street to the Addition. For nearly three hours, every buzzard or crow that appeared in the eastern sky brought yells, cheers, and cries of "There he is!" At five o'clock the man-made bird arrived, banked away from the SP track, circled the crowd, and fell onto the ground. It was swarmed over by the excited throng; its planes, already shaded by signatures added at Lacoste and Sabinal, darkened further from the onslaught of an army of autographers. Mayor F. H. Rheiner welcomed the aviator and praised the *Vin Fiz* machine as the greatest example of twentieth-century scientific achievement.

"Some weather you have here," Cal complained, looking somewhat wilted. "One minute it's freezing, and the next it's burning up. Give me the ocean to die in—it would be more merciful."

"You think this is hot?" said Mayor Rheiner, unable to resist a Texas rejoinder. "Why, son, last week I saw a dog chasing a jackrabbit, and it was so hot they both was walking."

A local businessman, C. C. Veltmann, offered a supply of gasoline at 15¢ a gallon, which was accepted and filtered into the tank on the airplane. The Vin Fiz special braked to a stop at the Sansom depot; Charley Taylor, Frank Shaffer, and Charlie Wiggin hurried over to assist with inspection and refueling. Taylor again berated Cal for "pouring coal oil into the engine. That's probably the cause of half our crack-ups."*

After twenty minutes on the ground, Cal took the air to circle above the crowd and drive the airplane through five minutes of dips and banks. To the south he could see Mount Inge and the ruins of Fort Inge at its

*The Wrights recommended 64-octane Crown gasoline "to promote proper combustion and to preserve a uniform temperature in the motor at all altitudes." Lubrication with Hoilboil oil was advised.

base. Encampments of cavalry units (patrolling the Mexican border) were evident along the Leona River. To the west, the SP track cut through the mesquite toward the now-setting sun. Cal aligned the flying machine with the rails and at 5:30 P.M. headed for Spofford and Del Rio.

It was past six o'clock—the last glints of the sun retreating from the sky—when the *Vin Fiz* bumped down on the east side of Spofford, forty miles from Uvalde and 132 miles west of San Antonio. That distance earned $528 from Armour & Company, a sum deKrafft was prompt to collect from Ed Merritt. Cal was greeted by Sheriff Salmon; Mr. Zuehl, the depot agent; Mr. Leroy Elledge, the six-foot ticket agent and cashier for the SP Railroad; and most of the ranch hands and Mexicans who resided in Spofford. Neither the single hotel in town (a dilapidated two-story structure with broken glass in every window) nor the Van Noy Café appealed to the Vin Fiz camp. It was decided that the party would pass another night on the train.

For supper, to spare their guests the ordeal of another ham-and-beans meal dispensed by chef Ed Davis, Messrs. Salmon, Elledge, et al. prepared a feast of barbecued goat. Bench tables were strung out end to end ("for a quarter of a mile," wrote Charlie Wiggin), and everyone within walking or riding distance was invited. Liberal doses of lemon juice rendered the otherwise gamy fare palatable to the visiting "tenderfeet." Cal donned the ten-gallon Stetson presented by Sheriff Salmon—and added six inches to his towering stature. Mr. Zuehl, bedecked for the occasion in wing collar, ascot tie, and four-button suit, spoke of the value of trains as navigational guides for airplanes and predicted that the SP Railroad would become the leader in this field. To the accompaniment of Frank Shaffer's banjo, the full assembly sang "Sweet Adeline," "Casey Jones," and "In the Shade of the Old Apple Tree." Mabel had heard, while in San Antonio, a new song written by the singing waiter whom she and Cal had seen at Nigger Mike's Place in New York's Chinatown. Titled "Alexander's Ragtime Band," it had the whole country tapping to its cry of "Come on and hear." Shaffer had already learned to plunk out its syncopated rhythm. When the singing and barbecue fires died out, Cal was asked to recount some of the more memorable adventures of his journey. A bonfire was kindled; by its flickering light, the group watched the aviator as he spoke of his crashes at Middletown, Salamanca, and Huntington, the bullfight at Bobo, the belligerent eagle out of Forth Worth. In response to several questioners, he denied that he carried a coffin on the train in anticipation of his demise.

Late at night a particular news item chattered into the Spofford telegraph office. Cal was there to read it: In the long-delayed fourth game of the World Series, the Philadelphias had conquered Christy Mathewson and the Giants at Shibe Park, 4–2. New York was "outpitched, outhit, outplayed, and simply outclassed." Connie Mack predicted that his team would "wrap it up" the following day at the Polo Grounds.

As Cal retired to his stateroom where Mabel was already asleep, the stewards claimed his store-bought trousers. George-2 unstitched the hems and resewed them at a more appropriate length. "Mr. Rodgers is a proper gentleman," both stewards agreed, "and should have a proper suit."

Nine o'clock Wednesday morning found the aviator prepared for takeoff into a crystalline blue sky free of the barest trace of a breeze. Charley Taylor declared the *Vin Fiz* in better shape than when it was shipped from the Wright factory in Dayton. A path between two barbed-wire fences had been cleared of catclaw, mesquite, and stunted oak stumps, and the machine positioned at its fore. "I was a bit skeptical about this roadway," said Cal later, "because it was not very wide; barbed-wire fences and telegraph wires were on either side, and a few stumps were left. . . . But the crowd was lined up along the fences, and even the babies and dogs seemed on their best behavior." He advanced the spark and moved forward.

The aircraft reacted sluggishly and was still rolling heavily when it reached a series of bumps in the road. Several children had squeezed through a gap in the fence and were running alongside. Angling to avoid them and struggling to control the machine through its jarring lurches, Cal bounced the *Vin Fiz* onto a cactus. One tire was punctured by several prickly spines. The machine swerved and slammed into the barbed wire. It hung there impaled, like a museum bird frozen on a pedicel. Cal, too, sat frozen. Then, unhurt, he climbed down from the driver's seat, dropped to his knees, and stared at the ground. After a few silent moments he rose and, as if to demonstrate his old élan, called out, "Fix her up, boys. I'll be ready."

Both left warping wings were smashed and shredded of fabric. The two propellers and skids were destroyed. "Fix her up, hell," said Charley Taylor. "With the parts we got left, we couldn't fix up a donkey cart."

"Well," Cal pointed out. "the bottle of Vin Fiz is still in one piece. That's at least one good omen."

(Another good omen, the two stewards subsequently told themselves, was that the aviator's sole two-piece business suit had weathered the crash without a tear.)

Leroy Elledge walked up, and Cal asked, "Who are those dad-blamed children?"

"They're mine," said Mr. Elledge. "I'll have to teach them better manners."

Mechanicians and crew were at first unable to loosen the crumpled machine from its entanglement with the wire fence. Two cowboys rode up, lassoed the wreck, and offered to pull it away using "real" horsepower. They were quickly dissuaded. The barbed wire was cut away and the airplane dragged from the fence and up a dirt street to the spur behind the freight depot. Taylor, Shaffer, and Wiggin set about their work of reconstruction. The jackrabbit mascot was booted into the desert with spits and shouted imprecations.

> *When this machine was being built I wanted to have the skids a bit lower so as to give the propellers more clearance for just this sort of country. After both propellers were broken, the motor began roaring, but I finally got it shut off before it did any damage. Upon looking over the wreck I find I'll have to put on a new lower left plane, two new skids, and the tail framing. I thought I had left the hoodoo behind, but it seems to have caught up. I must be the only aviator on earth who had a tire punctured by a cactus spine.*

Taylor was relieved to learn that Spofford boasted a skilled carpenter, Marcos Vela Gonzalez. Sr. Gonzalez was enlisted for rebuilding the principal structures (no spares remained on the hangar car; a list of needed parts was wired to Dayton with delivery ordered for Tucson). With lumber from an apple crate, he soon fashioned new spars and braces, then helped sew sections of fabric and wielded brushes from the glue pots over his handicraft. Work continued throughout the day and, under the lights of the freight depot, into the night.

Mabel, after noting that her husband was uninjured, suggested that the best thing in Spofford was the road out of town. At sunset she, Cal, deKrafft, and Ed Merritt motored to Fort Clark and took supper at the Bracketville Café, where they enjoyed the famous Terrill chicken spread and carried portions back to Spofford for the delectation of the crew. The old Negress at the café had been "feeding the hungry" for thirty-seven years. "Let's bring her along and leave [chef] Davis in Bracketville," deKrafft proposed.

The Spofford telegraph office was closed when Cal returned from Bracketville; two telegrams and a note were tacked to the office door.

The note informed him that the Giants had edged the Athletics 4–3 in a ten-inning battle in New York. Pinch hitter Otis Crandall was substituted in the tenth and delivered the victory blow. "We've got our momentum," said Tug McGraw. "If we can beat them in Philly tomorrow, we'll have them back here for the last game, and we'll wrap it up."

The first telegram, from John Rodgers at Pasadena, stated that arrangements had been concluded for a formal ceremony in Pasadena before ending the voyage at a coastal city. Lieutenant Rodgers had surveyed the area and selected Tournament Park as the most befitting landing site. With D. M. Linnard, owner/manager of the Maryland Hotel, he had inspected the roof of the hotel for a means of accommodating an airplane there. On behalf of his cousin, John Rodgers had accepted Linnard's offer of $1,000 for a flight over the Maryland but expressed doubt regarding an additional $500 for a landing on its roof. He had explained to Linnard that an airplane does not alight like a bird but requires space to lose its momentum, 100 feet or more even with a precise touchdown point. "If accomplished," Los Angeles newspapers underscored, "it would be the first landing in history on the top of any building." Lieutenant Rodgers was quoted as saying that he had "every confidence Calbraith Rodgers will complete the trip across the continent. There is no substitute for 'stick-to-itiveness,' and he has it in abundance. He will reach Pasadena within the week."

The second telegram, addressed to Charley Taylor, had been sent by Dr. Stephen Easley of the Good Samaritan Hospital in Los Angeles. Mrs. Henrietta Taylor, it read, remained in serious condition, and her husband's presence was, again, urgently requested. He would remain with the expedition, Taylor resolved after some deliberation, but in the event of another delay would immediately take his leave.

Early Thursday morning, after another night on the special train (currently dubbed "the Vin Fiz Hotel"), Cal was put into a railroad motorcar and sent off to explore the territory to the west. He traveled as far as Comstock, twenty-five miles beyond Del Rio, and reported that "besides mesquite and chaparral, all I could see was chaparral and mesquite. This part of Texas was not laid out with a view to accommodating aviators in their flights." Upon his return at 10:00 A.M. he found his mechanicians testing the rebuilt *Vin Fiz Flyer* and performing final adjustments. Cal told correspondents on the train that he would "hightail it" out of Spofford at "eggzackly" one o'clock (betraying a bit of the Texas jargon he had absorbed).

The crash at Spofford, Texas.

The Mercersburg football team, 1897. Cal Rodgers third row, second from left.

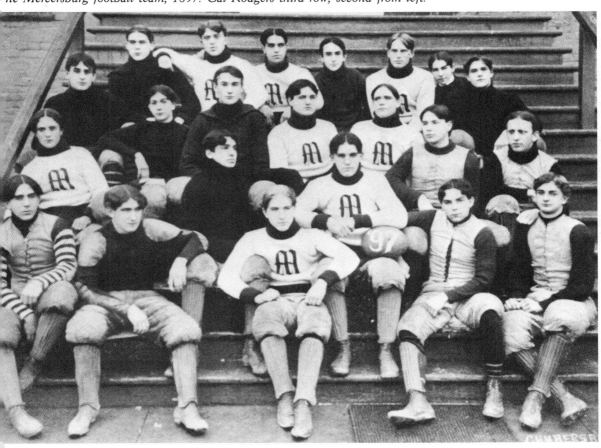

Mabel Graves, age 21. National Park Seminary, Washington, D.C. (COURTESY GEORGE A. WHITING II)

Imperial Junction, Calif. Rebuilding the engine by cannibalizing.

Hole in block after cylinder blowout over Salton Sea.

Jimmy Dunn in the Palmer-Singer automobile. (COURTESY MEL ANDERSON; THE ARNOLD COLLECTION)

Pasadena, Calif., Nov. 5, 1911. Cal Rodgers on telephone to Associated Press. D. M. Linnard at left.

Pasadena, Calif., Nov. 5, 1911. Cal Rodgers in Victoria Electric with "Rose Queen" Irene Grosse. (COURTESY BOB BROOKS)

Takeoff from Marfa, Texas.

Crew members by the wreckage at Compton, Calif. Fourth, third, and second from right: Charlie Wiggin, Jimmy Dunn, Frank Shaffer. (*COURTESY MEL ANDERSON; THE ARNOLD COLLECTION*)

Cal Rodgers recuperating from the Compton crash, Hotel Maryland, Pasadena, Calif. Mabel Rodgers at right, Mrs. Sweitzer at left. (*COURTESY NATIONAL AIR AND SPACE MUSEUM, SMITHSONIAN INSTITUTION*)

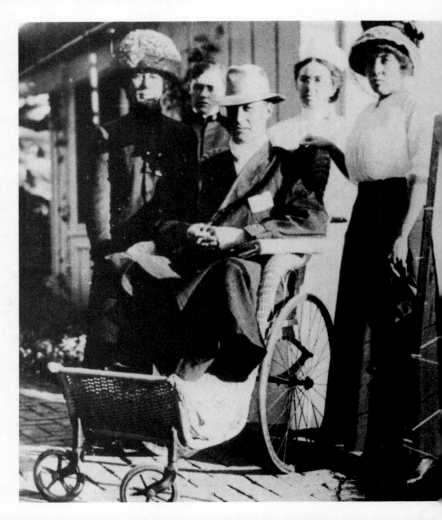

Cal and Mabel Rodgers "on the town" in Los Angeles.

Triumph! Cal Rodgers in the surf at Long Beach, Calif. (COURTESY NATIONAL AIR AND SPACE MUSEUM, SMITHSONIAN INSTITUTION)

Flying the Wright "B" around Long Beach, Calif.

Long Beach, Calif. Apr. 3, 1912. The fatal crash. (COURTESY LONG BEACH INDEPENDENT PRESS TELEGRAM)

I finally got my machine repaired and in good shape and after looking around found a better flying field. I had to cut down a few bushes and clear the field of stumps and debris. When I started the motor I found her pulling very well, which was a great satisfaction to me, considering what bad country I had before me. I got into the air in good shape and worked up to an altitude of 3,000 feet.

For the first time since the beginning of the transcontinental trip, Cal lifted off at the announced minute. The entire party on the train cheered in unison.

I soon overtook my special and passed it making Del Rio at 1:34 P.M., doing the 37 miles in 31 minutes—with a leading beam wind I made good time all the way. I got a purse here for a landing, otherwise I should have gone right on.

Del Rio, a community of adobe *jacales* and 5,000 people on the verge of incorporation as a town, reposed, as its name implied, on a bank of the Rio Grande. Cal could discern the river several minutes before he sailed by the Waterloo flatlands with conical-shaped Round Mountain off his left wings and, his skids nicking the tips of a prickly-pear thicket, skittered in a swirl of dust onto the abandoned parade ground of Camp Del Rio. More than 2,000 people had trekked out to the ground, most by "shanks' mare." A few wagons and family surreys banded at one end of the field. Three automobiles could be seen, one the fire-engine-red three-seater Brush, its wooden wheels (on wooden axles) fitted with pneumatic tires, that served—upon the purchase of 10¢ worth of candy at the cigar store —as a children's joyrider about the streets of Del Rio. A number of burros looked on impassively, each trailing a travois of sandals, beadwork, or other handicraft of the Mexican Indians who bartered such goods at the trading post. The clatter of the *Vin Fiz* engine, the first heard in Val Verde County, frightened children and horses, the former into screaming, the latter into bucks and frenzied gallops. Miss Byrdie Henry, twenty-five, principal of the Del Rio Junior High School, rushed about reassuring her students and younger teachers. County Judge Clyde McDowall, standing for mayor of the proposed township, formally welcomed Cal to Del Rio. Behind him stood five-foot-tall Miss Ouida Hymans, the "Del Rio Sweetheart," who presented the aviator with a rose and balanced herself on an upended apple crate to fix a kiss on his chin.

Cal was particularly intrigued by the "Mexican flavor of the scene" and, after the EX was refueled and checked over, hoisted himself onto the driver's seat and flew south across the Rio Grande over the village of Las Vacas. The 400 inhabitants of that pueblo were transfixed by the appearance of a flying machine less than fifty feet above the three stores and customs house of the plaza. Cal turned back over Del Rio and rocked his planes as the Vin Fiz special chugged from the SP depot.

Some in Del Rio were not unhappy to watch him disappear from view. (Bartenders had been persuaded, for a consideration, to serve only Vin Fiz carbonated grape drink during the aviator's visit, but few bottles of the soda pop passed over the counters of their saloons.) Most Del Rians were indelibly impressed by the airplane and its driver; local whittlers were moved to carve toy versions of the *Vin Fiz* machine, and for a time "aviator's headgear" was fashionable among the citizenry.

Set again westward along the Sunset line of the Southern Pacific at 2:50 P.M., through the Big Bend country* across the Amistad Reservoir, the special train, confined to a snaking track, was unable to pace the airplane, propelled at speeds up to 70 mph by animated currents.

> *The railroad twisted and wound in and out, but I laid the most direct course possible, leaving the track on one side and the Rio Grande on the other. The scenery was wonderful and rugged—especially the Pecos Canyon, over which the next to the highest bridge in the world was built. This is a most dangerous flying country. There is nothing but mountains, cliffs, and precipices; the deep canyons produce swirling air currents. Even on the level stretches I couldn't see any safe landing places by reason of the sagebrush, mesquite, and chapparal.*
>
> *I flew over the border into Mexico at the same time the train left Del Rio. I soon left the train behind, crossed back into the U.S. and then flew across into old Mexico again. I did this three different times during the trip.*

The Rio Grande in places was manifest merely as a wide, winding strip of white sand, baked and glaring in the sun. Its quicksands, Cal had been told, had swallowed cattle and sheep, horses, wagons, and the men who rode them. Beyond the river he observed only scattered cattle and an occasional Mexican or Indian who stood transfixed to stare up at the noisy apparition in the sky.

Stations agents and tower men reported the biplane's passage as if clocking a train. At 3:10 P.M. the *Vin Fiz* was registered over Comstock

*So-called because the Rio Grande here carves an immense dip to the south. Spanish explorers referred to it as "el desplobado" (the unpopulated place).

and at 3:40 over the Pecos River where it drains into the Rio Grande near Langtry (founded and named by Judge Roy Bean—the "Law west of the Pecos"—in honor of Lily Langtry, the devastatingly beautiful English actress he loved but never met). The citizens of Langtry had been unable or unwilling to raise a $50 fee for the transcontinental enterprise. Langtry's attractions—the Jersey Lilly,* the "hanging tree"—were deemed sufficient unto themselves to warrant a landing. Such proved not to be the case; the airplane flew by at 3,000 feet, and the train whipped by twenty minutes later without slowing.

Oct. 26, Thursday. Langtry, Pumpville. Oil running low, landed Dryden 4:20 P.M.

Finding the train would not arrive here until 5:00 o'clock, I hopped it around and got some poor cylinder oil. With the assistance of the natives I strained it into the tank, got the fans spinning and took the air again at 5:10 o'clock.

The final twenty-one miles to Sanderson, a sunbaked railroad repair-and-crew-change point of some 500 souls, were covered in eighteen minutes.

The full community of Sanderson collected on the Mexican School Square to welcome the coast-to-coast aviator. Not until 7:30 P.M. did mechanicians and crew arrive from the railroad yards—the train having been slowed by the serpentine roadbed and by a steer that had strayed onto the track and would not be intimidated. A guard was posted at the machine, and Cal rescued from the crowd ("I had to protect my machine for more than two hours and go hungry until my special arrived").

Distance traveled for the day totalled 174 miles in an astonishing 147 minutes—an average rate of 71 mph.

The Vin Fiz camp passed Thursday night on the train. Chef Ed Davis was importuned to vary his monotonous fare, but excepting the predestined steak, a wider range of provisions was unavailable. Reporters and other passengers again conferred on him the "Throw him off the train" Award (a daily ritual) and vowed to drown him in a giant vat of beans.

A dispatch at the telegraph office that evening described the sixth and final game of the World Series as "a tragedy and a farce." The Phila-

*The Jersey Lilly (the extra *l* courtesy of an itinerant sign painter) was the combination courtroom/saloon where Judge Bean dispensed his whimsical and autocratic justice. Bean had died eight years before.

delphias had humiliated the New Yorkers 13–2, the most decisive defeat for the Giants in all the 1911 season. Wrote Damon Runyon: "A little of that soft, slow, slobby music, professor. All right, let her go. The tumult and the shaking dies. The players with the dough depart. The dope, to our own intense surprise, was wrong. Be still, oh aching heart. There are some dollars that we bet. (Extremely pianissimo.) Let us forget. Let us forget." Moaned Tug McGraw: "What can I say? Tell me, and I'll say it." Cal's wager with his cousin John represented a few of the dollars lost.

A telegram from Mrs. Sweitzer in Pittsburgh had been relayed from Spofford to Sanderson: "TRIED TELEPHONE STOP IMPOSSIBLE STOP READ OF CRASH STOP IF MUST FLY FLY CAREFUL STOP KEEP WARM EAT WELL END."

Friday morning, flight was prevented by a 30-mph norther. Charley Taylor could defer his departure no longer. He clasped hands with each crewman and with each official on the Pullman. He charged Shaffer with responsibility for maintaining the *Vin Fiz* ("The motor is getting worse and worse—it's running so hot, you can fry an egg on it") and admonished Wiggin to behave himself. "Take care of your man," he commanded Mabel. In an uncharacteristic gesture, he embraced Cal and seemed on the verge of tears as he spoke his wishes for good fortune. Not a warm, friendly man, Taylor was respected by all. Every member of the expedition turned out to wave farewell when he boarded the morning passenger train for the West Coast.

With the machine in the "pink of perfection," the party lay about, waiting for the wind to subside. The *Sanderson Times* editor recommended the abundance of duck in the area and volunteered the loan of his 12-gauge shotgun. At ten o'clock Cal, deKrafft, Merritt, and Benell drove off in the Palmer-Singer on a determined hunt to expand the party's diet. "Even if we bag a duck," deKrafft complained, "that slop-cook would probably make it into a ham-and-bean stew."

Not a duck was sighted in two hours of combing the hills and flatlands around Sanderson. However, at one point a mountain lion sprang from a brush-filled ravine and scampered across the path of the Palmer-Singer. DeKrafft, Merrit, and Benell sat frozen; Cal grabbed for the shotgun, but the mountain lion was already out of range before the blast urged it to a yet swifter retreat. "Damn!" said Cal. "You can't kill a cat that size with a shotgun." He instructed deKrafft to purchase a .30-caliber rifle "so that we'll be ready the next time some big game comes our way." (De-Krafft nodded, and the request was forgotten.)

Mabel was delighted to find a tennis court, unpaved but quite usable; she corralled the Sanderson postmistress, the comely Miss Genevieve

East, to amuse herself at the game for an hour or so. Mabel overwhelmed her taller and younger opponent. When Cal returned, empty-handed from the duck (and lion) hunt, he, too, engaged Miss East in a set of tennis. One reporter watching the match suggested that if tennis balls were in short supply, they might substitute some of chef Davis's meatballs.

With no pressing matters to occupy their energies, Cal and his managers were able to catch up with the aviation news and other events from several days' newspapers. At Kitty Hawk, after extensive repairs, Orville Wright had hung the motorless buzzard biplane motionless 200 feet in the air for over a minute—in the teeth of a gale blowing in from the Atlantic Ocean. Said Orville, "The correctness of our theories has been demonstrated. . . . At one point, the machine even moved backward over the earth!"

Bob Fowler had become the first aviator to fly into the territory of Arizona. He had landed at the baseball park in Yuma on Wednesday before a crowd of 2,000 and predicted that he would reach Tucson, 260 miles eastward, by Friday evening. At last report, however, he had experienced engine problems and had opted for a new motor. Newspaper accounts referred to "Fowler's Flying Circus." "It was the only way I could get a special rate from the S.P.,"* Fowler explained. "There was no provision for an air race, so I told them we were a traveling vaudeville troupe."

In Mexico, General Zapata had defeated the *Federales* at San Gorgonio and was demanding surrender of the capital from President-elect Madero.[1] In China, revolutionaries had captured Kwang Chow. The Manchu government was reported in a state of demoralization, and rumors abounded of the emperor's death or abdication.[2]

Friday evening the Palmer-Singer racer narrowly escaped destruction, and Jimmy Dunn with it. Dunn was returning the auto to the hangar car and had driven up the ramp and out onto the platform extended through the opposite door over the main track. He looked up to behold an express train bearing down on him at full speed. Only the swiftest reaction enabled him to slam the vehicle into reverse gear and tromp on the accelerator. The platform was decapitated as the express train hurtled by. The rear wheels of the Palmer-Singer missed the ramp rails, and the auto tumbled backward, its rear axle broken.

---

*The railroad charged 25¢ a mile for the ten persons (including newly acquired manager Charles Young and excluding the Grundy family) accompanying the West-to-East enterprise. Another 15¢ a mile was levied to haul the baggage car.

At 5:30 A.M. on Saturday, Cal bounded from his stateroom berth and pounded on the hangar car to awaken his crew.

> *I wanted to get started by daybreak so I could make El Paso, 312 miles, if possible. I had my doubts about getting out of Sanderson because of puffy winds and the place being completely surrounded by mountains. Where I started was a wire fence on the left with houses [at the far end of the Mexican School Square], but it was too late to avoid hitting the fence. I was disgusted. . . . Luck was against me. I looked the machine over and found I had torn off the lower left warping plane and had smashed both skids and panels.*

Without Charley Taylor's practiced hand, Cal pitched in to help Frank Shaffer and Charlie Wiggin repair the damage. So rapidly did they labor that a new wing was attached, and the aircraft again pronounced in "shipshape and Bristol fashion" shortly before eleven o'clock. Scattered clouds dotted the sky, and a light norther had sprung up. Temperatures still tarried in the fifties. It was decided that in view of such splendid conditions, the train would be accorded an advance start over the hilly terrain ahead. In the unlikely event of a mishap on takeoff, Cal would telegraph the next town for the train to double back. The *Vin Fiz* was pushed onto a mud street away from the fence. Shaffer and Wiggin ran for the boxcar, and Cal was left to fire his engine with the assistance of the Sanderson natives.

> **Oct. 28, Saturday. Take-off Sanderson 11:42 A.M., now on Mountain Standard Time. Miles of grazing land. Taylor, Marathon. Landed Alpine 1:21 P.M., 101 miles in 99 minutes.**
>
> *My special had left three-quarters of an hour ahead of me, and I gained it past Marathon. The railroad runs uphill for about ten miles at this point. I had to climb also to keep my elevation on account of the mountains. When I had about reached the summit I noticed a line of clouds close to the ground and feared that I would run into a cloud bank. The railroad winds considerably, and I had to keep a close outlook. Just at that point I ran into a heavy white mist which enveloped me completely. I was worried and afraid I would lose my direction; I could hardly see my hand before my face. I did not know when I should get out of the clouds, and my gasolene was getting low, and it kept me guessing. Finally I cut through them and was delighted to see the ground. However, I was compelled to fly low in order to avoid the clouds, especially over the mountain ridges. On top of one of them I saw a magnificent stag. It looked at my machine for a moment, then galloped into the black brush.*

Cal swung over the Alpine Courthouse to the northeast and dropped into a pasture on the Kokernut ranch north of town. As he plopped onto the ground, one wheel struck a rock and suffered a punctured tire. Thirty minutes passed until Shaffer and Wiggin rushed up from the special train. A band of school children had surrounded the airplane, and from it a fourteen-year-old girl, Hallie Crawford, dashed in to inscribe her signature. Her action triggered a rush for the machine, and the fabric of the *Vin Fiz* grew darker yet with penciled scrawls.

At two o'clock, after the flat tire had been replaced, sunshine dissipated much of the mist, and Cal took the air for Paisano Pass, at 5,080 feet elevation, the summit of his route across Texas. He cleared the pass with an altitude of 300 feet.

Marfa,* the seat of Presidio County, although but twenty-six miles from Alpine, was not reached until 3:00 P.M. because of the slow climb and because of a dark cloud that diverted Cal for several minutes.

Virtually every inhabitant of Marfa (over a thousand people lived in the treeless, *jacal-*fringed town) turned out to see the *Vin Fiz* swoop onto the flat between the stock pens and the cemetery. The machine was immediately roped off by Sheriff Milt Chastain and his assistants. Frank Shaffer and Charlie Wiggin ran up (a propeller chain drive wanted replacement), and Harry Sanger claimed the crowd's attention with shouts of "Hear ye, hear ye" through his megaphone. Ed Merritt handed a bottle of Vin Fiz grape drink to Cal, and the aviator delivered a speech praising the "delicious coolness of the new blend of fruit juices, sold everywhere for five cents." He stoically drained two swallows from the bottle. Samples were not passed around.

While crew members wheeled the airplane to a field more secure against sudden shifts in wind direction, Cal was taken to the Bon Ton Restaurant, where the proprietor, "Dolores" Moreno, a 300-pound *hombre* with a three days' growth of beard, served dinner. Every youngster in Marfa was on hand, some perched astride the burros (known as "Marfa taxis") allowed to roam freely through the streets. One group trailed Shaffer and Wiggin, aspiring to autograph the plane fabric. Another followed Cal to the Bon Ton to gape at the celebrated transcontinental flier and try for a souvenir (Cal's scarf was stolen, and two buttons were yanked from his coat). A third group traipsed to the depot and asked to see "the coffin carried on board and the famous actress who accompanied Mr. Rodgers."

*Named after the servant girl in Dostoevski's *Brothers Karamazov*.

To a reporter from the *Marfa New Era*, Cal vowed that he would try for El Paso before dark, but might be forced to spend the night at Sierra Blanca or Fort Hancock. He mounted the airship, now repositioned for advantage in the swirling wind, lit another cigar, rolled forward over the hard caliche soil, and took the air westward at 4:01 P.M.

Oct. 28. Valentine 4:38 P.M., Van Horn. Landed Sierra Blanca 5:40 P.M.

At Van Horn, Mrs. Emmaline Barrow stood in the center of her melon patch to watch the *Vin Fiz* pass by. In her arms she held her white Manx, Buttermilk. She raised the cat above her head so that it, too, should have a view of the airplane.

A confusion in dispatch orders halted the Vin Fiz train at Van Horn. Despite a subsequent 70-mph run by engineer Otis Bobick, it arrived at the tiny hamlet of Sierra Blanca fifty minutes behind its leader. Thoughts of further travel were surrendered, and the party resigned itself to another night in berths, passenger seats, and on the floor of the hangar car. "This state is longer than any three others in the Union," said Cal. "I've been flying more miles than I can count and I still can't see the end of it." I seem to be passing over the same town again and again, the same church towers, the same bunches of children wigwagging their arms."

Bookkeeping for the day's flight showed 231 miles in 229 minutes, a stretch exceeded only by the 234 miles traversed between Springfield, Illinois, and Marshall, Missouri, more than two weeks earlier.

Chef Ed Davis celebrated the achievement with servings of omelets and diced ham. His efforts accomplished little to nullify the petition to have him replaced. "Unfortunately," deKrafft told correspondents, officials, and crew members, "he comes with the train—and his price is the only one we can afford."

A wire from John Rodgers confirmed that contracts for the landing in Pasadena had been signed. Two hours later another telegram bore Lieutenant Rodgers's regrets that his request for a second extension of leave had been emphatically denied. He would, perforce, immediately entrain for the East Coast. His message concluded: "I can't be at the finish in person, but I'll be there in spirit. Clear skies all the way."

Puffy and billowing winds swept over Sierra Blanca early Sunday morning. But he would not be deterred, Cal insisted.

My first start from Sierra Blanca was unsuccessful because some people and an automobile got in my way, and I was compelled to stop. So I changed my position, but was caught by several tumbleweeds that bounced into my face and onto the machine when I started to take off. I changed my position again and finally had a clear field. I took the air at 9:00 A.M. . . . bound for El Paso.

Approaching Fort Hancock, Cal again could discern the Rio Grande; the SP track veered to the northwest to parallel the river's bank. Then, as if sight of the river affected its workings, the *Vin Fiz* motor began sputtering. Cal brought the machine down in a field two miles west of Fort Hancock's old military post. It lost momentum while still ten feet up, fell, splintered both skids, and cracked the engine's water jacket. The gasoline tank tore loose and dropped on his neck.

Cal staggered from the machine in pain. Several bystanders ran over and helped him to a sitting position on a nearby tree stump. When the special train arrived five minutes later, Mabel massaged his neck while Frank Shaffer and Charlie Wiggin assessed the damage. "Fix her up, boys, I'll be ready," Cal mumbled weakly.

Panels and skids were quickly repaired; the tank was reattached. Major operations were obviously ordained for the engine. It was agreed that it would function for a time—likely to El Paso, where better facilities were available, and where it could be either reconstructed or replaced at greater leisure. Not yet fully recovered from the blow to his neck, Cal climbed back onto the seat of the machine and took off from the Fort Hancock field at 1:45 P.M.

Just as I was getting off the ground I scared up a rabbit. He just missed a propeller. Maybe I should have hit him; then the chef could have worked up a rabbit stew for the boys.

Less than two minutes after he took the air, Cal felt a hot, damp sensation high on his neck. He swiveled about—a spray of oil from the motor splashed over his face and ran down his goggles. He squeezed his body into the driver's seat and strove to shield himself from the oily mist. Eyes slitted against the oil that seeped under his goggles, he struggled to hold the machine on a course northwest along the Rio Grande, wiping —or smearing—his goggles every few moments against his forearms. A strong headwind had sprung up, and an hour and forty-seven minutes were required to negotiate the sixty miles to El Paso. By then the oil supply was spent and the overheated engine was groaning and rasping.

A crowd of 7,000 persons was waiting at Washington Park on the east side of El Paso. From the fire department came three long blasts on the fire whistle, the prearranged signal to notify the citizens of El Paso del Norte that the long-anticipated cross-country flier was approaching. No police protection had been provided, and, when the *Vin Fiz* was sighted, people excitedly scattered over the field. Cal, nearly blinded from the shower of oil, dipped the machine over the racetrack enclosure, searching for a space clear of running and jumping bodies. However he maneuvered, he encountered scores of people beneath and in front of him. He rose above the park, spiraled about while the crowd screamed and waved, then selected a patch of ground on the north side of the SP tracks at the edge of Evergreen Cemetery. The terrain was rough and bisected by barbed-wire fences, but Cal swerved around the obstacles and bumped to a stop with right wings draped over an adobe wall bordering a row of tombstones. Numerous doves, accustomed to more placid company, flapped from their roosts in nearby trees. The crowd at Washington Park was already streaming across the tracks in a pell-mell dash for the cemetery.

Cal staggered from the *Vin Fiz*, stiff from the blow to his neck and from holding a cramped position throughout the flight, oil-splattered over his face and body, his new flying togs soaked to a solid black luster. The special train had halted a hundred yards away, and mechanicians and crew rushed out. They were taken aback by the black-faced aviator in black clothes, an aviator last observed with white face and brown suit. Cal assured them that he had not permanently changed color and left them to protect the airplane against the swarming throng. His feet squishing the oil that dribbled into his shoes, he made his way to the Pullman, where Mabel was next to be startled by his appearance. With her helping hand, he scrubbed himself thoroughly and dressed in his second coat and a pair of trousers (inadequate) borrowed from Stewart deKrafft.

The train proceeded meanwhile to the downtown station, where Cal and Mabel were met by S. A. Sinderoff of the El Paso Chamber of Commerce. Cal was given no time to recuperate. The aviator and his wife, with Mr. Sinderoff and two other local officials, were immediately driven across the border to the bullring of Ciudad Juárez.

The first of the four bulls on the program of the Juárez corrida for October 29 was scheduled for 3:40 P.M. Opening ceremonies were delayed—Cal was escorted into the arena at 3:45 by manager "Paquiro" Alonso—awaiting the appearance of *el aviador transcontinental, el hombre famoso de aves, el conquistador de los cielos. El aviador* was conducted through two parades around the ring, while 1,500 aficionados threw flowers and hats and waved handkerchiefs at him. Matador Fidel Díaz dedicated his bull to the visitor from north of the border.

Cal's first experience on Mexican soil began with the adulation of a crowd, but ended in retreat. Left queasy and faint by the ritual killing, the honored guest departed the arena after the second corrida. It was not the same, he told Mabel, as the bullfighting he had engaged in at Bobo, Indiana. (Mabel, however, confessed to a certain sensual feeling from viewing the spectacle.) Before returning across the river, Cal stopped at a *tabaquería* to purchase several boxes of Mexican *cigarros* (one to be mailed to Charley Taylor in Los Angeles).

The Vin Fiz party ensconced itself at the St. Regis Hotel, an especially welcome respite from five consecutive nights on the train. Cal and de-Krafft were confronted there by Mayor C. E. Kelly, W. L. Gaines, local manager of Armour & Company, and others who berated them for the aviator's failure to alight at Washington Park. DeKrafft explained that there was no intention to break faith with the people and that Rodgers's action had probably saved the lives of one or more citizens of El Paso.

Waiting at the St. Regis Hotel was a letter, postmarked Thursday morning (preceding her telegram), from Mrs. Sweitzer in Pittsburgh. "I cannot tell you," she wrote, "how distressed I was to read of your dreadful accident in the small town of Spofford, Texas. I would have been less affected had I been at your side. Worry is elastic—the farther you are from the one you love, the more powerful is the pull on your emotions. . . ."

In the early evening a telegram arrived for Frank Shaffer. His wife, in Lima, Ohio, had contracted a serious illness. Shaffer wired for confirmation, then prepared to take his leave—little more than two days after Charley Taylor had, perforce, departed for his wife's bedside. "It seems there is an epidemic among mechanicians' wives," he said. Again, each passenger in the Pullman and in the hangar car lined up to shake his hand and bid him farewell. Mabel kissed him warmly. Cal embraced him and said, "You're a man I can rely on. You have a job with me anytime you want it—as long as I am in the aviation business." Shaffer promised to rejoin the Vin Fiz party as soon as his wife's health permitted and, regardless of circumstances, would follow the group to California for a postflight reunion. He was driven to the SP depot and placed on the next train east.

Seventeen-year-old Charlie Wiggin was now chief mechanician. "It's all yours, kid," Cal told him. He could obtain assistance from Leo

McNally and Virgil Howey, each of whom could offer some experience with machinery, but competent servicing of the *Vin Fiz Flyer* seemed doubtful. "At least," Wiggin observed, "not one of us has a wife."

On Monday morning, examination revealed that the engine had been shifted one-half an inch backward, throwing the machine out of balance. A cracked cylinder wanted replacement, and the skids were found to be misaligned. In addition to structural corrections, it would be necessary to hoist, overhaul, and remount the motor. It was apparent that takeoff could not be effected before Tuesday morning. The hangar car was pulled back near the Evergreen Cemetery, where the *Vin Fiz* still leaned against the bordering adobe wall, and, with Cal contributing his skills, repair work began on the engine.

About fifty youngsters hovered about the disabled flying machine to watch the work in progress. Some of them hustled around, fetching funnels, stepladders, rags, wrenches, etc., and feeling quite important. Others, energized by the flying-machine craze that now swept into El Paso, had constructed their own "flying tops"* and launched them into the air from time to time. Occasionally an overzealous lad would edge in for a quick signature on the planes. "Hey, get back!" Cal yelled. "How would you like it if I came to your home and wrote my name on your piano?" A moment later, with a good-natured smile of resignation, he pointed out a bare space on the elevator surface and invited another inscription. Charlie Wiggin was more practical; when Cal withdrew for an afternoon of rest and sightseeing in El Paso, Wiggie exacted 5¢ from anyone who wished to affix his signature to the machine.

To reporters from the *El Paso Herald,* Cal pronounced himself pleased with the condition of his airplane and specified his departure for eight o'clock Tuesday morning, the thirty-first. What were his plans after reaching Los Angeles? He had received several offers, he said, to continue flying up the West Coast as far as Oregon. Such offers were under consideration, but his ambition lay in the construction of an airplane factory and a school near Los Angeles. The machine to be manufactured would be called the Rodgers-Wright biplane and would be patterned after the Wright Flyers, albeit with improvements developed through his own experience in flying coast to coast. Charley Taylor, now in Los Angeles and formerly chief mechanician at the Wright factory in Dayton, would assume that capacity

---

*A tin can was flattened, cut into a propeller shape, and mounted on a wooden thread spool. With a cord, the spool was spun like a top and released to soar 30 or 40 feet upward.

at the new aviation company.* Cal himself would teach flying to novice aviators.

"Why pick Los Angeles?"

"I was there once years ago. As I recall, it never rains, and the orange juice is free."

"Do you enjoy what you are doing?"

Cal paused for reflection. "There are some love affairs that are so intense, they burn themselves out. I don't know if I am close to that point."

"Are you going to fly back to New York?"

"Not for all the tea in China. Not for all the fish in the sea."

In late afternoon Cal and Charlie Wiggin strolled down to an isolated section of the Rio Grande. "Race you across," challenged Wiggie.

Temperatures in El Paso did not exceed 63° for the day. Cal was game despite the cold. "You're on, kid," he said, and the two men stripped and splashed their way across the shallow river dotted at this point by sandbars. "Down by the Rio Grande,"† sang Cal, still fascinated by "the Mexican landscape."

Cal and Wiggie were observed and followed shortly by crew members from the hangar car. A playful free-for-all ensued, with each man splashing water on the others. Then all hands banded together against their leader and ducked him in the cold river. Mabel soon located the party; she pulled on her heavy riding boots and waded in to join the frolic. She was promptly baptized alongside her husband.

The group gamboled and sang its winding way back to the train. Depressing thoughts and clinging hexes, it was agreed, had been washed away in the river.

After supper at the St. Regis Hotel, Cal read newspaper accounts of Fowler and of the Wrights and retired early. Bob Fowler had finally taken his leave of Yuma and before setting down at Maricopa had remained aloft for four hours and twenty-six minutes, an American endurance record (by eight minutes). At Tucson, while aiming for the baseball diamond of the University of Arizona, a puff of breeze had struck his planes and floated the *Cole Flyer* into the grandstand. Several hundred spectators scattered like a covey of quail, and none was injured.

*Los Angeles was already the site of aircraft manufacturers Glenn L. Martin, Harry S. Dosh, and the Eaton brothers. Gage and the Eatons also offered flying instruction.
†A ditty based on Frank Desprez's poem.

The forward structures of the airplane were demolished. "It is treacherous country still," said Fowler while helping to pull the wreckage from the bleachers. "The atmosphere is very light and so full of air holes that an aviator must be constantly on his guard to keep out of trouble."

At Kitty Hawk, North Carolina, Orville Wright, his nephew Buster Wright, and Alexander Ogilvie dismantled the buzzard machine, distributed its fabric covering to local housewives, and boarded a train for Dayton. Orville Wright described the "buzzard" as "essentially a Model EX biplane of the kind C. P. Rodgers is now using in his flight across the country, but modified as far as the heads and tails are concerned. Instead of the familiar horizontal heads or lifting planes, a single canvas plane is mounted six feet out in front at right angles to the main lifting planes. This is our automatic stabilizing device—in effect a jib sail attached to an airship instead of a sailboat." Further tests with the buzzard machine would continue at Simms Station.

Late Monday evening, aboard the last passenger train from San Antonio, Mrs. Sweitzer arrived in El Paso. After leaving San Antonio the previous Sunday, she had reached Pittsburgh Tuesday night. Two days were devoted to legal and personal affairs. Then, Friday afternoon, appropriate laments for the late Harry Sweitzer having been uttered, condolences having been registered by friends and relatives, the last will and testament having been read and executed, related documents having been signed and registered, Mrs. Sweitzer raised her veil and made haste for the B&O station. Three days later, after transferring to the Union Pacific Railroad and thence to the Southern Pacific line, she materialized— triumphant—at the St. Regis Hotel to reclaim her position with the Vin Fiz expedition.

At her side was a twenty-two-year-old beauty from Pittsburgh, an heiress to wealth and social standing, an offspring of irreproachable bloodlines, a damsel clad in the latest examples of *haute couture*. "This," said Mrs. Sweitzer, "is my traveling companion, Miss Lucy Belvedere."

"An unexpected surprise," said Mabel, with (perhaps deliberate) redundancy. She smiled at the young lady, summoning every tittle of charm and self-control instilled in her by Miss Finch's capable staff.

Cal's charm rose to the surface more naturally. "Miss Lucy," he murmured, bowing and kissing her hand in his most courtly manner.

It was arranged that Mrs. Sweitzer and Miss Belvedere would occupy the second stateroom of the private Pullman; Stewart deKrafft and Ed Merritt removed to berths. Some eyebrows were raised among the Vin

Fiz contingent, but the only comments uttered were highly flattering to Miss Lucy Belvedere.

"It was a delightful trip," Mrs. Sweitzer remarked for Mabel's benefit. "Whoever said that traveling in the West is dangerous for women certainly is uninformed. . . .

"Thirty-seven years ago I came to Arizona Territory." Here Mrs. Sweitzer turned to her son. "That's why I especially wanted to be with you—where your father and I lived after we married. It is important to be acquainted with your predecessors. You can't know where you are going unless you know where you have been."

Cal nodded his appreciation of his mother's thoughtfulness.

"And where did you find that terrible suit of clothes? . . ."

Tuesday morning the Vin Fiz party prepared for ascent from the edge of Evergreen Cemetery. The special train, parked at the Stanton Street Station, had been reprovisioned and thoroughly aired. The Negro stewards had carefully cleaned and refurbished Cal's oil-soaked flying suit in a solution of petroleum naphtha ("Not much of an improvement," allowed Mrs. Sweitzer). A supply of eggs and fresh vegetables was stored in chef Ed Davis's ice locker. Cuspidors vanished again lest they incite Mrs. Sweitzer's wrath. Mabel disposed of her Sobranny cigarettes— "Other women smoke; Amy Lowell even smokes big, black cigars," she complained to Cal. "I'll wager there would be no objection to Miss Lucy smoking."

G. J. Guyette replaced Frank Maud of the Sunset route as trainmaster and prepared to direct operations over the remaining stretches of the railroad. El Paso marked a journey of 3,204 miles from Sheepshead Bay, Long Island. A thousand miles remained—a thousand miles through mountains and deserts—to the edge of the continent. Between Texas and California lay the territories of New Mexico and Arizona, the land that had often been described to Cal as a young boy, the land where his father, the first bearer of his name, had served in the army of the United States —as his mother had needlessly reminded him.

The immediate itinerary called for a stop at Deming, New Mexico Territory, and thence to Bowie, Benson, and Tucson, Arizona Territory, for a possible meeting with Bob Fowler. At 10:41 A.M., October 31, two hours and forty-one minutes after the announced time, Cal lifted the *Vin Fiz* from the east side of El Paso, flew a line over the city, by the crumbling face of Commanche Peak, across the Rio Grande as it curves to the southeast to define the Texas-Mexico border, and onto the final segments of his transcontinental journey.

Thomas Hanly of the *New York American* had accompanied the expedition from its beginning. "The one certain thing about an aeroplane," he wrote, "is its uncertainty. Nothing else so far constructed, manufactured, or put together is so fragile. . . . [An aeroplane] can do the unexpected more times in a given number of minutes than any other thing on earth or above the earth. Compared with a flying machine, a frivolous woman is a Rock of Gibraltar.

"If there is anyone who can handle such a contraption, it is Cal Rodgers. He has taken to it as if he were raised in the air and was a little brother to the eagle. . . . He has the attributes of the sturdy, honest classes that first came to America—which helps to explain why he keeps going. He will get to Los Angeles and he will be all right when he lands. . . . It is the machine that is unsteady and doubtful. It is Rodgers who has the stamina and the strength. He is a man of iron constitution."

10

Rodgerses and Perrys— Heritage of Valor

CALBRAITH PERRY RODGERS, through two main stems of his family tree, could trace his descent from some of the most distinguished figures in U.S. military history. The adventures and derring-do of his ancestors were the primers of his youth. At the Rodgers family home in Havre de Grace, Maryland, the stern, uncompromising features of his bemedaled forebears stared down at him from rows of portraits in the gallery hall. Throughout his life he bore the ghosts of heroes past.

Though no Rodgers or Perry had crossed with the *Mayflower,* they did not lag far behind in reaching the New World. The Rodgers line was established in America by John Rodgers, a native of Scotland who arrived in the 1750s to settle along the banks of the Susquehanna River in eastern Maryland.* A zealous advocate of the cause of liberty, he fought with gallantry and bravery as a colonel of militia in the Revolutionary War. Of

---

*Proprietor of the village tavern in Havre de Grace, he could trace his lineage back to the Middle Ages and could recite details of the Rodgerses' first entry into Great Britain with William the Conqueror. One ancestral namesake commanded the vessel that rescued Alexander Selkirk (Robinson Crusoe) from the island of Juan Fernandez.

his nine children, two—John Rodgers and George Washington Rodgers —became commodores of the U.S. Navy.

John Rodgers, the second, displayed a fascination with the sea from an early age and at thirteen sailed on his first vessel (after echoing his father's oath that neither he nor any of his descendants unto the tenth generation shall touch a drop of alcoholic spirits). At nineteen he received his first merchant command. Upon one of his passages to Europe, his ship was borne by adverse winds and currents into the North Sea. Provisions nearly exhausted, three men frozen to death, his crew refused to climb aloft to secure the icebound rigging. The young officer stripped off his jacket and shirt and ascended the mast himself as an example for the men. He rose to command of the flagship USS *Constitution*, ever mindful of the unspoken maxim of the Rodgers succession: "Failure is more to be feared than death."

George Washington Rodgers also proved an officer who would lead, not drive, his men to battle. In 1809, while visiting at his elder brother's home in Greenleafs Point, he struck up a friendship with then-lieutenant Oliver Hazard Perry, a commander in Commodore John Rodgers's squadron. It was Lieutenant Perry's sister, Anna Maria, however, who gained his deeper affection. Their marriage, the first of several between the Rodgers clan and the Perry clan, produced four sons, all of whom served in the United States Army or Navy.

The Perrys had been rooted in America by Edward Perry, a Friend who emigrated from England about 1639, married Mary Freeman, a member of one of the First Families of Plymouth Colony, and settled in Sandwich, Massachusetts. His descendants held to his firm Quaker beliefs until a great-grandson, Christopher Raymond Perry, broke the pacifist tradition by enlisting first in the Continental Army and subsequently on Yankee privateers. In 1799 Christopher Perry received a captain's commission in the U.S. Navy commanding the *General Greene*. One of his junior officers was his firstborn son, thirteen-year-old Midshipman Oliver Hazard Perry.

Fourteen years later Oliver Hazard Perry, then bearing the rank of commodore, defeated the British squadron under Captain Barclay in the battle of Lake Erie and thereby gained his greatest fame. To cap this American victory, the first after a series of disasters, he sent to General William H. Harrison the message "We have met the enemy, and they are ours." He died of yellow fever at Port of Spain, Trinidad, three days beyond his thirty-fourth birthday.

Matthew Calbraith Perry followed in the wake of his eldest brother to enlist as a midshipman. He, too, fulfilled a distinguished naval career, certified by the rank of commodore. His distinctive achievement, negotiation of the first treaty between the United States and Japan, gained him world renown. In two visits to the Japanese Islands in 1853 and 1854, Commodore M. C. Perry (known as "Calbraith" to his friends and as "Old Bruin" to his sailors) carried President Fillmore's letters to the emperor and compelled the Japanese to receive American ships and to recognize American trading interests.

"Before you could get a Perry to abandon his mission," wrote a newspaper editor, "the Devil would have to drag him 'round Good Hope and 'round the Horn and 'round perdition's flames." Echoed Anna Maria Perry Rodgers, "In our family, ambition is the only virtue, sloth the only vice."

In 1814 Matthew Calbraith Perry had married Jane Slidell (scion of a wealthy and influential New York family). They continued their mutual tradition of large families with an issue of six daughters and four sons. One daughter, Caroline Slidell Perry, married August Belmont, a Jewish emigrant from Rhenish Prussia, who had settled in New York as a representative of the Rothschild banking house. Another daughter, Sarah Perry, espoused Robert Smith Rodgers, second of the eleven offspring of Commodore John Rodgers. Robert and Sarah begat five children: Jane Perry Rodgers, Robert Slidell Rodgers (who became an attorney in Kansas City), Frederick Rodgers (admiral, USN), John A. Rodgers (admiral, USN), and Calbraith Perry Rodgers (captain, U.S. Cavalry.)

Calbraith Rodgers, the third son, was born July 1, 1845, on his father's farm in Harford County, Maryland. He was fifteen years of age when his father, commissioned a colonel, and two elder brothers took up arms for the Union forces. "Mollycoddlers who would not fight for their country are not worth a heap of horsepies," said the colonel as he marched away. Calbraith was left in charge of the farm, a younger brother and sister, and his family's business interests. Thus prevented from enlisting in the Civil War, he secured an appointment to the army in November 1866 as a second lieutenant in the Fifth Cavalry.

In the 1869 battle of Summit Springs, Calbraith Rodgers gained distinguished mention for his actions. For two years, beginning in 1871, he was detached from his regiment for recruiting service in several eastern cities. He was thereby afforded opportunity for reunion with his brother John Rodgers, already a commander in the U.S. Navy. At a party in Pittsburgh, Pennsylvania, at the home of Martha and Alexander Chambers (cofounder with his brother David of the Pittsburgh Glass Works), the two young officers met their hosts' daughters, and subsequently married them

—Calbraith with Maria Chambers in 1873, John with Elizabeth Chambers in 1880. When he rejoined his regiment in the Territory of Arizona in December 1873, Lieutenant Calbraith Rodgers was accompanied by his undaunted bride.

After a two-year term as quartermaster at Camp Grant in Arizona Territory, Lieutenant Rodgers fought with his regiment in the 1876 Sioux campaign in the Wyoming and Dakota territories. He was promoted to captain, led his company at the battle of Slim Buttes, in engagements against the hostile Sioux near the Big Horn Mountains, and against the Nez Percé in the Wind River country.

On August 1, 1878, he was summoned to temporary duty at Fort Russell, Territory of Wyoming. His wife and two young children, John Perry and Martha (known as Patty), traveled with him and took up residence at the garrison of Fort McKinney. Three weeks later—on August 23—while in command of an Indian scouting party, Captain Rodgers was standing in the entrance to his pitched tent on the Fetterman Road, twenty-five miles north of Rock Creek Station, Wyoming Territory, when he was struck by lightning and killed.

Mrs. Maria Chambers Rodgers was four and a half months pregnant at the time of her husband's death. She returned with her children to Pittsburgh after the military funeral. There, on January 12, 1879, she gave birth to Calbraith Perry, Jr., the namesake preordained.

Each Perry, each Rodgers was imbued from childhood with the knowledge that his forefathers had been living in—and had helped to elevate —America for generations. His heart beat strong with the sense that this ancestry rendered him enviable above other men, that destiny would sound a summons to his soul.

Despite her state of widowhood—or because of it—Maria Rodgers heard the angels' trumpets yet more keenly than most of her kinsmen. She raised her three children as a domineering but loving mother. Not until they were grown did she consent to marry again—to Harry Sweitzer, a Pittsburgh businessman. "My children are my life," she reiterated to friends and relatives, and pledged to rear them with all the privileges of class and money to which they were entitled. From her father's interest in the Pittsburgh Glass Works, Mrs. Rodgers received a substantial if not munificent annuity, and the U. S. Army added a widow's pension of $20 monthly plus $2 for each of her three children.

At the age of six, her third child, Calbraith, contracted scarlet fever. His recovery was effected with permanent damage to his sense of equilibrium; hearing was materially impaired in one ear, slightly in the other. He also suffered a slight speech impediment; the rhythm of his voice changed —uneven, like the whinny of a curious horse. A significant turn was noted in the boy: From an outgoing, boisterous child, he grew into a reticent, reserved, even shy young man. Two visits to a pediatrician in Paris failed to mitigate his affliction, and he and his mother accepted the reality that he would be unable, in consequence, to pursue their common dream of a military career. Mrs. Rodgers, at the moment her son was born, had clearly perceived the shape of his life. Now fate was distorting that shape.

Young Calbraith's life was punctuated by ringing reminders of his illustrious lineage and the obligation to perpetuate its distinction. Family socials were frequent; in such gatherings, it was said, one couldn't fire a shot without sinking an admiral, a ship designer, or, at the very least, a water commissioner. Family funerals were often graced by congressmen, cabinet officers, foreign ministers, and other titled officials. Short of completing his twelfth year (November 1890), Calbraith was taken to New York City to attend final rites for August Belmont; J. Pierpont Morgan, Grover Cleveland, and New York governor David Hall were among the twelve pallbearers. Several months later he was again in New York, for the burial of William Perry Rodgers, secretary of the Municipal Consolidation Commission. On the eve of his thirteenth birthday, he suffered through lengthy obsequies in Washington, D.C., for Rear Admiral Christopher Raymond Perry Rodgers (brother of William Perry Rodgers) and witnessed interment at the Naval Academy. As each member of the clan was gathered unto his ancestors, his heirs—particularly the younger lads—were exhorted to pick up and raise yet higher the fallen standard.

Summers, school holidays, and occasional weekends throughout the year, Calbraith was packed off to the Sion Hill home of his aunt and uncle in Havre de Grace, a locale he preferred to his mother's house in the smoky air of Pittsburgh. His closest companion at these times was his double cousin, John Rodgers, two years his junior. (John A. and Elizabeth Chambers Rodgers had begat three sons: Alexander, John, and Robert Perry.) The two boys amused themselves in the cavernous yawn of the mansion's drawing rooms, only occasionally restrained by the disapproving stares from the ancestral portraits that lined the halls and stairways, the tut-tutting grandfather clocks, and the white Ionic pillars that could support the earth.

During his early school years, Calbraith was unable to find a discipline suited to his fancy. Mrs. Rodgers saw to it that he was steeped in family history, but, beyond his sixteenth birthday, she could effect no further inroads on his mind. He had decided that he could not stand in his father's shoes and that, ergo, he would not try.

In September 1897, Cal enrolled at Mercersburg Academy, Mercersburg, Pennsylvania, 120 miles from his Pittsburgh home. He lodged on campus at the Main Hall and concentrated on the athletic field to the detriment of his studies. At the position of left guard on the academy football team, he performed with more energy than skill. Six feet three inches and 175 pounds, Cal was the heaviest and tallest athlete on the team (and the only player to top six feet). He joined several social and sporting groups on the Mercersburg campus and was generally regarded as a friendly chap somewhat addicted to practical jokes.

A reputation for recklessness was acquired when a group of upperclassmen extended a plank across the twelve foot chasm between two three-story buildings and dared their juniors to cross it. Cal Rodgers was the only student to accept the challenge.

In February 1898, after a single semester, he left the academy, telling his mother that he was "not progressing toward my real goal in life."

That goal remained elusive. He and his brother John Perry (known as Perry to his friends and relatives) discussed plans for traveling to Alaska, where they would acquire both fortune and adventure (in the Klondike gold rush). The execution of such plans was effectively squelched by Mrs. Rodgers.

For several years Cal resided in New York City, either with relatives or in small Manhattan apartments subsidized by his mother. Mostly, he expended his energies on various sporting activities. He met Columbia University football coach George Sanford and, when Columbia returned to gridiron competition for the '99 season (after a hiatus of eleven years), faithfully attended each Saturday's game. He was present at—and for years afterward recounted his recollections of—Columbia's startling 5–0 upset over Yale (October 28, 1899).

An opportunity for a trip to Japan arose in 1901 when his uncle, Admiral Frederick Rodgers, was invited for a ceremony commemorating the advent of Commodore Matthew Calbraith Perry. Cal evinced a lackadaisical attitude, however, and was dropped from the party. Admiral Rodgers and Japanese premier Viscount Katsura duly delivered memorial addresses on the site of the reception hall at Kurihama, where Commodore Perry was first received by the emperor's plenipotentiaries.

To compensate her son and to expand his knowledge of America, Mrs. Rodgers (about to become Mrs. Sweitzer) paid for a holiday trip to the West Coast. Cal arrived in Los Angeles via the SP Railroad and was put up at the Hotel Van Nuys (where President McKinley was housed during his tour of the West). "This city has little to recommend it," he wrote. "Although 100,000 souls call it home, they do not much show themselves, and the atmosphere is one of a small village. . . . While electric trolleys are in general use, at least one horse car remains. . . . Attractive young ladies are apparently excluded from the environs. . . ."

Cal continued up the Pacific Coast to San Francisco, where he found the climate more to his liking: "The ladies here are quite friendly and are usually seen sunning their teeth at the smallest excuse. And there are no shortage of establishments that cater to the tastes of young men." After a month Cal boarded a Union Pacific train to return to the East Coast, having, in his words, "upheld the family honor."

In September 1899, John Rodgers, following his service in the Spanish-American war, had secured an appointment as a cadet at large to the Naval Academy at Annapolis. Cal took up sailing and was presented by his mother with a twenty-eight-foot sloop. As a gift for his twenty-third birthday, she advanced a year's dues at the New York Yacht Club. Cal was elected a member thereof on February 13, 1902, sponsored by his uncle, Admiral John A. Rodgers. The following year Midshipman John Rodgers, recently graduated from his Annapolis studies, was also admitted. A fellow member and one of the founders of the club was their cousin-once-removed August Belmont, Jr.

John Rodgers served on a series of naval vessels and as a recruiting officer in Puget Sound, Washington. He received his ensign's rank in February 1905, and three years later was commissioned as a lieutenant, S. G. Cal, meanwhile, had focused his energies on motorcycle racing. He purchased a 1904 Harley-Davidson cycle and, through the maintenance and repair of that vehicle, became adept at the mechanical work he found to his liking. He entered sundry competitive racing events, rarely finishing with a cash prize. As his most notable achievement, he drove his motorcycle over a 500-mile course between New York City and Buffalo in a time of eighteen hours.

Cal's other interests ranged over automobile racing, motorboat racing, polo, and rifle competition. He proved adroit at each activity, but never with the promise of gaining primacy. He continued his general unemployment, supported by a monthly allowance from his mother. That formidable personage, married to Harry Sweitzer since 1901, assured him of an "ever open door" to her home in Pittsburgh. Cal's sister had married W. Albert Pease, Jr., a New York real estate broker, in 1902; she, too, welcomed him to her Hempstead, Long Island, home whenever he drove up, the roaring of his Harley-Davidson engine heralding his arrival. When not staying with his mother or sister, he would often sojourn at the apartment of his cousin John in Washington, D.C., or at Sion Hill in Havre de Grace.

He was not averse to lengthy tours on his Harley-Davidson, occasionally driving between Washington, D.C., and Pittsburgh or between Pittsburgh and New York. In New York City, he would, at whim, race his cycle from the Battery through Bowling Green, along lower Broadway, across Longacre Square (renamed Times Square in 1904), and as far north as the mayor's residence (first Seth Low, then George McClellan) at Archibald Gracie's country estate on the East River at Eighty-eighth Street. He would speed by "Apple Mary" (who, in return for a copper or nickel, never gave an apple), wave at the doughboys who strolled the Battery streets on leave from Governors Island, and draw disapproving stares from the footmen along "millionaires row" (the blocks of expensive, lavishly adorned private mansions that covered much of Fifth Avenue from Fiftieth to Eightieth streets).

Shortly after he had acquired his first cycle, Cal had taken to wearing a stiff-brimmed cloth cap and smoking long cigars. He was developing a reputation as a "playboy"; divers lady friends found the tall, broad-shouldered, narrow-hipped, taciturn young man to their liking, although none won the approving eye of Mrs. Sweitzer.

In the early fall of 1905, perhaps to remove her son from the embraces of his fancy New York ladies, Mrs. Sweitzer invited him to join her and her husband on a cruise from New York to the Bahamas and the Caribbean. The party rented a cottage in Nassau for two weeks and a small yacht that Calbraith could pilot about the nearby islands. On one such excursion the Sweitzers' craft passed a boat rented by the Graves family: Frederick Graves; his wife, Isabelle; their son, Frederick; and their four daughters, Mabel, Bess, Irene, and Sallie. Mrs. Graves, intent upon waving at her fellow vacationers and perhaps preoccupied with the continuing burden of four unmarried daughters, toppled overboard. Cal leaped to her rescue and pulled her aboard the Sweitzers' boat. Thus it was that he met, at one thrust, the entire Graves family. Thus it was that he and Mabel Graves began an acquaintanceship that, within a year, blossomed into marriage.

Mabel had just turned 23. Openly flirtatious, she was not rightly a member of the "fast" sorority but spoke in the accents it approved of. After the chance encounter off Nassau, she and Cal dined together, sailed together, and swam together in the surf at Hog Island. When the

Graveses continued to Cuba on the next stage of their holiday, daughter Mabel had arranged a rendezvous in New York with her new beau.

Mrs. Sweitzer was not at all enamored of her son's amatory entanglement—"a teacup romance," she sniffed. Mr. Graves dwelt as a banker of some prominence in Bennington, Vermont. He had become casually acquainted with Rudyard Kipling during the writer's stay in that city and could command some degree of social stature. He—and consequently Mabel—claimed descent from Thomas Graves, commander of the British fleet at Boston. Mabel listed herself as a Bennington socialite. To certify that appellation, she had enrolled at Miss Finch's School for Young Ladies and had graduated with the school's first class (her previous schooling was acquired at the National Park Seminary in Washington, D.C.). These pretensions failed to impress Mrs. Sweitzer, who regarded the ebullient young lady as a predator in pursuit of her son. When Mabel was noted with a trace of rouge and rice powder and the whisper of a floral scent, Mrs. Sweitzer lectured her that such artifices were appropriate for actresses and fancy women, not for the girl who would grace her son Calbraith. Mrs. Sweitzer's disapproval of the Graves girl took the form of arranged introductions between her son and other young ladies, who in her opinion were more befitting his heritage and promise.

In the summer of 1906, shortly after the death of Mrs. Isabelle Graves, without prior announcement, Cal and Mabel were joined in wedlock. A justice of the peace performed the ceremony. Mrs. Sweitzer, to her agony, was presented with a *fait accompli*.

Marriage did not alter Cal's mode of living. The couple stayed at hotels or at the homes of friends or relatives, rarely in one location for more than a few weeks. Mr. Graves attempted to lure his son-in-law into real estate ventures in Bennington by offering choice parcels as inducement, but Cal evinced no inclination to plant himself in Vermont—or elsewhere. He and Mabel played tennis, sailed his sloop around Long Island Sound or down to Chesapeake Bay in summer, and avoided talk of the future. Mabel was content: "Whatever Calbraith wishes is what I wish," she wrote to her father.

Mabel's interests lay in art, music, and theater, although she had acquired little more than a dilettante's perception in any one discipline. When in New York City, she would attend—with friends—Alfred Stieglitz's "291" Gallery at Fifth Avenue, or Koster and Biel's Music Hall just west of Herald Square on the Great White Way, or one of the phonograph parlors on Third Avenue, where for 5¢ she could listen to a Gramophone for over an hour.

With Mabel thus engaged, Cal would patronize the six-day bicycle races at the Garden's "Squirrel Cage" or pass his time along "Automobile Row," which was developing on Broadway north of Fifty-second Street. Smith and Maybley's automobile salesroom particularly enthralled him with its selection of vehicles from Panhard and other European manufacturers. Automobiles were gaining currency in New York streets. The first metered cabs appeared in October 1907, and the elegant black hansom cabs began their decline.

When Cal and Mabel dined out, it was frequently at Nigger Mike's Place with its singing waiters or at one of the Chinese restaurants on Mott Street. Afterward they would stroll about through the gaudily painted, lanterned shops of Chatham Square. Weekends might encompass drives into the countryside, attendance at one of the amusement parks popular in Coney Island—Steeplechase Park, Playland at Rockaway Beach, Dreamland Park (its magnificent columns and arches burned to the ground in May 1911), Luna Park, with its castles, palaces, and temples limned in electric lights—or at Balmer's Great Atlantic Bathing and Swimming Baths.

Over the years from 1906 to 1910, Cal Rodgers continued his efforts at sporting competitions, both on land and at sea, but acquired no substantial rewards thereby. His destiny confronted him like a puzzle with a critically missing piece. Money remained a perennial problem, albeit he seemed unable to concern himself with financial matters until they piled on his doorstep. "It don't make anny diff'rence whether or not ye have money," he mimicked Mr. Dooley (the only literary character he could quote). "If ye're born to be rich ye'll be rich, an' if ye're born to be poor ye'll be poor."* For failure to pay his dues, he was dropped from the New York Yacht Club for four months in 1907 until Mrs. Sweitzer heeded his pleas and restored the payments.

Friends and relatives progressed in business or in military rank and urged Cal to consider an endeavor with greater prospects than those of racing cycles or boats. Lieutenant John Rodgers, carving a career in the U.S. Navy, entered the engineering branch, received instruction at the Naval Torpedo Station at Brooklyn and Sag Harbor, and served as engineering officer on the *St. Louis.* In 1909 his brother Alexander Rodgers sought adventure in Alaska and was lost.† His remaining brother, Robert

---

*From *Dissertations by Mr. Dooley* by Peter Finley Dunne.

†In July 1910, Rear Admiral John A. Rodgers, then commandant of the Bremerton Navy Yard at Puget Sound, retired from active duty to search the Alaskan wilderness (unsuccessfully) for his son.[1]

Perry, earned credentials as an architect and showed promise of success in that profession.[2] Cal's brother John Perry, after squandering a sizable fraction of his mother's resources on stock-market transactions, borrowed yet additional funds and decamped first for Paris and then for South Africa in search of gold.

In his brother's absence, Cal bore Mrs. Sweitzer's full gravamen that her sons were not fulfilling the potential bequeathed to them. Each was born, she reiterated, not as a man apart; each was fused eternally with his ancestors. Mrs. Sweitzer, ever a rallying point for *noblesse oblige*, retained an unclouded vision of the past and how it should intersect with the future.

A telegram from John Perry invited Cal to enlist in his treasure hunt. Her elder son, Mrs. Sweitzer lamented in a letter to her daughter, had "thrown himself astride the horse of adventurism [sic] rather than bridling the animal." She forbade Cal from following in his footsteps.

Withal, on March 23, 1909, Cal sailed from Hoboken aboard the steamer *Hamburg.* * At Durban, South Africa, he was met by John Perry. ("Durban is a surprisingly neat, well-kept city . . . everywhere one sees rickshaws drawn by white-coated coolies.") Five hundred miles of rail carried them through the Orange Free State into the Transvaal and Pretoria.† There, Cal was introduced to John Perry's "associate," Jaime Vinhales, a Portuguese "agent" who claimed to have worked for both Cecil Rhodes and Barney Barnato.

Vinhales accompanied them to Johannesburg ("low, dirty, ramshackle buildings; a maze of crooked, dirty streets; men of color wherever you turn") and thence by ox wagon to his "secret mine" in the Witwaters-rand.‡ This mine, so Vinhales swore, had been abandoned despite a profusion of gold veins that lay beneath its surface.

South African gold, the two brothers soon learned, was not California gold—to be gleaned by prospectors with shovel, cradle, and sieve. Gold in "the Rand" was embedded in cement-hard quartz; to extract it, Vin-

---

*The most celebrated passenger aboard the *Hamburg* was Theodore Roosevelt, who, having entrusted the country to his chosen successor, William Howard Taft, was bound for an extended African safari. (Members of the New York Yacht Club toasted the health of African lions with the anticipation that Teddy might provide one of them a satisfactory meal.) T.R. returned to New York June 18, 1910, to the greatest public reception ever seen, with tens of thousands chanting, "Teddy, Teddy!"

†The Union of South Africa was formed the following year (1910).

‡Afrikaans for "White Waters Rand," an area 170 miles long by 100 miles wide south of Pretoria.

hales sold them explosives, drilling equipment, and cyanide chemicals.

For three months Cal and John Perry excavated tunnels and shafts and hacked at the matrix of quartz rock, living more belowground than above —without detecting a trace of gold ore. By August they had exhausted their funds. A letter to Mrs. Sweitzer pleading for financial support brought only the offer of passage home.

John Perry scoffed at the thought of failure. "In this country," he told Cal, "they have never heard of a Rodgers or a Perry. You can be whatever you want to be." He had picked up rumors of diamondiferous deposits along the Vaal River and, with another "agent," departed in further pursuit of his dream. Reared with the same family icons, Cal, too, knew the personal dangers of failure, but his roots absorbed no nourishment from the mines of South Africa. He returned to the U.S.—and the welcoming embraces of his wife and mother. Still he sought an appropriate stage to act out the drama within him.

Of all the members of the Rodgers and Perry clans, there was one, August Belmont, Jr., who had unquestionably attained great wealth and high repute (he had financed the first subway in New York City and was president of the Rapid Transit Subway Construction Company). On August 10, 1910, he and Cal encountered each other at the New York Yacht Club. Since Cal was mechanically inclined, Belmont advised, he should consider the design and manufacture of automobiles as an enterprise appropriate to his talents. (Other investment counselors at the club disagreed. The automobile "craze" would peter out, they maintained, as had the earlier bicycle "craze," which had seen 10 million bicycles on the road at the turn of the century.) Belmont urged Cal to develop means to overcome some of the vehicular machine's inherent disadvantages. Relief was needed, he asserted, from tire blowouts, spark-plug defects, carburetor troubles, transmission difficulties, and other assorted ailments that required each motorist to be his own mechanic. Cal promised to ponder the possibilities of automotive improvement and to report his conclusions. He never did.

Always there seemed to be a shadow that fell between the reaching and the grasping, the aspiration and the realization. Past the age of thirty, Cal Rodgers saw no focus to his future. He continued to live on the cusp between gossamer illusions and bedrock reality. He continued his search for the jeweled sword he could pull from its vise of stone.

Throughout the years of Cal's manhood, the vehicle he was ultimately to ride to his end was spreading its wings in uncertain flight. At first and

for some time, aviation gained little more notice in the world than did
C. P. Rodgers. When it was not ignored or ridiculed, it was clouded by
personal attacks, publicized disputes, claims of patent infringements, and
a plethora of misconceptions.

Few newspapers chose to print the story of the world's first powered
flight at Kitty Hawk, North Carolina, December 17, 1903, and the few
that did so confused the facts that comprehension was improbable. Editors had been misled by earlier reports and were skeptical of allegations
that man could fly. The two brothers, Wilbur and Orville Wright, who
claimed the achievement were unknown. Not many readers took cogni-
zance of the report.

For two years the Wrights continued their experiments in aeronautics
around the Huffman cow pasture near Dayton, Ohio, developing a succession of advancements, notably the banked turn. By the end of 1905 they
had reached the stage of twenty-mile flights at speeds of 38 mph. Yet so
ingrained in man's deepest consciousness was the impossibility of flight
that no printed account or rumor could gain credence. Even some of those
who witnessed a machine in the air over Dayton concluded that what they
had seen was a *trompe l'oeil* without real significance.

Efforts to arouse the U.S. government to the new invention met with
entrenched apathy or with tepid responses. Negotiations with the U.S.
War Department, the British War Office, and the French Army all fell
before the financial demands of the Wrights, their mania for secrecy, and
their overweening righteousness. Engaged in these matters of business,
neither Wilbur nor Orville Wright took wing for a period of two and a
half years (from November 1905 to May 1908). Even the most sensitive
ear could detect no whisper of public awareness, curiosity, or comprehension of aeronautics.

The focus of aviation progress shifted to Europe and specifically to
France, where Louis Blériot, Henri Farman, and the Voison brothers
staked out claims to the aeronautical supremacy believed by the French
to be their rightful dominion. Concerned by this competition, the
Wrights acted to assert their superiority (French aeronauts had spoken
skeptically and condescendingly of the Wright brothers' "alleged"
flights). In the summer of 1908 Wilbur demonstrated the *Wright Flyer*
before delirious crowds at Le Mans (125 miles southwest of Paris), and
Orville performed the first tests of an aeroplane for the U.S. Army—over
the parade grounds of Fort Myer, Washington, D.C. Heavier-than-air
flight was now an actuality accepted by the Western World.

Also in the summer of 1908 Glenn Curtiss had publicly flown the *June Bug** (on July 4—the first "officially observed" powered flight in the U.S.). The Wrights, now faced with their first American competitor, countered with a patent-infringement lawsuit.

Incessant litigation oozed through the courts and dampened the spirits of other designers who struggled to move from the shadow of the Wrights.[3]

Because of the litigation and because of their continued reluctance to sanction open demonstrations, the Wrights rejected a request from the Aero Club of America to represent the United States at the Reims Air Meet in August 1909. Curtiss accepted in their stead and scrambled to build the *Golden Flyer,* the entry with which he won the James Gordon Bennett Trophy.

With Reims and with the American Meet at Dominguez, the airplane swept onto the stage of history. Its outlandishness and very impracticality endowed it with miraculous, almost religious, overtones. Somehow, it was the harbinger of a glorious new world.

In Glenn Curtiss and Louis Paulhan, aviation found men who could arouse public interest, public support, and public participation. The next step demanded someone who could stir the crowds to adulation and hero worship, someone who could perform a feat of aeronautics so daring and so magnificent that the last remaining skeptic would fall to his knees in genuflection.

By the end of 1910, aviation had not yet been introduced to its sworn champion. The office was a risky one; thirty-seven candidates had been killed in their attempts to master the skies. Calbraith Perry Rodgers, future suitor to the goddess of glory, was scarcely conscious of his intended's existence. Introductions came five months into the year of 1911. The affair began at once. Its climax resounded throughout the world on November 5, 1911, from the infield at Tournament Park, Pasadena.

*Curtiss had formed an association with Dr. Alexander Graham Bell and others to design and construct a succession of flying machines, of which the *June Bug* was the third.

11

Triumph at Pasadena

WEST OF THE Rio Grande, Cal soared by the rugged and bluish Franklin Range at close to a mile-a-minute rate, a slight breeze favoring his course. Ninety miles and 100 minutes from east El Paso, he worked into the Mimbres Valley, circled gracefully around the city of Deming, New Mexico Territory, and lit on the SP right-of-way southeast of the Harvey House. Bulletins of the aviator's progress had been posted in the window of the *Deming Headlight,* and about 1,000 persons hailed the birdman upon his arrival.

The special train followed the *Vin Fiz* closely into Deming (where thirty years earlier the SP and the Santa Fe were joined to form the second transcontinental railroad). Charlie Wiggin and Leo McNally refueled the engine, administered a quick inspection, and replaced a broken magneto spring. Mabel sold a few postcards (no stamps) and, with a wary eye, scouted Lucy Belvedere as the young woman sashayed out to join the admiring circle around the airman. Mrs. Sweitzer engaged in conversation with the Reverend H. M. Bruce. "I breathe a prayer for Calbraith's safety every minute he is in the air," she told him. Responded the Reverend

Bruce: "I am sure he needs your prayers more than do earth-abiding men."

Train and airplane departed Deming simultaneously at 1:50 P.M. under a sky of the deepest blue in nature's palette. From Deming's altitude of 4,342 feet, the *Vin Fiz* spiraled several times over the fields of yucca to the west while the locomotive chugged up a grade and through a cut between Red Mountain and Black Mountain, the latter with a peak at 5,422 feet. Twenty-six miles from Deming, amid some of the most rugged and magnificent terrain in the U.S., lay the 4,584-foot pass of the Continental Divide.*

West of the crossing, the train accelerated into a steep, twelve-mile descent shackled with a succession of horseshoe bends. Engineer "Poochey" Frederickson raced through the tight curves "hell-bent for salvation." Those in the Pullman and hangar car were flung about like tenpins. Luggage scattered onto the floor. Dishes and glassware in the kitchen compartment shot from their shelves. The stewards, George and George, fell to their knees with pious laments. Mabel was passing the adjoining stateroom and was flung into her mother-in-law's arms, their first embrace in five years. Lucy Belvedere swooned onto her panel bed, suffering a case of the vapors. Conductor C. C. Carter turned pale and grabbed for the emergency brake as it seemed that the cars would lift from the rails. But Frederickson would not be deterred; he scorched by a water tank scheduled as a stop and then was forced to steer through curves with even greater speed, relying on his momentum to reach the next tank. Frederickson was exultant at the end of the run. His passengers were less enraptured. Mrs. Sweitzer threatened a formal complaint to railway officials.

At Lordsburg,† N.M.T., thirty-eight miles beyond the divide, a traveling carnival had pitched its tents, rides, slum joints, grab stands, and girlie shows just south of the railroad tracks for its annual encampment in Hidalgo County. Almost the entire population of Lordsburg strolled its midway, ogled freaks in its sideshows, competed in gaffed contests of skill and chance, and partook of other lures touted by the carnie talkers. With anticipation of the cross-country airplane at keen pitch, the Southern Pacific agent had agreed to sound the switch-engine whistle (the signal for a fire alarm) as soon as the flying machine hove into view. Even before the whistle blew, men and boys had climbed the water tower and to the

---

*A principal motive underlying the Gadsden Purchase of 1853 was to obtain this lowest crossing point of the divide.

†Formerly Lordsborough, named for a construction engineer with the SP Railroad.

roofs of boxcars and buildings to peer eastward through cupped hands or binoculars.

They first saw a moving black blob. Although no airplane had previously favored Lordsburg, pictures of Wright biplanes had been printed in the *Lordsburg Liberal,* and the blob did not conform to expectations. As it approached, the phenomenon resolved itself into a genuine airplane attended by a murder of crows. Large birds—even eagles—that trespassed the crows' feeding grounds were thus discouraged. The technique proved unavailing with the mechanical bird.

By the final blasts of the switch-engine whistle, the carnival midway was deserted. The town populace converged on the baseball park, where sheets of linsey-woolsey had been laid out to form a large *X.* Numbers were increased by ranchers and farmers from Redrock, diggers from Shakespeare near the "85" mine, even homesteaders from Animas, thirty-four miles to the south. By the time the *Vin Fiz* dipped over the diamond, the crowd had covered the area so thoroughly that its escorting crows would have found difficulty in landing. As Cal circled back to the east, the link chain to the spark-advance treadle snapped. He pulled the compression-release cable and volplaned into a field about 800 yards north of the railroad track.

Soon surrounded by a frenetic mob, Cal remained in his seat. Several carnies came up to stare at the goggled, leather-clad figure, a freak from another world. The aviator, in turn, was particularly fascinated by the lady snake charmer who stood before him, a python draped from her neck. He asked if hers was not a dangerous profession. "It's not a big drop," she said, "if you fall off a snake."

Some of the more avid youngsters in Lordsburg, unable to find space for their names on the lower warping plane, brought up a stepladder to inscribe the upper plane. One lad cut loose the cap to the gasoline tank (the spare had been chained to the tank after the original cap was stolen at Scranton, Pennsylvania) before crew members arrived from the special train to shoo him away. Inspections by Wiggin and McNally showed nine rollers lost from one of the drive-chains (out of thirty-four). Were two adjacent rollers to break, the three men knew, the chain tended to climb the sprocket—a potential for disaster. "Never mind, boys," said Cal, "we'll fix it at Willcox."

Mabel sold a few postcards and souvenir pennants. Lucy Belvedere remained aboard the Pullman, the earlier lurching of the train still echoing in her stomach.

Cal was interviewed by Don Kedzie, editor of the *Lordsburg Liberal.*

New Mexico, Kedzie told Cal, had modified its new state constitution and would soon be admitted to the U.S.[1]—probably before another airplane paid its respects to Lordsburg.

"What does the area have to recommend itself?" asked Cal.

"Well," said Kedzie, "we have more tarantulas, more centipedes, and more vinegarroons than anywhere else in the Union."

"I'll remember that," said Cal.

During the interview Wiggin scampered off to a local greengrocer and persuaded the man to contribute a large potato to the enterprise. The potato was wedged into the gasoline tank, and Wiggin, mimicking Charley Taylor, pronounced the machine ready for flight.

Cal waved his arm, and the crewmen pulled down on the propellers.

> **Oct. 31, Tuesday. Take-off Lordsburg 3:25 P.M. Across Pyramid Mountains, Stein's Pass (into Arizona Territory). San Simon, Bowie. Landed Willcox* 4:45 P.M.**
>
> *I had never seen a sky so vivid, a view so vast and empty that it seemed only my aeroplane was alive in the world. Time runs a different course in this country. You have the feeling you could fly on for a thousand years.*

Dropping to earth 100 feet from the Willcox depot, the *Vin Fiz* lost momentum while still ten feet up and split both skids on contact. Further examination revealed a broken magneto spring and two increasingly toothless propeller chains (eleven rollers were now missing from one chain and five from the other). Cal's hope of reaching Tucson and meeting Bob Fowler was tabled for the nonce, unrealized.

Upon registering at his Tucson hotel Monday evening, Fowler had written, "By air from Los Angeles. No Word from Rodgers yet." Now, learning of Cal's stop in Willcox, he announced that he would delay his departure for one day to vouchsafe the encounter. The West-to-East flier was, in any event, awaiting shipments of essential components from Dayton (to replace those smashed at the baseball bleachers Monday afternoon). It was proposed by Tucson aviation enthusiasts that the two birdmen take the air simultaneously to fly from the city in opposite directions. The possibility of a joint exhibition was also under discussion.

News services, in reporting the day's progress of the *Vin Fiz*, had been uninformed of the stops at Deming and Lordsburg. Consequently, it was given out that "Aviator C. P. Rodgers, going west on his transcontinental

---

*Named for Gen. Orlando B. Willcox, a hero of the Battle of Bull Run.

aeroplane flight, today broke the world record for sustained flight. He remained in the air six hours and four minutes in traversing the 222 miles from El Paso to Willcox." The story was not corrected until the following morning.

Cal's landing site at Willcox bordered the Hooker ranch, and Colonel Hooker (brother of General "Fighting Joe" Hooker of Civil War fame) was present to escort principals of the aviation party the fifty feet to the two-story Willcox Hotel (the tallest structure in town). The hotel staff had prepared a special "Flying Halloween supper" in honor of the day and the spellbinding visitor it brought from the skies.

Mrs. Sweitzer held forth during the supper. Her previous arrival in Willcox, she recalled, had been by army wagon. Then (1873) there was not a mile of railroad track in all the Arizona Territory. Willcox, now home to over 100 people, was merely a stagecoach stop at the time. To reach Camp Grant,* twenty-seven miles to the north, she and her husband, Lieutenant Calbraith Rodgers, had traveled more than four hours by buckboard through country menaced by outlaws. Life in those days was hard and hazardous; the women were far hardier than those of today (a sideways glance at Mabel). But Mrs. Sweitzer at age fifty-six would not exchange her life for one with modern comforts. "Memories," she concluded, "make the food that nurtures the soul in its old age."

Hay-wagon rides around the Hooker ranch were scheduled after the evening's repast; the wagons were pulled by hackney ponies under the charge of a "witch" or "warlock" in sackcloth and conical cap. The colonel warned that his property had been invaded by goblins and bogies that were lying in wait for anyone wandering off into the darkness. Mrs. Sweitzer maneuvered Cal and Miss Lucy onto one wagon and pulled Mabel onto another. The party charged away into the night, Mabel wedged grimly between Mrs. Sweitzer and Stewart deKrafft. "Doesn't she look lovely," smiled Mrs. Sweitzer, her eyes following Miss Lucy's cloche bonnet, graced for the occasion with orange and black plumes.

Not until midnight did the last wagon—carrying Cal and Lucy Belvedere, flushed and out of breath—return to the Willcox Hotel. Cal tendered thanks to the townfolk for their hospitality and allowed that a grand time was had by all. Mabel seethed but said nothing.

After a comfortable overnight rest (the hotel's management had fashioned a special extension for his bed and had installed in his room a repoussé copper bathtub), Cal found Charlie Wiggin and Leo McNally

*Abandoned by the Army in 1905.

still tinkering with the motor at eight o'clock in the morning. A jack-o'-lantern sat on the driver's seat of the airplane, its grin a reminder of the previous night's merriment. Rollers on the drive-chains had been replaced, and the chains removed and soaked in hot tallow and graphite. Cal added his own hands to the work, and in two hours the chains were remounted, and the engine was restored to working condition. Another hour passed before Henry Morgan, president of the Wilcox Bank & Trust Company, appeared with the promised $75 purse.

With the single four-room school dismissed, every child in Willcox stood solemnly to watch the alien figure minister to the amazing flying machine and then mount its saddle. "Who wants to hold the planes?" Cal called out to the clusters of youngsters. A wild scramble ensued. Joe and Ed Kenester seized one end of the lower plane; Harley Windsor grabbed the other end and kicked at his competitors. The propellers were spun; Cal yelled, "Let her go, boys"; and the machine rolled forward. The Kenester brothers dropped away. Harley Windsor held on, half running, half stumbling. "Let go, let go!" Cal screamed at him. Windsor held fast to the wing tip, his feet dragging along the ground. At 11:05 A.M. the *Vin Fiz* ascended from Willcox. Harley Windsor was sent sprawling on his stomach in the salt grass.

Southeast over Cochise and Dragoon Pass, at 4,613-foot elevation, the highest point on its transcontinental route (twenty-nine feet higher than the crossing of the continental divide), the *Vin Fiz Flyer* dealt out a sparkling performance—"not a miss to the engine, not an erroneous quiver," said Cal. The prevailing strong wind through the pass abated and offered a quartering component. A few puffs of cirrus clouds scurried across the upper sky, as if to a private rendezvous. At Benson, the SP track curved back to the northwest and up along the Pantano Wash into Tucson. Cal covered the ninety miles of this course in 110 minutes and, in accordance with the prearranged program, steered his machine toward the University of Arizona.

> As I passed over the campus I saw Fowler's machine in which he had his accident. It looked more like the Wrights' old kiwi bird than a "flying circus."

Bob Fowler had arranged to view his rival's approach through the university observatory's six-inch reflecting telescope. As the image of the *Vin Fiz* gained resolution, Fowler staggered back from the eyepiece. "My

God," he exclaimed, "it's flying upside down!" Astronomers assured him that optics, not aeronautics, bore responsibility for the inverted airplane.

Thousands of students packed into the athletic field and surrounding grandstands. Cal entertained them with dips, glides, wheelings, and pivotings; they responded with a collegiate yell—three cheers and a "tiger."

After a wide arc to the southeast, the *Vin Fiz* descended at 1:05 onto a clearing on Ninth Street beyond Fairmont Avenue. Reporters soon found the aviator and demanded an explanation of why he had not landed at the campus, where his fellow aeronaut stood waiting.

"I wouldn't have tried it for all of Hearst's prize money," said Cal. "The grounds were too crowded, and I did not want to swoop down there and kill or injure some people."

To a reporter from the *Star*, Cal volunteered that he felt a special warmness for Arizona since his father, Captain C. P. Rodgers of the Fifth Cavalry, had been stationed in the territory during the Indian campaigns.

The assemblage around the airplane was soon augmented by buckboards and surreys that had brought people from outlying ranches and settlements into town for celebration of All Saints' Day.

An automobile carrying Bob Fowler dashed up, and Fowler sprang out to grasp the hand of his competitor and extend hearty congratulations: "Well done, old man, it was a beautiful flight."

Cal congratulated Fowler on his record-breaking performance between Yuma and Maricopa.

"It's nothing compared to what you've achieved," Fowler returned. "What do you advise for the rest of the trip?"

Cal paused to eye his aerial colleague, a lean six-foot human dynamo he had just met for the first time. "Give it up," he said.

Thus passed the "moment of history"—the distinction unique to Tucson—when the two transcontinental fliers crossed paths, bound in opposite directions, setting records as they proceeded.

Neither aviator's mother was at the scene. "A pity," said Mrs. Sweitzer unnecessarily. "I think we would have found much in common."

Fowler returned to the University of Arizona campus and announced that he would be delayed until the next day, repairing broken stanchions and replacing yards of rotted canvas. "But I'm going to New York," he declared. "You can bet your life on that." He denied with vehement emotion printed accounts that C. P. Rodgers had broken his record for sustained flight.

Fowler was asked by his manager, Charles Young, for his assessment of the much-acclaimed Calbraith Rodgers. "I don't know what grinds the gears inside of him," replied Fowler. "Maybe he should have his stuffed shirt ironed."

The Vin Fiz train arrived at the SP depot at 1:20 P.M. Charlie Wiggin and Leo McNally had no difficulty in tracking the conflux of people to where the *Vin Fiz* was parked, and they set to work tightening bolts and plugging another oil leak that had developed en route. Other crew members, meanwhile, loaded into the hangar car parts that had been ordered at Spofford and shipped from Dayton to Tucson by rail express.

SP officials arranged for a new locomotive, No. 1393 of the Nogales branch, to be coupled onto the special. Engineer C. E. Olden replaced "Poochey" Frederickson (to the passengers' relief), and C. R. Williams took over from C. C. Carter as conductor.

Cal adjourned to a nearby café with John Mets, president of the Tucson Chamber of Commerce, for a quick lunch. It was undecided, he said, whether or not he would stop in Phoenix—his more likely, direct route proceeded westward from Maricopa to Yuma (the "Gila Monster route"). At that moment the matter was under discussion between Stewart de-Krafft and Louis Garesche, the Armour & Company manager for the capital city. Mr. Garesche, who had boarded the special train in Willcox, bore with him a possible $1,000 offer for a landing on the Phoenix Circus Grounds.

At 2:51 P.M., less than two hours after his arrival ("Aviator Rodgers Says 'Hello,' 'Good-bye,'" headlined the *Tucson Citizen*), Cal took the air from the Ninth Street "runway" and headed northwest into a flawless azure sky.

> *I flew over the railroad station and noticed that the train was not ready nor the engine even in sight. I thought it strange, for I had given orders to have everything ready and the train to start when I did. I found out later that they did not attach the engine until 35 minutes after I had left. There had been great rivalry between Tucson and Phoenix, and the general passenger agent probably wanted to keep me in Tucson overnight.*

Nov. 1, Wednesday. Across the Tortolita Mountains. Red Rock, Picacho. Casa Grande. Downed at Maricopa.

Some eighty-three miles beyond Tucson, the engine of the *Vin Fiz* began coughing and then spurting founts of oil. Cal yanked at the emergency cable and began a spiraling volplane. Below, a dot on the map became the tiny community of Maricopa. The *Vin Fiz* skidded onto a dirt road across from the Maricopa Post Office. It was 4:30 P.M.

For several moments Cal and the flying machine were attended by a pervading stillness. No stirring of life was evident in the sunbaked terrain. Only a two-story hotel, the depot building, and a broken line of undistinguished, featureless adobe structures disturbed the ubiquitous desert. Just as Cal was concluding that he had landed in a ghost town, several residents —Dallas Smith, the stationmaster; his wife, Suzy; "Maricopa Slim" Powers, the railroad "dick"; and the five children of the Drake family— ventured forth to stare silently at the alien apparition. Dallas Smith held himself incumbent—in the absence of a town polity—to express acknowledgment of the event. "Welcome to Arizona," he offered. "Are you planning to settle down here?"

Cal only stared at him, but Smith was not expecting a response. "All we really need here," he continued, "is water and some good people."

When this remark, too, went unanswered, Smith reconsidered: "Of course, that's all that hell needs."

Darkness had descended by the time the Vin Fiz contingent pulled into the Maricopa station. Engineer Olden had been alerted that the flier was on the ground someplace short of Phoenix, and he reduced speed as he approached each town. He spotted the unmistakable rangy figure with long cigar and reversed cap standing unattended on the station platform.

In his stateroom, Cal undressed and again surrendered the suit purchased at San Antonio, again smirched with oil, to the Negro stewards for another cleansing with petroleum naphtha. Stewart deKrafft quickly determined that facilities at Maricopa's lone hotel (the McCarthy) were incommensurate with unexpected arrivals. Another night of cramped sleeping quarters was to be suffered aboard the train.

At supper, Cal, his wife, mother, and Lucy Belvedere shared one table in the Pullman car dining area. Only Cal demonstrated an appetite. "Why don't you show Miss Lucy around the hangar car, dear," suggested Mrs. Sweitzer. "I'm sure she would be interested." "Why, I'd admire to," Miss Lucy confirmed, as she rose from the table and took Cal's arm. Mabel watched them leave and was not disappointed to hear Mrs. Sweitzer murmur, "Don't they make a lovely couple?"

Others on the train also found little enjoyment in the evening meal. With provisions in a thin state, chef Ed Davis was able to muster only a meager supply of ham and beans. At least, sighed his disgruntled clientele, it would be the final supper on the train, since Thursday night would see Yuma, and Friday night, November 3, the metropolis of Los Angeles.

Wiggin and McNally repaired the *Vin Fiz* engine and replaced four rollers broken from the drive chain. ("If one of these chains ever breaks," said McNally, "it'll lop off a wing—like it was attached to a parboiled chicken.") At 9:44 Thursday morning Cal took the air to fulfill his engagement in Phoenix, thirty-seven miles to the north (although the possible $1,000 offer had materialized as $250). "I had a terrible dream last night," he told Mabel as he left the Pullman. "It was so real, you could draw a picture from it. My engine quit just as I reached Tempe, and I crashed onto the track in front of the train. I think I was killed. . . . That's the first really bad omen thus far."

The special train was switched on to the Maricopa & Phoenix line, an SP subsidiary, and gave chase across the Gila River Indian Reservation toward the Southern Pacific branch line at Tempe. On board, Mabel apprised deKrafft of Cal's dream and beseeched him to "do something." DeKrafft ridiculed her fears but, faced with incipient hysterics, consented to hold the train short of the Tempe switch point until report of a sighting was received.

Cal, meanwhile, had dipped the *Vin Fiz* over a troop of ostriches at the Tempe Ostrich Company farm (a major commerce of the Salt River Valley).[2] The big birds panicked at the skyborne menace, flocked to the wire fences of their pens, and pushed their necks through; "Ostrichboys" on the field brandished their shepherd's crooks at the airplane. (A story later circulated that several ostriches had hanged themselves in this fashion.)

The *Vin Fiz Flyer* was first sighted over the Salt Mountains just south of Phoenix. Eight thousand persons were awaiting the aviator at the Circus Grounds immediately north of the Churchill School on Taylor Avenue. Cal gradually descended from his 2,500-foot altitude and, passing over the downtown section of Phoenix, picked out the Circus Grounds, where Louis Garesche and other Armour & Company officials stood waving large flags as beacons to the man in the air. At little more than 100 feet, Cal circled the area, searching for a space free from the blanket of frantic, screaming bodies. Six times he circled, as low as twenty feet, yelling profanely—to no avail—at those who seemed intent upon tackling the airplane if it dared to land. Eight constables assigned to clear a lane for the machine were unable to cope with the unheeding throng. "Ain't seen nothing like it in these parts since the flood of '91," said one old-timer. Finally, Cal elevated his planes and sailed off to the northwest.

For a time many in the crowd refused to acknowledge that the birdman would not turn back to the Circus Grounds. Others, realizing that their own actions had driven him away, jumped into automobiles or raced after him on horseback or on foot. He dipped to earth over a mile away in an alfalfa field south of the territorial fairgrounds. First to reach him was J. Gordon Shackelford, eleven, a pupil at the Churchill School, who had ridden to the Circus Grounds on his pony and then, divining the aviator's design, galloped off to the fairgrounds. Cal pushed up the fur-rimmed goggles on his forehead and relit his windblown, half-smoked cigar. As he dismounted from the seat, he bumped his head on the stanchion and cracked a lens in the goggles. He removed the goggles, examined them, and said to Shackelford, "Here, kid, you can have them." After delivering himself of several epithets to reporters from the *Phoenix Gazette* regarding "those maniacs at the Circus Grounds," Cal stepped into an automobile driven up by Louis Garesche. He was whisked downtown (where street paving had begun) "to look things over from a ground view" and to take luncheon with city officials.

J. C. Adams, manager of the new Hotel Adams, offered a free meal and lodging in exchange for the aviator's appearance on the roof of his hotel. Joe Wickersham of the Christian Men's Business Association suggested that Cal might appreciate a respite at one of the famed sporting houses along Jefferson Street—featured this week was "Irish Annie," the girl with the green pubic hair and "a shamrock tattooed on her * * *"

Cal declined both offers (the latter probably bringing to mind the two painted ladies at Kyle, Texas), pointing out that he had intended to gain Yuma the night before and that the side trip to Phoenix would cost a full day if he did not depart shortly. "The lightness of the air," he said, "makes it necessary to fly along the ground at a greater distance than when the air is denser. It also makes landing more perilous."

By the time Cal was driven back to the airplane, most of those at the Circus Grounds had found their way to Six Points and the alfalfa field. *Vin Fiz* crewmen had inspected and refueled the machine. Cal grandly declared that his next hop would span over 200 miles: "I am confident I can reach Yuma before nightfall. If I can't, though, I'll probably land at Gila Bend." At 1:20 P.M. he rose into the "light air" of southwest Arizona.

The *Vin Fiz* took up a course due south across the Salt River and over the Salt River Mountains. Cal had been advised that, should he lose sight of his train along the M&P, he could orient himself with Montezuma Peak (below the Gila River) on his right side and would then intersect the main line of the Southern Pacific. In the event, a slight change in wind direction caused a drift to the west around Montezuma Peak, and Cal came upon the main track closer to Mobile than to Maricopa.

Those on the Vin Fiz special were notified by the Maricopa station agent that the EX flying machine had not been sighted since its takeoff from Phoenix. They searched the northern sky vainly, aware that the mountainous terrain in that direction was unlikely to deal kindly with an emergency landing. Nervous apprehension invaded each member of the party. Mrs. Sweitzer wrung her hands and paced the corridor of the private varnish. Mabel walked forward to the hangar car to seek reassurances from the crew.

Not until 3:30 did a telegraphed message arrive from Sentinel stating that the cross-country airplane had just passed over that point. Directly, another problem presented itself. Engine No. 1393 refused to take up the chase, crippled by a broken coupler (irreparable outside a roundhouse). Trainmaster G. J. Guyette wired to Tucson for another locomotive.

A second traveling party—the "Polly at the Circus" company—was also marooned in Maricopa at this time, its boxcar relegated to a siding, pending the settlement of debts owed the railroad. Members of the two groups commiserated with each other. The company's manager proposed that his boxcar be coupled in with the Vin Fiz train—"Wherever you're going, it's better than here"—in exchange for "lifetime" free passes. DeKrafft declined. However, two "Pollys" pled their case so convincingly that he relented—"We have a lot in common with a traveling circus."

Ed Merritt objected ("The Vin Fiz name should not be associated with a cheap carnival troop"), but was overruled. When the new locomotive arrived from Tucson, the circus boxcar was coupled between the hangar car and the private varnish.

The *Vin Fiz Flyer*, meanwhile, was slicing its way through the aerial ocean with a vengeful persistence. Below, a rumpled sea of rock and sand threw up shimmering heat waves that danced to unheard rhythms. Ahead, streaks of cirrostratus—fractures in the inverted bowl of the sky— stretched to the far end of the Arizona flatlands. An unfriendly land, it seemed to Cal, one that left the aviator above it feeling vulnerable, exposed. He could simply disappear in such a land; no one else in the world knew of his whereabouts and would not know until he reappeared, if he ever did. There were no ties to the earth here. . . . He dipped the flying machine to skim the desert floor, watching his shadow leap from dune to dune. . . . That was one benefit of climbing the sky, he thought once again—his shadow was left behind. As Al Welsh had pointed out at the Wright Flying School, not until he touched the ground did it reattach itself, an unwelcome encumbrance. . . .

Back at a safe altitude, the benison of the sun on his brow, Cal wedged a pencil into the spark-advance cable and dangled his legs below the forward crossbar. With the track clearly etched on the parched landscape, he needed no pilot train. The *Vin Fiz* was complete unto itself.

Over the formless expanse of desert, the aviator's sense of time eroded, almost suspended. The engine obeyed its own chronology—between Aztec and Mohawk it coughed briefly and died, its last drop of gasoline consumed. Cal pulled the compression-release cable and looked about for a hospitable landing site. From 2,000 feet he volplaned toward a section house in a "village" of three shacks along the track. Stoval Siding, as the "village" was called, did justify a single telegraph operator. "Gasoline?" said that worthy in some surprise, unable to shift his gaze from the "prehistoric beast" that had dropped onto his doorstep. "We got water, but we don't got no gasoline here."

Cal wired Maricopa and learned the quiescent status of the Vin Fiz special. He then wired the SP depot in Yuma for a supply of gasoline to be dispatched with the next train east. After further wires between SP agents at Yuma and Maricopa, it was decided to comply with his request. Not until 6:40, however, did an express reach Stoval Siding with the gasoline. Cal and the telegrapher unloaded the fuel, and Cal invited himself aboard the express for a hasty supper before it departed. "It's my own damned fault," he said of his delay at Stoval. "Now, I'll probably not get to Los Angeles before Saturday morning." There were, he calculated, 317 miles remaining.

Cal flopped onto a bunk in the section house and was soon asleep. The Vin Fiz train did not arrive until almost midnight. Those on board had had no evening meal, excepting a few scraps scrounged from a farmhouse near Maricopa by "Polly at the Circus" members (the ice locker was empty, and the chef did not look kindly on the additional mouths attached to the train). On the Pullman, Austrian shades were lowered, and duvetyn curtains drawn; passengers retired soon after sunset. Only Mrs. Sweitzer left orders to be awakened at Stoval. She tiptoed into the section house and gazed at her sleeping son, unhappy at his haggard appearance. He had lost twenty pounds, she thought, and could not repress the further thought that every lost pound had shown up on Mabel.

Friday morning Cal and his mechanicians began work on the *Vin Fiz* at the sky's first brightening. Pausing to study the machine as it rested on a level stretch of desert sand, Cal remarked, "I think only the rudder and elevator planes are originals; everything else has been rebuilt." "More than once," added Charlie Wiggin.

Cal and the *Vin Fiz* proved objects of curiosity for the circus performers, while the aviator seemed nonchalant at the presence of the extra boxcar and its strange cargo. "If you would consider flying your machine as part of our show, you have a job," offered the manager. Cal expressed disappointment that "Polly at the Circus" did not include a snake charmer. He admonished the midget who was crawling over the lower plane (shrilly proclaiming that he would fly the machine higher than its regular driver dared) and turned back to his work.

The Eastbound Limited passenger train paused at Stoval's water tank each morning at 6:55. DeKrafft boarded its dining car on a resolute mission of mercy. He emerged bearing a large carton whose contents drew joyous celebration from passengers on the Vin Fiz special. Calling out in triumph, he held aloft, item by item, steaks, fruits, wine, and half a dozen coconut pies. "Hallelujah!" yelled reporters, Vin Fiz members, and circus folk alike. "Let's cook it ourselves," Leo McNally proposed. "We'll take the chef's next meal and throw it overboard." DeKrafft demurred: "Better not—we'd poison half the coyotes in Arizona."

Mabel Rodgers proved even more inspired than Stewart deKrafft. Not daring to raise the issue of Lucy Belvedere with her mother-in-law, she had confronted the young lady directly to demand the real purpose of her presence with the expedition. "Why, whatever do you mean?" said Miss Lucy. Now, with a second train stopped on the adjacent track, and with Mrs. Sweitzer and her "traveling companion" attending the aviator, Mabel slipped into the adjoining compartment, stuffed Miss Lucy's elegant wardrobe (containing several scandalous sheath dresses and ladies' dainties of filigreed faille) into her three cases, and dragged the cases down the steps of the private Pullman and onto the rear platform of the Limited. There, she consigned the luggage to a puzzled porter ("Take them east—as far east as you can") and stood on the roadbed, watching the train recede into the distance.

Miss Lucy was mortified, diminished to tears and incoherence. She, too, stood on the roadbed gazing eastward, as if to catch sight of her vanished wardrobe and thereby recall it. Mrs. Sweitzer was indignant. Such erratic behavior, she trumpeted to one and all, was not the mark of a rational individual. And to what end?

"Let's get on with it," ordered Cal after both the ruckus over Mabel's coup and the jubilation over deKrafft's had subsided. "Three hundred and seventeen miles to go." He climbed onto the driver's seat and rose from the Stoval water station at 7:30 A.M.

I got away in good shape, and my special left at the same time I did. I was in hopes it would stay with me today, but I soon ran away from it. My motor was running fine. I cut across one range [the Copper Mountains] that the railroad had to run around and saved a few miles thereby. It was not long before I picked up Yuma in the distance, and I was soon over it.

Yuma was scheduled as a stop for breakfast. It received, instead, a handful of Vin Fiz leaflets from 4,000 feet and a few extra puffs on one of Cal's Mexican cheroots ("El Ropos," snorted crew members). Several hundred people waved and beckoned for him to alight; from his altitude they went unseen.

Yuma is 140 feet below sea level,* and this is the worst part of the desert that I have come across so far, being very sandy and rolling. I could see hills of sand fully as large as mountains. The land here is as empty as the sky.

At 9:00 Cal flew over the Colorado River on the northern edge of Yuma. The *Vin Fiz* had entered California. Clumps of turnip-colored clouds lined up along the Arizona side of the river, marking the end of a light, soupy sky. To the west, nothing but flawless stretches of resplendent blue could be seen above the horizon. "I thought it must be a state ordinance," Cal told Mabel later. "No clouds permitted beyond this line."

Nov. 3, Friday. CALIFORNIA! Pacific Standard Time. Northwest along Yuma Plain. Drylyn, Acolita, Tortuga, by western edge of bald-pated Chocolate Mountains. Salton Sea.

The painted sky, the clear air, the monotonous drone of the engine, all combined for a near-hypnotic effect: a poetry of space and freedom, with nothing to intrude between the individual and the infinite. Cal allowed his mind to drift, flying along the edge of time.

Some sixty miles into California, Cal's gaze upon the world that might be—or should be—was wrenched abruptly to the world that loomed beneath his feet. Without a warning indication, the *Vin Fiz* was rocked by a blowout of the engine's No. 1 cylinder. The explosion tore out the crankcase, bent the shaft, and demolished the magneto. Several large chunks of metal shot by Cal's head; metallic shards pierced his left shoulder. His arm numb, he tried to manipulate the elevator lever with his knee. The motor was thrashing itself asunder as the wind cranked the

---

*Actually Yuma lies 140 feet above sea level.

propellers; the machine heeded its commands with parlous sluggishness. Hot oil spraying from the gap in the crankcase covered his face and goggles and dribbled under his collar. With one hand and his knees, he maneuvered the *Vin Fiz* into a plummeting spiral two miles back along his path.

> *It was only providence that saved my life. I could have come down in the Salton Sea. I could have been killed by the pieces of flying metal. The only decent landing place I could see in all those sand dunes was near a few boxcars and a couple of shacks by the track. I volplaned in from 4,000 feet and succeeded in making a very good landing in a very bad place.*

The "very bad place" was Imperial Junction.[3] Its population comprised three telegraphers (for round-the-clock shifts), a station agent, and their wives; about twenty farming families lived within a radius of three miles. It also could boast of a post office (situated in a boxcar) under the charge of Mrs. Claire Hobgood,* wife of the second-shift telegraph operator, Fred Hobgood. All eight inhabitants of Imperial Junction watched, wide-eyed in astonishment, as the *Vin Fiz* fell from the skies and, at 9:25 A.M. (P.S.T.), skidded along a gravel stretch beside the railroad track.

Mrs. Hobgood beheld the oil- and blood-streaked aviator and telephoned for a doctor. Telegraphed messages were sent, under Cal's direction, to the SP depot in Yuma and to Lawrence Peters at the Maryland Hotel in Pasadena. Peters managed to place a telephone call to the Imperial Junction Station, but Cal's "good" ear was still buzzing from the clatter of his engine, and he was unable to converse.

The special train, after a slow, winding journey from Stoval Siding, was only then puffing into Yuma. Its passengers (except for Lucy Belvedere, who sulked in her room) were entertained by jugglers, acrobats, "Middle-Eastern" dancing by the "Polly" girls, and leaps through a hoop by a dog costumed as a tiger. Passing the hat collected a sum of nearly $6 for the troop.

While the circus boxcar was being uncoupled, information arrived that the aviator was down and had suffered severe injuries. Engineer Olden was urged to full speed toward Imperial Junction, Mabel and Mrs. Sweitzer vying in their laments as they neared the scene where their loved one lay "dying."

Their loved one, meanwhile, had recruited Fred Hobgood and three

---

*Authorized by Postmaster General Frank Hitchcock Nov. 7, 1910, with Mrs. Hobgood as postmistress, it was possibly the smallest post office in the U.S.

other men to lift the flying machine onto a pile of intercrossed railroad ties (to facilitate its repair). He then paced, fidgety, up and down along the track, awaiting the arrival of the Vin Fiz special.

Passenger train No. 10 of the SP stopped for water at Imperial Junction. Faces peered through half-drawn curtains at the lanky, oddly dressed figure, one arm dangling, that strode the length of the train oblivious to their stares. Through windows on the other side, passengers could observe a real airplane squatting—somehow—in a nest of timbers.

After the No. 10 train had departed, Cal, unable to tolerate the inactivity, began tinkering with the engine, running his hand through the jagged opening torn by the explosion. "The cause of the trouble," he reported, "was that a small screw came loose inside the motor, causing a connecting rod to break in two and thrusting a hole through the crankcase."

When, at noon, the Vin Fiz special screeched into Imperial Junction, Mabel and Mrs. Sweitzer were craning their heads through windows. What they saw was the aviator, his new suit once again splattered with oil, circling his stranded machine to assess the extent of damage, pondering the problem of its reconstruction, and furiously puffing on a cigar. A doctor arrived from Brawley minutes later and, while Mabel and Mrs. Sweitzer soothed the object of their affections, extracted bits of metal from Cal's shoulder.

"He's OK," deKrafft informed reporters who had inquired about the aviator's condition. "Anything less than death we classify as a minor accident."

Charles Wiggin and Leo McNally immediately began rigging a pulley to dismount the engine. Cal, changed into his second suit of clothes, his arm in a sling, directed the operation and worked at whatever one-armed tasks he could meet. A few parts were salvaged, and, combined with the alternate motor (still not repaired fully from the crash at Kyle, Texas), the semblance of a power-producing mechanism was regained.

Both Wiggin and McNally were dubious of its ability to push the airplane into Los Angeles. "Only 184 miles to go," said Cal. "For that distance, I'll flap my arms if I have to."

"You've only got one to flap," Wiggin pointed out.

It was recommended by the mechanicians that the final leg of the journey be postponed until a new engine could be delivered from the Wright factory. Cal vetoed the proposal. "I'm leaving here by noon tomorrow—period," he told Robert Yost, Jr., a special correspondent from the *Los Angeles Examiner*, who had joined the entourage of newsmen on the now overcrowded Pullman. Yost wired his newspaper that "Cal P. Rodgers will arrive Pasadena Saturday, Nov. 4, between 3:00 and 3:30 o'clock. Preparations to receive him should be organized to that schedule."

"From the Atlantic Coast 47 days earlier," wrote Yost, "this intrepid man-bird has traversed 4,034 miles in 4,702 minutes—three days, six hours, 23 minutes—a time faster than that of the fastest express train, faster than the flight of crows. He now stands on the edge of history, about to complete his Promethean effort to master the continent.

"Why does he do it? Why does he pursue a personal odyssey that matches the public one? He is not Captain Ahab. He is motivated not out of vengeance for a lost limb but from a lost commitment to generations of heroes. It might prove easier to regain a limb."

Groans of anguish from officials and reporters preceded yet another night on the special train. The feast procured by deKrafft had been quickly devoured. Chef Davis had reprovisioned his larder during the stop at Yuma, and again there was no shortage of ham, beans, and eggs. Stung —at last—by the aspersions to his culinary skills, he baked a dozen apple pies that were relished by his severest critics. "Who says I can't cook?" he demanded. DeKrafft was not taken in. "Even the great masters can have an off-day," he said.

Mabel and Mrs. Sweitzer enjoyed more comfortable accommodations and superior cuisine. The two ladies had been invited by D. M. Linnard to pass the night at the Hotel Maryland in Pasadena, and there to await the expedition's arrival. They were urged by Cal to accept the invitation; his arm and shoulder, he assured them, were mending nicely without further nursing. Lucy Belvedere would accompany them, whence she would arrange for immediate transportation eastward in pursuit of her fugitive finery. Cal enjoined Charlie Wiggin to escort the ladies and to keep the peace among them. Miss Lucy still quivered nervously whenever Mabel approached within stone-throwing distance. Mrs. Sweitzer would neither forgive nor forget; the temperature of her regard for Mabel hovered well below its normal level. Wiggin promised to exert his authority if necessary. The quartet boarded a passenger train for Pasadena.

Later in the evening Hearst correspondent Yost attempted another interview with Cal but was unable to elicit much information. "Outwardly, Rodgers is a cold man," Yost complained in his story, "warmed only by an inner sun. He would not be out of place on display at the waxworks. It is almost impossible to get more than a word at a time out of him. He will start to answer a question and then suddenly remember something and either drift off into his thoughts or break abruptly to walk over to where his flying machine is parked and stand there staring at it. Without doubt, that machine is the center of his universe. He is flying when he eats. He is flying when he sleeps. . . ."

Wrote Thomas Hanly: "Not much given to conversation at any time, Cal P. Rodgers grows ever more reticent as he nears his goal. . . ."

Shortly after 5:00 A.M. Saturday, as daylight was breaking over the Imperial Desert, Cal arose to inspect the *Vin Fiz* once more and to help remount the remaining engine. He was attired in his spare suit coat and the one pair of trousers extant (the stewards had labored into the night sewing the coat ripped by engine fragments, but the result had not met with Mrs. Sweitzer's approval; the trousers had withstood their third "dry cleaning" in six nights).

Over the protests of Leo McNally (the "fourth-string quarterback"), who pleaded that the machinery was hurting for another day's work, Cal announced that he would take off as soon as a proper starting site could be found. Crew members fanned out to survey the vicinity, while Cal downed a breakfast of fried eggs. A dry wash a short distance away was selected. Shovels and pickaxes were borrowed from a railroad section gang; a lane was leveled and filled in several places. The biplane was then carried across the tracks and wheeled into position. Cal arrived, pronounced the location unsatisfactory, and drove off in the Palmer-Singer to conduct his own survey. He returned an hour later to inform the crew that he had located a suitable space on the shore of the Salton Sea.

> We had to wheel the machine about three and a half miles and we had to cut our way through sagebrush and mesquite the whole distance. It took us two hours to cut and to drag the machine—very hard work and quite tiresome. After finally arriving at the beach, all the men danced a war dance to celebrate and for pure joy at getting there without any damage to the aeroplane.

At 10:07 A.M. Cal removed his arm from the sling, climbed into his machine, and took the air. Almost immediately he decided that the engine sounds held ominous overtones, and he glided back to earth several hundred yards away. McNally tinkered with the motor, and again—at 10:27 A.M.—Cal lifted the airplane from the desert floor. For the second time he dropped to the ground, still unwilling to trust the machinery. A magneto plug was changed while Cal told Yost, "It's better to be sure of this engine. . . . I'll make one stop at Beaumont, the top of the grade, 105 miles from here. The rest will be easy—sailing over the valley to Los Angeles 80 miles on." At 10:45 A.M. the third takeoff succeeded, and the *Vin Fiz*, with a graceful spiral, rose from the shore of the Salton Sea.

Soaring to an altitude of 1,000 feet, Cal flew directly over the recently formed inland ocean,* shortening his distance from that along the railroad track. A three-quarters headwind sweeping out over the desert through the mountain passes reduced his speed to 45 mph and drew moiré patterns on the glistening surface below him. Over Indio and Palm Springs, he winged his way, his machine casting fleeting shadows on barren mountain slopes, hot white sands, and desert cactus.

On the special train, deKrafft's anxiety over the condition of the airplane provoked him to request a stop at each telegraph office en route for a quick word with the local operator regarding the aviator's whereabouts.

Cal was sighted by residents of Banning shortly before one o'clock. The aircraft was droning along smoothly, seemingly with perfect poise. At a point directly over the Banning Railroad Station, they saw it suddenly veer to the south, the driver tugging desperately at the levers with one hand while his other hand attended the engine. They saw the machine bank over a cluster of pine trees. The planes were seen to tip over to one side. Spectators thought the machine on the verge of flipping over. It disappeared below the horizon south of Banning, and townspeople rushed in that direction, expecting to find the craft wrecked and the aviator injured or dead.

> *Just as I reached about the worst part of the San Gorgonio Pass my magneto began to work loose from its fittings and threatened every moment to come off. It was very aggravating as there were no landing places available, and there were powerful eddys of wind. I had to jolly my machine along and try to keep my motor from breaking loose altogether. As I finally worked to the outskirts of Banning, I started to make a landing. But my magneto succeeded in breaking loose and my motor stopped. I had to volplane into a plowed field. The spirit is willing, but the machine is weak.*

Those first reaching the field were greeted by the sight of both airship and driver in upright positions. Cal was chewing on a black cigar and glowering at the rapidly growing assembly. A local baseball game in progress had been disrupted by the sounds of the airplane; both spectators

---

*From 1905 to 1907, floods from the Gila River, a tributary of the Colorado, tore through irrigation channels and filled the previously dry seabed (destroying thousands of homes and farms).

and players had deserted the ball park to attend the more curious spectacle.

Cal concluded that his most serious problem was a leaky radiator. He dispatched a willing youth for a carton of laundry soap and recruited the Banning baseball players to carry the *Vin Fiz* into another, firmer field. With the laundry soap poured into the radiator, he prepared for takeoff. At that moment Leo McNally and Virgil Howey arrived from the special train. It was discovered that a connecting rod had worked free; opening the crankcase hatch disclosed worn-out bearings.

Cal sighed and turned to the crowd: "I'm starved. Any food around here?" He was promptly escorted by Constable Joe Toutain to the Banning Hotel, where an impromptu meal was spread before him. Harvey Johnson, editor of the *Banning Record,* approached the table to note the aviator's words. "This altitude creates a very healthy appetite," Cal commented, devouring a second helping of cake, "and I don't always get as much to eat as I did here. My train is always, naturally, a few hours behind. There is not a train in the country that can keep up with me. Therefore I have to run chances about reaching the towns ahead as per program. It is a most difficult thing to prophesy anything in aviation."

George Wing and George Fountain, operators of Banning's only garage, were enlisted to expedite repairs on the *Vin Fiz* engine, but after two hours it became apparent that the machine would not take its leave of Banning that afternoon.

In Pasadena, eighty miles to the west, D. M. Linnard, the Maryland Hotel owner, had organized a gigantic spectacular show of welcome. Ten thousand persons had gathered in Tournament Park. Emotions had reached a liturgical pitch as people now accepted as imminent reality the arrival of a man who had flown the entire distance from New York. By two o'clock the grandstands and bleachers were filled. A contest between the Reds and the Whites of the Pasadena Polo Club had been arranged and claimed the crowd's attention while Mr. L. F. Benton, in Linnard's chauffeured Simplex auto, flitted between the Maryland and the park bearing messages. Shortly before three o'clock, telegraphed word represented that Cal P. Rodgers was about to ascend from Banning and would land at Pasadena in two hours. After this intelligence was announced, the polo players again combatted, the band played, and the brigade of newspaper photographers sent out for flashlight outfits.

In front of the judges' platform stood a brilliant black electric Victoria laden with flowers. In it sat Mabel Rodgers and Mrs. Sweitzer. Mrs. R. D. Davis, wife of the president of the Board of Trade, and Miss Irene

Grosse, the Rose Festival Queen, prepared to present the bouquets to the transcontinental aviator.

What kind of a man is your husband?" reporters asked Mabel.

"Mostly a stubborn one," she said. "He has reserves of strength and will above the ordinary man."

"Does he take himself seriously?"

"Well, he always has. But now it shows, I think."

"Has he changed in other ways?"

"Well, he used to sleep very soundly. Now he wakes up in the middle of the night. Sometimes he seems to have fallen into a pit in his mind and is trying to climb out."

"Nonsense," Mrs. Sweitzer interjected. "He is the same boy he always was. I should know."

Mr. Linnard, Mr. Benton, and Vin Fiz advance man Lawrence Peters continued to telephone and telegraph SP agents with queries about the airman's whereabouts. At five o'clock the polo match concluded, but the crowd waited patiently. The indefatigable Linnard had mapped the center of the field with bedsheets from the linen supply of the Maryland. Now he rounded up a hundred lanterns and deployed them to spell out the word "Pasadena."

Finally, at sunset, a telephoned message from Banning informed Linnard that the aviator would be unable to depart Banning until the following morning.

"Give all these people rain checks," said Linnard to his aides. "We'll put on a better show for them tomorrow."

More disappointed than the fervent crowd, Mabel and Mrs. Sweitzer each decided that another night apart from their Calbraith was intolerable. They boarded the next passenger train back to Banning. No railway fare was available for Charlie Wiggin, who remained in Pasadena. Lucy Belvedere had departed, and with her the prospect of open warfare between wife and mother-in-law.

During supper at the Banning Hotel, Cal learned that Fowler, over the past three days, had flown from Tucson to Benson and thence to Bisbee, Arizona Territory. He was expected to reach El Paso by Sunday. Harry Atwood, in Worcester, Massachusetts, vowed to go Cal P. Rodgers one better by flying across the South American continent. If successful, the trip would net him $100,000, he claimed. "I may cross the Andes Mountains," said Atwood, "but that will depend on what conditions are prevailing."

Cal found little time to peruse the news, as he was besieged by platoons of reporters from Los Angeles. What did he plan to do when the trip was over? he was asked most frequently.

"I'm ready for the simple life," said Cal. "All I want now is a $20-a-month bungalow near Los Angeles and a Chink who can cook."

He refused to discuss the numerous aviation fatalities that had plagued the last several months. "There is an enhanced safety in flying at high altitudes," he asserted, "since most mishaps can be managed if given the opportunity to recover or volplane and avoid wires and other obstructions. The whole thing is in keeping cool. Aviation is no sport for a timid person, but when something happens, if one does not get rattled, there is little danger. I expect to see the time when we are carrying passengers in flying machines from New York to Los Angeles in three days. This will mean more than 100 miles an hour, and the riders will have to be boxed in because the wind blasts one awful at that speed. Even with my goggles, the wind creeps in and tears at my eyes.

"Even if passengers are not carried, they will learn someday to put a box around the driver[4]—if only to keep his cigar from going out."

Howard Benell, the transportation manager, had attained some accomplishment as an artist. Cal's prognostication struck him (and others) as so preposterous that he sketched it out—a barrel covering the operator seat, with two slots for the driver's eyes and a hole for his cigar.

Mabel and Mrs. Sweitzer arrived, conferred loving words on the object of their affections, and withdrew to rooms at the Banning Hotel. Others in the Vin Fiz party made a huddle in the private Pullman. Cal toiled in the hangar car of the Vin Fiz train, tinkering with the engine, wrapped in his private thoughts. His face, drawn with concentration, was a study of unspent emotions; he chewed roughly on his cigar. Not until after midnight did he drop his tools and retire to his stateroom. The voices of deKrafft, Merritt, and others could be heard discussing anticipated events of the morrow. Irritably Cal yelled at them to stay quiet and ordered all lights on the train turned out. No one argued with him.

Sunday morning, November 5, dawned at Banning, California, with a temperature of 40° and a high wind that whipped over the pass at Beaumont six miles to the west and funneled eastward through a narrow valley. A heavy fog scattering from the west told those familiar with local weather patterns that the Los Angeles basin lay under a cloud cover.

Over his suit coat, Cal fastened a leather vest and a pea jacket of heavy canvas. He ate an unusually hearty breakfast, topped off with his usual glass of cream. Mabel fussed over his clothing and adjusted his tie. Mrs.

Sweitzer then rendered her inspection; she brushed imagined lint from his jacket and readjusted his tie. "You have to look your best at Pasadena so that I will be proud of you," she admonished him.

On impulse, Cal again climbed into the hangar car for a few last licks to the engine. At nine o'clock McNally and other crew members hoisted the cobbled-together airplane motor into the Palmer-Singer auto and, with Cal, drove to where the *Vin Fiz* was parked, a mile from the SP depot. Several hundred people, including a group of Indians from the Malki Reservation four miles away, were already gathered at the machine.

With little more than two hours of labor, the engine was remounted onto its platform on the lower plane, and wires, chains, and bolts were accorded final adjustments. "It needs more work," said Leo McNally, "a lot more work."

(To cap the gasoline tank, McNally had replaced the potato requisitioned at Lordsburg with a fresh potato: "It's given us better luck than a regular cap.")

Harry Sanger, decked out in houndstooth suit and a homburg hat with a feather in its brim, raised his megaphone for the final time to extol the virtues of "the finest blend of grape juices, at only five cents, Vin Fiz. . . . Vin Fiz."

While Sanger was assaulting spectators with his pitch, the entire crew of the hangar car lined up for a handshake and embrace with the man they had followed across the country. "We are with you, one and all," Al Dietrich told Cal. Supply-keeper Edward Sutton was choked with emotion: "That man—he can chase the birds right out of the sky."

Cal was cautioned that aerial maneuvers would prove difficult between the sheer, mile-high walls of the San Gorgonio Pass and that he would encounter the worst wind of his California flight at the 3,000-foot summit at Beaumont. Jabbing a fresh cigar between his teeth, adjusting his light-brown cap, yellow isinglass goggles, and black gauntlets, he climbed onto his seat, yelled, "Let her go, boys," pressed the magneto-spark treadle, and aimed the machine toward the boxed valley. The *Vin Fiz* fought for altitude, bucking against the wind, hung for a moment, then lifted and straightened its path. The time was two minutes past noon.

The special train departed the Banning Station a minute later. Ed Merritt and Howard Benell joined Mrs. Sweitzer on the observation platform. Mabel shut herself up in her compartment. Others in the aviation party chewed matches and exuded an aura of apprehension. At the Beaumont summit, the airplane disappeared in a low-lying haze.

When the haze lifted moments later, the machine was no longer in view. Engineer Olden charged his locomotive up the grade. Rounding a curve, those on the train sighted the *Vin Fiz* squatting in a large wheat field and Cal hurrying toward the tracks. (He had alighted in a field of the Stewart ranch, where Bob Fowler had halted more than a week earlier.) The train stopped, and Cal explained that a nipple on the feed line from the gasoline tank had broken; the entire supply of gasoline had poured out. Ten minutes had passed since the takeoff from Banning. He had advanced less than five miles.

While the tank was under repair, Cal fueled himself with a slice of pie brought up by Mabel. At 1:02 P.M. he took the air again and winged out over the pass. The Vin Fiz special again started in pursuit. Down into the valley flew the airplane, quickly outdistancing the train. Thousands who lived between Banning and Los Angeles had positioned themselves along the line of the SP tracks. They waved at figures on the train and pointed upward to indicate that the aviator was ahead and flying well.

> Nov. 5, Sunday. Redlands Junction 1:29 P.M., Colton 1:35 P.M., Bloomington, 1:40 P.M. Engine sputtering. Landed Pomona 2:07 P.M.
>
> *The pass was very narrow, and I could see on either side of me two mountain ranges, but not very far as it was hazy. When I got through the pass, the country began to take on a more fertile appearance. It really was very beautiful, and I noticed immediately that I was getting into civilization again. The orange groves were showing up all around and making a very beautiful view. The earth as well as the sky had a texture of friendly softness.*

Cal was engulfed by 2,500 excited people at Pomona. Thirty minutes later the train reached the depot; McNally and several crewmen hurried out to the field where he stood calmly smoking a cigar and chatting with Charles Walker and Laurence Wilson, president of the Board of Trade.

"Nothing wrong," Cal told McNally. "I just wanted to look her over, get some gasoline and oil, and catch my breath before the final hop."

McNally inspected the ragged, bobtailed airplane. "Nothing wrong?" he asked incredulously. "The bearings are gone, and there's not a spare left; the cylinders are about to go; the connecting rods and magnetos are as loose as goose feathers; and there's enough fabric hanging from the planes to make a dress for Miss Lucy; and I count fifteen rollers missing —two together in one spot, and you know that means the chain is likely to work loose and slice the aeroplane in half. You cannot fly this machine."

"Never mind," said Cal. "It will hold for twenty miles."

"It may not hold for twenty yards," McNally insisted.

Said Cal: "This machine has carried me for more than four thousand miles. Now if I have to, I'll carry it."

"Leastways," McNally pleaded, "fly it straight. Don't turn any capers when you get to Pasadena. If you get to Pasadena."

Cal smiled. He climbed onto the seat, glanced at the bottle of Vin Fiz secured to a brace, and signaled for the propellers to be turned. "Betsy," he addressed the machine, "they're waiting for us. Don't let me down now."

McNally and Howey, at either wing tip, could not hear his voice, but they saw his mouth frame the words "Let her go, boys."

The *Vin Fiz Flyer* shuddered and moved to the wind. Its engine went unheard by its driver as the world and time stopped once again. Only the beating of his heart persisted, its sound alone in the emptiness, rising above the flying machine, pulling it into the sky.

> *I got started again at 3:25 o'clock, but had a very hard time getting away as we could not make the people get very far back. They persisted in giving me only a narrow lane to take the air. It was rough ground, and there was danger of losing control of the machine and killing someone. I finally got away, spiralled over the field to gain altitude, and headed for Pasadena. Below I could see people lining the tracks as far as the horizon. There was a slight ground haze making a second, shadowy horizon above the natural one. Then it disappeared, and the sky seemed to get brighter and brighter. . . .*

At Tournament Park, 10,000 people had jammed onto the grounds, and another 10,000 milled about on nearby streets. They had come on foot, on bicycle, by automobile, on horseback, by horse-drawn surrey, by streetcar, by virtually every conceivable conveyance that could be mustered for the occasion. They streamed through the Arroyo Seco from Los Angeles, from the mountains to the north, from the farmlands to the east. They came from beach communities to the west and south. Cars of the Pacific Electric line bulged with people clinging to poles on the steps. Children, the middle-aged, the elderly, all flocked to the park. The poor, who could ill afford the 25¢ admission, came, as did the rich, who had reserved boxes. Scores of society ladies and gents joined front-row box parties arranged through the Maryland Hotel.

Early arrivals secured seats in the grandstand and soon filled its capacity of 5,000. "Owners of cars who are willing to lower their tops will be given preference in the front rows in order not to interfere with the view of spectators in the grandstand and boxes," read the printed announcement.

From the first hours of the day through the afternoon, the flow of traffic continued. By 3:30 P.M., when word was flashed that Cal P. Rodgers had descended and risen again from Pomona, the allotted number of patrons had been exceeded, and more were demanding entrance. In the grandstand, on the field, and on the streets, necks stretched, eyes turned upward, straining, scanning. . . .

At seven minutes to four on that cool, gray Sunday afternoon, a ten-year-old boy in the uppermost row of the bleachers at Tournament Park, Pasadena, beheld in the eastern sky a tiny speck, too small to be distinguished from a bird. But he knew—without question he knew—that he had espied the first flying machine of his life. At full lung power, the lad shrieked, "Here he comes!"

Almost simultaneously, every steam whistle in the city blew. Every fire bell, every school bell clanged. Every church bell pealed. Every auto horn was honked; every siren cranked up. Alarms wailed. Klaxons screeched. Ceremonial cannon on the courthouse lawn thundered their salute. A hemisphere of cacophony, of stentorious, uproarious sound, welled outward from the city, echoed from the foothills, rattled windows, startled flocks of birds.

At the park, 20,000 people went hysterical. They jumped up and down. They yelled and wigwagged their arms. They pounded one another on the back and pointed again and again to the growing object in the sky. They went frantic. They went rabid.

Within seconds, they were able to discern first the broad forward planes of the machine, then its rudder and elevator planes. With a lull in the clamor from 20,000 throats, the roar of the airborne motor became audible. Instantly the crowd renewed its shouting and drowned out the sound from above. The *Examiner* Newsboys' Band struck up a fortissimo rendition of "Come, Josephine, in My Flying Machine."

Approaching at an altitude of 1,500 feet, Cal swung from the Southern Pacific track to the northwest and descended until, at 300 feet, he flew directly over the park. As the thousands of frenzied people were able to distinguish the aviator himself, his long legs spilling out of the seat onto the framework of the airplane, pandemonium prevailed. The grandstand shook from 5,000 jumping bodies. Grown men lost control of their emotions. Several women fainted.

In the *Vin Fiz*, Cal could feel the furor, the mass hysteria that reigned on the field below. He sensed his own pulses, throbbing in harmony to the engine. Chains whipping over sprockets joined in the celebration. Infused, he bit through his cigar.

Each labored beat of the engine punctuated music the world would dance to. Ancestral spirits that had stowed away beside him bowed to that music. Shadows that had faded were now buried. He had done what no man had done before. His path, like a scroll of history, unfurled behind him across the country. He had scaled the cliffs of Olympus, had journeyed from failure to hero, from sinner to saint.

His heart pounding, his engine coughing, sputtering, wheezing with exertion, Cal drove the machine through a wild and perilous series of corkscrew banks and turns. He dipped, heeled, spiraled, performed Dutch rolls, ocean waves, and tailstands to kiss the sky; he cajoled the biplane through a "Texas Tommy." He demonstrated for the thrilled, screaming masses the most astounding, hazardous exhibition of aerial maneuvers yet seen in the history of aviation. At each moment spectators gasped and marveled at the sight. At each moment they anticipated the tragedy threatened by the daredevil stunts. At each moment the intrepid birdman "trumped Death's Ace."

Twice Cal circled the field. Then, suddenly, he swooped down, skimming the top of the bleachers, and bounced onto the field alongside the array of bedsheets opposite the club cottage. On first contact a tire blew; this time it didn't matter. A skid cracked as the machine slithered along the grass; it was scarcely noticed. As the *Vin Fiz* came to rest, its motor shuddered and died; a spout of steam hissed from the radiator. It mattered not at all.

The entire assembly fell silent—holding its collective breath—as if to absorb the sensation before it. . . . From New York, from the Atlantic Coast, from the far side of reality, a man had propelled himself through the air. Here he was—in touchable fact.

And then they rushed him.

M. H. Ready, the announcer, shouted through his cheerleader's megaphone to "keep back from the infield." He was knocked down and trampled. Fourteen policemen, "Pasadena's finest," lined up behind the ropes, clubs in hand, ready for the charge. They were overwhelmed, inundated in the flood of humanity that ignored their flailing clubs and fists. Men stumbled and went down and were heedlessly stepped upon by those blindly pushing toward the machine. Officials punched and pummeled at the waves of people that beat over them. Chaos triumphed over every attempt at order.

On the judges' platform, Linnard, Lawrence Peters, and Joe Newborn clasped hands and danced a Highland fling. The Newsboys' Band dropped its instruments and dashed onto the infield, maddened, like everyone else present, with excitement.

Linnard found Chief of Police Ed Kirschner, and together the two men rallied the force of policemen and plowed their way to the side of the besieged aviator. Cal was pressed back against the airplane, which rocked sharply from the crush of people around it. Hands stretched out to grasp him, to pull at his clothes. An adolescent girl staggered away, squealing in ecstasy, "I touched him! I touched him!" Hundreds of others nearby shrieked to reach the man who had conquered the air across the continent. Linnard and the policemen formed a tight circle around him and wedged their way through the melee. To negotiate the 100 yards back to the judges' stand required twenty minutes as thousands more strove for contact with the birdman.

Cal was delivered to the Victoria automobile, where Mrs. Davis and "Rose Queen" Irene Grosse presented him with a bouquet of roses. He looked embarrassed and mumbled words of thanks through his chewed-off cigar stub.

Linnard brought out a telephone from the platform. It was connected to the Associated Press office in Los Angeles. Still deafened from the clatter of the engine and now from the tumult of the crowd, Cal was unable to comprehend a syllable of speech. He uttered a few unintelligible words into the mouthpiece and handed the telephone back to Linnard.

Someone had obtained a gigantic American flag and managed to bring it forth. It was draped over Cal's shoulders. He was hoisted, protesting, into the Victoria. The automobile, driven by Pasadena's Mayor Thum, moved forward on a triumphal parade around the track.

In the grandstand, people acclaimed their hero and the star-spangled banner he bore so befittingly. Some applauded as he passed; others trembled with rapture or danced about. Many stood silently, choked with emotion, helpless as tears blurred their eyes and slid down their cheeks.

On the field, the Victoria Electric moved slowly, hemmed in and convoyed by a howling mob seemingly bent on self-destruction. Reporters pulled at bodies, trying for a few words from the idol of the entire nation.

Finally, after the second circuit, a reporter from the *Examiner* broke through and jumped onto the running board.

"What about the prize?" he yelled at Cal. "The Hearst money?"

"Never mind the money," Cal yelled back. "I did it, didn't I? I did it!!"

12

Coast to Coast and Beyond

CAL WAS DELIVERED from the delirious crowd at Tournament Park by D. M. Linnard in his chauffeured Simplex. He was taken to the Maryland Hotel, where his wife and mother waited anxiously in the forefront of several hundred more enthusiasts. Mabel dashed forward, hurled herself into his arms, and delivered a resounding buss. Cal beamed at her, returned the kiss, and then turned to embrace his mother, who wedged between them.

"Are you tired, Calbraith?" asked Mrs. Sweitzer.

"Oh, not much," said Cal cheerily, and then more quietly, "I guess I am quite a bit tired after all."

"I knew you would do it, Calbraith," Mabel interposed.

Pushed through the crush into the lobby, Cal signed the register, "Cal P. Rodgers, New York to Pasadena by Air."

"Now, what can we do for you?" offered Linnard.

Cal—the only unruffled person in Pasadena—turned to him calmly and, puffing on his cigar, said, "I would like a glass of cream and a cracker."

"What," he was asked, "is the secret behind such a strenuous accomplishment?"

"Simple," said Cal. "You just keep going till you get there."

Reporters and photographers soon gained admittance to his hotel room. Did he think other aviators would soon cross the continent as he had?

"It's easy," said Cal, "but I don't believe it can be done in thirty days —not for a long time yet. I do not believe my flight will be duplicated for a year or two."

"How do you manage to light your cigar in the air while going at the rate of an express train?"

"Nothing to it. You merely have to smoke all the time, lighting one cigar from the other."

"What is your single-day record for cigar-smoking aloft?"

"Nineteen. Wind makes the cigars burn faster."

That evening, at a supper arranged by D. M. Linnard to present the celebrated birdman to newsmen covering the McNamara trial, Linnard announced that "Rodgers has made no immediate plans. He is glad to rest for a few days here in Pasadena where he is so welcome." Cal reciprocated by predicting that Pasadena would one day become the site of an aerodrome, the principal transfer point for air travel from New York to San Francisco. "For the present," he said, "I want to confirm that I don't consider the trip complete until I have actually touched the Pacific Ocean. That will probably be at Venice, but it depends on the business conditions."

Monday morning Cal was driven to Tournament Park by Linnard to inspect the *Vin Fiz*. The machine had survived, more or less intact, the onslaught of the Sunday afternoon crowd. It stood, roped off at one corner of the field, in tatters—broken struts, dangling wires, strips of fabric hanging from the planes—less the proud bird that had spanned the continent than a bedraggled warrior home from the Crusades. Between its skids lay Charlie Wiggin. He had slept through the night, his arms embracing a set of wheels. "Someone had to protect her," he said. "Besides, it didn't seem right for her to be alone when everyone else was celebrating." With Wiggie's help, the aircraft was stripped of its skin and removed to a small warehouse nearby. Its engine was detached and taken to Walter Hansen's machine shop for thorough reconditioning.

The Vin Fiz special train, at Armour's insistence, was disbanded, its locomotive returned to the Southern Pacific, the Pullman *Orkney* to the Chicago & Alton. Armour officials estimated that the cross-country expedition had cost the meat-packing concern more than $180,000 and expressed doubt that sales of their Vin Fiz drink would justify such a sum. No further expenditures would be indulged.

The hangar car was retained at a siding of the Pasadena depot. Linnard promised that he would contract another private train to accompany Cal on the final leg to the water's edge.

A telegram was dispatched by Stewart deKrafft to William Randolph Hearst, stating that although the thirty-day time specification had not been met, the feat itself was overwhelmingly successful—for which Mr. Hearst was to be congratulated. No response was received from the publisher.

Newspaper editorials competed for superlatives in describing the aviator and his transcontinental flight: "By sheer pluck and determination, he annihilated the distance between our oceans." . . . "Defied the laws of nature." . . . "Emblazoned in every history book of world events." The *Los Angeles Examiner* printed a full-column editorial:

> *Not alone Los Angeles, but all the world applauds the tall bronzed young man who came down from out of the upper strata yesterday after writing history on the clouds. Even though his original quest, the Hearst prize, was not won, young Rodgers has demonstrated that the aerial passage of the continent is not only possible but an accomplished fact. He takes place with the great pioneers of history, with those men who in sports or warfare or civic life have stood forth from the ranks of their fellow man and made their impress on the affairs of the world. . . . Through every variety of weather, the pelt of hail, blinding rain and snow storms, fierce blasts of squalls, and the obverse of desert haze and heat, this stouthearted airman has completely traversed a continent. . . . His feat will give a fresh impetus to the science of aviation and has killed forever the bugaboo of the mountain ramparts supposed to blockade an American transcontinental flight. . . . It brings into early possibility the passenger aeroplane and the realization that the airship is no longer a mere toy. . . . Calbraith P. Rodgers—Los Angeles and the world takes off its hat to you.*

Monday night the Vin Fiz entourage convened for a private supper—its last gathering—at the Maryland. Ed Merritt presided as host on behalf of Armour & Company. He and Cal bade farewell to each of those returning East. Charley Taylor, whose wife still lay ill at Good Samaritan Hospital, attended, as did Frank Shaffer, who had arrived only hours before and whose wife was recovering in Lima, Ohio. While waiting for dessert to be served, Stewart deKrafft arose, proposed a toast in memory of chef Ed Davis, and deliberately poured a glass of water onto the floor. His audience cheered lustily and followed suit.

Well after the party concluded, about 3:00 A.M., Cal, in company with deKrafft, Frank Shaffer, and Charlie Wiggin, drove the Palmer-Singer from Pasadena to the beach at Venice. He steered the auto over the sand to within a few feet of the waves. A listless surf rippled onto the shore, breathed out its asthmatic hiss, and receded. Cal stood on the wet sand for a moment, staring at the waters streaked with silver from a gibbous moon; then, with a thin smile, he stepped lightly into the automobile and drove back to Pasadena.

Throughout the week Cal was fêted at luncheons and dinners and at schools and colleges in the area. Between such activities, he answered some of the scores of telegrams and congratulatory messages that flooded in from various parts of the world. August Belmont, Al Welsh, Harry Atwood, and the Wright brothers were notable among the senders.

Tuesday the seventh was "Wiggie the Kid's" eighteenth birthday. Mabel purchased a vanilla-frosted layer cake decorated with a ring of eighteen candles. "You're a man, now," Cal told him. "I can't call you 'kid' anymore."

At a supper party Wednesday evening at the Maryland, a representative of William Randolph Hearst was introduced and expressed "Mr. Hearst's desire to present Calbraith P. Rodgers with a loving cup in honor of his historic achievement." Cal declined the proffered cup and, in words not suitable for newspaper print, delivered his opinion on the subject of the Hearst offer and the man behind it.

Of the several beach communities bidding for the distinction of terminating the transcontinental flight, the city of Long Beach posted the most generous offer: $5,000 from the chamber of commerce. A landing on the beach east of the pike was specified for Sunday afternoon, November 12. Almost immediately after signing the contract, Cal was besieged by a delegation from the Pasadena Ministerial Union, demanding that he change his flight from Sunday to a weekday ("You cannot serve God and skylark in a flying machine"). Long Beach ministers, following the lead of their Pasadena brethren, also condemned the Sunday flight ("Long Beach does not seek the reputation of a Sunday circus town"). Cal dodged the delegations ("They'd stop the birds from flying on Sunday, if they could") and, with part of the money advanced for the Long Beach flight, purchased for Mabel a white Mercer runabout. The model was similar to that owned by Fire Chief Higham in Middletown, New York, and openly admired by Mabel.

For the twenty-seven-mile jaunt from Pasadena to Long Beach, two special cars of the Southern Pacific had been arranged by D. M. Linnard. The train would leave Pasadena at 2:30 P.M. Sunday and would depart Long Beach at 5:00 P.M. for the return journey. A total of 125 prominent persons were invited on board.

Sunday, November 12, the *Vin Fiz Flyer*, again reassembled, rewired, and retuned to flying condition, its planes again boasting clean white fabric, a cap for the gasoline tank replacing the potato requisitioned at Lordsburg, was pushed onto the polo field of Tournament Park. Charley Taylor, who had supervised its reconstruction, cautioned against stressing the airplane near its limits. "It's still a worn-out old bird," he said. "It'll hold for one last hop," Cal declared as he climbed onto the machine for a 3:30 P.M. takeoff. "Now, for the last time—let her go, boys."

Skies over the Los Angeles basin were dull, overcast with layers of cirrocumulus. A slight haze prevailed at lower altitudes. Only a soft breeze could be felt at ground level. Before proceeding toward his destination, Cal circled the airplane at a steep angle around the Hotel Maryland. Then he turned for the Arroyo Seco, passed over the Cawston Ostrich Farm to the cheers and waves of people assembled on the Salt Lake Bridge, flew directly above Mount Washington, and then skimmed over the foothills, veering eastward to pick up the Pacific Electric rails.

A thousand feet over Eastlake Park, the motor began to hiss; it sputtered violently, then stopped. Cal released engine compression and spiraled to a small valley a mile northeast of Covina Junction. He quickly diagnosed the problem as a leaky gasoline feed pipe; vibration had split a soldered joint near the engine. He removed the pipe, carried it to a nearby farmhouse (where it was wrapped with wire), and returned to the flying machine. Meanwhile several hundred men, women, and children, many of them from the nearby Union Fertilizer plant, had arrived on the scene and crowded about the craft. Cal appealed to the responsible citizens to restrain their more rambunctious neighbors. The arrival of several deputy constables enabled him to reattach the feed pipe without interference.

His labors concluded, Cal asked assistance in pushing the machine up a hill to the east, from where he could effect a takeoff. As many men and boys as could lay a hand on it lent their efforts. Some difficulty was then experienced in attempting to restart the engine. The sparker refused to function properly, and several minutes were lost to ineffectual trials at inducing the pistons to cooperate. The propellers were pulled through and the engine fired; however, it seemed to those in the crowd familiar with mechanical devices that the motor sounds were irregular and of false pitch. Nevertheless, an hour after he descended at Covina Junction, Cal again took the air for Long Beach, where a multitude of 50,000 awaited his appearance.

Twilight was creeping over the eastern skies as Cal sailed over Boyle Heights to the Slawson Junction. He angled eastward to Watts and then into view of spectators at Compton, who soon heard the intermittent splutter of his engine. Losing altitude, he crossed over Artesia Street at about 200 feet, sighted a line of high-tension wires along the road, and banked at 45°. About 100 feet from the ground, the machine suddenly veered to one side and plummeted. It struck head-foremost into a ploughed field.

Cal was thrown forward, his head buried in dirt. The gasoline tank tore loose and slammed onto his back, pinning his chest to the ground. The chain guard tumbled across his neck. The engine sheared from its mount, smashed through the radiator, struck the earth, and came to rest on his legs, which protruded beyond the rear planes as the machine tumbled over onto his body. The bottle of Vin Fiz was wrenched from its wires.

Within two minutes James Orr, owner of the ranch on which Cal had crashed, and Herbert Mulherron, the ranch foreman, reached the scene. No sign of the aviator was in evidence. Fearing that the wreckage, now soaked with gasoline from the burst tank, would explode with fire, Orr and Mulherron pulled at sections of the collapsed machine, searching for its driver. "I first thought he might have gotten out," said Orr later. "We could see nothing of him. I was about to leave when I heard a noise under the front plane. Then I knew Rodgers was under the thing."

Orr and Mulherron tore at the plane fabric until they uncovered the form beneath the wreckage. Their first impression suggested that Cal was beyond human assistance. Only the body was visible, the head wedged into a furrow. "As we looked through the hole, we saw him move," said Orr. "We realized then that he was only hurt."

The two men pried the engine and gasoline tank from Cal's body, dragged him from under the crumpled airplane, and scooped out clogs of dirt from his mouth and nostrils. His face was cut, one side burned from the engine; his clothes were soaked with gasoline. For a brief moment he regained consciousness to ask, "Where is my cap?" They carried his limp body a quarter-mile to a road along the southern boundary of the ranch.

The first automobile to appear was driven by Frank J. Carlisle, business manager of the *Los Angeles Express*. Carlisle helped to load the aviator into the rear seat and then rushed him to the Compton office of Dr. A.

L. Holcombe. As he was being lugged onto the doctor's table, where his mangled clothes were cut from his body, Cal again stirred to consciousness and muttered, "How far do I have to go?"

At Long Beach, with dusk blanketing the scene, bonfires were lit along the landing enclosure. Mayor Windham, the Reception Committee, other dignitaries, and many in the immense crowd fidgeted impatiently. The Pacific Electric line had switched every extra car onto its Long Beach run, and the "Big Red" coaches were lined up at the terminal like giant pismires.

The crash of the biplane occurred shortly after five o'clock. Almost an hour passed before word reached Long Beach that the transcontinental flier was down at Compton, twelve miles to the north. Details were not available in the first meager reports. Charley Taylor and Frank Shaffer jumped into the Palmer-Singer racer and started for Compton. Mabel, Mrs. Sweitzer, and others in the private party assembled by D. M. Linnard rushed for the Southern Pacific train, which was given a clear track north. Many in the disappointed gathering at the beach drifted to their automobiles or ran for the Pacific Electric cars. Yet others refused to leave, feeling vaguely that the famous birdman would somehow overcome whatever difficulty had befallen him and appear in a blinding flash over the Long Beach pier.

Taylor and Shaffer were first of the aviation group to reach Dr. Holcombe's office. News of the accident was flashed to Pasadena; arrangements were made to transport the aviator to that city's General Hospital. Dr. Holcombe's examination indicated a possible broken right ankle; sprained left ankle; a severe twisting of the back; bruises and lacerations of the right shoulder and side; rib fractures; and bruises, scratches, and gasoline burns over the face. Shortly before seven o'clock Cal was lifted into an automobile and driven to the chartered train. He was semiconscious but failed to recognize his wife and mother as they scrambled from the train to his side. Both women hovered near him, hysterical with anxiety.

Dr. Holcombe accompanied his patient through the trip to Pasadena. It was decided that Cal could be adequately treated at the Maryland Hotel, and he was removed to his quarters there in an ambulance. He was conscious but delirious. "Did I make a good landing?" he asked several times from the stretcher. Two physicians, Drs. F. C. E. Mattison and A. T. Newcomb, were called to administer their services. Their examinations confirmed Dr. Holcombe's diagnosis and revealed further injury to the base of the spine and a slight brain concussion. Opiates were administered, and the doctors reported their charge to be resting easily. Mabel remained near her husband until after midnight when two nurses arrived to attend him. Mrs. Sweitzer stayed through the night, dozing on a chair next to her son's bed.

Total tranquillity with minimum movement was prescribed for at least thirty days to facilitate recovery. "My patient is to be kept extremely quiet," said Dr. Mattison, "and not to be disturbed by the press. His only statement is 'I will get to the ocean before I quit.'"

Regardless of the doctor's orders, newsmen converged on the aviator early the following day. "When I started to fall, I knew at once what was happening," Cal told them while sitting up in bed, his back propped by two large pillows, smoking a huge cigar for which he had bribed a nurse, "and then my mind went blank. I neither knew how far I fell nor how long it took me to fall. I didn't even know what was the matter. . . . I seemed to have been frozen as far as mental sensations are concerned. . . . I don't recall any feeling of fright—only an absolute absence of thought. . . . 'Ethereal asphyxia' is what I call it. It lurks in the pockets of the upper air strata and creeps irresistibly upon the senses of the aviator, lulling him into dreamy unconsciousness. I believe this same thing caused the deaths of Arch Hoxsey, Ralph Johnstone, Eugene Ely, and a number of others who have fallen to their deaths by losing control of their craft. . . . The one thing I know for certain is that I will complete the job when I am recovered—probably in a week."

As for the airplane, "The machine was all worn out, and the bearings gone," said Cal. "I knew it before I started and I only flew on so as not to disappoint the crowd at Long Beach. I do not blame my mechanicians."

Numerous messages of condolences were received at the Maryland Hotel.* Aviators in the U.S. and Europe telegraphed expressions of sympathy and empathic feelings. Several ministers wrote their belief that the accident was a sign of God's disapproval of Sunday flying.

The tangled mass of wire, engine parts, and frame that had been a modern flying machine was piled onto a truck and hauled to the sun parlor at the end of the Pine Avenue pier in Long Beach. Charley Taylor diagnosed the cause of the crash as a clogged fuel pipe and estimated the

*A telegram from the Wright brothers in Dayton read, "Our sincere sympathy and best wishes for a speedy recovery. Your general performance was so extraordinary as to be almost incredible, even to those who understand its difficulties." (To a friend in New York, Orville Wright wrote, "That man Rodgers was born with four horseshoes in his pocket.")

cost of reconstruction at over $4,000: "The only portions we could salvage in one piece are the tail elevator, the vertical rudder, and the two propellers. It will require almost a week to rebuild the airship." The hangar car was transferred from its Pasadena siding to a track at Long Beach, and Taylor, Shaffer, and Wiggin detached parts from the "B" machine for adaptation to the EX. Additional components were ordered from the Wright factory.

The bottle of Vin Fiz was not found in the wreckage. Crew members, at Cal's insistence, were sent back to the Orr ranch to search for it—without result. "There are a million bottles of the stuff all over the country," Cal was told. "I want that one," he persisted. A second search uncovered the bottle, buried some yards from the crater scooped out by the airplane.

For the next three weeks Cal lay abed or was trundled about the grounds of the Maryland Hotel in a wheelchair, all the while puffing huge black cigars and chafing to regain his feet. He passed much of each day acknowledging telegrams and writing notes to people he had met on the cross-country trek. A special letter of gratitude was addressed to Ricardo Vela Gonzalez, the carpenter in Spofford, Texas. To Elsie Alexander, the young girl in Great Bend, Pennsylvania, who had dashed out to Carl's Flats with her just-washed hair streaming behind her, he wrote: "My dear little friend. You do not mind if I call you my little friend, do you? I just wanted you to know that I completed my flight, and I have not forgotten your shining beautiful hair. It was one of the pleasures of my trip, and one day, when we were having a light rain, it seemed as though I could see your hair in the rain ahead of me. I could see it very plainly, just as it was when I was there. Your friend, Cal."

An hour of one day was allotted to a tailor summoned by Mrs. Sweitzer to the Maryland. Cal was measured and shortly presented with two brown business suits, a "get-well" gift from his mother.

During this time of Cal's convalescence, Bob Fowler had continued eastward across Texas. Stranded in the shifting sands of Mastodon, N.M.T., for eight days, he had dismantled the *Cole Flyer* and reassembled it on the deck of a railroad handcar. With its propellers whirling full force, the pickaback machine gained a speed of 45 mph along the track. At that point, Fowler observed a freight train puffing around a bend directly ahead. It was too late to stop without a collision. He pulled back on the elevator lever, and the airplane shot into the air. He missed the oncoming freight by several feet. The handcar was derailed.

In spite of delays at Mastodon and elsewhere, Fowler expressed hope that, with Rodgers's machine broken at Compton, he would become the first aviator actually to complete the span from ocean to ocean.

By the end of the first week in December, Cal could no longer tolerate his inactivity. He gained Dr. Mattison's permission to proceed—with the proviso that both ankles be encased in plaster casts. "The casts won't bother me," said Cal. "I can fly with my feet amputated if necessary, and I'm going to finish this flight if it kills me." A new date was quickly negotiated with the Long Beach Chamber of Commerce: December 10, a Sunday. Formal reception ceremonies were canceled owing to renewed protests of the ministerial associations.

Sunday afternoon offered generally clear skies—a respite after an overcast Saturday and drenching rains earlier in the week. Cal was driven in the Palmer-Singer to a field near the Orr ranch, where the *Vin Fiz*, again gleaming white, had been towed earlier. He was accompanied by Charley Taylor, Frank Shaffer, Charlie Wiggin, and Mabel. The machine was accorded a scrupulous inspection and declared in excellent shape for the twelve-mile flight. Cal hobbled about on crutches, double-checking every wire, every bolt, every part of the aircraft he could reach. The bottle of Vin Fiz was again in its rightful place.

At Long Beach, 50,000 persons gathered for the second time, eager for the spectacle of Rodgers's landing on the beach and also for the advertised escort of two additional flying machines. Again, extra Pacific Electric cars were pressed into service, and again hundreds of private automobiles flocked to the beach community. Several automobile parties had been organized to depart from the Hotel Maryland. Mrs. Sweitzer rode with one of these groups.

At 3:30 P.M. word was received at the Compton field that aviator Frank Champion had flown from Long Beach to Dominguez Field, where Beryl Williams had already mounted his machine. A time of 3:50 was affirmed for the takeoff of all three airplanes. Precisely at that moment, Cal, having strapped his crutches to the forward edge of the lower plane, lit a cigar, waved at his wife and mechanicians, and called out, "Let her go, boys." At Dominguez Field, Frank Champion switched on the 60-horsepower engine of his Blériot monoplane. Only yards away, Beryl Williams urged forward his Curtiss biplane.

Lifting from the Compton field, Cal circled back over the Orr ranch to pick up the thread of his journey and headed for Signal Hill, where an outsize blue flag had been planted as a marker.

Over the Del Mar Hotel at 3:55 P.M., he was spotted by observers on the roof of the auditorium. A great cheer rose from spectators on the beach. The Municipal Band, seated in the half-finished new grandstand by the pier, struck up a lively air.

As he crossed over the shore of the Pacific Ocean, Cal was joined by Champion and Williams in their machines. The three airships maneuvered to within 100 feet of each other, and the thousands of onlookers shouted themselves hoarse at the stupendous spectacle of an aerial caravan. Champion saluted Rodgers by dropping three copies of a letter addressed to the transcontinental aviator.* The three envelopes fluttered into the water.

Cal dipped the *Vin Fiz* to within a few feet of the ocean and flew along the surf line so that the spray from the breaking waves christened the machine in symbolic triumph. As his purpose dawned on the crowd, deafening whoops and hurrahs issued from 50,000 throats. He veered over the "Walk of a Thousand Lights" and descended to the roped-off area at the east end of the beach. At the same time, the forward ranks of the multitude broke through the restraining ropes. Police and National Guardsmen were swept away. Several persons were trampled, and many had clothing torn and hats crushed in the overpowering charge. A group of policemen encircled the airplane and with considerable force held the throng at bay while emergency ropes were brought in as a barricade. Cal fumbled through his pockets for a match and lit his largest and blackest cigar. Then he unfastened his crutches and climbed down from the driver's seat. He had been in the air fourteen minutes in the twelve-mile flight from Compton, capping a voyage of 4,231 miles.

First to reach him was Mrs. Sweitzer, who screamed at policemen, "Let me through! I'm his mother! I'm his mother!" She threw both arms around her son's neck, exclaiming, "Oh, Calbraith. Calbraith, my boy, I'm so glad it's over." She was alternately laughing and crying.

Mabel Rodgers and the mechanicians drove up in the Palmer-Singer. Mabel was escorted through the crowd to her husband's side. Her face was beaming. "I'm so glad—so proud of you. You are indeed my hero," she said, embracing him before the cheering thousands.

Reporters bulled their way to the aircraft and demanded a statement. "I said I would complete this flight and I have done it," Cal responded. "It has been a hard strain . . . but I am proud to have blazed the way to the Pacific Coast by the air route. . . . It points out what air travel will mean to the next generation."

---

*It read, "Congratulations on the completion of your coast-to-coast trip. Best wishes for your continued success."

Photographers clamored for a picture of the travel-scarred airplane in the ocean. To oblige them, Cal again strapped his crutches on the lower plane and perched on the driver's seat as the *Vin Fiz* was pushed a few feet into the surf. He handled the levers of the machine and puffed cigar smoke at the photographers.

A wild scramble of the onlookers followed this scene. The force of the thousands in the rear struggling for a glimpse of the aviator and his machine pushed scores of people, many of them handsomely gowned women, knee-deep into the water.

Cal was taken in charge by Secretary W. I. Camp of the Long Beach Chamber of Commerce and driven to the Hotel Virginia (at the west end of the beach). There, he was feted at a dinner attended by many notables of the city. Secretary Camp proclaimed him "the Balboa of the Air, a man with a long cigar and an even longer record of accomplishments." Both Mabel and Mrs. Sweitzer delivered short speeches about their experiences en route from New York, and Lawrence Peters summarized the problems of an advance man. No one addressed the essence of the magnificent achievement whose culmination they had just witnessed. It was, finally, a triumph of determination over logic, of sentiment over sense.

In his own brief speech, Cal declared that he had no plans for the immediate future, and probably would rest until fully recovered from the injuries sustained in his fall at Compton.

When Cal and his entourage returned to the Maryland only shortly before dawn—after a night's celebration at Ship's Café in Venice—a pile of congratulatory telegrams had already accumulated. Cal selected first the one from Al Welsh. It read, "Don't stop now. Only the Pacific lies ahead. You can make it."

Cal's activities over the next three weeks were not strenuous, and he was able to discard his crutches before Christmas. He agreed to a request from the Tournament of Roses Association to participate with his flying machine in the association's New Year's Day extravaganza.

Pasadena's Twenty-third Annual Tournament of Roses parade took place on January 1, 1912, in an atmosphere of semitropical warmth. At the appointed moment of ten minutes past 10:00 A.M., the nation's most celebrated aviator drove his transcontinental flyer along Colorado Street at 700 feet. From the airplane poured a shower of 10,000 carnations. Below, a mad scramble ensued, one that shamed any department-store bargain rush, as 150,000 persons lining the parade grounds fought to claim the fluttering petals.

"There were queens without number in the parade," wrote a reporter for the *Pasadena Star*, "but none was the absolute queen. This year a king reigned, the monarch of the air who has glorified American history by his epoch-making flight from New York to Pasadena, crossing the continent along the uncharted airlanes. Calbraith P. Rodgers, ruler of the air, replaced the Tournament Queen and was the aerial monarch of the greatest fete that ever beautified a New Year's morn."

One of the fifty rose-petal-covered floats in the long procession— viewed by Cal from the judges' stand—depicted Calbraith Perry Rodgers in his cross-country airship, dipping his feet in the Pacific Ocean (represented by a tub of water). The feature of the nighttime show and parade was a "reproduction" of the great naval battle on Lake Erie in 1813 between the American fleet under Commodore Oliver Hazard Perry and the British flotilla under Captain Barclay. Fifteen ships were portrayed in floral arrays, and two-thirds of a ton of fireworks were exploded in the pyrotechnic display that simulated the battle. Cal stood and applauded as the float of his famous ancestor passed by.

For the first days of the New Year, Cal's schedule showed only blank pages. Mabel, on the other hand, was fully engaged with social affairs, parties, and sporting events (tennis with Mae Sutton, whom she had met at the Maryland). She attended the opening at the Mason Opera House of *Miss Innocence* and was introduced to its leading lady, Anna Held. Her confidence with her white Mercer swelled, and she exercised her prowess by warming its tires through the streets of Pasadena. On January 3 she was flagged down by a police officer for exceeding the speed limit by double. Mabel explained that she was still a novice driver and identified herself as the wife of the transcontinental aviator. The officer dismissed her with a warning and a request to convey his congratulations to her husband.

In Boston, Harry Atwood informed the press that—in place of his flight across South America—he would attempt to span the Atlantic Ocean in the spring. With a special hydroaeroplane and a newly designed 150-horsepower engine, he planned to alight on the water each sundown and take the air again at dawn the next day.

At the end of the first week of 1912, Mrs. Sweitzer received word that Isabella Bolton Perry Tiffany had died in Baltimore (January 5) at the age of seventy-seven, the last survivor of Commodore Matthew Calbraith Perry's ten children. Mrs. Sweitzer regretted that she could not pay her respects by attending the funeral. Said Cal: "I have paid my respects ever since I can remember. I am due some return payments."

January 12, 1912, marked Cal's thirty-third birthday. A party that evening found the honoree submerged in a slough of depression. "My father died at this age," he muttered darkly. Mabel shrugged off the remark, but Mrs. Sweitzer caught its full impact. "I know," she sternly lectured her son, "better than you do."

On January 13, at his bride's King George Street home in Annapolis, Lieutenant John Rodgers bound in matrimony Miss Ethel Greiner. The wedding stirred naval social circles because of vehement opposition from both the bride's mother, Mrs. Richard M. Greiner (aghast that her daughter's future depended on the driver of a flying machine), and the groom's mother, Mrs. Elizabeth Rodgers (dismayed that the Rodgers name should be conferred on a member of a lower social class). Immediately after the ceremony, the newlyweds departed for San Diego, California, where John Rodgers had been ordered to report January 20 "to establish a Naval Aviation Camp at North Island." A stop of one day in Los Angeles for a reunion with Cal and Mabel afforded Cal his first emotional lift since the New Year's Day parade.

The third air meet at Dominguez Field was scheduled for January 20 to 28, 1912. General manager Dick Ferris had predicted the most grandiose demonstration of aeronautics ever held. Never before and likely never again, he promised, would Americans behold such a number of world-famous birdmen gathered in one nest. One of the first invitations had been extended to Cal P. Rodgers, and the transcontinental aviator had indicated his acceptance.

As the date of the meet approached, Cal and Dick Ferris exchanged increasingly heated words. By January 15, Ferris became exasperated over what he regarded as Cal's supercilious attitude and issued a statement to the press: "This afternoon I sent Rodgers word that unless he signed an entry blank and agreed to fly every day of the meet, it will be necessary to vacate the hangar he is now occupying and make room for the aviators now compelled to house their machines in tents at Dominguez. Rodgers seems to have formed the opinion that no aviation meet can be held without him. He is mistaken. If he enters the meet, he will have to abide by all the rules and regulations."

Cal refused to commit himself to a specific schedule of flights. Twenty-four hours before the meet's opening ceremonies, he was ordered to remove his two biplanes from the Dominguez field hangar. "This action is due," Ferris stated, "to a case of mutinous conduct recently developed by Rodgers."

Cal transferred the *Vin Fiz* and the No. 27 "B" to a warehouse in Long Beach (the hangar car had been repossessed by the Armour Company in mid-December) and informed his wife and mother that the family would return, at least temporarily, to the East Coast. Temperatures in Los Angeles through the week hovered in the mid-eighties; in Washington, D.C., a reading of 13° below zero was recorded. Mabel had immersed herself in the Southern California milieu but, as ever, expressed willingness to accompany her husband whither he would go. Mrs. Sweitzer had long grown ill at ease in the same environment; further, she welcomed any opportunity to separate her son from his flying machines. A friend had mailed her a clipping from the *New York Times* of December 31, 1911, that detailed aviation deaths since Lieutenant Thomas Selfridge was killed in 1908. There were 136 names on the list, 99 of which were entered during 1911.* Mrs. Sweitzer did not discuss the matter with Cal, but pointedly left the *Times* clipping in his room at the Maryland.

The family packed its bags and boarded a train for New York on Saturday, January 20, the opening day of the Dominguez Air Meet.

For Saturday evening, January 27, Cal had been invited to a dinner hosted by the Aero Club of America at Sherry's, where President Taft was the guest of honor. Robert J. Collier, president of the club, told the 332-pound chief executive that the Aero Club was ready to commission the building of a roomy airplane that could carry him the next time he went "swinging around the circle." Then, on behalf of the club, Collier and Taft together presented Cal with a gold medal for his unparalleled feat of aeronautics and recalled to the assembly that the Aeronautical Society had previously awarded a medal to William Randolph Hearst for the $50,000 purse that instigated the transcontinental flight. It was, said Collier, "what our friend Joe Weber would have called 'a good offer.'" President Taft congratulated Cal, shook his hand, commented that he was indeed a man to look up to, and departed.

It was shortly after this time that Bob Fowler reached the Atlantic Ocean. At Weatherford, Texas, he had triggered a cattle stampede while landing on the prairie and was almost trampled when the cattle turned toward his downed machine. At Iola, Texas, he had survived a 60-mph windstorm by sheltering the *Cole Flyer* behind a barn. Reaching Beaumont, Texas, he took off with R. H. Sexton as the operator of a moving-picture camera; the city and the forest of oil derricks surrounding it were

*After Selfridge in 1908, 4 aviators were killed in 1909, and 32 in 1910. Of the 99 deaths in 1911, 26 were American. The increase in fatalities was ascribed both to the increase in the number of aviators and to the influx of amateur fliers who were not competent to battle tricky air currents, "holes in the air," and other dangers confronting the airman.

photographed, and the pictures exhibited two weeks later (by Sexton) in New York City. From Jennings, Louisiana, he flew vials of typhoid vaccine to Evangeline, a flood-isolated village where an epidemic of typhoid raged. Christmas Eve found him in Paradis, Louisiana, where, landing after dark in the town square, he sparked rumors among local youngsters that Santa Claus had come to Paradis. New Year's Eve brought him to New Orleans (flying the twelve miles from Ama, Louisiana, he rose—for the second time—from a handcar on a railroad track); he circled over the spot where John B. Moisant had met his death a year earlier. Into the new year, through Mississippi, Alabama, Georgia, and Florida, he continued, despite crashes, misfunctioning machinery, and blustery weather. On February 8, 1912, he landed at the Moncrief racetrack at Jacksonville, Florida. Aviators Max Lillie and Harold Kantner, both performing exhibitions at the track, greeted him in the air and escorted him onto the field. Nine days later, on February 17, 122 days and 2,517 miles from Los Angeles, he fulfilled his promise, largely forgotten by the world, and flew a final short hop to the surf at Pablo Beach. Cal did not deign to wire congratulations.

At the end of February, Mabel entrained to Bennington for a week's visit with her father. Cal spoke vaguely of a trip to Stockholm for the forthcoming Olympic Games. The Aero Club of France had posted a $100,000 prize for a flight across the Atlantic. Cal discussed the offer with several friends but dismissed it as impractical. Mrs. Sweitzer returned to her home in Pittsburgh and began planning for a round-the-world cruise to recover from the rigors of cross-country train rides and anxieties from her son's ventures.

Early in March Cal and Mabel again embarked for the West Coast and were welcomed back to their previous quarters in the Hotel Maryland. D. M. Linnard was on hand for another entertaining dinner. Cal held a few cursory discussions with Charley Taylor about their prospects of forming an aeronautics company and school, but nothing materialized. "The main hazard in aviation," said Cal, "is starvation." Ultimately, he concluded, aviation is for aviators, not for the public. Taylor decided to return to the Wright factory at Dayton as soon as his wife's health permitted. Of the crew that accompanied the transcontinental enterprise, only Frank Shaffer and Charlie Wiggin remained to tend the two airplanes and reminisce with Cal, shoring up the memories of their experience.

The fragile celebrity, acquired so quickly, seemed about to crumble. A letter from Stewart deKrafft in Chicago reminded him that, as they had agreed in private conversation, yesterday's heroes belong to yesterday. "A nation drunk with admiration can sober up quickly," deKrafft wrote. "When you have flown as high as you can, there is only one direction you can go." DeKrafft had once asked: "What will you do when the tumult and the shouting dies, when the Captains and the Kings depart?"* There was no answer.

Throughout his life, Cal had been torn between two conflicting aspects of his character—the untroubled cavalier and the dedicated torchbearer of his ancestor's fame. Now the gulf between them seemed wider than ever. The line between heroes and fools, between courage and stupidity, seemed thin indeed. Previously, when he looked in a mirror, he was looking *for* himself—for some quality beyond the image. Now he looked *at* himself; the quality of transcendence was missing, vanished beyond the looking glass.

The Wright "B," "Old No. 27," was assembled and tuned to working condition. The bottle of Vin Fiz was transferred from the EX to a brace on the "B," and, for $2 each, Cal carried passengers for brief excursions a few hundred yards out to sea and over the Long Beach Pike.

At long last he was able to fulfill his pledge to Wiggin given during his first aerial exhibitions the previous July—on April 2 he began instructing his junior mechanician in the art of driving an airplane.

On Wednesday, April 3, there were two customers awaiting Cal's services for an afternoon flight. A circuit of the area was described with G. B. Harris, an elderly gentleman visiting southern California from Vancouver. When the "B" landed on the salt flat near the warehouse, Shaffer and Wiggin noted a peculiar hollow sound to the engine. Edmund Allyne, president of the Aluminum Casting Company of Cleveland, the other scheduled passenger, also commented on the irregular sound. "Just oil it up, kid," Cal told Wiggin. Cal seemed in high humor and bantered with Mr. Allyne for thirty minutes while Shaffer and Wiggin tinkered with the "B."

Cal inspected the machine and advised the two mechanicians that he would test it aloft before hazarding a passenger. He lit a cigar and mentioned casually that he would return in a few minutes. He rose from the salt flat at three o'clock and started east toward the amusement pier.

As always when an airplane flew from the Long Beach shore, it attracted a number of onlookers. Among those who followed Cal's course this time was Mamie St. Germain Parker. Mrs. Parker, who had witnessed the *Vin Fiz* at the Phoenix Fairgrounds, had removed to Long Beach in

*From Kipling's *Recessional.*

December. Through the glass enclosure of the refreshment parlor, where she had paused for a soda, she watched Cal thread a line between the roller coaster and the "Shoot the Shoots" and swerve toward the bathhouse. His low altitude and near-miss alarmed those watching on the beach. He continued to the west and flew by the Virginia Hotel, where he cleared the tennis-court fence by three feet. Guests at the hotel marveled at his daring. After another mile westward, he circled back and retraced his path over the coaster pier, this time at a height of 250 feet. A flock of sea gulls approached the machine, and to avoid its course, Cal dipped downward at a perilous angle of 45°.

Ahead loomed the seventy-five-foot-high double-decked Pine Avenue pier. With the wind blowing from the west, directly behind him, it was all but impossible to recover from the drop and climb over the obstruction. Fifty feet above the ocean, Cal was seen to work frantically at the lever controls. The machine did not respond but plunged at a yet steeper angle. Cal covered his face. His cigar fell from his mouth. The Wright biplane slammed into the surf thirty feet from the shoreline in about three feet of water. The engine sheared from its mount and struck Cal in the back, breaking his neck. He died instantly.

The bottle of Vin Fiz was shattered.

EPILOGUE

Calbraith Perry Rodgers became the 147th flier to meet death in an airplane. The fatal accident occurred only a few feet from the spot where he had concluded his historic transcontinental flight less than four months earlier and where residents of Long Beach planned to erect a monument to his achievement.

His body was disentangled from the wreckage and examined by a physician, Dr. S. A. Stone, who was among those watching the flight. Dr. Stone confirmed the cause of death.

Souvenir hunters raced into the water to pirate sections of the machine. Only the engine, propellers, and a few other components, were salvageable. Remnants of the "B" were carried by Frank Shaffer to the warehouse. Examination of the engine revealed that a disconnected terminal had disabled one of the four cylinders. Said Frank Shaffer, who had had a full view of the fatal dip: "Cal, I am sure, knew that death was staring him in the face on the last 100 feet."

(Several weeks later Shaffer announced that he had found the body of a sea gull wedged so tightly between the rudder and the tail framework that it was necessary to break the rudder to remove it. Consequently, he said, the control wire had snapped when Cal attempted to veer the machine. None of the scores of eyewitnesses saw a gull strike the airplane, and no one other than Shaffer confirmed the existence of the gull's body in the wreckage.)

Mabel was at the Hotel Maryland at the time of the accident. Notified of her husband's death, she was unable for a time to comprehend the reality of it. Then she burst out crying hysterically, "Oh, it is true. I always warned him. I knew it would happen this way." She was prostrated and could not suffer a trip to Long Beach. D. M. Linnard summoned two physicians to attend her.

Cables to Mrs. Sweitzer failed to reach her for more than a week. Cal had earlier received a letter from her as she traveled through India. She was reportedly somewhere in the Orient.

Lieutenant John Rodgers drove up from San Diego to take charge of funeral arrangements; he promised Mabel that he would never fly again. Services were held at the Turner & Stevens Chapel in Pasadena. Pallbearers were Lieutenant Rodgers, Stewart deKrafft, Lawrence Peters, Frank Shaffer, Charlie Wiggin, D. M. Linnard, Clifford Turpin, and Phil Parmalee. The Reverend Leslie Learned of All Saints Episcopal Church delivered the sermon. DeKrafft spoke for those who had traveled the train cross-country (quoting Hamlet): "He was a man, take him for all in all, I shall not look upon his like again."

DeKrafft also summed up the speculation regarding Cal's fatal crash. "It wasn't suicide," he said, "but it wasn't an accident either."

"I'm not afraid of death in an aeroplane," Cal had said only days before. "When it comes, if it does, it will have no hurt. When I fell at Compton, I made sure of that. The minute an aviator begins to fall he experiences . . . a state of what seems unconscious bliss. If death follows, an aviator doesn't know what has happened to him."

A telegram from Cal's sister, Mrs. Patty Pease, directed burial in the family plot near Pittsburgh. Mabel, John Rodgers, and Frank Shaffer departed for that city with the body.

The route taken retraced that which the Vin Fiz expedition had tracked on its transcontinental journey. At each location where Cal had landed, the train slowed, and the casket was displayed on a flatcar. People —far fewer than before—stood by the tracks to pay homage to the hero they had cheered only months earlier. Men doffed their hats, and children threw flower petals at the casket, which was covered with a huge American flag—the same flag that the hysterical crowd in Pasadena had draped over his shoulders on November 5.

Calbraith Perry Rodgers was interred in Allegheny Cemetery, Pittsburgh, Pennsylvania. A six-foot-four-inch tombstone was set on his grave, the inscription reading:

> *I conquer*
> *I endure*

Official Log
of the Vin Fiz
(from train dispatchers' sheets)

Date	Leave	Stops	Arrive	Comment
Sept. 17	Sheepshead Bay, N.Y.		Middletown	
Sept. 18				Crash on takeoff; machine wrecked
Sept. 21	Middletown		Hancock	Wrecked skids
Sept. 22	Hancock	Carbondale, Pa. Throop Scranton Great Bend Binghamton, N.Y.	Elmira	Lost
Sept. 23	Elmira		Hornell/Canisteo	Crash on landing
Sept. 24	Hornell/Canisteo	Olean	Redhouse/Cattaraugus	Wrecked machine on takeoff from Redhouse

Sept. 28	Salamanca	Meadville, Pa.		
		Warren, Ohio	Kent	Broken skid
				Delayed by
				storm
				(Sept. 29)
Sept. 30	Kent	Mansfield		
		Marion	Bobo (Rivare), Ind.	
Oct. 1	Bobo (Rivare)	Geneva	Huntington	
Oct. 2				Crash on takeoff; machine wrecked
Oct. 5	Huntington	Aldine	Hammond	Broken skid
				Delayed by weather
Oct. 8	Hammond	Chicago, Ill.	Lockport/Joliet	Cracked skid
Oct. 9	Lockport/Joliet	Streator		
		Peoria		
		Middletown	Springfield	
Oct. 10	Springfield	Nebo		
		Thompson, Mo.	Marshall	
Oct. 11	Marshall	Blue Springs	Kansas City, Mo.	
Oct. 14	Kansas City, Kans.	Moran		
		Russell Creek, Okla.	Vinita	Delayed by wind
Oct. 16	Vinita	Muskogee		
		Northtown	McAlester	Cracked cylinder
Oct. 17	McAlester	Durant		
		Pottsboro, Tex.		
		Bonita		
		Gainesville	Fort Worth	
Oct. 18	Fort Worth		Dallas	
Oct. 19	Dallas		Waco	
Oct. 20	Waco	Granger		
		Austin	Kyle	Engine explosion
Oct. 22	Kyle	San Marcos	San Antonio	
Oct. 24	San Antonio	Lacoste		
		Sabinal		
		Uvalde	Spofford	
Oct. 25				Wrecked machine on takeoff

Date				
Oct. 26	Spofford	Del Rio		
		Dryden	Sanderson	
Oct. 28	Sanderson	Alpine		
		Marfa	Sierra Blanca	smashed skids, torn plane, first takeoff, Sanderson
Oct. 29	Sierra Blanca	Fort Hancock	El Paso	Smashed skids at Fort Hancock
Oct. 31	El Paso	Deming, N.M.		
		Lordsburg	Willcox, Ariz.	
Nov. 1	Willcox	Tucson	Maricopa	
Nov. 2	Maricopa	Phoenix	Stoval	
Nov. 3	Stoval		Imperial Junction, Calif.	Engine exploded
Nov. 4	Imperial Junction		Banning	Loose rod, worn bearings
Nov. 5	Banning	Beaumont		
		Pomona	Pasadena	
Nov. 12	Pasadena	Covina Junction	Compton	Wrecked machine
Dec. 10	Compton		Long Beach	

Appendix B

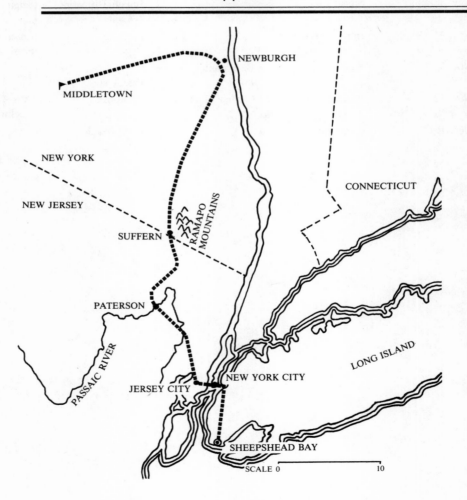

NEWBURGH

MIDDLETOWN

NEW YORK

NEW JERSEY

CONNECTICUT

SUFFERN

RAMAPO MOUNTAINS

PATERSON

PASSAIC RIVER

LONG ISLAND

JERSEY CITY

NEW YORK CITY

SHEEPSHEAD BAY

SCALE 0   10

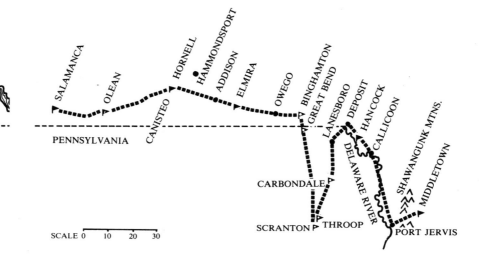

LAKE CHAUTAUQUA

SALAMANCA

OLEAN

CANISTEO

HORNELL

HAMMONDSPORT

ADDISON

ELMIRA

OWEGO

BINGHAMTON

GREAT BEND

LANESBORO

DEPOSIT

HANCOCK

CALLICOON

SHAWANGUNK MTNS.

MIDDLETOWN

PENNSYLVANIA

CARBONDALE

DELAWARE RIVER

SCRANTON THROOP

PORT JERVIS

SCALE 0   10   20   30

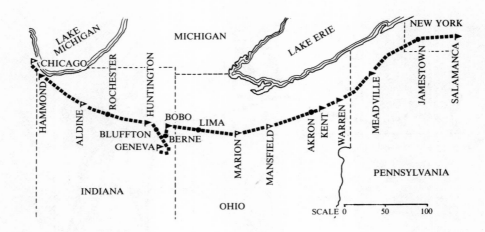

LAKE MICHIGAN

MICHIGAN

LAKE ERIE

NEW YORK

CHICAGO

HAMMOND

ALDINE

ROCHESTER

HUNTINGTON

BOBO

LIMA

BLUFFTON

BERNE

GENEVA

MARION

MANSFIELD

AKRON

KENT

WARREN

MEADVILLE

JAMESTOWN

SALAMANCA

PENNSYLVANIA

INDIANA

OHIO

SCALE 0   50   100

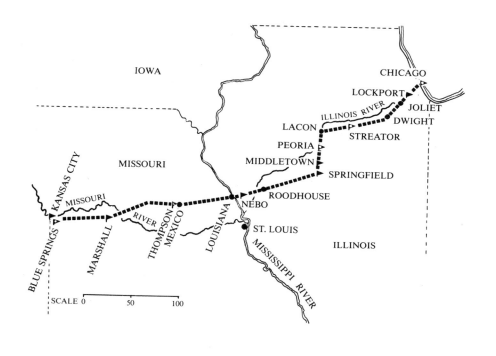

IOWA

CHICAGO

LOCKPORT

JOLIET

ILLINOIS RIVER

LACON

DWIGHT

STREATOR

PEORIA

MIDDLETOWN

KANSAS CITY

MISSOURI

SPRINGFIELD

MISSOURI

ROODHOUSE

RIVER

NEBO

BLUE SPRINGS

THOMPSON

MEXICO

LOUISIANA

ST. LOUIS

MARSHALL

ILLINOIS

MISSISSIPPI RIVER

SCALE 0   50   100

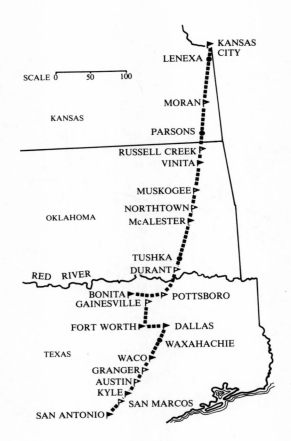

KANSAS CITY
LENEXA

SCALE 0   50   100

KANSAS

MORAN

PARSONS

RUSSELL CREEK
VINITA

MUSKOGEE

OKLAHOMA

NORTHTOWN
McALESTER

TUSHKA
DURANT

RED   RIVER

BONITA   POTTSBORO
GAINESVILLE

FORT WORTH   DALLAS
                WAXAHACHIE

TEXAS

WACO
GRANGER
AUSTIN
KYLE
            SAN MARCOS
SAN ANTONIO

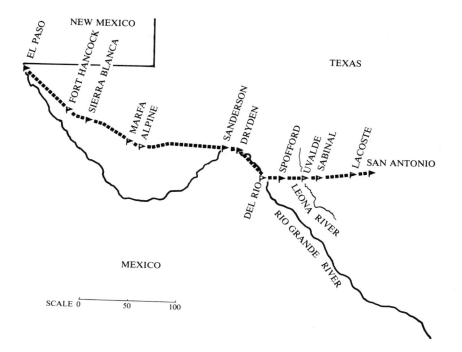

NEW MEXICO

EL PASO

FORT HANCOCK

SIERRA BLANCA

MARFA
ALPINE

SANDERSON
DRYDEN

TEXAS

SPOFFORD
UVALDE
SABINAL
LACOSTE
SAN ANTONIO

DEL RIO

LEONA RIVER

RIO GRANDE RIVER

MEXICO

SCALE 0   50   100

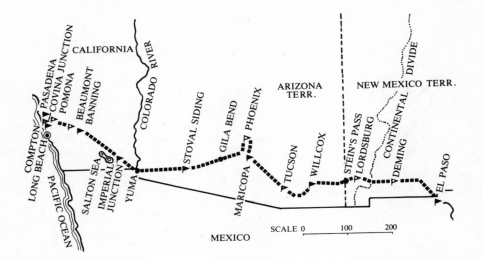

COMPTON
LONG BEACH
PACIFIC OCEAN
PASADENA
COVINA JUNCTION
POMONA
BEAUMONT
BANNING
CALIFORNIA
SALTON SEA
IMPERIAL
JUNCTION
YUMA
COLORADO RIVER
STOVAL SIDING
GILA BEND
MARICOPA
PHOENIX
ARIZONA
TERR.
TUCSON
WILLCOX
STEIN'S PASS
LORDSBURG
NEW MEXICO TERR.
CONTINENTAL DIVIDE
DEMING
EL PASO

MEXICO

SCALE 0   100   200

Appendix C

Statistics

Precise data were not compiled even by the Vin Fiz expedition itself. The following figures represent best estimates.

Total distance flown (railroad mileage): 4,231 miles

Actual flying time: 82 hours, 4 minutes

Average speed: 51.56 mph

Elapsed time, New York to Pasadena: 49 days
New York to Long Beach: 84 days

No. of landings: more than 80 in 76 different towns

Gasoline consumed: 1,230 gallons

Greatest distance covered along route in a single day: 234 miles, Springfield, Ill., to Marshall, Mo.

Greatest distance flown in a single day: 315 miles, McAlester, Okla., to Fort Worth, Tex.

Longest time in the air: 2 hours, 40 minutes, Kansas City, Kans., to Moran, Kans.

Longest single hop: 133 miles, Stoval, Ariz. Terr., to Imperial Junction, Calif.

No. of planes used: 18

No. of propellers used: 8

No. of skids broken: 20

Appendix D

Notes
Ex Post Facto

Chapter 1—Sheepshead Bay—Up and Away

1. Eddie Lynch, the 14-year-old boy who was last to touch the *Vin Fiz* as it rose from Sheepshead Bay, became interested in mechanics, founded and served as president of the Edward A. Lynch Machinery Co., Wynnewood, Pa.

Chapter 2—Love at First Flight

1. The *Pennsylvania* was an armored cruiser. The practice of assigning state names exclusively for battleships was not instituted until shortly before World War I. The *Pennsylvania* was at that time renamed the *Pittsburgh.*

2. In a 1925 interview, Samuel Perkins, the kite's inventor, recalled his selection of Lt. John Rodgers for its first operational test: "I [had] received a wire from Secretary of the Navy Meyer to proceed aboard the USS *Pennsylvania* in San Francisco harbor and make experiments with the man-carrying kite. Rear Adm. [Charles] Pond was then Captain of the *Pennsylvania,* and he instructed me to pick the naval officer who would make the tests. I looked them over, and there was one who was my man. I liked him immensely, mostly because he did not tell me what wonderful things he would do if I gave him a chance. Some of the others thought it would be an easy matter to go 1,000 feet in the sky and keep their minds on what they could see rather than on themselves. [Lt. Rodgers] thought he could do it, but

wasn't so sure. I knew, for I'd been up in them, that if you are fearful, your chances are better of doing a good job; so I selected him. And that's what got him interested in air and subsequently to Dayton. . . ."

3. Wright-Patterson Air Force Base now includes the area of Simms Station.

4. Wing warping is a particularly inefficient method of lateral control. While it alters the spanwise distribution of lift, it also alters the drag of the wings, producing a tendency for the airplane to skid; further, it prevents proper bracing of the wings for rigidity. The Wrights persisted in the use of wing warping although ailerons had been known for several years. Alberto Santos Dumont was first to incorporate ailerons (in the 14-*bis*); his experience was noted and adapted by Louis Blériot (1908). In America, ailerons were invented independently by Dr. Alexander Graham Bell and used on *White Wing*, the 1909 aircraft constructed by Bell's consortium, the Aerial Experimental Association.

5. The Wrights were likely the first to realize that a propeller is not a screw but a rotating wing—with an appropriate airfoil section and also a spanwise twist (so that it presents a constant—spanwise—angle of attack). Their propellers achieved a 66-percent efficiency in converting torque to thrust; modern engineering has added another 20 percent to their performance.

6. Much of the Wrights' case in their patent suits against Curtiss and others rested on their invention of these coordinated controls.

7. In later models of the Wright "B," two complete sets of controls were used.

8. Lts. Arnold and Milling were assigned as the first flight instructors at College Park, Md., the Army Signal Corps's first flying school. On July 6, 1911, they were certified in tests at College Park, as army aviators Nos. 2 and 3, respectively (Lt. Frank Lahm was designated No. 1). "Hap" Arnold (1886–1950) went on to become the prime architect in the development of the U.S. Air Force. He retired from his 41-year military career in 1946 with the rank of five-star general of the army. Thomas Milling rose to the rank of brigadier general before ill health forced his retirement. He died in 1960 at the age of 73.

9. The Wrights' base of operations at Montgomery is now the site of Maxwell Field.

Chapter 3—Middletown and Mother

1. Considered the best aviator of his time, Lincoln Beachey died on Mar. 14, 1915, when he crashed into San Francisco Bay.

2. One characteristic of the early Wright engines was an inadequate airflow.

Chapter 4—Big Man, Big White Bird

1. After the defeat of reciprocity in the Canadian elections, Hearst broadened the concept to embrace South America. The Argentine government announced that it would begin a movement to include all nations. German officialdom declared its receptiveness. No action succeeded the rhetoric.

2. In the grandstand at Dominguez Field on Jan. 19, 1910, witnessing Hearst's flight with

Louis Paulhan, were William F. Boeing, who was already interested in aircraft design, and a short, wiry 13-year-old from Los Angeles named Jimmy Doolittle.

Chapter 5—O, Hi, Ohio and Windy Indiana

1. Prior to Nov. 18, 1883, time of day was prescribed by each community independently. On that date, a uniform system of time went into effect (generally), promulgated by the railroads. Eastern standard time centered at the 75th meridian west of Greenwich, England; central standard time at the 90th; mountain standard time at the 105th, and Pacific standard time at the 120th meridian. Specific time changes were defined at towns served by the railroads. Not until Mar. 19, 1918, did Congress pass the first federal legislation establishing a national time standard.

2. The Commercial Club was the forerunner of the chamber of commerce.

3. In 1916, Art Smith provided Japan with its first intensive introduction to aviation. His reckless exhibition of aerobatics, including an inside loop, stirred up a craze for flying throughout the Far East.

4. Although "strap watches" had been known for several years, they did not find public favor until World War I.

Chapter 6—The Great Chicago Air Show

1. Beachey's altitude record stood unsurpassed for three years.

2. Directional stability is the effect that impels an airplane to head in the direction it is moving. Turning stability impels it to move in the direction it is headed, avoiding a skidding or sideslipping turn. By adding blinkers (the two vertical panels below the upper wing), the Wrights sought to increase turning stability. Attaching the blinkers forward, as on the "A," accomplishes this purpose, but reduces directional stability. With the blinkers at the center of gravity, turning stability is increased without affecting directional stability.

3. The Menger later became the Taft Hotel.

Chapter 7—A New World Record

1. Founded in 1874 (at Lake Chautauqua, N.Y.), the Chautauqua movement soon evolved into a vigorous private enterprise of popular education. Serious lecturers, humorists, magicians, popular music companies, play-readers, and preachers presented a variety of offerings under the general rubric of "Culture." The entertainers traveled to small communities in a tallyho, a supersize spring wagon with seats along the side and roof with seats and space for luggage. Tent Chautauqua (audiences sweltered under a large brown canvas tent) flourished for 20 years after the turn of the century.

2. The Kaw River is currently known as the Kansas.

Chapter 8—Katy All the Way

1. Sixteen years later, Ryan Airlines (founded by T. Claude Ryan but recently sold to B.

Franklin Mahoney) was engaged by Charles Lindbergh to build *The Spirit of St. Louis.* T. Claude Ryan later formed Ryan Aircraft Corp.

2. Ten stamps are known to have survived to this writing. Each is valued at several thousand dollars.

3. Amon Carter was Fort Worth's first citizen. His name graces parks, schools, buildings, sports arenas, and plaques in abundance. He was largely responsible for the aviation interests of his close friend Will Rogers. The International Airport at Amon Carter Field serves the Fort Worth area.

4. The Chicken Ranch, opened in 1844, was not closed by the law until 1973, thus becoming the oldest, continually operating nonfloating bordello in the nation. Known throughout the world, said to have slept two presidents and scores of senators, it inspired the Obie award–winning musical production *The Best Little Whorehouse in Texas* and, subsequently, the motion picture of that title.

Chapter 9—Down by the Rio Grande

1. In 1911, the 34-year-old dictatorship of Porfirio Díaz collapsed, and Mexico entered a period of revolution. Francisco Madero, who succeeded Díaz, was, in turn, murdered in 1913 by a clique that included his successor, Gen. Victoriano Huerta, a full-blooded Aztec Indian. Mexico's political cataclysm continued into the 1930s, through the regimes of Carranza, Obregón, and Calles.

2. The emperor abdicated the Dragon Throne in Dec. 1911, and a republic was declared. Sun Yat-sen was elected provisional president of China and was formally installed in office Jan. 1, 1912. For the illiterate masses, nothing was changed; the reality of power still lay with the military. A monarchy was restored in 1915; it vanished a year later. Struggles among internal factions and pressures from foreign interests, principally Japanese, held Chinese affairs in an apparently insoluble state of confusion until Chiang Kai-shek and the Kuomintang imposed their authority in the 1930s.

Chapter 10—Rodgerses and Perrys—Heritage of Valor

1. Alexander Rodgers was never found; his disappearance was never explained. In July 1910 Rear Adm. John A. Rodgers, then commandant of the Bremerton Navy Yard at Puget Sound, retired from active duty to search the Alaskan wilderness (unsuccessfully) for his son. He returned to active service for four months in 1918 as commanding officer of the naval unit at Harvard. He died Mar. 2, 1933, age 84, at his Sion Hill residence. He was bred in the old navy of "wooden ships and iron men." His death nullified a saying valid for a century and a third: "There has been a John Rodgers in the Navy Register ever since there was a navy."

2. In Feb. 1932, with his partner Alfred E. Poor, Robert Perry Rodgers won (over 34 competing architectural firms) the assignment to construct the Wright Memorial at Kitty Hawk, N.C.

3. Lawsuits brought by the Wrights for patent infringements were finally settled in 1915 in a decision handed down by Justice Learned Hand, rejecting the Wrights' claim of proprietary interest in fundamental aerodynamic principles.

Chapter 11—Triumph at Pasadena

1. After more than half a century of second-class status, New Mexico and Arizona were admitted to the Union as the 47th and 48th states on Jan. 15 and Feb. 14, 1912, respectively. Flag makers rejoiced.

2. Ostrich plumes were in great demand in 1911, selling for $20 to $40 a pound. Fashion began changing in 1914, and by 1920 demand for the plumes was virtually nonexistent. Shepherd's crooks were carried by the "ostrichboys" to ward off vicious kicks from the often irascible birds.

3. Imperial Junction is now dissolved into Niland, Calif.

4. Donald Douglas, after completion of the *World Stratocruiser* in 1924, noted: "Well, we've finally learned to put a box around the pilot."

Appendix E

Postmortems

The Principals

CALBRAITH PERRY RODGERS (1879–1912)

The impact of the transcontinental flight on the public mind had subsided sharply even before Rodgers's death—whether because of the commercialism associated with it or because the achievement compelled no immediate advance in aviation. So extraordinary was Cal Rodgers's flight that (except for Bob Fowler's odyssey) no further attempts at a cross-country air passage occurred until the technical advancements of World War I were incorporated into aircraft design. On October 8, 1919, Lieutenant Belvin W. Maynard ("the Flying Parson") departed Mineola, Long Island, in a DeHaviland 4 as one of sixty-five contestants in a round-trip transcontinental air derby sponsored by the Army Air Service; after three days, six hours, and four minutes, he landed at the Presidio in San Francisco (and then flew back to Mineola in three days, twenty and a half hours). In September 1922, Lieutenant Jimmy Doolittle flew coast to coast with but a single refueling stop. The first nonstop crossing of the U.S. came with Lieutenants J. A. Macready and O. G. Kelly, May 2–3, 1923, from New York to San Diego, California. These men knew of Cal Rodgers only as a dim memory.

Pittsburgh's first official airport, near Fox Chapel, was founded in 1925 and named Rodgers Field (it was abandoned in 1933). For the fifteenth anniversary of the flight, a bronze tablet, contributed by the Pittsburgh Aero Club to the Carnegie Museum, was unveiled by Mrs. Sweitzer. For the twenty-fifth anniversary, radio station WEAF featured reminiscences by Mabel Rodgers and some of the other participants. In 1961 the fiftieth anniversary was commemorated when the FAA designated the path followed by the *Vin Fiz* as "The Rodgers Skyway." Three years later—in 1964—Calbraith Perry Rodgers was inducted into the Aviation Hall of Fame in Dayton, Ohio.

MABEL RODGERS (1882–1972)

Mabel outlived everyone else associated with the first transcontinental flight, dying two weeks short of her ninetieth birthday. After marriage to Charles Wiggin, she titled herself "Mabel Rodgers-Wiggin, wife of the first cross-country aviator." The letterhead of her correspondence bore the full title. For sixty years after Cal's death, she strove to promote the great adventure from the back benches of history, where it had been so swiftly relegated. Her efforts met with unrelieved failure (even the U.S. Post Office rejected her plea for a Rodgers commemorative issue), and Mabel grew increasingly embittered, reduced to peddling slivers of wood allegedly from the *Vin Fiz.* She passed her last years —after Charles Wiggin's death—in a Miami, Florida, nursing home, indigent and unremembered.

MARIA CHAMBERS RODGERS SWEITZER (1855–1936)

Mrs. Sweitzer proved to be a survivor despite her maternal attachments. She devoted much of her remaining energies and fortunes to her elder son, John Perry Rodgers, who merely enhanced his reputation as a bent twig on the family tree until his life ended in July 1941. Her daughter, Martha C. Pease, died in October 1936, after a two-year illness. After Calbraith's death, Mrs. Sweitzer never again spoke with Mabel. She is buried in the Rodgers family plot in Allegheny Cemetery.

JOHN RODGERS (1881–1926)

After a week's leave of absence to accompany his cousin's body to the East, John Rodgers returned to the North Island Air Camp and thence to the Naval Academy from May to August 1912 for further aviation duty. At the importuning of his bride, he renounced flying and compiled sea duty with the USS *Illinois*, the USS *Nebraska*, and the USS *Paducah.* He transferred to submarines in 1916 and served with distinction during World War I; he was later awarded the Distinguished Service Medal. Promoted to the rank of commander in 1919, he regained his aviation assignments in 1922 to command the Naval Air Station at Pearl Harbor, Hawaii.

His marriage to Ethel Greiner ended in divorce in 1924. They produced one child, Helen.

In 1925, he piloted the first "successful" flight from the U.S. mainland to Hawaii. His seaplane, a PN-9, was forced down through lack of fuel 400 miles short of its goal (yet setting a distance record for seaplanes). Seawater was purified by means of a still that had been pressed on him by his mother, and a sail was rigged with fabric torn from the wings. He and his four crewmen then sailed and paddled their flying boat for nine days until they were picked up by a U.S. submarine fifteen miles east of Kauai.

Appointed assistant chief of the Bureau of Naval Aeronautics, he soon found that office work ill suited his taste and temperament and wangled command of an experimental seaplane squadron. Eleven days later, on August 27, 1926, while flying from Washington, D.C., to the Naval Aircraft Factory in Philadelphia, Commander Rodgers crashed his Vought VO-1 into the shallow waters of the Delaware River. He was pinioned beneath the engine and died in the nearby naval hospital. He is buried in Arlington National Cemetery.

STEWART IVES DEKRAFFT (1874–1927)

Substantial credit for Cal Rodgers's success should be assigned to Stewart deKrafft's organizational talents. Forsaking aviation after Cal's death, deKrafft turned those talents to theatrical presentations. He settled in New York City and became associated with Frohman Productions. He died of a heart attack while in Buffalo, New York, preparing for the opening of *Old Ironsides* at the Erlanger Theater.

CHARLES EDWARD TAYLOR (1868–1956)

Because of his wife's illness, Taylor remained in California for nearly a year, associated for a short time with Roy Knabenshue and Glenn L. Martin. In the fall of 1912, he returned to Dayton and continued as Orville Wright's general mechanic (Wilbur had died of typhoid fever on May 20, 1912). After his wife's death (1927), he moved back to California, invested in an unrewarding land-development project on the edge of the Salton Sea, and found employment with the North American Aviation Company and O'Keefe & Merrit Company (during World War II). From 1937 to 1941, he directed restoration of the original Wright brothers' home and shop at Henry Ford's Greenfield Village museum in Dearborn, Michigan. Taylor's last years were destitute. Ill from asthma and the infirmities of age, he relied on social security and an $800-a-year pension from the will of Orville Wright. He died on January 31, 1956, less than two months after a special fund had been created by members of the aircraft industry to support him for the rest of his life. He was interred in Valhalla Memorial Park in the San Fernando Valley, the "unsung hero" of man's first conquest of the air.

CHARLES WIGGIN (1893–1964)

When Mabel Rodgers returned to California after Cal's burial, she allowed Wiggin to teach himself the art of flying, first in the rebuilt "B" and then in the Wright EX. Wiggin flew the *Vin Fiz* at the 1912 Chicago Air Meet (September 12–21) and there obtained his FAI Certificate No. 175. In December 1912, he and Mabel formed the Rodgers Aviation Company in Wiggin's hometown, Atlanta, Georgia. Exhibition engagements were booked, featuring the *Vin Fiz* airplane (which crashed and was repaired several more times). In 1914 Charles Wiggin and Mabel Rodgers were married, welded together by their one great adventure.

Wiggin served as flight instructor at several government flying fields during World War I and continued active flying until 1925. He puttered through a succession of jobs—with the Thomas A. Edison Company (furniture division), Blue Crown Spark Plug Company, etc.—but gained prominence in none. He was plagued with financial exigencies through much of his life.

ROBERT G. FOWLER (1885–1966)

After completing the first West-to-East air crossing of the United States, Fowler, insolvent, meandered home via exhibitions for $5 plus meals (for himself and his crew). He acquired a Gage Tractor airplane, affixed pontoons to it, and on April 27, 1913, with motion-picture cameraman Ray Duhem as passenger, flew the fifty-mile length of the Panama Canal (thus achieving—technically—the first nonstop ocean-to-ocean flight). He then appeared at various theaters in the San Francisco area, exhibiting the first aerial pictures of the canal with his personal commentary. In 1915 he crashed his "Bluebird" airplane into San Francisco Bay and thereby sustained injuries that left him with impaired hearing. He joined the staff of the Curtiss Aeroplane Motor Company in Buffalo, co-founded the L.W.F. Company (with Edmund Lowe, Jr., and Charles Willard), then formed the Fowler Aeroplane Company in San Francisco. That enterprise was consumed in a 1918 fire, and Fowler engaged in a diverse series of projects for the remainder of his life. Like those of Rodgers, Ward, and other Early Birds, Fowler's heroic feats were soon forgotten by all but a small band of aviation enthusiasts.

The *Cole Flyer* was rented by a Los Angeles motion-picture company. Left untethered on the roof of a hotel where filming was in progress, the airplane was animated by a gust of wind and plummeted to the street below.

Jimmy Ward (1889–1956)

In 1913, Jimmy Ward formed the Ward Aviation Company at Chicago's Cicero Field. His exhibition team comprised Louis Gertson, Eugene Godet, and Blanche Scott. The team gained little audience, and Ward turned to cycle car construction. He served as senior-grade flying instructor in World War I and then ended his flying career. His fortunes declined to his death in a Chattahoochee, Florida, hospital.

Arthur L. ("Al") Welsh (1875–1912)

Better known as an instructor than as an exhibition flier, Al Welsh remained at the Nassau Boulevard. Wright School until April 1912. He was killed June 11, 1912, while flight-testing a military aircraft at College Park, Maryland. He is buried in Adas Israel Cemetery, Washington, D.C.

The Wright Type B—No. 27

The two-seater airplane was rebuilt by Frank Shaffer and Charlie Wiggin at the Long Beach hangar. It was purchased from Mrs. Sweitzer by Frank Shaffer and Jesse Brabazon, a Delavan, Wisconsin, businessman. Shaffer and Brabazon shipped the "B" to Lima, Ohio, where it was engaged in a series of exhibitions and passenger-carrying flights. In 1913 aviator Andrew Drew was induced to transfer his association from Max Lillie to the Brabazon-Shaffer Company as chief pilot of the "B." On June 12, 1913, he crashed the machine at Lima. Drew was killed, the airplane burned to ashes.

The Wright Model Ex—The *Vin Fiz*

For two years Mabel and Charlie Wiggin flew and exhibited the transcontinental aircraft. In 1914 Mrs. Sweitzer obtained a court ruling that awarded her possession of the airplane. She shipped it to Dayton with a request that Orville Wright restore it to prime condition that she might bequeath it to the Carnegie Institute. When she was unable to pay the costs of restoration, the *Vin Fiz* slowly rotted away while being cannibalized for other Wright machines.

In 1916, a year after Orville Wright had sold his remaining interest in the Wright Company, vast quantities of old airplanes and parts at the factory were destroyed as being of no value and occupying space. The *Vin Fiz* shared this fate—except for pieces of fabric stripped off by Charley Taylor.

When in 1927 the Carnegie Institute decided to resurrect the machine, odds and ends were stitched together and a wooden "engine" was emplaced. In 1933, this *"Vin Fiz"* was lent to Chicago for its International Exposition. Paul Garber, curator of the Smithsonian, then arranged for the craft to be transferred to his institution, where he restored it to a condition closely resembling the original, using—as far as possible—similar materials and following the Wright construction procedures. He mounted a Wright engine flown on a Type B. This *Vin Fiz* hangs at the Smithsonian's National Air and Space Museum in Washington, D.C.

ACKNOWLEDGMENTS

Special thanks for special contributions:

"Tiny" Broadwick
Bob Brooks
E. Wayne Cook
Col. Carl J. Crane
Gen. Jimmy Doolittle
Paul Garber
Esther Griffis
A. Stevens Halsted
Margaret Haring
Erik Hildesheim
Prof. Frederick Hooven

James Jacobs
T. H. Johnson
Jack Keasler
Stuart Lancaster
Edward A. Lynch
Perry Rodgers Pease
Ruth Reinhold
Bob Steele
Adm. George van Deurs
E. D. ("Hud") Weeks
Mrs. George Wheaton

and John Curran for the inception.

To the following eyewitnesses (in approximate geographic order), each of whom freely contributed their recollections of the *Vin Fiz,* this book is gratefully dedicated:

Perry Pease
Eddie Lynch
Gordon Keyes
E. Wayne Cook

Robert T. Nelson
B. A. Wilder
George Wildrick
Elsie Alexander (Weibler)

349

Grover Hermann
Valleau Curtis
Edwin Hermann
James Allen McGuire
Fred Witaker
Edward A. Mooers
Mrs. Julia C. Seaman
John Hover
Geral Kelleher
Mrs. Frances Hilpert (Higgs)
George A. Hempstead
Harold Pendorf
Roy D. Monroe
Warren J. Buck
Paul Weisshaar
James Paul
Nicolas B. Siccama
Milton G. Pulis
Edna Williams (Cook)
Neil S. Rogers
Victor E. Orn
A. L. Slyve
Henry J. Drescher
Carl Thierfeldt
Howard C. Crater
Donald Bethune
Lloyd R. Foster
Mabel Noyes (Miller)
Charles A. Dickson
William A. Vincent
Henry J. Meek
Clair R. Yaw
M. A. Buckley
John A. Nutt
Mrs. Helen C. Kellogg
Harold M. Kreason
Hazel Kreason (Richtmyer)
Bill Seaman
Mrs. Margaret G. Gibb
Mrs. Adelene Lake (Dingman)
Keith M. Rowley
Kenneth E. Taft
Paul Johner
Howard Wise
George Milne
William J. Prangs
F. D. Jackson

Margaret Smith
John P. Stephens
J. W. Ferris
C. S. Overly
Leonard J. Whitacre
Harold C. Long
Tony Meyer
M. M. Maxwell
Jay S. Cairns
Frank E. Lawrence
Mary Landis (Ralston)
Grant Beckwith
"Mud" Gardner
Mrs. Gladys A. Warner
Russell E. Green
Walter A. Simpson
Harry E. Latimer
Harold H. Hunter
C. B. Thompson
Robert S. Oberly
Hawley C. Calvin
Floyd M. Conrad
Blanche M. Foth
L. Harold Caldwell
Luke Scheer
Margaret Lovett (Smith)
Emerson L. Watkins
R. W. Hendrick
A. C. Armstrong
Mrs. Lucy Searfoss
Mick Montague
Nina Cooper (Pipes)
Leroy Ogden
E. C. Steinheimer
Jacob D. Esch
Lewis C. Esch
Dr. Henry D. Esch
Dr. T. H. Winans
Dolph A. Hickerson
Evans Franklin
Leo Peck
R. T. Dinsmore
Pearl Erickson (Scott)
T. Claude Ryan
M. H. Litherland
Erwin Buess
Clarence Sittel

C. J. Stroman
Dick M. Jeffries
B. B. Hunter
Mrs. Issac Newton Millhollon
W. Turner Harwell
Walter B. Smith
Flavia Day (Swearengin)
Calla Day (Enlow)
Dr. Donald Day
Oscar Haas
Virgil Patterson
Joe B. Lindsey
Jeff Tidwell
Charles H. Powell
S. B. Compton
W. W. Curry
Edwin L. Harding
W. H. Hagerty
Aubrey F. Sapp
Queenie Sapp (Bone)
J. Henry Simpson
Mrs. Jessie O'Rourke
John L. Davis
Katherine Stiewig (Washburn)
Lewis P. Kell
Beulah Belle Bennett (Dickson)
Thomas V. Philip
Hallie Crawford (Stillwell)
Mrs. Helen Mitchell

Mrs. M. T. Bennett
Eugene F. Montgomery
Howard G. Christensen
Frederick S. Wing
K. K. Henness
Mrs. Mamie St. Germaine Parker
J. Gordon Shackelford
Sam R. Falvey
Roy F. Martin
Albert Schwertner
Minnie Schwertner
Mrs. E. M. Fisher, Sr.
John E. Lee
Mrs. Eleanor Ellison (Maurer)
Dr. Charles Maurer
J. R. Arken
Mable Dailey (Ehlinger)
Byrdie Strahle (Phillips)
Paul H. Rodin
Mrs. R. C. Courtney
Margaret Elledge
Ricardo Vela
Stella Garlick
T. H. White
Claire Hobgood
Sylvester H. Clark
Mel Anderson
Richard Millar (first to touch the
   Vin Fiz at Long Beach)